The Political Economy of Power Sector Reform

T0340282

Over the last fifteen years the world's largest developing countries have initiated market reform in their electric power sectors from generation to distribution. This book evaluates the experiences of five of those countries – Brazil, China, India, Mexico and South Africa – as they have shifted from state-dominated systems to schemes allowing for a larger private sector role. As well as having the largest power systems in their regions and among the most rapidly rising consumption of electricity in the world, these countries are the locus of massive financial investment and the effects of their power systems are increasingly felt in world fuel markets. This accessible volume explains the origins of these reform efforts and offers a theory as to why-despite diverse backgrounds-reform efforts in all five countries have stalled in similar ways. The authors also offer practical advice to improve reform policies.

DAVID VICTOR is Professor of Law at Stanford Law School and Director of the Program on Energy and Sustainable Development at Stanford University.

THOMAS C. HELLER is Lewis Talbot and Nadine Hearn Shelton Professor of International Legal Studies at Stanford University.

The Political Economy of Power Sector Reform

The Experiences of Five Major Developing Countries

Edited by

David G. Victor and Thomas C. Heller

CAMBRIDGE
UNIVERSITY PRESS

CAMBRIDGE UNIVERSITY PRESS
Cambridge, New York, Melbourne, Madrid, Cape Town, Singapore, São Paulo, Delhi

Cambridge University Press
The Edinburgh Building, Cambridge CB2 8RU, UK

Published in the United States of America by Cambridge University Press, New York

www.cambridge.org
Information on this title: www.cambridge.org/9780521865029

First published 2007
This digitally printed version 2008

A catalogue record for this publication is available from the British Library

ISBN 978-0-521-86502-9 hardback
ISBN 978-0-521-10070-0 paperback

Contents

Figures

Tables

Notes on contributors

DAVID VICTOR is Professor of Law at Stanford Law School and Director of the Program on Energy and Sustainable Development at Stanford University. The Program, launched in September 2001, focuses on reform of electric power markets, the geopolitical consequences of newly emerging global natural gas markets, energy services for the world's poor, and managing climate change and other environmental consequences of modern energy systems. Much of the Program's research concentrates in Brazil, China, India, Mexico and South Africa. He teaches energy law and regulation at Stanford Law School.

Previously, Dr. Victor directed the Science and Technology program at the Council on Foreign Relations in New York, where he remains Adjunct Senior Fellow and Director of the Council's task force on energy. At the Council his research focused on the sources of technological innovation and the impact of innovation on economic growth. His research also examined global forest policy, global warming, and genetic engineering of food crops. His Ph.D. is from the Massachusetts Institute of Technology (Political Science and International Relations), his B.A. from Harvard University (History and Science).

THOMAS HELLER is coordinator of the Rule of Law Program at CDDRL, a CESP senior fellow, and the Lewis Talbot and Nadine Hearn Shelton Professor of International Legal Studies at Stanford. His work focuses on international law and political economy, law and development, energy law and policy, and environmental law.

Heller has been on the Stanford faculty since 1979 and has served as associate dean of the Law School (1997-2000), deputy director of FSI (1989-1992), and director of the Overseas Studies Program (1985-1992). He was a member of the faculty at the University of Wisconsin from 1971 to 1979, and served as co-director of the Center for Public Representation in Madison, Wisconsin, during 1976-77. He has been a visiting professor at several institutions, including Hong Kong University (2003), the European University Institute (1992-93 and 1996-99), the Catholic University of Louvain (1998), and the Center for Law and Economics at the University of Miami (1977-78).

He was previously a fellow of the Humanities Research Institute at UC-Irvine (1989), a Kellogg National Fellow (1981-83), and a fellow of the International Legal Center at Bogota, Colombia (1968-70). He received an AB from Princeton University in 1965 and an LLB (law degree) from Yale University in 1968.

VÍCTOR G. CARREÓN-RODRÍGUEZ is chair of Department of Economics at the Centro de Investigación y Docencia Economicas (CIDE). He has been a professor of economics at CIDE since 1998.

ADILSON DE OLIVEIRA is a professor of economics at the Institute of Economics at the Federal University of Rio de Janeiro. He is a member of the editorial board of *Utilities Policy*, has consulted for several Brazilian energy companies, and has advised the Brazilian Ministry of Energy on power industry reform. Prof. de Oliveira holds a Ph.D. in development economics from Grenoble University in France and a specialization degree in energy economics from the Institut Economique et Juridique de l'Energie.

ANTON EBERHARD is professor at the university at the Cape Towns school of Business. He teaches executive courses in the management of reform and regulation of infrastructure industries in Africa. For seven years, he was a Board Member of the National Electricity Regulator of South Africa. He founded and directed the Energy and Development Research Centre at the University of Cape Town between 1989 and 1999, is a foundation member of the Academy of Science of South Africa, and serves on numerous councils and boards including the Western Cape Regional Electricity Distributor. He is also an editorial board member of the *International Journal of Economic Regulation and Governance*.

ARMANDO JIMÉNEZ SAN VICENTE was Director of Energy Policy of the Secretary of Energy in Mexico. Dr. Jimenez received his Ph.D. from the London School of Economics (LSE) in 2002 where he worked on the political economy of tax collection in Mexico and the constraints on reform.

JUAN ROSELLÓN is currently the Repsol-YPF-Harvard Kennedy School Fellow at Harvard University, and a tenured professor of the Department of Economics at the Centro de Investigación y Docencia

Economicas (CIDE). He has also held faculty positions at the Program on Privatization, Regulatory Reform and Corporate Governance at Harvard University (1997–2000) and at Princeton University (2001).

RAHUL TONGIA is a research faculty member at Carnegie Mellon University in Pittsburgh, PA. His research interests include energy, power, networking and telecom infrastructure development in developing countries. He holds a Bachelor's degree in electrical engineering from Brown University and Ph.D. from the Department of Engineering & Public Policy at Carnegie Mellon University.

CHI R. ZHANG is the current Cambridge Energy Research Associates, Inc. (CERA) Director of China Energy. His research focuses on China's evolving electric power and natural gas markets. Prior to joining CERA he was head of China research for the Program on Energy and Sustainable Development at Stanford University. Dr. Zhang holds a Ph.D. in economics from Johns Hopkins University and has worked at the Institute for International Economics in Washington, DC, the Monterey Institute of International Studies and the Institute of World Economics and Politics at the Chinese Academy of Social Sciences in Beijing, China.

Preface

Over the last fifteen years the world's largest developing countries have initiated market reforms in their electric power sectors. This book evaluates the experiences in five of those countries – Brazil, China, India, Mexico, and South Africa. These five are important in their own right, as they have the largest power systems in their regions and their consumption of electricity is among the most rapidly rising in the world. They are the locus of massive financial investment – from domestic and foreign sources, both public and private – and the effects of these power systems are increasingly felt in world fuel markets. In addition to their intrinsic importance, these countries reveal important variations in reform efforts. Their power systems have been organized in distinct ways, have different primary fuels and technologies, and have been reformed under quite different strategies.

In the pages that follow, we explain the origins of these reform efforts and proffer a theory as to why – despite diverse backgrounds – reform efforts in all five countries have stalled in similar ways. We also suggest that our theory may have more general application to electricity reform beyond these five countries and also to reforms of other network industries.

In the broadest sense, this book advances four arguments. First, we suggest that these five countries initiated reform efforts at approximately the same time not simply because "markets" were a fad or that market-oriented elites controlled key governments and multilateral institutions such as the World Bank. Rather, a series of investment crises created political opportunities that reformers exploited in their push for markets. And while every country story varies, some elements are common across the five case studies. In most countries, electricity had become politicized and thus tariffs for politically favored groups were set at levels that did not cover costs. At the same time, many of the economies of scale that led to ever-declining costs faced technological exhaustion. The state enterprises that ran the power system got squeezed between inadequate revenues and rising costs, and state budgets were increasingly unable to cover the difference – especially for governments that were also struggling to manage the consequences of the 1980s debt crises. With a country in financial crisis it was easier to make the politically difficult choices that are intrinsic to power market reform – for example, raising tariffs and privatizing state enterprises.

Second, we show that all these countries articulated their reform strategies with reference to a "textbook" model of power sector reform – one written largely on the basis of the successful reforms in England and Wales. In practice, each country followed its own strategy in pursuit of that textbook outcome. Some started reform efforts with distribution companies; others focused on generation and transmission. Some sought large-scale privatization of the power sector, while others focused their attempts on attracting private enterprise in special niches as "independent power producers (IPPs)" that sell electricity to the grid under state-backed long-term contracts.

These varied reform strategies have not had much impact on the actual functioning of the power sector. Much more important than reforms in the power sector have been reforms in other parts of the economy – notably in state budgeting and capital markets. Wherever states have imposed hard budget constraints and where firms face real opportunity costs of capital the electric power sector has generally become more economically efficient, regardless of the particular reform strategy that the government has pursued. Other complementary reforms have also played important roles. For example, the progress with judicial reform helps to explain why some regulators have been able to issue meaningful orders while others find their dicta ignored by firms and enterprises that know the courts will not back the regulatory authority.

Third, each study has examined the effects of power sector reform on the various elements of the "social contract" that has long existed between society and state-dominated electric power systems. This contract includes varied investments in public purposes, such as the supply of low-cost electricity to poor households, as well as public goods such as protection of the environment and investment in innovation. Many analysts have feared that power sector reform would undermine that contract because profit-oriented firms would focus on their bottom line rather than these broader public services. We find little support for that fear because reformers, in practice, have generally adopted a wide array of complementary policies such as special subsidy programs and tax incentives that have sustained (or even expanded) investment in social services.

Fourth, we argue that early in the reform process a special class of firms and enterprises emerges to play a dominant role in reform. These organizations, which we call "dual firms" are marked by their strong interest in *avoiding* full-blown reform, for they thrive in the murky middle ground between the old state-dominated system and a fully open and competitive private marketplace. Dual firms, we argue, are distinctive because they are governed to perform two tasks simultaneously. On the one hand, they are able to mobilize the political connections needed to get plants financed, sited, and dispatched and to obtain the subsidies and payment guarantees that are necessary for profitable infrastructure investments. Simultaneously on the other hand, these firms are efficiently managed so that the resources they obtain are not squandered through poor operations and bloated payrolls. Performing both these tasks is exceptionally difficult; some of the organizations that do it have arisen originally through state ownership (e.g., China's Huaneng Power, Brazil's Petrobras, South Africa's Eskom, and India's National Thermal Power Corporation); others trace their origins to private enterprise (e.g., India's Reliance and Tata companies). Power sector reform has differed from the textbook model not simply because it is technically difficult to create private markets. Rather, power reforms have stalled because these dual firms know that they thrive best in the partially reformed world and have the ability to prevent full-blown restructuring of the sector.

We thank the many collaborators and reviewers who have participated over the nearly three years of this study. We launched the effort at Stanford with a February 2003 meeting on the experiences with power sector reform, at which the authors presented early drafts of their studies. Thanks to the chairmen, speakers, and discussants at that meeting for their focused critique of our methods and results: Ralph Bailey, Don Baker, David Bodde, Jim Bushnell, Ralph Cavanagh, Robert Crow, Craven Crowell, Zhou Dadi, Alberto Diaz, Shyam Divan, Alex Farrell, Charles Feinstein, Leo Feler, T.J. Glauthier, David Holloway, Arvind Jadhav, Stephen Krasner, Ron Lillejord, Hugh McDermott, Granger Morgan, Alberto Pani, Dionisio Perez-Jacome, Jayant Sathaye, P.R. Shukla, Jonathan Sinton, Bernard Tenenbaum, Jim Williams, Mason Willrich, Frank Wolak, and Kurt Yeager. We and our collaborators are grateful to the many follow-up meetings with officials in government and industry as well as academics.

In parallel with this study, the Program on Energy and Sustainable Development (PESD) participated in two studies on related topics. One focused on independent power projects (IPPs) was ably led by PESD's Erik Woodhouse. As the present study will show, IPPs are typically the primary vehicle for attracting private capital for investment in new infrastructure, and thus a retrospective on the IPP experience is an essential complement to the full examination of power sector reform that is presented in this book. In addition to Erik, we are grateful to the many other scholars who participated in the IPP study: Felipe Araujo, Efe Cakarel, Katia O. Karpova, Joshua House, Peter Lamb, Luciano Losekann, Alejandra Nuñez-Luna, Adilson de Oliveira, Jeff Rector, and Pei Yee Woo. PESD also collaborated with Anton Eberhard and Katharine Gratwick at the University of Cape Town who studied the IPP experience in Africa. The IPP study, although funded mainly by PESD, benefited from a seed grant from the Bechtel Initiative on Global Conflict and Cooperation through the Freeman-Spogli Institute for International Studies; we thank John Weyant and Bob Crow for their efforts to initiate the work on IPPs with the Bechtel funding.

Second, in parallel with this study PESD also collaborated with Prof. P.R. Shukla at the Indian Institute of Management (Ahmedabad) to examine the effects of power sector reform on technology choices in two Indian states. We thank the U.S. Agency for International Development for funding that study and for the continued support of the USAID team in Delhi: Richard Edwards, John Smith-Sreen, Sandeep Tandon, and Glenn Whaley. We are especially grateful to our collaborators Debashish Biswas, Tirthankar Nag, and Amee Yajnik. That study on two Indian states mirrored an earlier study, funded by the Electric Power Research Institute, that examined the effects of power sector reforms on electric technologies in three Chinese provinces, and we thank our colleague Michael May who co-led that effort and contributed in many ways to the present study.

Finally, and most importantly, we thank our collaborators and PESD's main funders. Our collaborators have been notably patient with our lengthy review and extensive editorial process. We have been blessed with generous and consistent programmatic support from the Electric Power Research Institute and BP, plc. We also thank the staff at PESD including Rose Kontak for overseeing and implementing the final stages in this undertaking – she has managed the production process and also played an instrumental role in the final rounds of editing. Others at PESD have also been exceptionally helpful, notably Becca Elias and Bob Sherman; we are also grateful to Josh House who helped oversee the project in its earlier stages. Our editors at Cambridge University Press, Chris Harrison and Lynn Dunlop, were a pleasure to work with throughout the publication process.

David G. Victor and Thomas C. Heller
Stanford, California
December 2005

1 Introduction and overview

David G. Victor and Thomas C. Heller

Over the last three decades a wave of market reform has spread to nearly every aspect of modern economic activity. Reformers have sought to replace state control with private enterprise and market competition in air transportation, telecommunications, banking, ports, railroads, food service, and sundry other activities. Even Russian vodka, for decades a guiding spirit of the planned economy, is today a product of private entrepreneurs rather than solely state enterprise.

Yet markets do not arise or function spontaneously. To deliver on their promise, they require ancillary institutions, such as banks, regulatory agencies and courts that must operate in steadfast but subtle ways. This book is part of a growing literature that seeks to explain how that institutional context affects the origins and operation of markets. Our interest is the political economy of the shift to markets – that is, how political forces interact with institutions to affect how markets function in practice. The perspectives of political economy, we will argue, explain why the real outcomes from attempted market reforms have often diverged sharply from the economist's theoretical ideal.

Infrastructures have proved to be a particularly challenging area for the introduction of market forces. Infrastructures are marked by high capital costs and require long time horizons that can make it especially difficult to attract private investors who are wary of their ability to earn an acceptable return. The services supplied by infrastructures – such as telecommunications, electricity, and running water – are often highly visible politically, which raises the risk that governments will intervene if markets, left alone, deliver outcomes that are politically inconvenient. Indeed, heavy infrastructure has long been viewed as a central function of government, especially in countries where the state is strong and occupies a large space in the economy. It has also proved difficult to replace the state with private enterprise because infrastructures usually display strong economies of scale, which arise through network interactions that are prone to natural monopoly. Even where governments find ways to open infrastructure for private investors and operators they must still monitor closely the behavior of private firms to detect, punish, and deter monopoly behavior – tasks that are demanding even when regulators are highly competent.

Despite these obstacles, some infrastructures have been the locus of successful market reforms. They include the auctioning to private firms of the concessions to run toll roads, airports and ports. Telecommunications offers the most striking success with reform of a network industry – thanks to a variety of technological innovations that have eased the entry of new competitors and created new products (such as wireless telephony) that old state-owned, wired telecommunications firms could not nimbly deliver. New services, competition across platforms, and lower prices in turn stimulated much larger demand and allowed for more contestable markets. Declining costs and improved service helped to sustain the political constituency for market reforms in telecommunications.

Electricity is proving to be among the trickiest of all network industries for reformers.[1] The network effects of large power grids, along with the massive economies of scale in modern central power stations, create high barriers to entry that (until recently) had made electricity the epitome of natural monopoly. The prohibitive cost of storing electricity requires that all power systems be managed literally at the speed of light – a characteristic of systems that many had thought would require synchronized central management rather than the looser and decentralized coordination that are hallmarks of most markets. Unlike telecommunications, no technological revolution has swept over electric power generation to catalyze a fundamental change in business structure; across most of the world the core technologies for delivering electric power have changed little since the 1950s (or earlier).

Despite these challenges – high capital costs, political visibility, network monopoly effects, technological stasis and daunting regulatory tasks – reformers have found ways to introduce market forces into the business of electricity. One track for reformers has involved the model that dates to nearly the beginning of the electric power industry: regulated franchises. Indeed, a few markets – notably in the United States and Hong Kong – never abandoned this mode of regulated enterprise even as the rest of the world turned power systems over to state managers during the twentieth century. Following this model, private firms would operate the entire integrated electric power system, earn a guaranteed return on their investment if they perform well, and be subject to the oversight of

---

[1] The literature on reforming electric networks is large. For introductions see Newbery, 1999, pp. 199–279; Carbajo and Fries, 1997; Gray, 2001; Asia Pacific Energy Research Centre, 2000; Wamukonya, 2003; Bradley, 1996; Bacon and Besant-Jones, 2002.

regulators. Some analysts even suggested the regulator could be eliminated if franchisees would be required periodically to bid for their service (e.g., Demsetz 1968).

This track, however, suffered from many deep flaws. It depends on regulators that, in practice, are often unable to function independently. Even where regulators are strong and competent they often find it difficult to obtain full information on the firm's costs and thus are prone to make mistakes that either allow excessive returns or, in the opposite, regulatory rules that do not allow a sufficient return to encourage fresh investment. Moreover, a guaranteed return provides strong incentives for firms to over-invest in favored projects and reliable staid technologies. Thus regulated franchises, it was thought, tended to squander capital and to avoid innovation (Averch and Johnson 1962). To fix these problems, experts on regulation have developed a wide array of new schemes – often loosely called performance-based regulation – that give the regulator and the firm, alike, a stronger incentive to behave more efficiently. None, however, has solved the fundamental problem that regulators have incomplete information and are subjected to political forces that make it difficult to provide credible long-term commitments.

The second track for reformers offered the promise of fuller efficiency through market competition. New ideas advanced since the early 1980s have shown that some aspects of electric power systems were not natural monopolies and could be made more efficient through market competition (e.g., Joskow and Schmalensee, 1983). In a classic integrated power monopoly – whether owned by the government or run as a private franchise – the entire system is owned and operated as a single entity (see figure 1.1). The new insight of these market reformers was that some power functions – notably the generation and final marketing of electricity – could be transformed to allow the entry and market competition of many private firms. Generation, especially, could be highly competitive because the number of power plants is usually large and the barriers to entry (and exit) are not prohibitive.[2] By contrast, transmitting electricity from generators via high voltage power grids to final users is replete with network effects and prone to monopoly. That is because

---

[2] Moreover, in the twenty years since these ideas were originally developed a series of technological and financial innovations have reduced the barriers to entry for many types of generators. Technologically, thermal power plants have declined in size due to the wider availability of natural gas and innovation in gas turbines that have sharply reduced the capital cost required to build a thermal power plant. Financially, more efficient capital markets and improved financial instruments have made it easier to fund the construction of single power plants – usually in the form of independent power projects (IPPs).

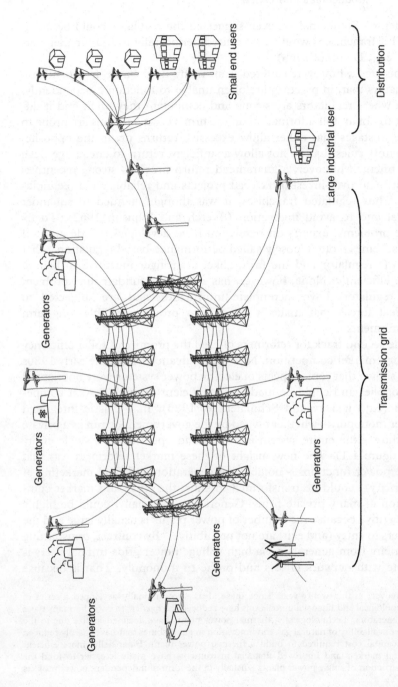

Figure 1.1. An electricity network: generation, transmission and distribution

alternating current grids that interconnect generators and distributors operate as a single organism with power looping and flowing in all directions, making it difficult (but not impossible) to atomize the system into individual competitive units. Similarly, the function of distributing power to millions of final users is also prone to monopoly because the rights of way, power poles and lines have high fixed costs that make competition difficult except for very large users that can afford to acquire their own lines and transformers needed to interconnect directly with the power grid. Thus the transmission (grid) and distribution functions would be left in the hands of the state or operated as private franchises according to the strictures of a state regulator. No country in this study has operated these infrastructures other than as state enterprises, although Mexico and Brazil have some private franchises for individual power lines. The function of marketing power to users could be competitive so long as companies that bought power from generators and sold it to final users could be assured "open access" to the monopoly-prone grid and distribution system.[3]

Britain's market-oriented Thatcher government was the first to apply these insights on a large scale. It unbundled the integrated state enterprise into several competitive generators. It also created twelve distribution companies, each with its own exclusive franchise area. The transmission system was maintained as a single enterprise owned by the state. Generators and distributors were required to trade power through bidding in a common pool or through direct contracts. (Most bulk power was sold through competitive long-term contracts with relatively stable prices; smaller quantities were traded on the more volatile pool market as needed.) Large users, too, were allowed to purchase their power directly from generators and through the pool. A new regulator, the Office of Electricity Regulation (Offer), was established to oversee the whole enterprise – to monitor possible collusion by generators and distributors and to set rates for the parts of power system that remained governed as natural monopolies.

The great experiment in England and Wales saw rates fall sharply, especially for large users. The decline in rates correlated with market reforms, but the actual causes were complex. Some of the decline was rooted in factors exogenous to the power sector reform, notably a decline in the cost of coal (from reforms that broke the unions in that sector) and the unexpected availability of natural gas from the North Sea. However, much of the decline in rates was due to the power sector reformed.

---

[3] For an accessible introduction to current theory and practice of power sector reform see Brennan (2002).

Table 1.1. *"Standard textbook model" for electricity sector reform*

1. Unbundle	Separate generation, transmission, distribution and marketing of electricity.
2. Privatize	Sell those parts of the system amenable to competition to multiple private firms.
3. Create regulatory institutions	Setup independent regulators to oversee market conduct in the competitive industry and to regulate the monopoly-prone parts of the system.
4. Create markets	Allow markets to function for parts of the system that are amenable to competition.

The experience in England and Wales has revealed some dangers in the design of electricity markets. These include the risk that single firms can exert "market power" – the ability to affect prices for the whole market by their actions alone or in tacit collusion with others. As regulators learned about these and other flaws in their market, they crafted substantial adjustments to trading rules and oversight mechanisms. Nonetheless, the England and Wales experience is widely (and rightly) seen as a success, and that experience (along with the theory of power market reform) has established a model for reform in other part of the word.

Out of this theory and practice arose what we call the "standard textbook model" of electricity sector reform, consisting typically of four major elements (table 1.1). These reforms would begin with government "unbundling" the functions of generating, transmitting, distributing, and marketing electricity. Then, the standard textbook model called for the state to transfer those parts of the system that were amenable to competition into the half of private firms. The standard textbook model required creating powerful new institutions – notably, independent regulators – to oversee conduct in the industry and regulate the monopoly–prone parts of the business.

For generators, the standard textbook model required the creation of markets such as power pools and provisions for power users and marketers to contract with generators. So long as many different generators have access to a transmission system capasle of moving ("wheeling") their the users of electricity could select among the diverse offers and the market would be competitive.

There were many variants on the markets that reformers sought to create. Some countries required power generators to sell their output to a single distribution company, known as a "single buyer" system. The most ambitious reformers, however, envisioned that multiple distribution companies and even individual users would compete and contract directly with the multiple competitive power suppliers. For very small users such as households and light industry the benefit of such competition would be small, and thus nearly everywhere those "captive" users have relied on the power distributor to obtain the best prices and services. Large users, by contrast, were encouraged to participate directly in electricity markets, adding competition to keep the system operating close to full efficiency. The standard model required creating powerful new institutions – notably, independent regulators – to oversee conduct in the industry and regulate the monopoly-prone parts of the business. Very few among even the most energetic reformers have actually implemented the full standard model. Nonetheless, the model and experience of England and Wales illustrated the great potential for markets – a shining city on the hill that has inspired reformers worldwide.

The vision and practice of power sector reform has spawned a vast and growing literature that, broadly, fits into four categories. First, there is a large literature on the design of competitive power markets. While some of this literature is purely theoretical, much is rooted in the actual experiences of reform – particularly of England & Wales, New Zealand, California and a few others (e.g., Joskow 1983, 2000; Newbery, 1995, 1999; Sweeney 2005, IEA, 1999, 1999a). Nearly all of the empirical literature focuses, by necessity, on jurisdictions that have done the most to restructure their power systems and thus this literature has a selection bias in that it is largely silent about the many setting, where market reforms have not advanced far. This literature also contributes to a broader economic literature on the operation and restructuring of network industries. It is this first literature, which derives its general theory from these much analyzed cases, that has given rise to the textbook model (Shy 2001).

Second, a small but growing literature has arisen in reaction to the optimism of the first. It has two strands. One strand has focused on the various ways that effective competition could fail to materialize (e.g., Apt 2005). Another strand questions whether reforms might intrinsically undermine certain important functions that state-owned power systems provide, such as low-cost access to power for poor villages, protection of the environment, or investment in research on new technologies (e.g., Dubash 2001, 2002; Goldemberg, 2004; and Lopez-Calva, 2002). We call these broader functions of power systems, which the market does not autonomously value on its own, the "social contract" of the electric power system. Many of the authors in this genre have been primed to find such erosions in the social contract, and thus this literature has kept a skeptical eye on the many dangers in market reform. However, a small body of research has examined the actual effects of power sector reform on the social contract (especially on access to energy services for the poor) and generally found that the shift to markets is not necessarily harmful and often is quite positive (e.g., Powell, 2000; and Victor, 2005).

Third, there is a rapidly growing body of empirical research on the actual practice of market reforms in countries that are early in the process of resturcturing. Much of this work is focused on individual cases (usually countries), although some part is comparative and few studies have applied statistical techniques to large samples. This literature has not emerged around any particular theory of market reform; nor has it established a theory (or collection of competing theories) to explain the reform process. Rather, most of these empirical studies are conceived as unique to each country and market (e.g., Estache, 1996, 1999; Guasch, 1999; Berrah, 2001; Dubash and Rajan, 2001; Ferreira, 2002; World Bank, 2003; Deloitte Touche Tohmatsu, 2004). Most adopt the textbook model as the end-point for reform, in part because reformers author much of the analytical literature and in part because the textbook is often the only star on the horizon. (One goal of the present study is to articulate other outcomes from reforms that are more feasible and likely in much of the world.)

The consequence of holding the textbook as the measuring stick for reformers is that much of case study research has concentrated on the yawning gap between the textbook goal and actual practice. Since the goal has been unquestioned in its attractiveness and feasibility, most of these studies aim to explain the failure to reach the shining city as a series of inconvenient obstacles. These impeding factors include "politics," poor "rule of law" and other "weak institutions" that impede efforts to put the state on the sideline and to provide space for markets to operate.[4] Studies that have given attention to these factors are usually anecdotal and suffused with the view that politics, law, and institutions are barriers to be cleared before launching the real work of implementing market designs that accord with the standard textbook model. By placing the textbook model in a prized position they bring this empirical literature into alignment with the first literature on market design. The lack of rigorous attention to these impeding factors as

---

[4] For example, a World Bank survey of international investors in reforming power sectors identifies a stable legal environment, government responsiveness, and regulatory independence as some of the most important factors to consider in infrastructure investment (Lamech and Saeed, 2003).

subjects worthy of analysis is particularly strange since political, legal and institutional forces are hardly transient or quickly and easily modified. In fact, as the studies in this book will show, such factors are the dominant ones in explaining the actual pace and character of market reforms in the electric power system in developing countries (see Yarrow, 1999 and Levy, 1996).

Fourth, a specialized literature has arisen in response to the many difficulties that have been encountered on the road to reform. This work has had one main branch, along with a few smaller offshoots. The main branch has focused on the problem of credibility in making commitments since the reform process is, in effect, a promise by government that reforms will create an environment in which prudently managed investments by private firms will allow for recovery of an acceptable return. Since those commitments often take the form of a contract, this specialized literature is part of a broader body of research on the management of risk in environments where it is difficult for the parties to enforce contracts (e.g., Levy, 1994; Irwin, 1997; World Bank, 1997; Henisz, 1999; Moran, 1999; Wells, 1999; Schiffer and Weder, 2000; Zelner, 2000; Kessides, 2004). Contract enforceability is particularly important for power infrastructures that demand massive capital investment upfront and offer a return through a stream of payments over a long period (up to 30 years) during which the investor relies on the host government and other counterparties to honor the original deal. This body of research has been particularly focused on contracting for independent power projects (IPPs), which are power generators built and operated by private companies that usually sell their output under a long-term contract. As we will show, many countries begin the process of restructuring by inviting investment in IPPs, in part because this step is seemingly the easiest to take and in part because most power sector reforms begin in the context of looming shortages of generation capacity. IPPs provide an interesting crucible for studying contracting because they are usually financed through special purpose vehicles on a limited-recourse basis, a structure that maximizes sensitivity to the credibility of contracts because lenders can look only to the project company and its revenue as collateral for loans (International Finance Corporation [IFC], 1999).[5]

---

[5] Project revenues are subject to a pre-determined (usually fine-tuned) allocation of project revenues to particular accounts dedicated to particular purposes or lenders; thus even small changes register loudly in the contractual structure that governs this allocation. Lenders often respond to developing country risk in a variety of ways that increases this sensitivity (Dailiami 2003; and Esty 2003). Additionally, as country risk deepens beyond the point of commercial viability, many sponsors and lenders turn to

Much of the literature on the problem of establishing credibility needed for long-term investment has viewed the issues through the lens of the "obsolescing bargain" (Vernon, 1971). Negotiating leverage in a large private infrastructure project shifts during the project life cycle. Initially, the host needs private investors and thus offers attractive terms. Once operational, the investors require a long amortization period to attain their expected return while the host has already secured what it needs. The original bargain has become obsolete. Theory predicts that the host will force a change in terms – either by outright nationalization or by squeezing revenue streams as far as possible – unless factors such as fear of a poor reputation create an incentive for discipline. As the incidence of wholesale expropriation declined (Minor, 1994; Harris et al., 2003), subsequent development of the original obsolescing bargain hypothesis primed analysts to be wary of subtler attacks on project value – often "creeping expropriation." Such attacks could be handled (so the story went) by careful contracting to close such loopholes and constrain government actions towards infrastructure investment (see Moran, 1999 and Powers, 1998).

Investors in IPPs and in other elements of the power sector, such as transmission lines and distribution companies, knew about these risks and had studied closely the earlier experiences with expropriation, such as the wave of nationalizations of natural resource companies in the 1960s and 1970s. In response, the architects of private participation schemes in the 1990s sought to improve the commercial and regulatory environment of the host country itself (Jadresic, 1999), as well as the incentive structure of particular transactions in order to bolster the stability of the long term contracts that served as the foundation for these investments (Green, 1993). Much of the literature in this area has centered on the work of a cottage industry of lawyers and financial advisors – project or structured finance specialists, privatization advisors, legal and regulatory reform consultants, and commercial arbitrators – who engineered the tools that investors thought were necessary to solve these problems (Wells, 2005).[6]

Smaller branches of this fourth literature have focused on solving other particular problems that arise in the process of market reform.

multilateral credit enhancements (such as guarantees from MIGA or OPIC) to increase the debt capacity of a particular project. One study finds that the availability of credit enhancements is the most significant variable associated with higher levels of debt in countries with weak institutional environments (Devapriya, 2003).

[6] For a full review and empirical assessment of the contracting issues, with a focus on IPPs, see Woodhouse (2006).

Among them has been the difficulty in creating truly independent and competent regulators. A small literature has arisen around the varied efforts to train regulators, but that work is mainly descriptive; to date, there has been no major analysis of the effectiveness of those programs. And a literature has arisen on alternatives to the classic regulator whose functions are based on independent judgment. Among the solutions proffered when regulators are unable to assure independence or sound judgment, is regulation "by contract" that, in effect, replaces many functions of regulation with contractual terms (Bakovic, et al 2003). Such solutions reveal that, at the core, the problems of making and enforcing credible commitments is an inescapable element of power sector reform.

This study

During the late 1980s and early 1990s nearly all of the leading developing countries announced plans to restructure their power systems (Bacon and Besant-Jones, 2002). In most cases, reformers turned to the standard textbook model as their guide. Yet today – well more than a decade later – the power systems in place bear little resemblance to that theoretical ideal. With few exceptions – principally, Argentina (until 2001) and Chile – market forces operate only at the margins of electric power systems that remain dominated by the state.[7]

Our goal is to explain this outcome – the apparent stalling of reform efforts – as a phenomenon in its own right rather than the unintended byproduct of residual barriers. At the outset of our study we adopted the working hypothesis that this outcome is due to structural forces that are rooted in the political and institutional context of developing countries. The studies will show that this context leads not to the ideal textbook outcomes, but to a hybrid – what we call a "dual market" – that combines some features of textbook reform with powerful residues of state monopolies. Indeed, we will suggest that the hybrid systems we observed in all these countries should not be considered aberrations or way stations to the shining city but, rather, stable and likely outcomes. In this book we explore (and build) the theories that could explain that outcome, as well as their implications for reform policy. We also suggest that more effort be given to explaining these hybrid outcomes and their

---

[7] Chile and Argentina are discussed below. In addition, a wholesale market is taking shape in the Philippines (Woodhouse 2005; Velasco 2006) and a few other nascent markets, such as in Columbia, are evident as well.

stability rather than the theoretical textbook that, so far, is rarely observed in the developing world. (Indeed, the textbook ideal is a rare species anywhere on the planet.)

To study this outcome we have selected a sample of five countries – Brazil, China, India, Mexico, and South Africa – from the approximately six dozen developing countries that have undertaken some form of power sector reform (Bacon, 1999).[8] We have focused on developing countries for two reasons. First, these countries are intrinsically important as the locus of most investment in the power sector in the coming few decades, the hosts of four-fifths of the world population, and soon the largest contributors to the world economy. Second, the institutions needed to support a shift to markets are likely to be most fragile and varied in the developing world as these countries, in general, are most recent and diverse in their efforts to deploy markets to allocate resources in their economies. These countries are thus a particularly interesting laboratory for examining the ways in which institutional forces affect the pace and operation of power sector reform.

In selecting this sample at the beginning of our study we were guided by our working hypothesis yet were confident that we did not know which factors would prove to be most important in explaining the partial reform outcomes that we observed across the developing world. Thus we identified four major attributes of the power sectors that, we hypothesized, would be important in explaining outcomes. Then we ensured that our sample allowed us to observe variation in each of those four dimensions.

Incumbent fuel

The cases in this book include power systems dominated by all three of the primary electricity generation fuels that dominate electricity generation in most of the world: hydro (Brazil), oil (Mexico), and coal (China, India and South Africa). We hypothesize that primary fuel

[8] There is no agreement on the exact number of developing countries that have attempted some form of power sector reform. By one count, the number is *fifty* – namely, all countries that have in place at least one IPP, since the existence of an IPP is an easily observed indicator that the country has undergone sufficient restructuring to allow, at least, some semblance of private investment. (The IPP is the easiest of such indicators since private investment in generation is usually much easier to manage than investment in distribution. Many countries also allow private ownership of transmission, but all of those also allow IPPs.) The IPP–linked definition is too restrictive, however, as it excludes countries that aim to restructure their power systems by creating ownership forms other than IPPs – as South Africa attempted (but largely failed, eventually settling on IPPs as the main vehicle for private participation). In many countries – for example, China – IPPs account for only a tiny share of power generation.

matters because the systems for supplying primary fuels are organized very differently, and each case study examines the interaction between the organization of the fuel system and the operation of the power sector. Coal requires an elaborate mining and transportation network (usually railroads, but barges in some cases) – itself often owned by the state. Hydro systems require massive capital expenditure and often benefit from integrated management of whole river basins that encourages (but does not require) operation by a single integrated enterprise. Once the capital is spent, the operating costs of hydro systems are low and it is particularly difficult for alternative fuels – where the cost of operation is much higher – to unseat the incumbent. Oil is the costliest major fuel; for oil exporters, fuel not burned to generate electricity can be exported for revenue, which can provide a strong incentive to shift to alternative fuels. Interestingly, in each case the "new" fuel envisioned by most policy makers is natural gas (see table 1.2). This common element across case studies allows us to observe the different ways that natural gas struggles to gain a market share, a process that is unfolding at the same time that a global market for natural gas is emerging (see Victor, Jaffe and Hayes, eds., 2006).

National governance

We found no simple and comprehensive metrics of governance since each country and society employs its own highly varied methods. However, the sample includes both federal systems (i.e., Brazil and India) that disperse and share power between the center and state or provincial elements, as well as more integrated governments in which electricity policy is controlled almost entirely by the central government (i.e., Mexico and South Africa). China reveals both patterns, as most provinces in China are integrated with the central planning system for electric power, but Guangdong province usually works alone. These differences in systems of governance matter for two reasons. First, in integrated systems it may be easier for reformers to gain leverage over the reform process and direct it strategically from the center, while reforms in federal systems may proceed in a more chaotic decentralized fashion. Second, federal systems offer the prospect of within-country variations that allow the analyst to show how outcomes are affected by factors that are present in one state or province while absent in others. Indeed, all three of the case studies on countries whose electricity policy is distributed between the central and state/provincial governments (Brazil, China and India) use differences within the federal system to reveal important factors at work.

14   *David G. Victor and Thomas C. Heller*

Table 1.2. *Reform strategies in the five countries.*[a]

Case	Dominant fuel (%)	National governance	Sector adequacy	Reform strategy
Brazil	Hydro (88)	Shared (mainly central)	Modest under-investment	Privatization of distribution companies to raise money for government budgets and create solvency; privatization of generators and provisions for IPPs; independent regulator.
China	Coal (78)	Shared (mainly central)	Chronic under-investment	Provisions for investment in IPPs; corporatization of state enterprises to raise money; nascent independent regulator.
India	Coal (75)	Shared (mainly federal)	Chronic under-investment	Provisions for investment in IPPs; restructuring of some distribution companies; guaranteed returns and payment security for national power corporation; independent regulators.
Mexico	Oil (47)	Central	Modest under-investment	Provisions for investment in IPPs; fuller reforms envisioned by government but stalled due to political and constitutional barriers; independent regulator.
South Africa	Coal (93)	Central	Surplus investment until recently	Corporatization of utility; reform of distributors in attempt to create solvency; aggressive electrification program to provide energy services to formerly disenfranchised citizens; independent regulator.

Note: [a] "Dominant fuel" includes the share of total power generation capacity by the fuel in [2004] as reported in [cite].

Adequacy of the power sector

A third dimension on which the case studies vary is the adequacy of the existing power system to supply electricity needed for growth. Our sample includes countries whose power sectors were unable to keep up with demand by the late 1980s (China and India), one in glut due to a history of overbuilding and weak economic growth (South Africa) and two in the middle (Brazil and Mexico). We anticipated that the adequacy of the existing system could affect outcomes for two reasons. First, if the lights are already flickering then the country's government may have few options but to launch reforms, especially if new sources of investment (private capital as well as funding from multilateral development institutions) are unavailable without a market-friendly context. Second, governments view electric power (and other infrastructures) as a crucial catalyst for economic growth, and they worry that weak power sectors will harm economic futures. Insofar as electric power creates such bottlenecks, governments with a mandate to restructive for economic growth would focus resources on reforming the electric power system as part of their larger mandate.

Reform strategy

Finally, we are mindful that literature on power market design has identified a wide array of reform strategies that are broadly consistent with the standard textbook model. There is no widely accepted typology of reform strategies, so we concentrated on three main elements of reform strategy that were already abundantly discussed in the literature. First, we ensured that our sample includes countries that began their reforms in the distribution sector (Brazil and to lessor degree South Africa), those that started with generation (China and Mexico) and those that did both at nearly the same time (India). This matters because the distribution sector is closest to the customer and reforms that raise prices to end users (which nearly always occur due to the history of undercharging for power in these countries) should be more likely to cause a political backlash. Moreover, if unreformed distributors are insolvent, then efforts to encourage private investment elsewhere in the power supply system may fail because investors in new generators, for example, will fear that they won't get paid. Second, we examined countries that encouraged new investments in generation mainly through private IPPs (Mexico), those without IPPs (South Africa), and those that sought to expand private power plants at the same time that they expanded the capacity of state-dominated power supplies (Brazil, China and India). The IPP-led strategy has been attractive to many reformers, but it has been can be difficult to implement because it requires host governments and their regulators to make credible long-term commitments. Moreover, because IPPs rely on private capital that usually demands a rapid recovery, IPPs require hard budget financing, a topic to which we return later. Thus, IPPs often appear more costly than existing (often state-owned) plants and force greater financial accountability in the power sector. Third, we examine different strategies for empowering regulators because independent regulation is a keystone to any reform that aims to remove the state from direct control over the power sector while, at the same time, preserving some semblance of orderly oversight to ensure that investors work toward the public interest. While all these countries created independent regulators as part of their market reforms, our sample includes wide variation in the practical independence, authority, and function of regulators. In Mexico, the regulator has great independence and competence but does not have the key authority to regulate tariffs. In Brazil, the regulator's independence has suffered in periodic bouts of politicization of the sector (notably after a power crisis in 2001–2002). In South Africa the regulator is vulnerable to high turnover and some scandal, but has improved markedly in recent years. In India, the experience with regulation varies widely across the states. In China, the regulator exists only as a formality, but has no influence on investment and operation in the power system. Table 1.2 summarizes these reform strategies.

Strengths and limitations of our sample

While our main interest in selecting the sample was to ensure variability in key factors that might explain outcomes, we note that our sample countries all share the common attributes of having the largest economies and among the largest populations in their regions (table 1.3). For their sheer size they are intrinsically important. In the 1990s these nations alone added 240 gigawatts (GW) of generating capacity – nearly half of the world's total increase in generating capacity. By 2003, China alone had in place 356 GW of generating capacity – the world's second largest electric power system, behind only the United States (EIA 2006). Yet, average power consumption in these five countries is only 1830 kWh per capita, or barely one-tenth the U.S. level. As these power systems grow, the consequences will be felt in world capital markets and in mankind's footprint on the environment. Already, these five countries account for more than one-fifth of the world's emissions of greenhouse gases.

We note that our ability to infer general conclusions from our sample of five countries suffers from at least three limitations. First, our small sample does not allow us to probe all combinations of the factors identified above. This limitation is intrinsic to the type of "medium N" research that is presented in this book. Our approach has an advantage over large statistical studies because it allows the exploration of factors that are difficult to measure systematically and which operate in complex ways within each case. This approach also has obvious advantages over individual studies or collections of studies that are not part of an

Table 1.3. *Key indicators for 2002 and 2003*[a]

Country	Population	Income (GDP/cap $, PPP)	GDP (Billion $)	Power supply (TWh)	Generating capacity (GW)	New fuel (%)
Brazil	177m	7790	492	345	76	Nuclear(4)
China	1288m	5003	1417	1641	338	Hydro(18)
India	1064m	2892	600	597	122	Hydro, Gas (11 each)
Mexico	102m	9168	626	215	44	Gas(32)
South Africa	46m	10346	160	218	41	Nuclear(5.5)

Note: [a] Fuel shares are a percent of total generation; "new fuel" is the most commonly cited alternative to the dominant fuel and, in all five cases, government has actively considered policies to promote the new fuel for the sake of fuel diversity. Total power supply and new fuel data are for 2002; the rest for 2003.
Source: World Bank, 2005; Energy Information Administration (EIA), 2005.

integrated whole in that it allows for some measure of generalization to other settings. However, we are unable to overcome all the limitations of a small sample. Where possible, the case studies have multiplied the explanatory power of the sample by comparing different stages of reform over time and by contrasting the experiences across different jurisdictions within the country.

Second, the study may suffer from numerous selection biases. In particular, we have selected cases from a universe of experiences that is marked by the *failure* to implement the standard textbook model. We have adopted this universe of cases because the purpose of our study is to explain that failed outcome. Nonetheless, we are mindful that there are examples in the advanced industrialized world – England and Wales, the PJM interconnection in the United States, parts of Australia, and soon perhaps much of the European Union – where the textbook model is being put into practice, often with substantial improvements in efficiency. Those examples, we suggest, are not directly relevant to this study, which aims to explain the experiences across nearly all developing countries where the institutional environment needed for markets to operate in the power sector is very weak. In such emerging markets, the rule of law is highly imperfect, truly independent and powerful regulators are extremely difficult to create, and it is very difficult to establish institutions in which rules rather than political interests determine outcomes. We do not intend our study to apply directly to settings where these market-forming institutions are much stronger – including the few mis-named "developing" countries such as Singapore and possibly Korea. However, in the conclusion we will suggest some ways that our findings may be universal to all settings. For about four-fifths of humanity, however, the results from this study have considerable relevance.

We are also mindful that our study omits the very few examples of textbook reform examples from the developing world – including the most often cited cases of Chile and Argentina. Chile is a special case because reformers operated within the special powers that arise in a military state, which allowed the government to quash opposition and also impose broad-based reforms. Moreover, a close look reveals that Chile has not really implemented the standard textbook model. The power system in Chile is dominated by a few firms, raising serious questions about market power. Chile's regulatory authority is seen as a model in the region; yet in-depth studies show that the monopoly aspects of the business still earn extraordinary returns (approaching thirty percent annually), far above what would be justified by Chile's relatively low-risk investment climate (Estache and Rodriguez-Pardina 1999, p. 11). This suggests that Chilean regulators have never been able to perform their central task – to set tariffs or create a market competition that fully serves the public interest. The more difficult challenge to our study is Argentina, where reforms under the democratic government of President Carlos Menem seem to illustrate that in a typical major developing country the textbook can be applied – albeit under reform-minded leadership with a political mandate for reform (Heller and McCubbins, 1996; Estache and Rodriguez-Partina, 1999). The problem with the Argentine example is that the very compromises that were needed to sustain the reform appear, in the end, to have undermined the achievements of reform. The financial crisis of 2001 has exposed foreign investors in the power sector to a dramatic devaluation, while keeping in place their hard currency-denominated debts. At the time of writing this, a new Argentine government responding to populist pressure is in the process of undoing the reforms in the power sector. As Argentina struggles with the effects of the recent macroeconomic shock, we suggest that the outcomes are becoming quite similar to experiences examined in more detail in this book.

Third, critics may argue that our sample of cases is biased because not enough time has passed to observe full reforms in the developing world. Thus we may prematurely conclude that reforms lead to a special stasis when, in fact, our sample merely represents five early snapshots on a long path to fuller reform. We will show that despite widely varied fuels, reform strategies, timing and starting points the outcomes appear to be similar. Moreover, we will show that in some cases reforms have actually retrenched and the state-dominated part of the power sector is reasserting its role. All these outcomes suggest (but do not prove) that the political economy we describe in this book reflects an equilibrium rather than a transient phenomenon.

The outline of each study

For each of the five countries, we enlisted leading social scientists and power sector experts to examine the causes and outcomes of efforts to introduce market forces. We asked each author to address a common set of research questions, introduced in more detail elsewhere (Heller and Victor, 2003). With full drafts in hand, we then led an intensive process of consultation and review – with seminars in each country that included presentations of case study drafts – and edited each of the studies into a common voice. Chapters 2–6 provide the studies, and here we summarize the four main elements included in each study, as well as the hypotheses that each of those elements allow us to probe. In the conclusion (chapter 7) we return to these four elements and use them to frame our main findings.

The historical context and the origins of reform

First, each case study places the organization of the power sector into historical context. In each of these five countries, electric service had similar origins in the late nineteenth century. Private for-profit ventures served lucrative customers, mainly in major cities and industrial areas, and as these power systems expanded in size and scope they became increasingly integral to the economic system. The state increasingly intervened to regulate and eventually assume ownership of the electricity supply industry; in most countries state intervention gathered steam in the 1930s and 1940s, an era of increasing state control in nearly every aspect of the economy. Governments adopted policies that were hostile to private ownership, while at the same time lavishing state resources on politically favored state-owned enterprises (SOEs).

Managers of these early power systems expanded their infrastructure to meet exponential growth in demand by tapping the fuel that was locally most abundant and least costly to deploy – coal in China, India and South Africa; hydroelectricity in Brazil; and oil in Mexico. Whatever inefficiencies arose because of state control were typically offset by the ever-increasing economies of scale and scope in the power sector. Thus nearly everywhere in the world the price of power declined (at least until the 1970s), a fact that allowed governments to supply a politically visible service at ever-more-attractive prices while reinforcing contemporary assumptions that electricity was a natural monopoly that required state ownership and control.

One of the most striking observations from the studies that follow is that in each, the impetus for reform arose at approximately the same time – around 1990. We asked each author to explore the motivations for reform. To help frame the analysis, we articulated three rival hypotheses. One hypothesis is that the coincident arrival of market reform strategies reflected the global diffusion of a superior idea. Following the early academic work on markets for power and the demonstration of success in England and Wales, policy makers may have seen markets as a better option than state control in assuring that society applied its resources efficiently. In practice, this diffusion may be accelerated by certain elites – such as market-minded experts from the World Bank, consultancies and academia – but the prime mover, according to this hypothesis, is economic efficiency.

Another hypothesis views market reform as simply a trend. Like the failed import substitution policies of the 1960s or the statist architecture of public buildings such as airports in the 1970s, market-oriented reforms might simply reflect a new fad in economic organization (Meyer and Rowen, 1977; Megginson et al., 1994). For this argument to hold, those who embrace reform would focus less on the actual expected performance of reforms and more on the fact that all countries were undertaking reforms.[9] It was the thing to do. According to this hypothesis, elites were not merely a conduit for superior ideas but they were, in addition, the prime movers for change. When the ideas in vogue within elite circles change, so do the ideas in the field on the periphery.

A final hypothesis is that reform emerged from crisis. The accumulation of inefficiencies and the exhaustion of potential for cost-reducing improvements might have created crises during which domestic reformers perceived no viable alternatives except the move to markets. For this logic to hold, reformers would need to believe that markets were the only option, and reform would need to be correlated with the onset of crisis. Crisis would focus a spotlight on the problems of SOEs and also create a political opportunity that could be used to overcome opposition. In exploring this hypothesis, we asked each author to explain the origins and nature of any crisis that spurred reform. Did it

---

[9] Note that many participants in the wave of privatization in the 1990s embraced the process "on faith" with little in the way of empirical evidence to support either the timing or manner of the privatizations. There is a canonical argument that organizations establish legitimacy through adoption of formal changes that have little impact on factual performance.

arise inside the SOE as a consequence of its own operations and inefficiencies? Or did crisis stem from events outside and lift a tide of disarray and financial ruin that affected the power sector (and perhaps much else in the economy)? Nearly all the crises examined in this book are financial in nature since the power sector is such a large user of capital and, as we will show, control over the allocation of capital is fundamental to control over the sector. This hypothesis is based on the logic that power sectors might often be targets for reform – whether due to the economic advantages of reform or its faddish nature – but the "transaction costs" of reform are so large that only a crisis would allow the mobilization of resources needed to impose an alternative form of organization.

Reform strategy

Having established the historical background, each study then examines the reform process in detail. We expected (and found) that each country would follow its own idiosyncratic patterns in the reform process, and thus it would be extremely difficult to identify a general template. Instead, we asked each author to explain the choice of strategy that reformers put into practice. The standard textbook model for reform focused on the end point – namely, an unbundled, privately owned, and õ competitive power system – with much less attention on the steps that governments would (or should) take toward that end. Most governments that undertook power sector reforms articulated however vaguely, a long-term goal that reflects all the main elements of the textbook model. However, they made choices about the sequence of steps, what we call "reform strategy," and through the studies we explore whether the sequence affected outcomes. To frame the options, we identified three reform strategies that countries have followed in the past:

Big bang

The Chilean and U.K. models entail reform that was implemented rapidly and fully – putting generation, transmission and distribution services into private hands and creating competition where feasible, notably in generation and in service for large customers. None of the countries in our sample followed this approach because only a very few developing countries have pursued big bang reform. Below we will explain why those cases are likely to be special outliers.

Lead with generation

Some countries – in our sample, China and Mexico – began reforms in the generation sector. They did this either because it involves a limited number of industrial sites and potential firms and thus was thought to be politically and organizationally easier to implement, or because they assumed that they would face imminent power shortages that required urgent action to boost investment in generation. The latter logic, especially, usually leads to provisions for independent power projects (IPPs) that are often stand-alone companies operating a single cluster of generators that sell their electricity under long-term contracts to a state-controlled distributor. The early period of India's reforms followed this strategy, and South Africa is presently poised to proceed along this path.

Lead with distribution

Other countries – in our sample, Brazil – initiate reform from the distribution sector. These efforts are usually justified by the logic that distributors are wasteful in their operations and insolvent. They must become normal enterprises, able to pay their bills, before reforms anywhere else in the power sector will have practical effect. For example, according to this logic private investors would be wary of investing in new generators unless they had confidence that the purchasers of power would be able to honor their contracts. Some Indian states, along with the whole country in its most recent attempt at power sector reform, have followed this strategy.

Many other variants on these three strategies exist, of course. For example, countries that have led with generation have not fully ignored the insolvency and inefficiencies of distributors. South Africa has attempted some reforms in distribution (for example, by redrawing the boundaries around regional distributors to ease the task of subsidizing users who pay less than the cost of supply with more lucrative customers), even as the country's main reform strategy has focused on generation. In different states and at different periods of time, India has attempted both strategies. Brazil started with distribution services in some states and then moved to generation before the reform effort largely ran aground. Nonetheless, we pose these three strategies starkly so that we can focus on whether strategy actually affects outcomes.

The institutional context for markets

Fundamentally, market reform is an exercise in reinventing the role of the state in the economy and society. Moving to markets does not entail, of course, the complete abandonment of the state in the economy.

Rather, it shifts the functions of government toward regulation and oversight instead of the actual financing and operating of economic enterprise (Vogel 2003). Part of this shift is the dismantling (or decline) of state-owned enterprises (SOEs) and the creation of usually new or deeply restructured institutions such as independent regulators, judiciaries to settle disputes, and capital markets. Early in this project we developed stylized descriptions of two alternative forms of economic organization – what we called "state-centered systems" and "market-centered systems" – to help the authors of each case study explore how the changing role for government and organization of the economy might affect the process and outcomes from power sector reform.[10] Here we focus on just the three most important institutional elements: the setting of policy and regulation; industrial organization and management; and financing of capital and operating expenses.

Policy and regulation

The process of setting policy priorities is usually embedded within the SOE itself because the SOE in a state-centered system shares in the functions and identity of the state. Indeed, there may be no useful distinction between the SOE and the ministry charged with its oversight; elites in both may cycle easily and rapidly between jobs in both entities. In some countries, electric power SOEs are functionally identical to the ministry. Thus the enterprise becomes an extension of government's broader purposes, and the government relies on the SOE to supply a wide array of social services – in the extreme, child care, education, housing, "social safety nets," shopping and even restaurants. The state and civil society (themselves conceived as an integrated unit) focus on the firm in both the policy making and policy implementation processes. Social objectives, often extensive, blend goals like employment of idle workers, protection of the environment, and provision of energy services to poor areas into the daily production decisions of the firm. As with all SOE behavior, these varied policy goals may be negotiated through the continual interaction of firm management, government officials, and, in some cases, other state-organized actors such as labor or consumer

---

[10] That early description is discussed in detail in Heller and Victor (2003); the distinctions are intended as "ideal types" and thus actual reforms are likely to have attributes of both. The distinction drawn here between state- and market-centered systems grows out of a body of work in comparative corporate governance examining the origins, development and stability or adaptation of differing forms of firm organization (e.g., Hollingsworth, et al., 1997; Streek and Yamamura eds., 2001; Bratton and McCahery, 1999; Hall and Soskice eds., 2001). A mid-1990s World Bank report surveys the persistence of what we refer to as state-centered governance patterns in reforming countries (World Bank, 1995).

associations. Where a few firms dominate each industry, negotiations of a wide range of policy outcomes between the limited set of core actors is feasible. Outsiders play little role. Nor can outsiders judge enterprise compliance with public policies because policy outcomes are neither transparent nor expressed as independent norms of conduct. They are known only to insiders and directly monitored by administrative or industrial peer supervision. Additionally, when state firms implement policies they are generally compensated by politically orchestrated privileges, such as access to low-cost finance or market protections. Because of this practice, SOEs often strongly favor the visible delivery of public functions, as this allows managers to amplify the resources that they can capture from the state.

In contrast, in market-centered systems the policy domain is more often restricted in scale and externalized from the firm. First, in competitive markets, the effective formulation and implementation of any policy decision rarely devolves upon a particular firm or closed roster of state-chartered interest groups. Second, unlike state-centered systems where the executive branch of government is pervasive, market-centered systems have separately elected legislators that play a larger role in policy setting. Finally, basic policy decisions are implemented primarily in private market decisions between autonomous producers and consumers. Supplemental and exceptional policies must be institutionalized outside the invisible routines of an integrated state–firm network. Like the markets for capital, labor and goods, the policy process is a competition in which key players (e.g., firms, NGOs) comprise voluntary members; transparency and independent accounting are held at a premium. Independent regulators and judges adjudicate contested outcomes. Policy outcomes must be formulated through participatory processes, implemented openly and subjected to public review – even in highly regulated sectors like electricity.

Industrial organization and management

States (or their subordinate political jurisdictions) rarely create multiple enterprises that perform the same function in the same sector of the economy. Because the philosophy that underpins most state-centered systems is that the state enterprise's interests are identical to the public interest, competition between state-controlled firms is viewed as unnecessary and wasteful. Large, capital-intensive industries, including network industries that have characteristics of natural monopoly, are the jewels in the crown of such a non competitive political economy. Even where the nature of the goods and services provided by the industry do not bear the hallmarks of a natural monopoly, polities erect barriers to entry such as exclusive franchises and tariff walls. Where the state allows other firms to provide a service similar to that offered by a SOE, those firms are frequently small and incorporated into state-chartered industrial groups or associations in which the dominant (state-controlled) firm leads on price and market organization. Administered standards and other restrictions tilt the market to assure dominance for the state-controlled production. Prices and quantities are the joint products of political authority and market factors.

In a state-centered system key management decisions are made by insiders who are either government agents or acquire their authority from the state. Managerial behavior is directly monitored by line ministries; performance is usually measured by the expansion of gross output and employment. Prices, inputs, production levels, and other operational practices are administratively determined. The activities of the firm are viewed in technical terms. Key managers are usually trained in engineering and the natural sciences, rather than finance, law, management or economics. Internal accounting is poor or idiosyncratic and transparency to outsiders is, at best, opaque. The state and its agents manage labor supplies, with unions serving as instruments of coordination rather than confrontation.

In market-centered systems, the state does not disappear from the scene. Although the normal rules of market organization guarantee free entry and exit, even in competitive industries firm conduct is monitored by both government (e.g., antitrust regulation) and other market actors (e.g., private law suits and remedies). In the absence of collusion, it is assumed that prices and business strategies will emerge from market forces. Business associations, networks and corporate groups are voluntary, rather than state organized, and carefully watched as probable forums for illegally coordinated conduct. Whereas in state-centered systems the institutional organization of monopoly firms is integrated with that of the state, in market-centered systems the state creates regulatory authorities that oversee their prices and behavior – ideally in ways that create incentives for good performance that mirror incentives and outcomes that would exist in a competitive market.

In market-centered systems, management of the firm and the state are distinct activities. Corporate governance reflects the legal relationships that emerge from the nexus of complex contracts between the firm and private providers of capital. In the normal case, shareholders, including protected minority investors, decide on senior appointments and oversee operations through key firm managers. Monitoring of managerial performance is enabled by requirements of extensive disclosure, transparency, independent audits, and analysis by institutional investors, financial media, securities brokers and rating agencies. Senior managers are socialized in business schools to a norm of profit maximization and shareholder accountability. The state plays a role in governance through independent regulators that are specific to the sector as well as general regulatory authorities, such as those charged with detecting and detering collusion.

Finance

In a state-centered system, both investment approval and the requisite capital for new projects come from the state itself. Loans from state-controlled banks are usually offered at rates below what commercial markets would charge. Indeed, state banks are often run by managers with incentives to maximize throughput rather than accountability that reflects the true risk-adjusted cost of capital. Their own books make little distinction between loans that carry the expectation of repayment and loans that are basically capital grants. Firm managers typically work with "soft budgets" – if costs exceed returns, the state stands ready to supply the difference (Kornai, 2001). The state financial system, in turn, is organized to facilitate selective allocations of credit that align with political priorities. The state often represses consumer spending and alternative savings opportunities, which artificially raises aggregate savings that flow into state banks. The national government also acts as an agent in negotiating concessionary loans from multilateral development banks to complement domestic financial resources.

In market-centered systems financing simply reflects the risk-adjusted cost of capital obtained in diversified markets. Capital is potentially available through bank loans, public securities issues, or private equity markets, with average capital costs determined by competitive project evaluation across these several competing sources. Equipment, materials, and services are procured in competitive markets – often globally. Managers work with a hard budget constraint because any failure to meet targets for capital repayment, interest or dividend expectations threatens their control of the firm and raises their own cost of borrowing. In addition, while in some state-centered systems substantial internal capital may come from retained earnings that result from state-created monopoly franchises, competitive or independently regulated firms that exist in more market-based economies are less likely to be able to invest solely with retained earnings. Consequently, capital-intensive projects that require long payback periods may be especially disfavored in market-centered systems.

The demand for, and effects of, power sector reform are particularly intertwined with state financial systems. The integrated power systems that prevailed in all these five countries (and essentially all the world) were relatively invulnerable to problems that would arise if parts of the system could not cover costs. If an integrated power system lost money, as most did, the enterprise was nonetheless often able to remain viable so long as the government continued to provide some form of subsidy. (In many countries such subsidies took the form of tolerance of non-payment for other services supplied by the state, such as fuel.) By contrast, in an unbundled system each unit must remain financially viable. For those that are loss-making, viability usually requires either the setting of higher tariffs or provision of explicit (on budget) state subsidies-both of which can be difficult for governments to offer credibly, especially when reforms in banking, capital markets and public finance appear on the political horizon.

These problems of subsidy become particularly acute in electric power systems for two reasons. First, in all five of our countries (except oil-dominated Mexico) the incumbent power system is generally characterized by low operating costs. Thus the function of actually operating the system, which entails dispatching power plants to minimize immediate costs, is quite different from long-term investment. The differences are particularly striking where installed power systems are dominated by coal or especially hydro, which are systems that require enormous capital investment but cost little to run. Yet natural gas fired plants, which all five countries in our sample are trying to attract, are marked by lower capital costs and higher operating costs – attributes that are particularly attractive to private investors who are keen to invest in assets that entail a lower immovable investment that can be recovered quickly. Second, "new" power is generally more expensive than "old" power. Physically and financially, the difference between new and old power should be meaningless since electrons are fungible and tariffs on the entire system should be set at the marginal cost of additional supplies (i.e., "new" power). Politically, however, the differences are extremely important as groups vie to obtain their "share" of the existing, amortized, and low-cost power supplies, leaving others to bear the cost of the new sources.

These characterizations of the institutions and their functions that provide the context for power sector reform are incomplete and highly stylized. And we remain mindful that even where these categories can usefully describe attributes of political economic systems in different countries, the differences between countries and systems remain enormous. The Chinese Communist Party, the PRI in Mexico, or the Congress Party in India are not the same organization, although each has presided over a state-centered system with some similar attributes.

Nor, obviously, are market-centered systems identical to one another, as both Americans and Englishmen are constantly pointing out.

Social contract

Each study explores how the shift to private enterprise has affected a variety of other functions that integrated state-owned enterprises historically provided as a single package. We focus on three services in particular – electricity for low income households, protection of the environment, and investment in innovation – which we label collectively as the "social contract." All three of these services are forms of public services and goods and thus markets, on their own, are unlikely to supply them at adequate levels (e.g. Tjiong et al 2003; Victor, 2005).

Providing electric service for low-income households requires operating in areas such as slums and remote rural villages, where it is particularly difficult to profitably supply energy services. Yet, about 1.6 billion people (one quarter of the global population) have no access to electricity. Although that number has declined in absolute value and also as a fraction of the world's population since 1970, mainly due to extraordinary success in Chinese electrification, by 2030 it is expected that 1.4 billion people will still lack electricity (IEA, 2002a). Most of the un-served live in rural areas in developing countries (mainly in South Asia and sub-Saharan Africa). Governments are under intense political and moral pressure to address this issue, especially as they have become aware of the critical roles that electric services can play in promoting human development (World Bank, 2002b; Rufin et al., 2003). Under the old state-dominated system, many governments created special tariffs that subsidized low-income households. Governments also directed state enterprises to provide energy services for poor households. Under the state system, the state's monopoly on capital and investment allowed for the provision of services that would be risky or unprofitable for private companies to supply – for example, by building costly extensions of the grid to poor rural areas. In all the countries examined in this book, with the partial exception of Mexico, the transition to markets has required raising user tariffs so that they better reflect the real cost of supplying new electric services. Such increases can be unaffordable and disruptive to those who have become accustomed to cheap power. Many of the world's poorest operate through informal arrangements that may be difficult to accommodate when electric services are supplied by private companies that require formal incomes so that customers can pay tariffs (e.g., USAID, 2004). Such concerns are the root of many concerns that power sector reform will be harmful to the poor (e.g., Powell and Starks, 2000; Dubash, 2002; Goldemberg et al., 2004).

In addition to focusing on the effects of power sector reform in low-income households, each study also gives some attention to the effects of power sector reform on the environment and on innovation. The environmental consequences are strongly influenced by the fact that all these countries are looking to natural gas (the cleanest of fossil fuels) as a significant new fuel. Moreover, all these countries have also undertaken substantial efforts to regulate environmental emissions over the same period that they have implemented many other political and economic reforms. Disentangling the exact effect of power sector reform on the environment in this context is difficult. In terms of innovation, none of these countries has been the source of major new technologies for grid-based power systems. However, they have contributed to technological progress of the grid system and have pioneered same technologies particular to their setting, such as South Africa's pre-paid electricity meters. The effect of power sector reform on investment and innovation has been a major topic of concern in the advanced industrialized world (e.g., Morgan and Tierney, 1998). In the developing world, these concerns have been much less evident; nonetheless, each study explores how, if at all, power sector reformers have attempted to create special incentives to invest in innovation.

Conclusion

For long, the political, legal and institutional dimensions of market reforms have been viewed as "barriers" to be cleared. This view holds that with enough political will, an entrepreneurial leader, and credible policies these barriers can be overcome and reform can proceed. An ideal model is known. With enough effort the existing system can be shocked into a form that approaches that ideal.

We argue that that view of reform is much too simplistic. The difficulty of reform stems from the nature of state-centered systems – their financing, the many ancillary social functions that are performed by SOEs, and their systems of governance and control. Those attributes, we suggest, lead to predictable patterns of behavior in the reform process and explain why economic efficiency, alone, is unlikely to be an adequate motivator for reform. They also suggest that the process of reform is likely to become intertwined with reforms in other aspects of the economy, such as fuel markets, financial markets, accounting practices and corporate governance. Financing, in particular, appears to be the key variable.

In the concluding chapter (chapter 7) we revisit the main questions and expectations introduced in this chapter, and we focus on the outcome that is strikingly common across all the cases. We find no application of the "standard textbook model" in the five developing countries that we examine in this book. Rather, we find a reform that yields a distinct outcome – what we call a "dual market," combining attributes of the state- and market-based systems. The "dual market," we argue, is not a waystation to the standard textbook model but, rather, a stable equilibrium outcome. While not the most economically efficient outcome, the dual market arises and is held in place by strong political forces that favor a system in which parts of power generation and delivery are profitable even as other parts are plagued by nonpayment, inadequate investment, and economically inefficient operation.

We suggest that our dual market theory explains observations that emerge from the studies – such as why reformers have disproportionately focused on IPPs even though in most countries the need for reform more urgently applies to distribution companies. It also explains why certain types of firms – what we call "dual firms" – have thrived in this dual market even as many conventional privately owned enterprises have failed.

2   Political economy of the Brazilian power industry reform

Adilson de Oliveira

Introduction

After a long period of rapid growth the Brazilian power industry entered a period of stagnation and crisis in the 1980s. Ever since the 1930s a series of tariff rules and nationalizations had squeezed private investors from the market. In their place, state enterprises had assumed the function of distributing electricity in Brazil's twenty-six states; Eletrobras, owned by the central government, managed the transmission system and also generated much of the electricity in Brazil. Through its control over state funds for building power plants, Eletrobras pursued vast projects such as the Itaipu hydroelectric plant and assured low electricity prices as part of the government's policy of import substitution. In the shock of the oil crises and the Latin American debt crisis this system unraveled. Financing costs escalated yet tariffs were kept low; losses mounted.

The process of reforming the electric power system began after the new democratic government took power in 1990. But a more radical effort at reform arose only in the mid-1990s in response to two main pressures. One was the goal of reorienting the entire economy away from the import substitution policies towards a more competitive system that promised greater investment and economic growth (Diniz, 2003). As a first step the finance ministry induced several states to sell valuable electric assets to private investors and plug gaping holes in their balance sheets. Privatization of these jewel assets was made politically attractive to the states when coupled with loans that allowed their governments to finance projects that generated jobs and other political benefits. The finance authorities were singular in their goal of raising the maximum amount of hard currency and did not have any strategy for the industry after privatization. Indeed, ad-hoc regulations were adopted to inflate the value of the assets at the time of privatization; the rules were settled in a different way once private investors had committed to the market.

The second pressure for reform came from international trends in the electric power sector – in particular, the model of reform adopted in England and Wales (e.g., Surrey, 1996). International experts crafted all the major elements of the "standard model" of reform – continued privatization, open access to the grid, and competition in generation and in retailing – into a strategy tailored for Brazil. That strategy envisioned that private investors would assume key roles as owners and operators of the power system, under the control of an independent regulator. The role of government was to be limited to empowering the regulator and to providing strategic policy guidance.

In practice, restructuring has been much more difficult to implement than implied in the standard model. The privatization-for-cash approach to reform generated early income for the government but did not resolve key problems in making the power business a profitable and reliable enterprise. Through much of this period the architects of reform focused on profitability and investment; however, a drought in 2001 underscored the need to focus on reliability as well.

Brazil's hydroelectric system – which supplies 95 percent of the country's power when rains are flush – is run by a system operator embedded in a culture of integrated centralized management. Dispatch rules give priority to hydro over thermal power and aim never to spill water "over the dam" – multiple dams are operated as a single system even though the owners vary. An interlocking revenue-sharing mechanism makes dam ownership more like a guaranteed bond asset than separate, competitive enterprises. The principal risk in the system – that of under-supply during extreme drought, such as in 2001 – is shifted to the customer. A wholesale pool gives the appearance of competition, but in fact prices are artificial and generated by computer models.

This chapter explores the origins of the Brazilian power system and its transformation from a system initiated by private foreign investors in the late nineteenth century to one controlled completely by state-owned enterprises ("Historical Development of the Industry"). It then examines the mounting forces that generated pressure for reform and how the broader political and economic changes in Brazil shaped the reform process ("Restructuring the Electric Power System"). The most dramatic reforms were initiated by financial authorities who were interested in achieving macroeconomic goals. Interests that opposed reform – especially in the states, which feared losing politically valuable assets – sought to delay and redirect the reform process. At the same time, a large group of technicians in the power companies as well as a cadre of consultants with experience in power sector reform elsewhere in the world each pursued clashing visions for reform. The result was a hybrid power market that combined "reformed" elements – in which private owners compete for tenders and operate in an environment where many prices are artificially generated by computer – along with state-owned and centrally managed economy despatch.

In "Unresolved Issues: Fuel Diversity and Systemic Risk," we explore the consequences of this system and give particular attention to the problem of attracting investment in thermal power sources – notably natural gas. The political compromise that created Brazil's hybrid system was attractive to most of the powerful players who were present at the negotiations. Integrated and risk-dispersing control of the hydro system allowed incumbent generators to continue their operations largely unaffected and with virtually assured profits; foreign investors found these generators to be low-risk opportunities, and the treasury welcomed the resources from the privatizations. In a few states governments refused to dispose their distribution assets but generation remains largely a state-dominated one. The hybrid system that has emerged gives little voice to interests who were not well represented – potential new generators who could burn newly available gas resources. A few such plants have been built, but only the plants that have attracted special government subsidies or special gas contracts with Petrobras, the state-owned oil and gas company and take-or-pay contracts with distribution companies, have proved profitable; in most gas-fired plants dispatch rules and other provisions make it difficult for potential private investors to justify the expenditure.

So far the reform has produced a system that is remarkably similar to the old system – although a few names on doors have changed and there has been a net flow of resources into the treasury from privatizations. Assessing the effect of the reforms so far is difficult. It appears that the main benefits of reform have emerged not from full-blown competition – which does not exist in Brazil – but rather from creating a structure that produces much greater transparency about the economic and technical conditions of the power supply, as well as the costs and the dispatch rules that govern the system. Although the fundamental problem of creating incentives to invest in new power supply (other than hydroelectric plants) remains unsolved, in this new system the independent regulator – when allowed to exercise its authority – is much better able than its predecessors to exert control over the system for the benefit of consumers.

Historical development of the industry

Brazil is physically large (8.5 million km^2) with 170 million inhabitants, concentrated primarily in large cities along the Atlantic coastline

34   Adilson de Oliveira

Table 2.1. Key demographic and economic statistics

	1950	1960	1970	1980	1991	2000
Total population (millions)	51.9	70.1	93.1	121.61	149.9	170.1
Urban population (millions)	16.3	28.5	47.5	72.1	98.5	123.5
Number of Cities	1,887	2,764	3,952	3,991	4,491	5,507
GDP (1980 = 100)	11.8	24.0	43.7	100.0	118.1	151.8
GDP/capita ($)	899	1,359	1,861	3,260	3,124	3,538
Power consumption (GWh)	8,513	18,346	37,673	115,874	225,372	331,596

Sources: IBGE, Eletrobras, and IPEA.

(table 2.1). The Brazilian federal system shares power between states (each with its own elected governor) and the center. At the federal level, power is divided between the Executive – led by the President, who names thousands of political appointees to key administrative positions – and the Congress. In practice, nearly all key decisions lie with the Executive because powers in Congress are usually diffuse and difficult to craft into working coalitions.

As in most other countries, the earliest investors in Brazil's power industry were private companies that built exclusive concessions in large cities and for large industries – mainly in the industrialized and wealthier southeast of the country. A Canadian Group (Light) obtained the concessions for Rio and São Paulo in 1897; in 1927 a US firm (AMFORP) obtained concessions for several other large towns. The main source of generation – then and now – was falling water. Brazilian fossil fuels reserves are relatively scarce;[1] water resources are plentiful, except in the Northeast, and total about 260 GW of hydropower potential supply. The topography in the industrialized southeast is favorable for the construction of large reservoirs[2].

Without any single federal process for awarding public concession of power services, each municipality established its own rules. Typically,

[1] Coal reserves are in the extreme south (Rio Grande do Sul and Santa Catarina) but are of poor quality. Until the 1980s, oil and natural gas reserves were small but they increased substantially in the 1980s, after large oil field discoveries offshore from Rio de Janeiro. However, the country still is importing both fuels.
[2] Existing reservoirs are able to store up to 130 TWh, almost half a year at current consumption levels. The water flow can be streamlined during the year, increasing the capacity factor of the power plants and consequently their competitiveness as well.

investors operated within contracts that fixed maximum tariffs (reviewed monthly), with payments half in domestic currency and half in gold standard (*Cláusula Ouro*). Under this framework, the installed capacity of the power industry grew at 7.6 percent per year between 1900 and 1930. As shown in figure 2.1 (left panel) private investors dominated the industry.

The 1929 New York Stock Exchange crash had a profound impact on the Brazilian economy. Coffee exports, the single tradable Brazilian product in those years, dropped dramatically, pushing the economy into deep recession (Furtado, 1972). Growing urban middle class dissatisfaction with the political control exerted by the *coroneis* (landlords) culminated in an uprising that installed a revolutionary government with nationalist policies (Stepan, 1973). The new federal government eclipsed some of the powers of the twenty-six states. Successive Brazilian governments structured a fast growing but protected industrial sector. From the start, the role of foreign companies in energy supply was a political issue. Nationalists argued that energy was a strategic factor of production and could not be left to foreign control; liberals responded that foreign investors would bring technology and capital, both scarcely available in the country. As in Mexico (see chapter 5 by Carreon and Jiminez, this volume), the nationalists eventually won the conflict (Medeiros Lima, 1975).

The virtuous circle

In 1934, the federal government laid the cornerstone for development of hydroelectric power by adopting the Water Code, which assigned to the federal government the property rights of the hydropower potential of Brazilian rivers and the authority to regulate the power services. A National Council for Water and Power (CNAEE)[3] was created to regulate the industry, and the federal government introduced a cost of service (cost plus) tariff scheme. The water code discouraged private investment in the power business – notably, it calculated costs in nominal terms (Dias Leite, 1977), and the Water Code forced investors to absorb currency risks by abolishing the *Cláusula Ouro*.

The new tariff regime – along with other factors, such as continued world depression and the war in Europe – caused private power companies to curtail investment, and growth in generating capacity slowed (figure 2.1). Yet demand for power continued to soar due to

[3] Later, National Department for Water and Power (DNAEE) and, since 1996, National Power Agency (Aneel).

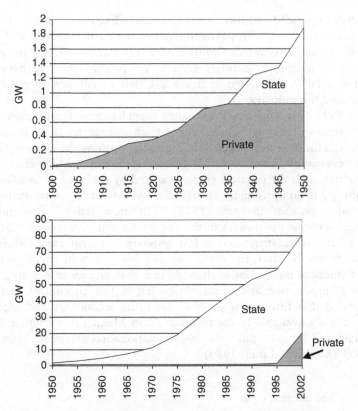

Figure 2.1. Installed capacity by ownership – 1950–2002[a]
Note: [a]Note the scale change.
Sources: IBGE, 1986; Aneel, 2003.

industrialization, urbanization, and economic growth, with the result that rationing of electricity was required in several cities, creating a serious problem for the emerging industrial sector. Public pressure urged a larger role of government in the power industry; federal and state governments invested in power projects with the goal of reducing the gap between supply and potential demand. Starting in 1945 (and extending to the 1970s) the federal government's investments formed four regional electricity suppliers – Chesf (1945), Furnas (1947), Eletrosul (1968), and Eletronorte (1972).[4]

---

[4] State governments created CEEE (1943) in Rio Grande do Sul, CEMIG (1952) in Minas Gerais, Copel (1954) in Paraná, and Uselpa and Cherp in São Paulo.

Although democracy was reinstated at the end of World War II, the industrialization strategy did not change. With private investors interested in the energy sector increasingly wary of Brazil, a consensus emerged between nationalists and liberals that state-owned companies should control the energy sector. Petrobras, a federal government monopoly, was created in 1954 to develop the incipient oil market. In 1962 the federal government created Eletrobras as a holding company for the four federally owned regional suppliers plus other electricity assets owned by the federal government.[5] Eletrobras also assumed the role of imposing compatible technical standards and coordinating development of the power system into a truly national interconnected grid.[6] Both of these state-owned enterprises operated with the mandate to spread the supply of modern energy sources at prices that would aid industrialization (de Oliveira, 1977).

Initially, hydropower projects were built with no coordination among power companies. In the 1960s, when different companies were envisaging the construction of power plants on the same river runs, the federal government engaged – with the financial support of the World Bank – a consortium of international engineering companies (Canambra) to craft a long-term coordinated development plan for the South and the Southeast power systems.[7] Using a fuel oil thermal power plant as a benchmark, Canambra concluded that thermal power plants would be more costly than tapping the available hydropower sites and thus advised that thermal power plants should be limited to a complementary role in the power industry.[8] The oil shocks made hydropower plants even more competitive and reinforced the perception among power policy makers that Brazil is a hydropower country.

The bulk of the conventional thermal power capacity is installed in the South, close to coal mines, but thermal power plants (burning oil products) also supply power to several isolated power markets, mainly in the Amazonian region. A nuclear power program, initiated at the end of

---

[5] Besides the nuclear power plants and the Brazilian share of Itaipu, Eletrobras had control of the four regional generation and transmission companies (Eletronorte, Eletrosul, Furnas, and CHESF), and minority shares in every other power company.

[6] Until then, each power company decided on its own technical standard, a situation that proved very difficult for the interconnection of the regional power systems of the country.

[7] Canambra comprises Montreal and Crippen, Canadian companies, plus Gibbs and Hill, an American company.

[8] Thermal power plants should be dispatched in periods of reduced rain fall.

the 1960s, never blossomed as it was constantly constrained by the unattractive economics of nuclear technology. However, with persistent support of the military and the Brazilian establishment for the peaceful use of nuclear power, the program did yield the construction of two nuclear power plants (600 MW and 1250 MW) in a single site (Angra dos Reis/Rio de Janeiro). A third power plant (1250 MW) has been under construction since the 1980s at the same site but still has not guaranteed the financing for its completion.[9]

To help finance the creation of a national power industry, in the 1950s Congress created a federal tax on power consumption (Imposto Único sobre Energia Elétrica, IUEE) and channeled the revenue into a National Electrification Fund – much as China today uses special national taxes to fund large power projects (see chapter 3 by Zhang, this volume).[10] A few years later, industrial consumers were ordered to supply compulsory loans for power projects, which became a small but not insignificant source of funding (figure 2.2).

Funding for power projects was designed to come from a tripartite system: one-third from taxes and "parafiscal" levies, such as the IUEE and compulsory loans,[11] one-third from retained earnings, and one-third from loans, such as from multilateral development banks and other sources. Most of these resources flowed through Eletrobras, which administered them according to its investment plan.

Easy access to low cost financial resources made it possible for state enterprises to expand generating capacity at 8.8 percent per year between 1945 and 1970 (see figure 2.1). The public sector gradually supplanted private investors who, seeing that tariffs fail to keep pace with inflation, were wary of unsecured currency risks.

In the early 1960s a fierce political battle between left wing (mainly socialist) and right wing (supported by the military) parties ended with the military removing civilians from government (Skidmore, 1969). The new regime, although radically right wing, did not change the industrialization and energy strategies of the past (Gaspari, 2002). Indeed, it

---

[9] The 600 MW power plant is a turnkey project bought from Westinghouse. The other two are the result of a comprehensive nuclear agreement between the Brazilian and the German governments that envisaged initially the construction of at least eight nuclear power plants and the development of the nuclear fuel cycle in Brazil. Although the Brazilian–German agreement was not formally rejected, it is a consensus that it will end as soon as Angra III is put in operation.

[10] Revenues were shared between central government (40%) and state governments (60%).

[11] "Parafiscal" include the compulsory loans that were technically loans (when given they were expected to be paid back), but state control over these financial flows meant that they were much less costly than market rate loans. In the 1990s, the compulsory loan mechanism was being phased out as part of an effort to make taxes more transparent.

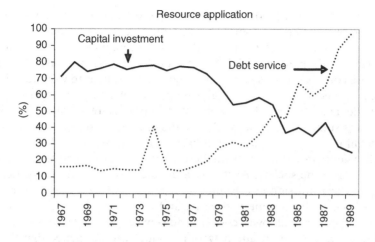

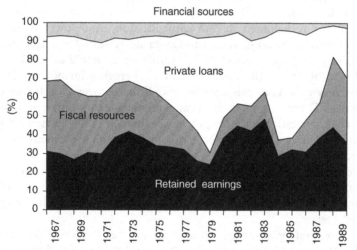

Figure 2.2. Financial situation of Brazilian power companies (1967–1989)[a]

Note: [a]The series are calculated by the sum of balance sheets' values of the Eletrobras Group. Other capital expenses are not available.

Source: Eletrobras.

deepened the federal government's control over generation and transmission by creating two coordinating committees – one for operating the interconnected grids (GCOI) and the other for planning generation and transmission expansions (GCPS) – both headed by Eletrobras. The aim of these committees was to induce all power companies to work together to explore economies of scale and scope (lower reserve margin, lower peak demand) offered by the interconnection of regional grids. The logic was similar to that adopted in all the other four countries examined in detail in this book: competition was seen as wasteful, and monopoly (under government control) the best means to extend benefits of electrification to the society. At the time the technology of electric generation and transmission also favored integration and monopoly control – indeed, costs did decline with scale and scope and productivity rose, allowing greater and lower cost electric service (de Oliveira, 1992).

Two regulatory innovations were introduced to guarantee that there was no financial risk for power projects. Nondepreciated assets could be annually reevaluated in line with inflation, and power companies were allowed a tracking account (Conta de Resultados a Compensar, CRC) in their balance sheet if their tariffs were unable to provide their legal rate of return (between 10 and 12 percent) on nondepreciated assets. Any deficits in this account should be recovered in future tariff increases. These new financial arrangements were intended to enhance the credit conditions of the power companies. They benefited both private and state-owned power companies but the movement for state control of the power industry was already unstoppable.

Even as the federal government centralized generation and transmission, the task of distribution was decentralized into the hands of the states (figure 2.3) – a reflection of the shared power in the Brazilian federal system.

The federal government had acquired a few key distributors (AMFORP in 1965 and Light in 1977) and sold some of these assets back to the states, with loans from the state-controlled National Bank for Development (BNDES). Where private incumbents did not already exist, states created new power companies. The central government's aim was to create a federally controlled enterprise that generated and transmitted power to state-owned regional distribution companies. (A similar model was already in place in England and Wales and was adopted in other countries such as India [see chapter 4 by Tongia, this volume].) Eletrobras occupied the central role in this strategy: its share of total investments in power sector investments rose from 32.6 percent in 1974 to 60.7 percent in 1983 (Memória da Eletricidade, 1995). The federal government eventually dominated the power business through

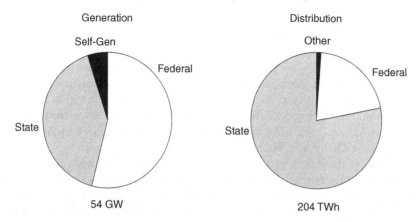

Figure 2.3. Ownership of generation (left) and distribution (right) assets

Source: Eletrobras, 1998.

Eletrobras' control of low-cost financing and the requirements of a coordinated, interconnected national grid. Unable to tap these resources, state companies gradually reduced their presence in the generation and transmission of electricity.

Conflicts emerge

The federal government strategy suited the majority of the Brazilian states but was not received well by the states that already had their own vibrant generation and transmission companies (Camozzato, 1995). The conflict of interests between Eletrobras and these state power companies became particularly intense in the 1970s as a result of two federal government decisions: the construction of Itaipu and the introduction of a single tariff system.

In 1973, despite the strong opposition of the Argentinean government, Paraguay and Brazil signed a treaty to construct a binational power plant (Itaipu).[12] Jointly managed by both countries but entirely financed by Brazil, the Itaipu power output (12,600 MW) is shared in equal parts by the two countries. Itaipu's tariff is based on its production

---

[12] Argentina's opposition was geopolitical and technical. Politically, it feared that Paraguay (traditionally a close Argentine ally) would become more closely integrated with Brazil – in fact, that political outcome has occurred. Technically, Argentina raised many objections – among them, the fear of downstream risk to Argentina from catastrophic failure of the dam and from water fluctuations. Some changes were adopted to address these technical objections, but the principal fear was geopolitical.

cost (nearly entirely the amortization of capital expenditure) and is fixed in American dollars. Because demand in Paraguay is insufficient to absorb its 50 percent share, Eletrobras committed to buy any Paraguayan surplus.[13] A law passed in Congress granted dispatching priority for Itaipu into the Brazilian market, forcing the state companies of the South and the Southeast to reduce their power plants' generation and to postpone their projects. (Similarly, in China large state-controlled projects have led the central government to mandate states to take the power [see Zhang and Heller in chapter 3 of this volume]).

In 1977, the government sought to reduce regional economic disparities by introducing a single tariff regime for the whole country. Even as the South and Southeastern parts of the country became wealthy and highly urbanized, the vast majority of Brazil's poor were dispersed in the North and Northeast with little access to modern opportunities, including electric power service.[14] A compensation mechanism forced low cost, profitable companies of the Southeast to transfer revenues to a fund (Reserva Geral de Garantia, RGG) controlled by Eletrobras and used to compensate high costs companies of the North and the Northeast of Brazil. Through this mechanism, Brazilians in different regions faced the same tariff structure – even though the cost to serve low-intensity and dispersed power users in the northeast was much higher than in the dense living, industrialized cities of the southeast. The military assured that both measures were accepted (if angrily) by the Southeast generation companies.

The financial effect of these measures was disastrous. Low and high cost companies alike saw no reason to control costs, which inflated rapidly. Tariffs should have risen in tandem since the basic tariff regime was based on costs. Formally, tariffs were regulated by the DNAEE, but in practice the finance ministry set prices. Concerned about inflation, the finance ministry refused to allow tariffs to increase according to costs. The *unreceived* revenue was placed in the CRC account for recovery in future tariff increases – allowing the power companies to show their guaranteed 10 percent rate of return on their balance sheets even as their cash flow dwindled. But this trick, which pushed actual recovery of costs into the future, did not fix the fundamental problem. Facing a sharply rising need for investment, the power companies (through Eletrobras and the government) sought loans overseas to

---

[13] At present, about 95% of Itaipu's electric power output is sold in Brazil.

[14] Today, almost three quarters of the population is living in urban areas, compared to 31.3% in 1950. Of today's 170 million population, 50 million Brazilians still live below the poverty line – the largest share located in the North and in the Northeast of the country.

supply the balance that lenders were happy to oblige as they saw utilities with supposedly guaranteed revenue streams and assumed that these loans were, in essence, backed by the state. In 1980, only 20 percent of the industry's financial resources went to service debt, a fraction that rose steadily (and peaked at 98.4 percent in 1989).[15]

The vicious circle

At the beginning of the 1970s, the Brazilian economy was growing rapidly (10 percent per year) but 80 percent of oil consumption was imported. When the first oil price spike deteriorated the country's external accounts, the military government launched an ambitious industrialization program intended to accelerate the process of import substitution (Castro and Souza, 1985). The assumption was that, in due time, investments in Brazilian industry would alleviate the need for imports; the surplus in the trade balance would then pay for the external loans that had financed these projects. However, this treadmill stopped short of maturity in the wake of the second oil shock and the Latin American debt crisis. The increase in the prime interest rate in the United States forced the devaluation of the Brazilian currency, inducing a spiral of inflation and fiscal deficit that disordered the macroeconomic fundamentals of the country (Carneiro and Modiano, 1990). Government policies forced the Brazilian economy into a severe economic recession to avoid defaulting on its loans.

In the context of economic recession, power consumption fell well below the forecasts of the early 1970s, which increased average costs as capital-intensive generators sat idle. Yet the Ministry of Finance, more worried about the rest of the economy, mandated tariffs below the rate of inflation (figure 2.4).[16] Power companies' net cash flow declined even as higher interest rates raised their financial obligations. The "three-thirds" financial strategy for the power industry collapsed. Lacking funding, several power projects had to be delayed, but no state

---

[15] This shift occurred despite the greater availability of special funds that could be tapped for construction, like the Global Reserve for Reversion ("RGR") fund to which each company is required to pay annually 3% of the value of its fixed assets. The nominal purpose of this fund was to handle the growing buyback obligations under the Water Law concession scheme, although in practice it became just another one of the "parafiscal" revenue resources. Typically, concessions were for thirty-five years after which time they reverted to the federal government, which was then obliged to compensate the owner (usually a private investor or state government) for the value of its nondepreciated assets. The fund still exists in Eletrobras' accounts and is used mainly to finance rural electrification projects.

[16] Legally, DNAEE was responsible for fixing power tariffs but in practice the regulator had to submit its pricing policy to the Ministry of Finances.

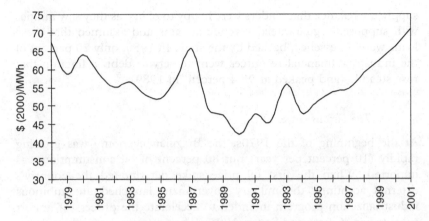

Figure 2.4. Average prices paid by final consumers
Sources: Eletrobras, Aneel, 2003, and Ipea.

power company was prepared to postpone its favorite projects voluntarily (see figure 2.5). Eletrobras found it difficult to play its central coordinating role as it was under constant accusation that it protected its own power projects – notably Itaipu – to the detriment of the state companies of the Southeast (Medeiros, 1993).

The state (provincial) power companies found a creative, although ultimately disastrous, strategy for their cash flow problem. Arguing that they were suffering the consequences of tariffs that the federal government had fixed below costs, the state of São Paulo power companies decided to withhold payments for the power supply of federal companies. Several other state companies followed the São Paulo strategy, with the result that power system accounts became a shell game with accumulated obligations parked in special accounts (CRC) that were rolled over and financed only because the federal government had complete control of the industry. No power project under construction was officially cancelled because of lack of funding; rather, nearly all were slowed with no economic or financial rationality in the decision. Outright cancellation of these projects, which provided visible jobs and achievements coveted by politicians, would have been politically too costly. The case of the Porto Primavera hydropower plant in Sao Paulo is particularly emblematic: from conception to the first power delivery took eighteen years!

In 1987, this serious situation prompted the Ministry of Mines and Energy (MME), with the support of the World Bank, to organize a

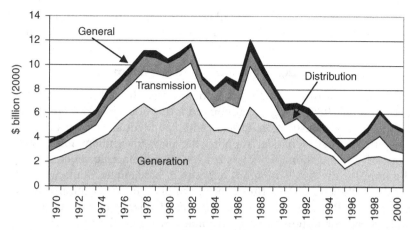

Figure 2.5. Investment in Brazilian power supply industry
Sources: Eletrobras, Ipea; Pinhel, 2000.

working group – the Institutional Revision of the Power Sector ("REVISE", in the Portuguese acronym) – to assess causes and remedies to the looming power crisis (Eletrobras, 1989). Among the problems they identified, three were particularly critical. First, politically appointed managers of the state-owned companies performed poorly and were not accountable to consumers. Moreover, managers had done little to protect environmental quality as they built ever-larger hydro projects. Second, the keystone coordinating role of Eletrobras was under fire —neither the state power companies nor Eletrobras' own regional subsidiaries accepted its role. Third, tariffs had been set to achieve economic, social and regional policies objectives but overlooked the crucial need of power companies' financial viability.[17] Remarkably, the REVISE report had not addressed the looming problem of a funding shortfall for capital projects, despite the fact that several power projects were lacking funds needed to sustain their construction schedule.

Participation in REVISE was dominated by government and the power companies. These stakeholders thought that the system was working well, with only a few fixes required at the margins – notably, they sought approval for higher tariffs and looked to government for larger funding allocations for investment in new projects. Just as the

---

[17] As the World Bank pointed out, because tariffs were kept artificially low state-owned power companies had to increase their loans, adding inflationary pressures to the economy (World Bank, 1992).

REVISE report was finalized Brazil went through a tumultuous period of political change and the recommendations were left sitting on the shelf.

Restructuring the electric power system

In the midst of the Latin American debt crisis, the military rulers stepped aside in 1985. Congress appointed a transition government, which led to a new constitution (1988) and Presidential elections (1989). Despite its fragile political support, the new government imposed an aggressive – and ultimately disastrous – macroeconomic shock therapy. To improve the fiscal situation, deposits in banking accounts were frozen for eighteen months. But, contrary to plan, inflation spiraled out of control and President Collor was impeached when evidence surfaced of widespread corruption in his government. Vice-president Itamar Franco took power and launched an innovative macroeconomic stabilization plan in 1994, coupled to a series of other liberal reforms (Pinheiro et al., 1999). Import duties were reduced; the National Privatization Program, launched by Collor, was accelerated. Improved confidence as well as the seeds of a liberal economy helped to reduce inflation from 47 percent a month at the beginning of 1994 to 35 percent a year within a few months. After several years of mediocre GDP growth, the economy gained momentum; GDP grew 4.5 percent in 1994.

As these larger political forces swept across the Brazilian government, power sector reform (figures 2.6, 2.7 and 2.8) came to the forefront of the political agenda. Three distinct efforts at reform in the electric power sector could be distinguished – each with quite different motivations. Together, these three attempts have yielded a hybrid market that is remarkably similar to the system that existed before reformers attempted to work their magic on the electric power sector.

Marginal reforms

The initial stimulus for reform of the power industry came from the political reforms embodied in the 1988 constitution. As part of the effort to make taxes on industry more transparent and to delink taxes from specific uses, these reforms included abrogation of the tax on power formerly destined to finance the power companies (IUEE). The new constitution also required that public service concessions, including electricity, be licensed through public auctions in an effort to make the industry more responsive to market forces. Collor's Secretary for Energy, a respected official from the World Bank, favored approaches that were consistent with the standard model for power market

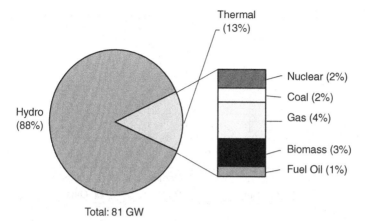

Figure 2.6. Installed capacity, 2003
Source: Aneel, 2003.

restructuring, but he found strong opposition to his ideas. Embattled and distracted by scandal, Collor devoted few political resources to the large privatization program he had initiated. By the time he and his successor Franco left office, the tidal wave of privatization had not yet reached the electricity sector.

In 1993, the government created SINTREL (the National Power Transmission System) with a requirement for open access to the grid in the hope that privately financed independent power producers (IPPs) would eventually enter the market. The government also passed a law declaring that power companies no longer had a legally guaranteed return for their investments;[18] rather, the cost-plus tariff regime was replaced by a regime in which prices would be reviewed regularly.[19] Power tariffs were almost doubled, to an average of $62/MWh; the national tariff equalization mechanism was abolished, and the federal government agreed to pay the state power companies approximately $26 billion in CRC credits that had accumulated on their balance sheets.

[18] The regime that would be used to review tariffs was not established. Nevertheless, there is a constitutional article that guarantees to any public concession the right to *economic-financial equilibrium of the concession*. It is not clear the exact meaning of this concept but the judiciary tends to admit that companies operating under concession have the right to a fair rate of return, although it is unclear how much this rate of return must be.
[19] These prices would be regularly reviewed by DNAEE to take care of inflation.

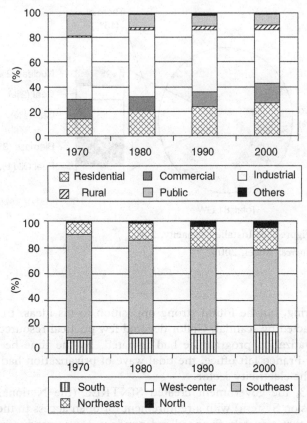

Figure 2.7. Electricity consumption by regions (above) and by consumer group (below)

Source: Eletrobras.

The net effect of these measures was to remove some of the financial distortions in the power system and to make the state companies financially viable enterprises – at least as long as tariffs remained in line with costs. But like REVISE before it, these reforms did nothing to change the fundamental structure of the industry or the incentives that affected most plant operators. The change in rules readjusted the role of the federal treasury in sustaining the industry by eliminating the CRC system and several special fees, but these changes were marginal – they offered no viable strategy for sustaining (private) investment.

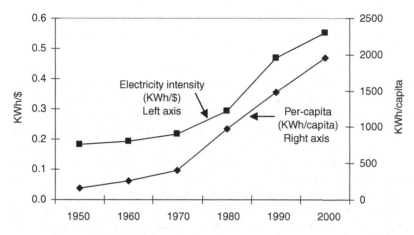

Figure 2.8. Electricity consumption per capita and per unit of GDP
Source: IBGE, 1986.

Reform through privatization

In 1995, restructuring of the power sector gained momentum around the mission of privatization. Taking advantage of his landslide victory in the election, President Cardoso was able to muster the two-thirds majority needed for constitutional amendments that would make it much easier to liberalize and privatize the energy industry. Those amendments removed Petrobras' legal monopoly on the hydrocarbons market and eliminated the rule that had restricted ownership of hydropower plants to Brazilians. (Since the 1930s, the Brazilian Constitution had stated that electricity was a public service; however, unlike in Mexico, the Brazilian Constitution never required that the state own all electric power assets [see Carreon, Jiminez, and Rosellon in chapter 5 of this volume]).

In the wake of these Constitutional reforms Congress passed a 1995 Law that voided all hydropower concessions made after 1988 as well as concessions granted before 1988 whose construction was not yet under way. Hydropower concessions that had lagged behind their construction schedule – as many had during the industry's perpetual financial difficulties since the late 1970s – were forced to show DNAEE that they could raise funds and complete construction, or lose the concession. Altogether, DNAAE recovered thirty-three hydropower concessions – a rich portfolio of projects ready for sale to private investors. To make these assets even more attractive the government adopted new institutions and rules – such as for IPPs – that reflected standard international practice. The Government also encouraged state power companies to organize consortia with private investors to finish construction on concessions that were behind schedule.

The BNDES occupied the central role in the privatization process, having sold steel mills, hotels, port facilities, and sundry other state-owned assets since the wave of privatization began in the early 1990s.[20] In the power sector the strategy of BNDES was to privatize distribution companies first; generation would follow; and, finally, transmission assets would be sold. First on the block were the distributors that, by accident of history, had become part of Eletrobras: Espirito Santo's Escelsa and Rio's Light.[21]

BNDES did not have a strategy for reform of the sector as a whole. It sought reform only insofar as privatization would provide fresh financial resources for the treasury. BNDES was looking for a reform that could elevate the price of the power sector assets. To estimate the market price of Escelsa, the first on the auction block, BNDES established a provisional tariff regime and required the auction winner to sign a concession contract granting that the future regulator could redesign the tariff regime. Not surprisingly, no international investor accepted these terms. However, a consortium of Brazilian private investors assembled a package that included distressed government debt that they used at face value (but had purchased at a steep discount on secondary markets) and won the auction with a bid that offered an 11.8 percent premium over the minimum price.

A tariff regime with much lower regulatory risk would be needed to attract more investors and higher prices. In the midst of privatizing Light, second on the auction block, BNDES adopted a price cap regime modeled on the system for regulating electricity distributors in England and Wales. Noncontrollable costs (e.g., wholesale electricity prices and taxes) would be passed directly to consumers; other costs (e.g., services and personnel) would be indexed to inflation, minus a factor "X" that reflected the expected rise in productivity each year. Investors would be allowed a fair rate of return plus any surplus they could earn above the "X" expected improvement in performance. Tariffs would be reviewed each year; the tariff baseline (along with the "X" factor) would be

---

[20] BNDES was created in the 1950s to finance long-term development projects, especially those related to infrastructure. Special levies on Brazilian salaries are channeled into BNDES, which also raises money in the international financial market.

[21] When AMFORP was nationalized in 1965 the Espirito Santo distribution company remained within Eletrobras. In 1977 the concession for Light – the distributor that served part of the Rio market and part of São Paulo – was about to expire and the assets were bought back by the federal government. São Paulo bought the portion that served its market, but the Rio portion was assigned to Eletrobras.

revised every five years, and the operator could request a special review if unusual circumstances prevented it from earning a fair return. The key to this whole system was the regulator; potential investors did not trust DNAEE, which was seen as a ward of industry insiders who did the government's bidding. Congress passed a law establishing in late 1996 a new independent regulator – Aneel (Agência Nacional de Energia Elétrica) – to replace DNAEE.[22] After these regulatory modifications, privatization of the distribution companies started to move forward, attracting several international investors.

Although formally under the umbrella of the MME, Aneel is financially and administratively independent from the government and is funded by charges levied on generators and distributors (plus any fines it collects from companies that don't comply with quality-of-service standards). A board of five directors is appointed by the federal government (and confirmed by Congress) for four-year terms. Aneel is assigned not only the task of regulating tariffs but also the licensing and controlling of power concessions; these multiple roles may yield conflicts of interest in the future. As regulator, Aneel must serve as impartial arbiter of disputes between the power companies and the government; however, as steward of concessions, Aneel also serves as the government's representative in the disputes.[23]

True to form, BNDES fixed the Light share in the initial tariffs to generate the highest market value[24] – the fair rate of return was set at 10 percent, and X was fixed at zero for the first seven years. (Zero was an implausibly modest value for X. At the time, most analysts thought that Light offered abundant opportunity for lifting productivity through improved collections and streamlining the workforce.) After an intense negotiation, a consortium controlled by international investors (EDF, AES, and Houston Power) paid the minimum price for a controlling share in Light, with a large fraction of their payment (70 percent) in hard currency to a government that was seeking to shore up its balance sheet.

The unions might have scuttled these two privatizations, but a BNDES-engineered compensation package blunted their opposition. A minority share for Escelsa and Light employees was offered by BNDES at a discount on the minimum price. Moreover, in both cases generous

---

[22] At roughly the same time, independent regulators were established for many other parts of the liberalizing economy, such as telecommunications.

[23] To solve this problem, Congress removed licensing power from the regulator and gave it back to the MME in 2004.

[24] With this goal in mind, government officials priced both transmission tariffs and power supply below opportunity cost to maximize Light's distribution share of consumer tariffs.

packages were offered for employees who left the company – in many cases through early retirement.

The next step was to sell distributors that were owned by the state governments. Governors and local politicians feared loss of the political patronage that accompanies power systems and opposed the move initially. However, state governors were facing large financial difficulties due to radical change in their fiscal situation following the Real stabilization plan. By offering soft loans in exchange for these governments' acquiescence to the privatizations BNDES bailed out these strapped states. The loans would be repaid with the proceeds from the privatizations, and each state could keep any extra revenues that remained.

The states of Bahia (Coelba) and of Rio de Janeiro (CERJ), whose governors were politically close to the federal government, accepted the BNDES deal. At the end of 1996, a consortium headed by Iberdrola (Spain) bought Coelba while CERJ controlling stocks were sold to a consortium headed by Chilectra (Chile). Both sales earned a premium (77.3 percent and 30 percent over their minimum prices, respectively).

The encouraging experience of these two states led several other state governors to see the BNDES upfront loan as an opportunity to acquire a financial windfall before the 1998 election. Changes in the constitution reversed a rule that had barred most officials from seeking re-election; politicians already in office were eager to raise funds and launch projects before voters went to the polls. The decision by São Paulo, the state with the largest power load in Brazil, to vertically disintegrate its power company and privatize its distributors and generators was widely seen as a signal that the BNDES strategy would be successful. Yet the rapid privatization by BNDES had alarmed incumbents in the industry who felt that privatization would harm their interests; they articulated those fears, along with power sector experts, by underscoring that electricity was a unique industry of national importance and the lack of a coherent strategy could harm the nation.

Power experts come in

BNDES viewed the existing stakeholders – in particular MME and Eletrobras – with suspicion and did not seek their advice during the privatization process. However, these interests were able to insert themselves into the privatization process by enlisting a consortium of outside consultants led by Coopers and Lybrand to prepare a comprehensive proposal for the reform of the industry. As detailed by Paixão (2000), this process marked the onset of the battle between BNDES (which sought rapid privatization) and the incumbent state-owned power companies (that wanted to protect their generation and transmission assets). MME acted as the interface between these two groups, with a slightly different objective: to ensure that needed investment in the power system would keep pace with demand during the rocky transition to a new organizational and financial model. The outcome of this process satisfied nearly all these core interests – BNDES, the incumbents, and MME – while not actually having much impact on the organization of the industry.

In contrast to the in-house process at BNDES, the MME consultation was highly participatory – at least within the industry, where all of Brazil's 60 power companies were represented. Thematic working groups presented their proposals in plenary sessions attended by 400 experts. Two issues dominated the discussion: the role of Eletrobras in coordinating funding within a privatized market, and decentralization of control over dispatch of generators and control of the transmission network.

BNDES argued that a privatized power industry allowed no role for Eletrobras as coordinator of funding mechanisms. (Extreme liberals within BNDES sought to shut down Eletrobras once its subsidiaries were privatized.) MME, however, argued that a central funding agent would still be needed for large hydropower projects and strategic transmission lines. Eletrobras offered its historical record of leveraging international funding for such projects as evidence that it was both competent and necessary. BNDES, which had not funded any power projects since the creation of Eletrobras in the 1960s, decided to finance large power projects once again to demonstrate that Eletrobras was not an irreplaceable keystone in the Brazilian power system.

Decentralization was more complicated. BNDES and MME alike sought the separation of transmission services from generators; both also sought to break the four large regional generation companies of Eletrobras into smaller enterprises. But their motivation for these views was quite different. BNDES sought the maximum price at the privatization auctions, where smaller firms would be more digestible and attractive to outside investors. MME was mindful of the need to improve efficiency in the power system, but it was more worried that no new hydropower plants would be built. The Brazilian energy policy was oriented towards the development of the large hydropower potential yet to be developed and there was a strong interest linked to the construction of hydropower plants.[25] Unless a mechanism existed to reduce the hydrological risk of hydropower plants, gas-fired combined

---

[25] Those with a strong interest in hydro plants included cement producers, dams and transmission lines constructors, and hydro turbines producers.

cycle thermal power plants would have a substantial advantage. These power plants had a lower capital cost and they could explore the large availability of hydropower in the wet years to reduce their fuel cost as well.

The state companies and the regional subsidiaries of Eletrobras strongly opposed the BNDES approach, arguing that cooperation among hydropower plants was needed to assure the efficient operation of the Brazilian hydropower system. Generators along a single cascade required coordination of water flows; moreover, coordination, they argued, would lead to a more reliable power supply as the risks of drought could be spread across the many different basins in the hydro system. The operator of the hydro plants ("GCOI", Portuguese acronym) estimated that "uncoordinated dispatch" – that is, market competition – could cause a loss of 30 percent of generating capacity due to spilled water and other operational inefficiencies (Santos, 1996). Of the state generators, only São Paulo – where the government aggressively sought the higher efficiency and lower power costs promised by privatization and competition – favored vertical separation and market competition for its power companies.

Conceiving a "Hybrid Market"

As debate over the many drafts of the MME plan droned on, the Real stabilization plan was in urgent need of more hard currency. BNDES pressured the MME to accelerate the reform process so that privatization of generators could continue, and in early 1998 the government created the key institutions for the new system: the National System Operator (ONS), a not-for-profit civil association of power companies that would dispatch plants and operate the transmission system,[26] and the Wholesale Power Market (Paixão, 2000). ONS is guided by a Board of Directors that includes representatives of each electric stakeholder group (generation, transmission, distributors, and "free" consumers[27]).

The key to understanding this system lies in the rules that ONS deploys when dispatching power stations, a process that is guided by computer models that aim for "least cost" operation. These same models also compute four regional spot prices (South, Southeast/Center-West, Northeast, and North) as indicators of the relative value of

---

[26] The government (MME) plans expansion of the transmission system, and Aneel offers new lines for competitive tender.

[27] Consumers whose peak load consumption exceeds 3 MW are free to shop around for their power supply; the remaining consumers (called captive) are served by their local distribution companies.

power at each node.[28] As operator of the system – not the long-term strategic planner – the ONS models focus on short-run marginal costs. Since hydro plants have nearly no operating costs whereas the operating costs at thermal plants are typically high, the system yields very low prices and minimizes the use of fossil fuels. This approach also corresponds with the hydropower engineering culture that dominates the ONS board – by this logic, the goal is to coordinate water flowing through cascades of turbines minimizing the water that spills past the turbines. Thermal plants, which reside outside this culture, are envisioned as backup facilities to be used only in periods of drought.

This approach implies that thermal power plants will remain idle for long periods of time, which is inconsistent with take-or-pay contracts for their natural gas contracts supply offered by Petrobras. To avoid this problem, these power plants were allowed to declare their power capacity as "inflexible" (i.e., must run).

To reduce the commercial risk to hydropower investors – a key aim of MME and BNDES – the concept of "assured energy" was introduced. Using historical rainfall data, Aneel estimates the total amount of electricity that the set of existing hydropower plants can generate during the worst historical hydrological period.[29] This amount, called the *assured energy* of the hydropower system, is divided among the hydropower plants[30] and each hydropower plant receives from Aneel a certificate of its assured energy. Although in wet years hydropower plants will produce much more than their assured energy, they can only contract their assured energy. The additional power, produced in wet years, called "secondary energy," is sold in the spot market – when waters are flush and spot prices are much lower than the contract price for the assured energy.

To guarantee each hydropower plant its assured energy cash flow in spite of the water actually flowing through its turbines, a financial mechanism (Power Reallocation Mechanism, MRE) was created for sharing the hydrological risk among hydropower plants. Whenever water flows are unfavorable for a particular plant, ONS dispatches another hydropower plant to assure that every plant "delivers" at least the assured energy listed on its Aneel concession.

This mechanism of socializing risk and revenue flows across the entire hydro system pleased BNDES. It transformed investment in a hydro plant from a risky venture that depended on variable rainfall and the actions of

---

[28] Aneel decided to reduce the sub-markets to two from the beginning of 2003: South/Southeast/Center-West and North/Northeast.

[29] This amount is estimated assuming 5% risk that the hydropower system will be unable to actually produce it.

[30] Based on the capacity factor of the hydropower plants.

possibly uncoordinated releases of water by upriver plants into a low-risk instrument, akin to a bond, that yielded a predictable stream of revenues. The mechanism pleased Eletrobras and the power companies because it augmented the economic competitiveness of their hydropower plants, and it pleased the MME because the same dispatch and revenue-sharing rules would apply to hydropower plants that were yet to be constructed, which would improve their economic competitiveness against hypothetical future thermal power plants. Traditional suppliers of hydropower projects also loved the move. Only investors contemplating thermal projects had reason to oppose this move, but they were not yet on the stage.

Financial transactions are cleared in a wholesale power market (MAE) that is functionally separate from the system operator and shown in figure 2.9.[31] Generators are free to sign bilateral contracts with distributors and with "free" consumers (large power users whose peak demand exceeds 3 MW), and power is also traded on a "spot" market. Real market prices emerge from the bilateral contracts, but the spot market is a fiction – its prices are generated by the same set of models utilized by ONS to dispatch generators and manage the transmission system. The models compute the opportunity cost of the water flow with data from the hydropower plants (availability, water flow, reservoir level, operational cost) and thermal power plants (inflexibility, availability, operational cost). Power plants are dispatched by merit order and the spot price is fixed by the last unit dispatched. Using projections for future demand and the most likely water flow, the spot price is currently calculated for a period of thirty days, though the aim is to have an hourly price.

Another "hybrid" aspect of this new market was a long transition process from the old "cost plus" plants to a new system based on opportunity cost. During a nine-year transitional period the existing power plants had initial contracts with distribution companies at the 1996 prices, indexed to inflation.[32] From 2003, one quarter of the power in these initial contracts has been released each year for sale in "old power" auctions. This transitional rule was considered necessary because the 1996 price of old power was roughly half the estimated long-term cost of new power supply ($40/MWh, based on gas-fired capacity as the most attractive and available hydro sites had been tapped already). Had power been priced at the real opportunity cost, tariffs

---

[31] An executive committee (Coex) with fourteen members indicated by the Assembly was originally responsible for managing MAE with the support of an administration company (ASMAE).

[32] The equivalent to $22/MWh, in the South and the Southeast, and $16/MWh, in the North and the Northeast, at that time. Itaipu has its price fixed in dollars, at much higher level ($34).

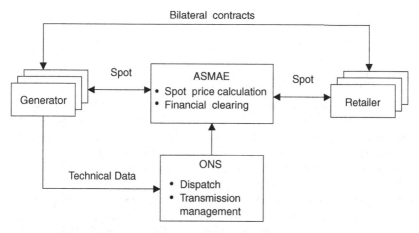

Figure 2.9. Market organization, 2000[a]

Note: [a]Power contracts are bilaterally settled but must be reported to ASMAE, where the power transactions not covered by contracts (spot trade) are cleared. Power flows in the inter connected grid are monitored by the ONS and informed to ASMAE.

would have increased sharply, an intolerable outcome to the inflation-minded government. During this transition period the new plants were free to negotiate contracts in the open market – an impossible situation for new investors contemplating gas-fired plants, unless they were able to sell power to regulated consumers of distribution companies.

Under this hybrid market system, distribution companies knew that in most years a very large surplus of hydropower secondary energy would be available in the spot market. The government feared that the distribution companies would seize this opportunity only to find themselves exposed to extremely high spot prices in dry years. Thus Aneel mandated that the distributors secure 85 percent (later 95 percent and currently 100 percent) of their power demand as firm bilateral contracts. Aneel also applied price caps to the power purchased by distribution companies – with perverse effects that we discuss later. The net effect of all these rules has been to reinforce the role of the spot market as a computer-generated phenomenon rather than a true market, with prices largely the result of administration rather than competition.[33]

---

[33] The market is affected by many other regulations that we do not discuss here. For example, to avoid problems of market power there are limits on the share that any investor group can hold in the Brazilian power market. (20% of the national market; 25% of the Southern or Southeast/Centerwest markets, and 35% in any other regional market.) Vertical integration is also restricted; distribution companies are allowed to supply up to 30% of their market through self-dealing with their own power plants.

Unresolved issues: fuel diversity and systemic risk

By the metrics that mattered to the key players, the restructuring process moved rapidly and was largely successful. By 1998, sixteen distribution companies, with a total annual service of 160 TWh, had been sold, along with 9.2 GW of capacity in four generation companies (table 2.2). CEMIG, the vertically integrated company of the state of Minas Gerais, was partially privatized, having sold a 30 percent share of its voting capital to investors. Copel, the vertically integrated power company of Parana state, and Furnas, one of the four Eletrobras generation companies, were both being prepared for privatization.

Licenses for new hydropower plants and transmission lines[34] were sold in public auctions by Aneel at premium prices, and several private investors asked for Aneel authorization to build thermal power plants.[35] The average annual capacity additions rose from a low of 1.080 Gw per year in the early 1990s to 2.800 GW per year from 1995 to 2000. The flow of funds to the power industry, one of the main objectives of the reform, was back.

Moreover, the newly privatized companies demonstrated better economic performance. A key measure of productivity – the number of employees per customer – was improving; most privatized distributors also decreased the number and duration of power outages (Aneel, 2003). The share of potential consumers with access to power had increased to about 95 percent. Crucially, the cost per MW of new hydropower installed capacity declined sharply due to improved control of construction and financial costs. (Thermal plants remained costly and hypothetical – we discuss that later in the chapter.) These improvements were evident not only in privatized firms but also in those enterprises still owned by the state and in the midst of preparation for privatization. Reform, it seemed, was delivering the envisaged results.

Nevertheless, one fundamental problem remained: in the zeal to privatize (and thus restructure) the system, no entity had assumed the task of long-term planning and policy guidance for the system as a whole. In the past, Eletrobras had played that role through its control of investment decisions, with MME providing additional support at the margins. In the restructured system, however, Eletrobras was in the midst of being broken apart, and its strategic planning functions eroded.

---

[34] Transmission lines offer the lowest monthly revenue requirement for the availability of their lines to the ONS. For users of the grid Aneel fixes tariffs that should produce revenues needed to pay the transmission line owners plus the ONS costs.

[35] Thermal power plants are not concessions; however, they require Aneel licenses to operate.

Table 2.2. *Brazilian power industry privatization (BNDES)*

Distribution co.	Market GWh 1998	Auction day	Price millions	$/MWh
Escelsa (F)	6,194	7/11/95	519	83.79
Light (F)	23,759	5/21/96	2,217	93.31
Cerj	7,208	11/20/96	587	81.44
Coelba	8,373	7/31/97	1,598	190.85
CEEE (N/NE)	5,213	10/21/97	1,486	285.06
CEEE (CO)	6,353	10/21/97	1,372	215.96
CPFL	19,045	11/05/97	2,731	143.40
Enersul	2,453	11/19/97	565	230.33
Cemat	2,718	11/27/97	353	129.87
Energipe	1,851	12/03/97	520	280.93
Cosern	2,590	12/12/97	606	233.98
Coelce	5,396	4/02/98	868	160.86
Metropolitana	35,578	4/15/98	1,777	49.95
Celpa	3,215	7/08/98	388	120.68
Elektro	6,407	7/16/98	1,273	198.69
Bandeirante	23,500	9/17/98	860	36.60
Celpe	7,018	18/02/00	1,004	143.06
Cemar	2,349	15/06/00	523	222.65
Saelpa	1,929	30/11/00	185	95.90
Total Distribution	171,149		19,432	113.54

Generation Co.	Capacity (MW)	Auction day	Price $ millions	Thousand $/kW
Cachoeira Dourada	658	5/09/97	714	1085.11
Gerasul (F)	3,719	9/15/98	880	236.62
Paranapanema	2,148	7/28/99	682	317.50
Tiête	2,651	10/27/99	472	178.05
Total Generation	9,176		2,748	299.48
Total			22,180	

Note: (F) denotes federal companies.
Source: BNDES.

MME was unable to fill the space. Aneel's mandate required that it serve as neutral arbiter rather than strategic planner. And BNDES remained obsessed with the mission of extracting the maximum price for privatized assets, and could not act as steward of the power system.

These problems were manifest in two tightly interlocking problems. First was the difficulty of attracting investment in new (gas-fired) thermal power stations. The other was the drought of 2001, which underscored the collective risk inherent in a hydropower system organized as in Brazil. The drought has focused minds on the problem and on "stop-gap" solutions (increased investment in thermal generation), but actual solutions are not yet on the horizon.

Fossil fuel markets

Historically, there was little connection between fossil fuel markets and the Brazilian electric power system. Eletrobras developed the power system assuming that hydropower resources (which were constitutionally owned by the state) were plentiful and that fossil fuels were scarce; Petrobras operated the oil market assuming that hydrocarbons were premium fuels that would not be used for generating electricity. Not surprisingly, conventional thermal plants occupied only a small share of the Brazilian power installed capacity and an even smaller share of actual power generated (figure 2.6).

Until the 1990s there were few thermal power plants connected to the grid, those that existed were located mainly in the south around the low-quality coal mines. These plants were dispatched when reservoirs ran low, and their owners were allowed tariffs that compensated for their cost of building the generating capacity that sat idle during wet years. The cost of the fuel for thermal generation was diffused to the society as a whole through a compensation mechanism (the fuel cost account, or "CCC"). All consumers paid into the CCC fund according to the grid operators (the GCOI, controlled by Eletrobras) estimated need for thermal power dispatch over the year.

That situation was expected to change as large amounts of natural gas became available. In the early 1990s the Brazilian government committed to purchase 30 million m^3/day of gas from Bolivia as part of a political deal (brokered in part with US pressure) that would bind Bolivia more tightly to Brazil while also offering a substantial source of revenue to Bolivia. This aspect was particularly relevant because it would facilitate the US fight for reducing the commerce of illicit drugs. The government instructed Petrobras to assemble a coalition to build a pipeline; not surprisingly, Petrobras found that no investor would participate without a firm take-or-pay clause built into the deal.

At the same time, major oil finds in offshore Rio had also generated large quantities of domestic associated gas. Saddled with all this gas Petrobras and the government scrambled to find markets. Mindful of its take-or-pay commitments to Bolivia and the wall of domestic gas on the horizon, the government adopted a broad policy goal of increasing the share of gas in Brazilian primary energy supply from less than 3 percent in the 1990s to 12 percent by 2010. The widespread use of combined cycle power plants elsewhere in the world – notably in Argentina, Chile, and the United Kingdom – had convinced the government that the massive new gas supplies would find a proper user in power generation.

The scheme for internalizing and diffusing the cost of thermal electric power generators had worked when the industry was integrated and the role of thermal electric generation was small. But 17 GW of thermal capacity mainly fuelled with natural gas, operating in a competitive electricity market, as the government envisioned for 2005, would be a different matter. The rude awakening for the government came when Petrobras offered thermal power plants the take-or-pay conditions of its contract for gas imports from Bolivia. Since their power would be more expensive than that from hydropower generators in relatively wet years, thermal plants would not be dispatched in most years.

With fuel in take-or-pay contracts, gas generators would have no choice but to declare themselves "inflexible" (must run) and thus were required to contract all of their power with buyers (distributors and "free" consumers). Moreover, Aneel had capped the prices for wholesale contracts that distributors would be allowed to pass to consumers. Any generator who fired with a long-term gas contract was, unable to make money, squeezed between the cap on electricity price fixed by Aneel and the natural gas price fixed by Petrobras in its take-or-pay contract.

For the potential generators of gas-fired electricity, the Brazilian market appeared to be a hydro cartel that was being perpetuated by the regulatory system. Moreover, gas users complained that gas from Petrobras was not competitive because the company was a monopoly[36] that attempted to pass the cost of the uneconomic Bolivian pipeline to its customers.[37] Gas supply was priced in dollars and indexed to international fuel prices, but electricity prices were regulated by Aneel in Brazilian currency – a risk that the sharp devaluation in 1999 made transparent to all. In this context, few investors were willing to build gas projects in Brazil.

In late 1999 ONS warned that Brazilian reservoirs were at dangerous levels, and the government adopted special subsidies to attract rapid

---

[36] Petrobras, for the time being, is the single supplier of natural gas in the country. The few trunk pipelines that exist are regulated by the National Oil Agency (ANP), but prices for gas are set by the government.

[37] The pipeline was made costly as result of the political decision to extend it to Southern Brazil despite the fact that gas demand would be low in that region and exports from Argentina were already projected.

construction of gas projects.[38] Except for these subsidized projects, gas-fired generators have not been an attractive prospect for outside investors. At this writing (2005), only 3.6 percent of total electric capacity is fired with gas despite bold visions from the government to raise the share for gas above 10 percent by 2010. An interruptible gas market would address many of these problems, but such a market is incompatible with an infant gas industry that has to find consumers for the large (and growing) Bolivian supplies.

Systemic risk

Under the old system, the federal government regulated the behavior of the concessionaires and the state governments dictated the conduct of their own enterprises. As the system grew to take advantage of the large economies of scale and the potential to spread risk across the entire country's water basins, Eletrobras oversaw investment planning and managed risk on behalf of the entire country – at times incurring the wrath of state generators (such as when Eletrobras put its own priorities of dispatching Itaipu power ahead of the others). Consumers were ultimately expected to bear the risk of improper investment strategies in the cost-based tariffs that they paid. When supply was excessive, consumers paid higher tariffs than necessary – the Averch Johnson effect of regulated utilities over-investing consumers' money in power systems – and when supply fell short, administrators forced reductions in consumption.

The reforms triggered by privatization have radically reallocated risk. Risk management is decentralized and there is no coordinated, strategic view of the future. There is no guaranteed rate of return for power generators and consumers do not face fixed tariffs. This new system was intended to shift more of the industry risks to generators and distributors which, as competitive firms, were expected to manage these risks better than state-owned enterprises. Unlike in the past, the Treasury would no longer be expected to provide funds for rash capital construction projects to avoid system risks that can be efficiently managed through the price mechanism. It took just a few years to discover that risk management in the power system is far more complex.

---

[38] In addition to subsidies from the government, Petrobras offered a hedging instrument that would reduce volatility in gas prices; however, the hedge raised the total price and made thermal power generation even less competitive. Moreover, BNDES offered soft loans for thermal power projects and Petrobras reduced the natural gas price for a set of emergency thermal power plants.

In practice, decentralization of risk management was proved far more complex for atleast three reasons. First, investors – especially those operating in foreign currency – are hardly equipped to manage large macroeconomic risks. For state-owned companies, currency risk was irrelevant because it was absorbed by the Treasury. For private companies, small shifts in currency or variations in demand are the normal part of business, but large variations have a devastating effect on the viability of investments.[39] Industry reformers neglected this issue, naively assuming that the Real macroeconomic stabilization plan would cement confidence in the currency. Large devaluations in 1999 and 2002 demonstrated that this assumption was wrong. These shifts in currency value also had large effects on the choice of technology – the consensus in early 1998 that thermal power plants could compete at the margin with new hydropower investments was completely reversed after the 1999 Real devaluation. Gas-fired plants required technology imports (with dollar indexed prices) and, in most plants that were envisioned, gas with dollar-denominated take-or-pay contracts.

Second, there was no clear responsibility for the inherent hydrological risks. Within the hydropower industry risk was managed through the mandatory MRE side-payments. ONS optimized the system, and the level of "assured energy" was a convenient benchmark for system planning. In most years the actual power available was far higher than the "assured" amount (figure 2.10), and ONS assumed that thermal capacity would be available in case of shortfall. But ONS did not have responsibility for assuring that such capacity was actually available.

There were no capacity payments to thermal generators; and the ONS was perceived as a hydropower club that sought, first and foremost, to shift risk away from the owners of hydropower stations. For example, under the ONS dispatch and the MAE clearing mechanism hydropower generators received additional revenues from their sale of "secondary energy" in the spot market, but they were allowed to deplete their reservoirs at no cost. As potential power was depleted from reservoirs, the scarcity cost of power increased and the spot price rose – which provided further benefit to hydropower plant owners, while penalizing consumers. A better system would force hydropower plants to offer compensation to society for the scarcity created when they release water

---

[39] Private investors can buy hedge in the financial markets to protect their cash flow from the risk of the domestic currency devaluation but its cost is prohibitive for large devaluations.

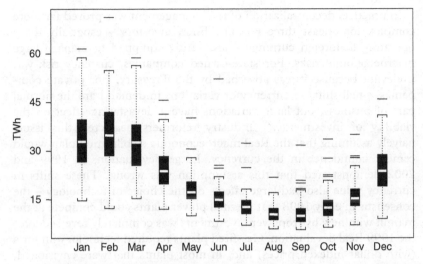

Figure 2.10. Seasonal and annual variation of hydropower production potential in the Southeast[a]

Note: [a]The upper and lower limits of the box-plot figure show the fluctuation in the energy inflow to the Southeast hydropower plants reservoirs in the 70 years of historical data (1933–2002). The white strip in the middle is the median. The red box represents the second and third quartile of data. The bars outside the limits are the outliers.

Source: ONS.

from the reservoirs – and/or compensation for thermal plants for the supply security that these power plants provide.

A third systemic risk surrounds the projection of demand for power. In the cost-recovery regime there was no economic risk when assumptions about future demand proved to be excessively bullish. Indeed, the Eletrobras' coordinating bodies usually assumed that economic growth would be buoyant, with the result that a substantial reserve margin was a constant feature of the Brazilian power system. This approach was justified by the fact that the social cost of power shortage would be much higher than the cost of over-investment in surplus, a solid argument when power consumption was growing rapidly[40].

The context is radically different in a competitive power market where there is no guaranteed return for projects and where (unlike in many

---

[40] The extra copy would not remain spare for long.

countries, such as in Argentina) the market has no system of capacity payments to compensate the builders of under-utilized "spare" capacity. Volatility in economic growth introduces additional risk to investors. And the power shortage of 2001 revealed still another unanticipated risk: when power prices rose to reflect scarcity, users found numerous ways to reduce their load. In all, about 10 percent of the load was shed permanently – about two years' total growth. Mindful of the problem of planning, the government created the Committee for Expansion Planning (Comitê de Planejamento da Expansão, CCPE) to amalgamate all of the companies' projections for future demand. The experience with CCPE underscored the severity of the problem: CCPE never actually operated.

The difficulty of the planning task is revealed when one attempts to estimate demand for power over the next decade and to use that estimate to develop a plan for supply. In the late 1990s Eletrobras forecasted power consumption at 589 TWh in 2010, on the assumption that the economy would grow at 4 percent annually over the period (Eletrobras, 1999). By their estimate, $ 4.7 billion in investment would be needed each year, half for power plants and half for transmission and distribution. Yet more recent demographic studies made after the 2001 census show a sharp reduction in the birth rate, suggesting that population will grow at only 1 percent a year. Power supply is already available to 95 percent of the population;[41] the period of heavy industrialization is drawing to a close; in recent years, GDP growth has averaged about 3 percent per year, which is much lower than the Eletrobras assumptions and the existing surplus of generating capacity is expected to be exhausted only in 2009. Taking all these factors into account, consumption closer to 440 TWh seems more realistic for the year 2010. For any individual project investor, the difference in projections (one-third) will determine whether projects exposed to market forces are profitable or money-losers. It is no wonder that the only place where privately owned generators have found profitable investments is in the hydro system, where insider control over dispatch and socialization of risk across all hydro generators made investments almost a sure winner.[42]

---

[41] The access to power supply is still very low in rural areas of the Amazonian Region (18 percent) and the Northeast (41 percent).

[42] Buyers of existing (i.e., "brownfield") hydro assets in the privatization auctions have generally found the investments worthwhile. Some purchasers of hydro concessions that had already been through project review found the investments profitable–because the risk that project review (including increasingly rigorous environmental review) was extinguished. But no wholly "greenfield" generators have turned a profit.

A case study: the 2001 drought

Ever since the 1930s, water regulation in Brazil has been oriented to serve hydropower generation, with other services (irrigation, transportation, and domestic and industrial consumption) somewhat subsidiary. In most places water supply was so abundant that these multiple services did not create conflict, but in the interior Northeast the water supply along the São Francisco River was already over-tapped by the early 1990s. Mindful of this tension, the newly elected new governor of Minas Gerais, Itamar Franco, seized the Furnas power plants in his state's territory – nominally to oppose the privatization but mainly to make clear his rivalry with President Cardoso.[43] His actions touched off a political row that halted the privatization of hydropower plants.

With privatization at a stalemate, private investors were also loath to build thermal plants – despite the fact that these plants would be essential to fill the power gap during dry periods. As it happened, this period of political crisis at the end of 1999 also marked the beginning of a drought. ONS warned the government that reservoirs were at a low level. Good rains that year partially refilled the reservoirs – averting crisis for a season (figure 2.11).

The Minister of Mines and Energy took command of the situation with a massive emergency action plan for thermal power plants. Through an opaque process he announced a list of thermal power plants, totaling 6.6 GW of capacity, that was eligible for special incentives. Pressure to extend these incentives more widely led investors to nominate a total of 17 GW of capacity (table 2.3). Several of these projects were joint ventures between private investors and Petrobras, the country's sole supplier of natural gas.

Although MME authorities were optimistic about the success of their thermal emergency plan, four reasons explain why private investors were hesitant. First, environmentalists were opposed to the inflexible dispatch of thermal power plants, which would waste hydropower capacity while fossil fuels were burned. Second, distributors were unwilling to give these generators a power purchase agreement at a wholesale price above the level capped by Aneel. In that context, MME had expected Eletrobras, as the wholesale power company of last resort, to absorb the difference in price – a very unattractive prospect for Eletrobras. Third, the incentives for investors included large loan packages from BNDES

---

[43] The battle in Congress for the constitutional amendment that allowed a second term for President Cardoso moved ex-president Franco from the government coalition to the opposition.

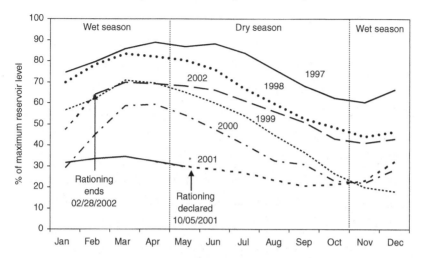

Figure 2.11. Depletion of Southeastern water reservoirs
(Jan/1997–Dec/2002)
Source: ONS.

earmarked for Brazilian-made equipment; yet a large share of the equipment in combined cycle power plants would need to be imported. Fourth, investors were wary of the risk in gas prices. Not surprisingly, few thermal power plant projects moved forward – in particular, only those projects that had joint investment with Petrobras, which offered interruptible gas supply contracts, went ahead.

At the beginning of 2001 the hydropower reservoirs were at historically low levels in the southeast and the northeast – the two largest hydropower regions. The 2001 rains were unfavorable – in the northeast the rains were the worst on record – and ONS projected that the reservoirs would be completely depleted before the beginning of the next raining season if consumption was not drastically reduced. (ONS suggested a 20 percent cut in consumption would be needed to avoid a collapse of the power system.) The Minister of Mines and Energy resigned; the President stripped Aneel of its regulatory authority and assigned a special task force, headed by the Minister of Civil Affairs, to manage the power crisis.

A consumer quota was introduced by the task force to induce the needed 20 percent in power consumption. Consumers would be liable for a substantial tariff penalty for consumption over their quota and those who exceeded their quota twice would have their power supply

Table 2.3. *Brazilian thermal emergency plan*

Power plant	Proposed capacity (MW)	Site	Investors	Operating capacity MW	Under construction MW
			Gas Cogeneration		
Vale do Açu	102	RN	Iberdrola/Petrobras	-	-
Sergipe	460	SE	Energisa/Petrobras	-	-
Termobahia	450	BA	ABB/Petrobras	-	-
Termorio	1,160	RJ	Petrobras/PRS/Sideco	-	1,160
Cubatão	950	SP	Sithe/Marubeni/ Petrobras	-	-
Rhodia Paulínia	100	SP	Energyworks	-	-
Rhodia S. André	88	SP	Energyworks/Pirelli	-	-
Alto Tietê I e II	230	SP	EDP	-	-
Capuava	220	SP	Rolls Royce	-	-
Valparaíso	240	SP	CVE - Soc. Valparaiense	-	-
Ibirité	850	MG	Petrobras/Fiat	235	452
			CCGT		
Dunas	120	CE	BP-Amoco/Repsol-YPF	-	-
Paraíba	460	PB	Gaspetro/Paraíba Gás	-	-
Termoalagoas	500	AL	Alagoas Gás	-	-
Termopernambuco	720	PE	Chesf	-	-
Vitória	450	ES	Escelsa/Petrobras/ CVRD	-	-
Norte Fluminense	725	RJ	Eletrobrás/Petrobras/ Light/Cerj/Escelsa	-	725
Cabiúnas	500	RJ	Petrobras/Light/Mitsui	-	-
Riogen	78	RJ	Enron	-	-
Poços de Caldas	1067	MG	Cemig	-	-
Juiz de Fora	480	MG	CFLCL	82	-
Santa Branca	500	SP	Eletroger	-	-
Vale do Paraíba	240	SP	EDP/Petrobras	-	-
Araraquara	550	SP	EDP	-	-
Paulínia	945	SP	Flórida Power/Petrobras	-	-
Paulínia II	500	SP	DSG Mineração	-	-
Carioba	700	SP	CPFL/Intergen/Shell	-	-
ABC	180	SP	El Paso/GE/Initec/ITS	-	-
Bariri	180	SP	CGEET	-	-
Cachoeira Paulista	350	SP	EDP	-	-
Indaiatuba	480	SP	EDP	-	-
Taquaruçu	300	SP	Duke Energy	-	-
Araucária	480	PR	Copel/Petrobras/El Paso/BG	480	-
Termocatarinense	750	SC	Petrobras/Celesc/ SC Gás	-	-

Table 2.3. (*cont.*)

Power Plant	Proposed Capacity (MW)	Site	Investors	Operating Capacity MW	Under Construction MW
Gaúcha	300	RS	Petrobras/Sulgas/ Techint/CEEE/ Ypiranga/RGE	-	-
Termosul	250	RS	AES Brasil	-	-
Campo Grande	480	MS	Enersul	-	-
Corumbá	340	MS	CVRD/Petrobras/EDP	-	88
Cuiabá II	180	MS	Enron	-	-
Termonorte II	426	RO	Eletronorte	-	180
Manaus	64	AM	Manaus Energia	-	-
Gas					
Termonorte I	100	RO	El Paso	-	-
Pitanga	70	PR	Copel/Gaspetro/ Inepar/Teig	-	-
Coal (C) and Petrochemical Waste (W)					
Cofepar (w)	616	PR	PSEG/Petrobras/ Ultrafértil	-	-
Figueira (c)	100	PR	Copel/C. Carbonífera do Cambuí	-	-
São Mateus (w)	70	PR	Copel/Petrobras	-	-
Sul Catarinense (c)	400	SC	Carb.s Criciúma e Metropolitana	-	-
Seival (c.)	250	RS	Copelmi Mineração	-	-
Candiota III (coal)	350	RS	Eletrobrás	-	-

Source: MME.

cut.[44] Small consumers who fell below the quota would receive a bonus and large consumers could consume above their quotas by purchasing surplus from those consumers who had made extra reductions. The trade of power quotas between large consumers was made at bilaterally negotiated prices – several bourses emerged to trade the quotas. Initially, prices were extremely high but converged progressively to about twice the normal level.

Consumers' reaction to task force measures was unexpectedly positive.[45] Average consumption dropped below the 20 percent quota, and the country avoided rolling blackouts. The 2002 rainy season was

[44] Large consumers, for example, were obligated to pay roughly $240 for each MWh consumed over their target.

[45] Domestic consumers who were able to reduce their consumption below the target received a financial bonus that was used to reduce their normal power supply tariff.

favorable and reservoirs rose to nearly normal levels. Moreover, moved by the perception that power shortage would result in high prices in the wholesale power market, thermal power projects that were already under construction sped up their availability to the beginning of the year 2002.[46] As the power supply moved back to glut the consumer quota was removed. However, the power crisis produced fundamental changes.

The drastic reduction in the industrial output forced by the power shortage produced a 2 percent drop in the expected GDP growth for 2001. Because the task force regulations disregarded contracts, substantial conflicts between generators and distributors arose. The government produced a grand settlement in which BNDES' loans to the generators and distributors compensated them for their financial losses, consumers saw their tariffs rise (2.9 percent for domestic consumers and 7 percent for large consumers), and the extra revenues were channeled back to the generators to repay the new BNDES loans.

Forced to reduce consumption, consumers changed to more efficient power appliances and altered their behavior. The market for efficient light bulbs, smart air conditioning, small generators for peak shaving and cogeneration boomed, producing a fundamental change in the level and shape of the power demand curve for Brazil. ONS estimates that these changes caused a permanent reduction in power consumption of at least 7 percent.

This change should not have caused persistent problems for generators. If the Brazilian economy had been able to resume its trajectory of growth the overcapacity would have been rapidly absorbed. Unfortunately, after a short recovery in the first half of 2002, another large devaluation of the domestic currency plunged the Brazilian economy into a new economic crisis. At this writing (2005) power consumption from the grid is hovering at a level barely above that of the year 2000, leaving roughly 5 GW of power supply capacity idle and increasing the average costs of the power companies. The large devaluation of the Real in 2002 required a sharp rise in domestic interest rates to prevent a further slide in the currency, and this further multiplied the costs of power. Several distribution companies are now in dire financial straights and are contemplating breaching their contracts with creditors and suppliers.[47]

---

[46] Keen to find consumers for its large take-or-pay natural gas contract in Bolivia, Petrobras is a partner investor in most of these projects.

[47] At the beginning of 2003 Eletropaulo (owned by the American firm AES) declared that it could not pay a loan of R$ 85 million to BNDES. After a long and difficult negotiation, BNDES and AES reached a deal in September 2003 that waived the interest charge ($118 million) due to the BNDES on the still outstanding principal of $ 1.2 billion.

For the government, the political cost of the power crisis was enormous. Consumers could not understand why they were penalized with higher tariffs when many actually exceeded the government's expected reduction in consumption. Investors were unhappy as well, with some foreign investors signaling that they wanted to sell their companies.[48] The credibility of the government's ability to assure provision of basic public services was seriously damaged by the power shortage.[49]

The political costs of the power shortage were paid by the government in the 2002 presidential election. The left wing opposition coalition won a landslide victory on a platform that included drastic reorientation of the power industry. Liberalization would give way to central planning; the privatization of power companies would be stopped. Private investors would be invited to participate in building new power supply – not least because the government could not afford that function – in partnership with state-owned companies. A variant on a cost-plus tariff regime would replace the wholesale power market pricing mechanism; average costs would be used to fix the power tariffs for consumers; visions of a tariff regime in which Aneel would gradually remove its caps and tariffs would be allowed to approach real long-term marginal costs were to be scrapped. The hybrid market would tip decidedly in the direction of more state control.

Mindful of all the difficulties with the reform process, the new government sought ways to return to the earlier era. While it is impractical to reconstruct the state-owned enterprises, the government is attempting to create a privately owned but state-managed power system. Power purchase agreements allocated through bids will be the norm. Central planning will decide the location and quantity of new power. Hydropower, the new government declared, would be the preferred technology for future projects; thermal power plants would be expected to adjust their output to the hydrological situation.

Yet the fundamental problems with this vision for thermal power – the systemic risk and the requirement for long-term take-or-pay gas contracts – are not altered. The wholesale power market will be replaced by a governmental administrator of contracts that will mix different power

---

[48] A small distribution power company (CEMAR), in the state of Maranhão, was actually abandoned by its foreign investor. Aneel is currently running the company and intends to restore the firm to financial viability and then sell it to private investors. This case reveals the many roles that Aneel is expected to play—at least, when the government does not suspend its authority (as during the 2001 drought)—and the conflicts of interest that may arise when operator, regulator and future auctioneer are all embodied in the same institution.

[49] President Cardoso declared that he was unaware of the risk of depletion of the hydropower reservoirs until April 2002.

plants prices to produce a single supply average price for the distribution companies – much as under the national tariff policy in the 1970s.

New power plants will be required to bid their output in yearly auctions, the first of which was held in late 2005. Although an auction mechanism is being used, Aneel is subjecting these power contracts to intense scrutiny such that, in practice, power costs are being indexed by generator type and by Aneel's sense of the price level that is politically tolerable. Distribution companies are prohibited from generating their own power to supply their consumers; instead, all are required to purchase 100 percent of their expected demand from generators through the "old" and "new" power auctions[50]. Since all of this auctioned power takes the form of long-term contracts, only relatively small amounts of power will be sold in the spot market to align supply and demand over short time periods. The required reserve margin was stipulated by the planning authority at 3 percent of the consumption forecast, and the cost of sustaining the margin will be passed to consumers through higher tariffs. Whenever needed, the Minister of Mines and Energy signaled in public conferences that the government intends to create a fund to protect investors from the currency devaluation.

All these elements are difficult to square. In 2003, Aneel started the first round of reviews of tariffs charged by distribution companies. Using a hypothetical "efficient" distribution company as a benchmark – a hypothetical one that, in fact, does not exist anywhere in Brazil – it fixed the new base rate for distributors. It estimated the factor X on the basis of the opportunities for scale economies and the quality of the service provided by the distribution company. The distribution companies strongly criticized Aneel's methods. The system taking shape looks much like the tariff rules that squeezed private investors and yielded the state-dominated system that created the mounting financing crises and needs for reform.

Conclusion

Although initiated by foreign investors, over the second half of the last century the Brazilian power industry was developed by state-owned companies. By removing protections against currency devaluation (Cláusula Ouro), the Water Code discouraged foreign investors by making it difficult to assure a fair rate of return (specially in hard

---

[50] Existing power plant sell "old" power and Greenfield power plants sell "new" power. Mew power plants receive thirty-five years contract for their output, while existing power plants receive contract uo to fifteen years. Old power plants can have up to 4 percent of the amount of their contracted power unilaterally reduced each year by the distribution companies.

currency); as the foreign, private share of the power system dwindled, the state-owned power companies emerged to fill the power supply gap.

State-owned power companies did not need to worry about currency risk; a dog's breakfast of domestic fiscal resources and international soft loans made feasible the rapid expansion of these state-owned enterprises. The interconnection of regional markets and the technological option for hydropower allowed for substantial economies of scale and scope that substantially improved the performance of the Brazilian power sector. Technologically and financially, this system favored centralization – a role that Eletrobras assumed.

Another turn of events, largely unrelated to developments in the power sector, produced a series of macroeconomic crises that eroded the financial situation of the federal government and key states. The immediate reaction to these problems – which were manifest, in part, in high inflation – was to keep power tariffs low, which exacerbated an already tenuous financial situation in the power sector. By the end of the 1980s there was a consensus within the government and the industry around the need for institutional reform; potential winners and losers from that reform were well organized, and the system that emerged reflected their interests – notably the interests of hydroelectric operators.

The transition to democracy included a radical shift in Brazil's economic development strategy. The import substitution policies that protected domestic producers were replaced by liberalization, privatization, and fiscal austerity. These pillars of reform also guided the effort at restructuring the power industry.

The need for a fresh inflow of foreign currency to support efforts to stabilize the Real led government to focus first on privatization – indeed, it initiated auctions of key assets in the power system before it had established a regulatory structure (or even a tariff). In this whirlwind of crisis and response, opposition to the privatization of distribution companies was weak and disorganized. State governors were wary of privatizing their companies but were convinced otherwise when up-front loans from BNDES were dangled for politically popular projects; employees were persuaded to accept privatization with generous financial packages for early retirement. Foreign investors, after an initial period of distrust, saw the price cap tariff regime introduced by BNDES as an opportunity to make a fair rate of return in a rapidly growing market. In their zeal to grab these assets, however, they overlooked the systemic risks – notably the risk that tariff regimes would be changed, that large currency devaluations would degrade their holdings, and a drop in power consumption that would make it hard to recover costs.

After privatizing some of the distribution companies, the privatization of the power generators proved much more difficult. Pressure from the domestic cluster of interest linked to the construction of hydropowers plants mounted to avoid the risk of a shift to thermal plants in the technological trajectory of the Brazilian electricity industry. The GCOI warning that uncoordinated (competitive) dispatch of hydropower plants could cause a substantial drop in their output led the government to adopt a mechanism that protected the owners of these plants from hydrological risk, moving this risk to thermal power plants. This approach raised the privatization price of the existing hydropower plants and increased the competitiveness of those to be built in the future but at the expense of the gas generators. Indeed, although these plants were essential to avoid the risk of power shortage in dry periods, they were not paid for the reliability they provided the power system.

Gas generators faced other difficulties in entering the market, notably with the fuel contracts that were available. The hydro-dominated system offered gas-fired plants the opportunity of profit only if they operated on an intermittent basis. But interruptible gas supply contracts were not available, a situation made worse, ironically, by the large volumes of take-or-pay gas coming into the Brazilian market from the government-backed Bolivia–Brazil gas pipeline.

While outside investors were abundant and genuinely interested in building gas plants, few such projects actually came to fruition. Without much thermal power, a high dependence on hydropower, and no entity providing the strategic planning and financing of last resort, it was simply a matter of time before a crisis hit. In 2000 Brazil narrowly averted that crisis; in 2001 it hit with full force.

Analysts should draw a few lessons from the Brazilian power reform experience. First, if large plans for reform are afoot then the new regulatory regime must be carefully designed and put into place before privatization starts. Brazil's federal government – BNDES in particular – was enamored of the short-term macroeconomic benefit of an up-front inflow of fresh funds to the Treasury. But its haste to sell has provoked fundamental flaws in the power system and caused long-term losses that will eclipse early gains.

Second, the introduction of competition to an industry that has long operated under a monopolistic regime introduces risks for power companies, and a regime is needed to share these risks. The incumbent clusters of interest will search for a regulatory scheme that protects them from risks and shifts risk to new players. The incumbent interests are typically well – organized and have ready mechanisms for voicing their views in the political arena while the newcomers struggle to find a voice.

Third, consumers place quite different values on the reliability of their power supply. The trade in quotas among industrial consumers indicated some consumers were prepared to pay more for reliable power supply while others readily curtailed their consumption in exchange for a financial reward (in the form of reduced power tariffs). Moreover, there is an enormous potential for end-user efficiency improvements that can be conveniently explored if the appropriate price signal is present.

Fourth, privatization of the power system does not remove the government's responsibility to assure reliability. There are systemic risks that no market player can assume individually, especially when foreign investors with exposure to currency risks are operating alongside local state and private investors. The government must assume these systemic risks; failure to do so will jeopardize the benefits of reform and also expose the government to an unruly electorate.

3 Reform of the Chinese electric power market: economics and institutions

Chi Zhang and Thomas C. Heller

Introduction

The People's Republic of China was founded in 1949 with only a primitive 1.85 GW electricity industry. It has since grown into the second largest electric power system in the world, with an installed capacity of 442 GW in 2004. The number of people who have no access to electricity has been reduced from 245 million in 1979 to around twenty million, less than 2 percent of the population. Nationwide, average per capita power consumption is about half the world level, and in China's largest cities the power system is up to world standards. Development has been particularly impressive since the boom in investment began in the 1980s. According to industry accounts, an estimated RMB 1.107 billion ($134 billion) was invested between 1981 and 2001 in new generation and delivery capacity. Three-quarters of this sectoral capital came from domestic sources, with foreign investment making up the rest.

This chapter explains this remarkable transition and explores the ways that institutional reform has affected the Chinese power sector. It begins with the founding of the People's Republic of China in 1949 and the adoption of Soviet-style administration of the economy. The government nationalized all industries, including electric power, and instituted five-year central planning with the goal of promoting industrialization. The central government planned the scale and location of all power projects, provided the funds for infrastructure expansion, operated the system and set the priorities according to which end-users were allocated electrical service. State-owned enterprises (SOEs) were not autonomous firms so much as administrative mechanisms for executing plans, without independent corporate status or claims to financial returns. The industry managed to grow at an average rate of 14 percent per year between 1953 and 1979 because electricity was given strategic importance in China's industrialization, and therefore was allocated massive resources from central government budgets. Despite growth, the industry was afflicted by the unavoidable flaws of central planning – economic inefficiency and, because prices were not accurate signals of cost, chronic shortage in power supply.

In 1979, the central government began sweeping market-oriented reforms that spurred economic growth, especially along the coast. Since the mid-1980s, reform efforts spread to the electricity sector, motivated by the hope of improving economic efficiency in the sector and the need to finance the added power delivery capacity needed to keep up with burgeoning economic growth. In many aspects power sector reforms have reflected the broader reforms of the Chinese economy that have gradually led to a declining state share of overall production and a reorganization of the residual state sector. Given the importance of energy to both growth and security, however, the Chinese central planning apparatus has been reluctant to relinquish control over the sector. At the same time, Chinese reformers have had an interest in what we have called in this volume the "textbook" model of electricity reform. It is the purpose of this chapter to show why, despite this professed interest, the actual record of change has been far more modest and complicated than the textbook would suggest.

We define in this chapter three stages of electricity reforms in China. The stages correspond principally to different organizational reforms that have been instituted in the search for capital and performance. In addition to these three periods of organizational reform, the chapter argues that the development of China's electricity sector can only be explained by the overlap of organizational reforms with broader macroeconomic cycles. These cycles have led from a critical shortage of electricity supply (1985–1997) to a brief period of lower demand when electricity was in glut (1998–2002), and finally to the current period of high renewed economic growth and a shortage of supply additions (2003–present). During long periods of shortage, Chinese reforms focus on getting new power on line as quickly as possible, and delegate much of the task of adding capacity to provincial and local authorities – a policy that has often pushed textbook reforms well into the background. During the period of surplus supply, political controversies sprang up over which plants would be dispatched; the central government used these controversies to reassert its authority and also to initiate planning for further organizational reform.

The first reforms specifically targeted at the power sector date back to 1986 when the central government partially decentralized investment authority. Local governments, state-owned industrial enterprises, and even private (including foreign) investors were invited to build new power plants that would supplement the state power system and help to satisfy surging demand. To make incremental investment attractive, the central government adopted a "cost plus" tariff for these new plants, which permitted an accelerated capital recovery and promised investors a competitive rate of return. In addition, various electric power construction and user fees were added to most end-user tariffs to fund still further investment and expansion of the power system.

This initial phase of organizational reform (1986–1997) successfully broadened sources of investment and raised badly needed capital for the electricity sector. Moreover, the reform changed the landscape of the electricity industry from a system exclusively owned and controlled by the central government to a dual system: at the core remained the dominant state planning system, but around the periphery emerged a decentralized generation system, owned by various levels of government (provinces to localities), industrial entities, and private ventures.

A second stage of reform began in 1997 in conjunction with a fresh campaign for fuller transformation of the whole economy to market forces. The focus of this second wave of reform was generally to separate government administration from business operations, which had been indistinguishable under central planning, and, in particular, to sort out the ownership of state enterprises among the central, provincial, and local governments. The central government erected the State Power Corporation (SPC) in 1997 to manage the state electricity system and eliminated (in 1998) the once all-encompassing Ministry of Electric Power Industry (MEPI). It vested the SPC with MEPI's business functions and assigned the administrative functions, such as system planning, to other government agencies. The SPC was later corporatized into a western-style holding company, with provincial subsidiaries that owned generation and transmissions assets across China.[1] Not all former MEPI electricity enterprises were brought within the SPC portfolio; the more modern and efficient facilities developed through central planning in the first reform period were retained. The SPC orchestrated in 1999 a limited experiment of wholesale market competition in six provinces.

This experiment was partially prompted by the unexpected glut of electric power following the macroeconomic slowdown in the wake of the Asian financial crisis. The SPC hoped that market competition could help lower electricity prices and increase sales, at the same time dispatching the more efficient plants in its own network. Instead, the experiment was halted in 2001 because of the quick return to rapid

---

[1] The Province of Guangdong is one exception. While its assets belong to the State Council, the provincial government and its power company were granted operating controls of the assets since the early days of reform and have been operating the system independent of SPC.

economic growth and a tighter market for electricity, which absorbed excess capacity and alleviated any immediate pressure for competition. However, the slack market had exposed enormous economic inefficiencies that arose from a system that was operated by politicized, often conflicting, agencies at different levels of government, revealing the flaws of the earlier organizational reforms. Those inefficiencies in system operations made it clear to the central government that the partially reformed industry needed further revamping.

Following intensive internal debate and international advice, the central government formally started the (still unfolding) third stage of electricity sector reform in December 2002. In theory, this third stage seeks to follow the "textbook" model by de-integrating utilities and exposing the sector to market competition. The vertically integrated SPC was broken up and its assets distributed to two government-owned grid companies and five state generation companies. All are controlled by the central government except for the regional grid company in the south, which Guangdong Province controls. The reform has also created an autonomous government regulatory commission that, to date, has few actual powers. The government is still contemplating the wholesale market design, the scope of power and responsibility of the regulatory commission, the possible continuing roles of central planning (including retail tariff setting), as well as industry structure and other issues associated with a functioning electricity market. Below these debates, economic growth has pushed demand to unprecedented levels and capacity expansion has taken off in a largely uncontrolled fashion. As reform has stalled, new power plants have been constructed by a wide range of state and private firms, with every kilowatt dispatched as quickly as it becomes available.

Since 1979 Chinese power sector reformers have been exploring a broad gray area between central planning and open markets. But there are few inviolable principles as guides in this uncharted space. Rather, a wide array of contextual factors and specific interests has determined the shape and speed of change. The two most influential factors in explaining the development of reform to this point are China's macroeconomic cycles and the central government's policies on the supply of state-controlled capital.

We hypothesize that during periods of high growth and strong demand for power the interactive effects of organizational reform and macroeconomic drivers will be largely formal or symbolic commitments to textbook reforms. The focus of policy will be on capacity expansion, which has successfully been provided since 1985 by decentralizing control of the electricity system to lower level governments that develop new capacity at the periphery of the central state system. Other reforms that might interfere with this established practice lose their priority. Conversely, in periods of macroeconomic decline, so far just observed once in the last two decades, we expect that the restructuring agenda will be reasserted and enforced by central government agencies that aim to protect their assets, usually by assuming that their plants are dispatched.

While much of China's reform effort in electricity is organizational, often with little practical consequence, the reforms of China's electricity sector are more than just formalities. Certain features of the system have been largely immune to reform. Finance has continued to be overwhelmingly from public, national sources. Politics still trumps markets in every forum for setting energy policy. And the central state has maintained its control of the core system of generation and transmission. Yet other elements of the sector's organization have varied, which have lessened the once near-exclusive influence of the central government.

First, the limited financial and political capability of the central government to keep up with growth in electricity demand during the period of high economic expansion has led to a partial relaxation of central planning and the emergence of more decentralized energy generation to meet residual demand not satisfied by the national power system. In effect, Chinese electricity development after the first reforms may be understood as a dual system, with a strong core of centrally planned and integrated utilities and a periphery of more varied, usually smaller, operators. This peripheral system has generally been built, financed, and managed by local levels of government, sometimes as co-investors with offshore Chinese or foreign investors. As proven during the second phase of reform, these new actors have the ability to contest and delay unwanted (re)centralization.

Second, the reorganization of the core state electricity system has created a new type of firm – what is called elsewhere in this book a "dual firm" – whose interests and capacities complicate the efforts of reformers. The five national generating companies in China have both extensive market power and political connections in Beijing. At the same time, these state-owned firms behave partly like private firms with management autonomy and publicly listed shares. If China were now to make any serious move in the direction of competitive electricity markets, these national generation companies – unchecked by China's ineffective competition law or power sector regulation, would hold enormous capability for oligopolistic manipulation of the market.

Two decades into China's power sector reforms, the structure of the Chinese energy sector is not yet determined. When economic growth has been fast, the central government has favored capacity addition over textbook reforms and relaxed its controls over local governments' ability to bring new power quickly on line. When supply has run ahead of demand, Beijing has pushed ahead with the design and enforcement of reforms, which have usually enhanced the market position of the central government's own generators. In addition to the pace of economic growth, the relative roles of the core and periphery in power development have also varied with the ebb and flow of federalism in Chinese politics as well as with national macroeconomic policies that affect the volume and sources of investment.

Electricity industry development

The Chinese electricity industry was born in the 1880s as various private and government investors built and operated scattered local systems. A British company built the first power plant in Shanghai in 1882. In 1888, the Guangdong provincial government of the Qing Dynasty installed an imported generator, becoming the first Chinese power producer. These early power plants used local coal to generate electricity for street lighting. Power soon spread to wealthy urban households – investors expanded nascent grids to serve large cities such as Shanghai, Tianjin, Beijing, Chongjiang, and Wuhan.[2] Over sixty years these local systems grew slowly as the country went through numerous wars and regime changes.

The founding of the People's Republic of China in 1949 brought about a significant change in the organization and rate of growth of the electricity industry, which stood at just 1.85 GW of installed capacity. The new communist government believed that public ownership of the means of production along with central planning of the national economy would overcome the inequality and cyclical recessions that plagued capitalist market economies.[3] Guided by this ideology, the new regime

[2] During this period, foreign power producers often held a dominant share over relatively weaker domestic companies. For example, in 1911, foreign companies owned 1.5 MW of the 2.7 MW total national capacity. In 1936, foreign companies owned 79% of 2.66 MW capacity in Shanghai, and accounted for 85% of power generation in the city. See, A Bright Cause: In Memory of the 120th Anniversary of the Chinese Electricity Industry, *China Electric Power News*, July 31, 2002.

[3] There were two basic forms of public ownership in China: assets owned by the entire population and assets owned collectively by the people directly associated with the assets (such as workers in an enterprise). Under the former form of ownership, the central government was the usual operator, while the latter was operated by provincial or lower

nationalized the electricity industry, as well as all other significant economic assets, and implemented the first five-year plan in 1953. The nationalized assets were assigned to and operated by various state-owned enterprises (SOEs) which combined generation, transmission, and distribution activities that usually encompassed province-wide service areas. These vertically integrated utility SOEs were placed under the administrative supervision of the MEPI.[4] Utility sector SOEs were never independent firms with management responsibility, the ability to allocate assets, and control over expenditure of their earnings. For the next three decades, until the 1980s, the central government was the exclusive investor, builder, and operator of the electric power system. The central administration's planning process dictated technological research and development, investment funding, power plant siting, design and construction, and even operating rules, complex tariff schedules, and the allocations of daily dispatch and end-user quotas. MEPI worked with the State Development Planning Commission (SDPC), China's chief economic planning and tariff-setting agency, in projecting demand for power, planning new projects to meet demand, and setting tariffs for new plants. It also interacted with various ministries and state banks to arrange the financing, construction, fuel supply, and staffing for the new projects. When the new plants were built, MEPI coordinated its operations with the State Economic and Trade Commission (SETC), which was in charge of production and supply for the entire economy, allocating and dispatching generation quotas and delivering power to end-users according to plans (Lieberthal and Oskenberg, 1988 see also, Lieberthal 1997 and Zhang et al., 2001). In essence, all demand and supply relationships in the entire chain of electricity supply were planned allocations among government branches, rather than market choices by business firms. Tariffs had little relationship to the real cost of supplying power or to scarcity. As is commonplace in central planning systems, electricity managers had an engineering background that encouraged attention to technological more than economic concerns; SOEs and their leaders also had governmental ranks. For example, the director of a large power plant could at the same time be a bureau chief-level cadre answering to the deputy minister of MEPI – an arrangement that ensured government control.

level governments depending on the size of the assets. Assets in the electricity industry as well as other important infrastructure industries predominantly took the form of the former.
[4] That the central government set up a ministry to operate an industry was not unique to the electric power sector. In fact there were many ministries under the Chinese State Council running industries, ranging from textiles to aerospace.

Not only were the SOEs government production units, but they also served to assure social welfare for their workers. Under the Chinese economic system, it was SOEs, or "Work Units" in Chinese terms, that built housing, schools, and hospitals for their workers and provided job security, life insurance, retirement benefits, and other services. An accounting scheme was designed by the central government to facilitate these services. In general, the government budgeted SOE revenues at a level sufficient to cover a wage adequate for workers to meet daily living expenses and to ensure that SOEs could provide comprehensive social welfare services free of charge.[5]

The Chinese government's massive industrialization strategy required an enormous expansion of the power system. To ensure the large supply of electricity for industrialization, the central government allocated large amounts of unpriced capital and set a low coal charge for the power sector. It awarded favorable low end-user tariffs for high-priority industries, with higher prices for less important sectors such as services. Through steady and prodigious oulays of capital, the government increased generation capacity to 80,000 MW by 1978 (see figure 3.1). A patchwork of five interconnected regional and several provincial level grids gradually evolved. Yet electricity supply still constantly lagged behind the growth of demand for power, and by the mid-1970s the national shortage of capacity was estimated at about 5,000 MW, or 12 percent of installed capacity.[6]

General economic difficulties associated with comprehensive central command, along with new political leadership, induced the government to begin market reforms in 1979. These general reforms sought to create commercially autonomous enterprises. They also included efforts to repatriate the revenues of SOEs though a nascent tax system, to encourage capital retention at enterprises for further investment, and to introduce more rigorous financial accounting (World Bank, 1994).

These reforms arrived slowly and selectively in the electricity sector. In 1986 the national government partially decentralized investment decision making and finance for new power plants in an effort to expand investment so that power capacity could meet rising demand. Provincial

---

[5] It often looked as though such services were free when in fact they were rewards in kind to compensate for low pecuniary wages under central planning. Changing compensation schemes and shifting social welfare services from SOEs to the market is one of the difficulties in reforming inefficient SOEs in China. Relieving SOEs of their social responsibilities requires outside-funded social programs to take over SOEs' accumulated liabilities in the form of employees' housing, health insurance, pension, etc. Foreign investors who buy into these SOEs often have not expected these liabilities.

[6] See the State Council 1975 circular "Speeding up the development of the electric power industry."

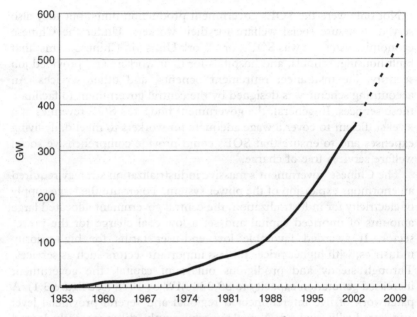

Figure 3.1. Generation capacity, 1953–2010[a]
Note: [a]The projection for 2003 to 2005 is based on 7% growth rate to reach the government 10th Five-year plan target which was revised upward in March 2003. Five percent growth rate is assumed for the second half of the decade.
Source: China Energy Statistical Yearbook, of various years.

and local governments, nongovernment enterprises, and foreign investors were all permitted to build additional power infrastructure that would supplement central government-planned projects. The result was an unprecedented expansion in system capacity and a shift in ownership. The combined share of capacity owned by these new investors rose from zero to over 50 percent of the national total in a matter of fifteen years, although the central government continued to be the single largest provider of power generation (as well as the sole operator of all long distance transmission and most local distribution systems). The growth effectively eliminated the nationwide chronic power shortage by the late 1990s and created the world's second largest electric power system.[7] In the second half of the 1980s and the 1990s, 15 GW capacity was added

---

[7] The turn of the power market from chronic shortage to surplus in the late 1990s was to some extent also associated with the unexpected slowdown of demand increase. The Asian financial crisis of 1997 and tight domestic monetary policy to control inflation slowed income growth and thus demand for electricity.

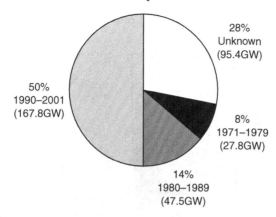

50%
1990–2001
(167.8GW)

28%
Unknown
(95.4GW)

8%
1971–1979
(27.8GW)

14%
1980–1989
(47.5GW)

Figure 3.2. Capacity by commission date, 2001[a]
Note: [a]"Unknown" includes capacity in 2001 that did not have a commission year. The 95.43 GW size is larger than the total national capacity in 1970, indicating they were not all old units built before the 1970s. Calculation assumes capacity commissioned during the 1970s was still in service in 2001.
Source: China Electric Power Yearbook.

each year on average (figure 3.1), which has given the Chinese electricity system a young vintage (figure 3.2).

Although power sector reforms in most countries have reinforced incentives to build ever larger power plants, the Chinese system is striking for the many smaller, less efficient units (less than 100 MW) which today account for more than half of the total installed capacity (figure 3.3). Some of these plants are the older legacy of the Cold War embargo, during which China received technical assistance mainly from the former Soviet Union and Eastern Europe. After China broke its diplomatic ties with the Soviet Union in 1960, its domestic development of Eastern European technology was slowed and interrupted by intermittent internal political chaos (Xu, 2002). In this period, power plants built under central planning were typically small in size and basic in technology; many of these plants are still in operation. The dominant force, however, is the recently built ones that are outside the direct control of the central government. During the first wave of electricity industry reform of the mid-1980s, local governments and nongovernment enterprises favored small power plants that were easy to approve, required low financing, short construction times, and supplied small franchised areas (Zhang et al., 2001). These small plants have thrived alongside the larger plants that were favored by the central government and became technically feasible as Chinese technology improved.

Hydro capacity

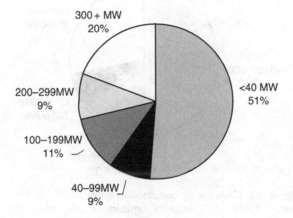

Fossil capacity

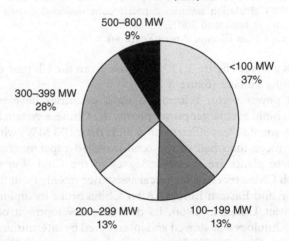

Figure 3.3. Capacity by unit size, 2004
Source: China Electricity Council, System Reliability Press Conference –
April 27, 2005. http://www.cec.org.cn/cec_kekao/zt/web/fb2.doc

Fuel structure

The Chinese electricity industry has always been dominated by local
coal and, secondarily, hydropower (figure 3.4). This reflects proximity
and, since 1949, a long-term energy policy that emphasizes energy
security through the promotion of indigenous energy resources. This
same policy has put enormous stress on China's energy transport

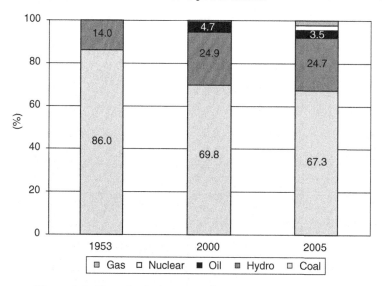

Figure 3.4. Capacity fuel structure[a]
Note: [a]Numbers for 2005 are calculated on the basis of government-planned development.
Sources: China Statistical Yearbook; 10th Five-year plan; Study of 2002 Electricity Industry Development, January 16, 2003; http://www. drcnet.com.cn

infrastructure. While China's coal resources are abundant, quality coal for power generation is concentrated in the north, far from the load centers in the eastern and southeastern coastal areas. Thus coal accounts for 40 percent of annual railroad and one-third of annual river and sea freight transportation. While China's hydro resources are abundant, their distribution is predominantly in the west, also widely removed from the coastal centers of demand. Development of hydro-power has been slow due to lack of funding and inadequate technologies for large hydropower stations.[8] Almost 80 percent of exploitable hydro capacity remains undeveloped.[9]

More recent Chinese energy policy has begun to look to alternative energy resources because of coal's adverse impact on the environment. Hydroelectricity is assuming new policy importance, which also serves

---

[8] The failure of the first large hydropower project in the 1950s, San Men Xia Hydro Station, and the withdrawal of the Soviet technical assistance in 1960 also adversely affected hydropower development.
[9] China's exploitable hydropower resources are estimated at 378.5 GW. (LBNL China Energy Data Book, 2001.)

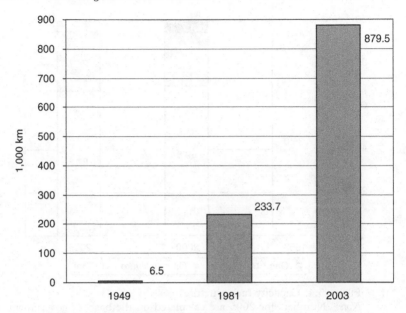

Figure 3.5. Length of transmission lines (≥35kV)
Sources: State Power Information Network, http://www.sp.com.cn/zgdl/
dltj/default.htm; China Electric Power Yearbook, 2004, p. 675.

the government strategy of investing in the poorer western regions. Moreover, the government now proposes to expand the use of natural gas for power generation. Close to 10 GW of new natural gas-fired generation capacity is planned for the 10th five-year plan period (2001–2005), including 2.0 GW in Guangdong Province using LNG shipped in from Australia, and 7.93 GW in eastern China using piped gas from Xinjiang. The inauguration of the 4200 km West–East gas pipeline between Xinjiang and Shanghai in 2004 helps in supplying natural gas to the eastern coast and will replace the equivalent of nine million tons of standard coal per year in new power plants. The first nuclear power plant, the 300 MW Qinshan (Phase One) in Zhejiang Province, was commissioned in 1992. By 2000, nuclear stations accounted for about 1 percent of installed capacity; many new plants are envisioned.

Transmission

Chinese central planning accorded high priority to transmission and distribution systems. Transmission lines (35 kV and above) have multiplied by more than a hundred times since 1949, with the most rapid growth in the last two decades (figure 3.5).

Table 3.1. *Transmission capacity ≥35kV in 2000*

kV	km	%
500	25,910	3.7
330	8,524	1.2
220	122,597	17.3
110	195,001	27.6
66	46,054	6.5
35	309,056	43.7
Total	707,142	100

Source: State Power Corporation, 2002.

Still, the grid is weak and the technology behind world standards (Xu, 2002). The first 500kV AC line was not installed until 1981, and high voltage (330 kV and higher) lines accounted for only 5 percent of the national transmission network (table 3.1).

Bottlenecks have arisen due to limited inter- and intra-provincial power transmission capacity. The weakness of both transmission and distribution (T&D) became further apparent when power suppliers were not able to reach a large number of rural end users even as a power surplus emerged in more economically advanced markets toward the end of the 1990s. Since 1998, in an effort to break the bottlenecks, the central government has begun to increase investment in the grid and distribution systems. A $23 billion investment in transmission and distribution is planned for the 10th five-year plan period (2001–2005) (Xinhua News Agency).

Electricity end uses

Since 1949 the Chinese government has consistently put an emphasis on heavy industry. Indeed, the industrial (manufacturing) sector accounted for over 80 percent of national power consumption in 1980; it continued to be the largest user in 2000, although broader economic reform in the past twenty years has catalyzed development of the service sector and also higher residential power consumption (figure 3.6). Unlike some other leading developing countries, such as India, China's power consumption in agriculture is very small (about 4 percent today) which reflects the high cost of power and the fact that farmers are not a politically powerful group in China.

Rural electrification

Rural electrification has long lagged behind the pace of national electricity development due to central planning that favored the

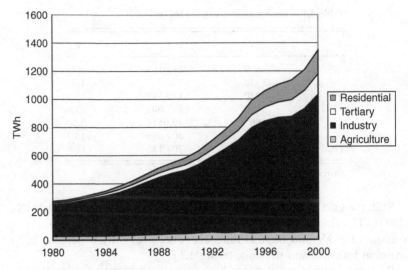

Figure 3.6. Electricity consumption by sector
Source: China Energy Statistical Yearbook (of various years).

manufacturing sectors. In China's first phase of growth, the national government's near exclusive focus on expanding electricity infrastructure to support industrial policy did not allocate much capital to promote rural electric power systems. Even though in the late 1950s and 1960s the central government set up rural power administration and initiated a few pilot rural electrification projects, the urban power shortages of the 1970s rendered these efforts short-lived and inconsequential (Yang, 2003). Rural areas were left to fend for themselves, and most analysts have concluded that the central government largely ignored rural electrification before 1980 (Xu, 2002, p. 74).

With little support from the central government, country communes and villages developed small (mostly hydro) local power stations during the 1960s and 1970s. By 1979, about 90,000 small hydropower stations had been built, with a total capacity of 6.33 GW (Smil, 1988, p. 64). These facilities averaged only 70.3 kW capacity, were unreliable due to seasonality, had no connection to major grids, and suffered high inefficiency with line losses as high as 25–30 percent.[10] In 1978, rural areas, which contained 70 percent of the country's population, consumed only

---

[10] Rural small hydro power is an evolving definition. In the 1950s, hydro stations with a capacity of 500 kW or smaller were considered small hydro. In the 1960s, small hydro power referred to stations with unit size of 500 kW or smaller and total capacity up to 3 MW. By the 1990s, the definition of a small hydro station increased to 50 MW.

Table 3.2. *Rural electricity development 1987–1994*

	1987		1994		1998
Rural capacity	MW	%	MW	%	MW
Small hydro	10660	66.9	15770	49.1	n.a.
Small thermal	2330	14.6	8180	25.5	n.a.
Diesel	2900	18.2	8060	25.1	n.a.
Renewable	40	0.3	80	0.2	n.a.
Total	15930	100.0	32090	100.0	44150
Rural generation	TWh	%	TWh	%	TWh
Small hydro	27.7	69.4	54.3	54.9	n.a.
Small thermal	10	25.1	38	38.4	n.a.
Diesel	2.1	5.3	6.5	6.6	n.a.
Renewable	0.1	0.3	0.1	0.1	n.a.
Total	39.9	100.0	98.9	100.0	132.1

Source: Ministry of Electric Power Industry, 1996, p. 46 and Wu, 2003.

13.3 percent of the national power, or 27.5 TWh. Of the rural population, 31 percent, or 245 million people, had no access to electricity in 1979.

Rural electrification has improved significantly since economic reforms began in 1979. Both installed capacity and power consumption have increased rapidly (table 3.2). Per capita rural residential consumption of electricity rose to about 64 kWh in 1998, yet this was still only one-eighth their urban counterpart. Every year from 1992 to 2001 twelve million people gained access to electricity.[11]

Several factors have contributed to accelerated rural electrification in the past twenty years. First, development of township and village enterprises (TVEs) increased the demand for electricity, especially from coal and diesel power, which are more reliable than run-of-the-river hydro stations. Indeed, table 3.2 notes the rising share of fossil-powered electricity in rural areas. The TVEs owe their origins to broader market reforms of the early 1980s that greatly increased agricultural productivity and made a large labor force redundant in the rural area. To prevent large-scale migration and problems associated with urbanization, the central government encouraged the farmers to remain in their towns and counties and set up manufacturing enterprises (i.e., TVEs) with the help of the local government. The TVEs have met with some economic hardships in recent years.

---

[11] Estimates of people without access to electricity range from 17.6 million (studies cited in IEA, 2002), to over 20 million (Yang, 2003) and 30 million (Wzng, 2004). The discrepancy amounts to 12.4 million people, or 0.8% of the Chinese population. The number used in the text is the median estimate.

Second, the central government introduced several programs to increase rural electrification during the 1990s, with campaigns like "400 Rural Electrification Counties," "Sending Electricity to Villages" and "Replacing Firewood with Electricity" (Wu, 2003; Yang, 2003).

Third, the development of the overall electricity system has contributed to rural electrification. Especially since 1998 when a power surplus developed at the national level and power costs declined, the central government has stepped up efforts to send electricity to rural areas. As a result, for the first time in Chinese history more rural electricity is provided by large national and provincial grids than by small disconnected local systems (Wu, 2003).

Environmental consequences

Rapid expansion of predominantly coal-based capacity and power generation has had severe environmental effects. By 1998, the power sector used 450 million tons of coal (25 percent of national coal consumption), emitted 6.97 million tons of SO_2 (30 percent of the national total), and 228.5 million tons of CO_2 (25 percent of the national total) (Zhu et al., 1999). It was also responsible for 80 percent of national NO_X emissions (Development Research Center, DRC, 2002, p. 71). SO_2 has been the most harmful, with national economic damage estimated between $7 and $13 billion in the mid-1990s.[12]

Chinese policy makers have enacted a number of environmental protection laws and regulations to address the problems associated with power production and to improve efficiency.[13] While enforcement has been weak, some progress has been made through policies that have had ancillary environmental benefits. For example, increased prices for electricity use in industry and de-emphasis of heavy industrial growth have lowered energy intensity (Sinton and Fridley, 2000). In addition, the recent long-term policy shift to diversify fuel sources has favored cleaner sources (notably gas, nuclear and hydro). Renewable energy, especially wind power, has been encouraged. Finally, the central government shut down many small, old (and dirty) thermal power plants in the late 1990s to alleviate the economic effects of the unforeseen power surplus, which also improved the environment. According to SPC data, a total of 10 GW of small thermal capacity was eliminated between 1996 and 2000 (SPC, 2002).

[12] See DRC (2002) chapter 3 for the source of literature. See also McElroy (1997), World Bank (1997).
[13] China's Air Pollution Control Law was promulgated in 1987. It has since been amended several times to tighten the control. The Electric Power Law of 1995 also provided for environmental protection in electricity development.

Electricity industry reforms

Reform to raise capital (1986–1997)

Since the central planning years the Chinese electricity industry has faced a long-term need for large-scale system expansion. Until 1986 the central government was the only source of energy investment financing, but the economic reform of the early 1980s gave rise to almost double-digit income growth. The gap between electricity supply and demand widened. According to government estimates, in 1979 the electricity shortfall amounted to only 10 GW of capacity and 40 TWh of generation. By 1986 it had grown to 15 GW and 700 TWh, respectively, equal to 17 percent of the annual power consumption. The shortage was especially severe in fast growing Guangdong Province – on the forefront of the broader economic reforms. According to Guangdong Energy Techno-economic Research Center (GETRC, 1999), lack of electricity forced many factories to shut for four days per week. The central government was unable to supply the financial and administrative resources required to satisfy surging power demand. The solution was to adopt reforms that would supplement traditional state capital by allowing entry by organizations previously barred from building power sector infrastructure. The reform included not only measures to broaden the sources of financing, but also an increase in electricity prices that would attract investors and special taxes that would supply funds for investment.

Regarding capital investment, the central government surrendered its long-term exclusive right to invest in electricity infrastructure and allowed sub-national governments, state-owned enterprises, and foreign companies to build and own generation facilities. The SDPC also decentralized the project approval process. While it still controlled approval of large projects and all projects involving foreign investors, projects smaller than 50 MW ($30 million) would require only the approval of provincial governments. Three variants of new power producers emerged around entities owned by provincial governments, local governments, and nongovernment enterprises. By the end of the 1990s, these new power producers accounted for 54 percent of the nation's installed capacity (figure 3.7).

Regarding tariffs, the central government established a special two-track pricing scheme for newly developed generators. For power plants built before 1985, with state capital grants covering the costs of equipment and construction, the SDPC set the tariff in an orthodox way that covered only the operating cost of power plants along with T&D. For new plants, the government fixed a tariff on a cost plus basis which guaranteed a 12–15 percent rate of return and allowed an accelerated capital

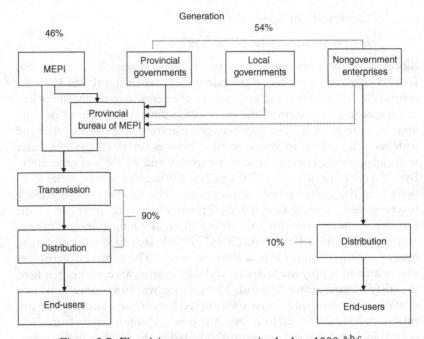

Figure 3.7. Electricity sector structure in the late 1990s[a,b,c]

Note: [a]MEPI and its provincial bureaus were replaced by SPC and its provincial subsidiaries in 1998. [b]Solid arrows indicate that the generating capacity was trusted to the Provincial bureau of the Ministry to operate, while the broken arrows indicate power generated from self-operated capacity was sold into the grid through the Provincial bureau of the Ministry. [c]Percentages represent shares of generation assets and electricity distributed respectively.

repayment schedule (usually over only ten years). The new pricing scheme acknowledged that new plants would be more costly because they did not have the benefit of subsidized capital nor cheaper fuel supplies that were awarded to plants built by the central government. In effect, the new policy entailed rate-of-return regulation with tariffs set for the conditions of individual generators. For new plants, nearly as many generation prices were adopted as there were new plants or units. Table 3.3 demonstrates the cost–tariff relationship of one representative power plant in Guangdong Province in the first period of policy reforms.[14]

Table 3.4 contains the national averages of these two tracks of generation prices. These higher tariffs were then passed on to consumers. The state was able to increase end-user tariffs with minimal resistance

---

[14] Our interview investigation of 25 thermal power plants in Liaoning Province revealed similar relationship.

Table 3.3. *"Cost plus" tariff of a representative power producer in Guangdong Province, 1999*

Capital cost		
Capital cost by capacity	Yuan/kW	6000
Interest rate	%	10
Payback period	Year	12
Annual capital cost	Yuan/kW	880
Operating hours	Hour	5000
Unit capital cost	*Yuan/kWh*	*0.176*
Fuel cost		
Coal	Yuan/ton	300
Coal consumption	gram/kWh	475
Unit coal cost	*Yuan/kWh*	*0.143*
O&M cost	*Yuan/kWh*	*0.002*
Total cost	*Yuan($)/kWh*	*0.321(0.039)*
Misc.	Yuan/kWh	0.018
Tax and Profit	Yuan/kWh	0.10
Tariff	*Yuan($)/kWh*	*0.439(0.053)*

Source: GETRC, 1999.

Table 3.4. *National average prices paid to power generators, 2002*

	$/kWh
Industry average	0.035
Capacity built before 1985	0.029
Capacity built after 1985	0.040
Vintage 1997 (62 plants)	0.050
Vintage 1999–2000 (70 plants)	0.043

Source: DRC, 2002, p. 46.

because most power users were state-owned enterprises and other forms of public companies that operated with soft budgets; to the extent that if these firms were unable to afford higher rates they would be bailed out by government or nonpayment would be tolerated. Unlike in Brazil, India, Mexico, and South Africa, consumers were not allowed to organize as interest groups to influence government policy making. (In some cases, such as Three Gorges Hydropower, the government even forced consumers to pay in advance for electricity that many of them would not even use.)

Finally, the central government added a fee of RMB 0.02 (0.24 US cent) per kWh to end-user prices across the nation to raise capital for an electricity construction fund. Half of the collections went

Table 3.5. *Guangdong urban area end-user prices, 1999*

End-users/ $ per MWh	Grid selling price	Power construction fee	Three Gorges fund	Extra local fuel fees	City fees	Total
Large manufacturing	65.46	2.42	0.85	13.77	1.69	84.18
Other manufacturing	79.35	2.42	0.85	14.37	1.69	98.67
Commercial	110.87	2.42	0.85	15.10	1.69	130.92
Residential	72.46	2.42	0.85	3.62	0.00	79.35
Agricultural irrigation	37.44	2.42	0.85	0.00	0.00	40.70

Source: GETRC, 1999.

to expand the generation and T&D capacity of the state system; the rest was given to provincial governments to set up power companies and build power plants of their own.[15] In addition to this general-purpose national fee, a wide range of special fees and charges were collected by both the central and local governments to finance specific projects such as the Three Gorges hydro project.[16] Table 3.5 shows the tariffs charged to different end-users in the urban area of Guangdong Province (see Wang et al., 2001; DRC, 2002; and Xu, 2002).

While Guangdong's prices are among the highest in the nation, it should be noted that Chinese electricity tariffs are high by world comparison – in striking contrast with Brazil, India, and South Africa, examined elsewhere in this volume.

The effort to attract new investment in the power sector coincided with important broader reforms in China's financial system. The government experimented throughout the 1980s and early 1990s with various mechanisms to allow SOEs to retain part of their operating earnings in order to increase autonomy and create incentives for additional investment. In addition, the central government gradually abandoned its practice of awarding capital from the state budget to state enterprises in favor of loans from state-controlled banks. At the margins,

[15] The central funds were administered by MEPI and, after 1997, the SPC (including its provincial subsidiaries). The provinces allocated their shares in various ways. For example, the Shanghai Municipal Government used its share of the collection to create Shenneng Corporation to invest in and operate power plants alongside the Shanghai Electric Power Company, a subsidiary of the SPC and therefore part of the state system.

[16] This part of pricing is often subject to local deviation and abuse. As SPC (2001) points out, a huge pricing problem is that provincial and local governments often change the electricity pricing and form their own pricing policy within their controlled areas without permission, after the SDPC had set the price for them (p. 111).

the central government even relaxed its traditional policy of repressing non-bank capital markets, which allowed politically selected state firms to raise funds through securities markets. For example, Huaneng International was founded by the central government in 1985 to access international equity markets for the building of power plants. The creation of domestic equity markets in 1992 further expanded the sources of financing for those electricity utilities and generators that had been granted state permission to list their shares. Access to equity capital became a new form of privilege for state enterprises (The *Economist*, February 6, 2003). More than thirty utilities have collectively raised about $1.8 billion in new equity funds (around 3 percent of total investment) according to some estimates. The former MEPI and its successor, SPC, themselves issued bonds to domestic investors in 1997 and 1998.[17]

This first stage of reform significantly diversified funding for the sector away from exclusive reliance on planned budgetary allocations to a variety of sources (table 3.6).

These new sources of capital supported construction of 226 GW of new capacity between 1986 and 2000. (For comparison, the total installed capacity in 1986 was 96 GW.) According to the SPC, $20 billion per year was invested in the electricity industry between 1996 and 2000 alone – 85 percent from domestic sources and the balance from foreign investors, including offshore Chinese (Wang and Chai, 2001).

The success in attracting new capital for power development never really signaled either a comprehensive restructuring of the electricity industry or a deep liberalization in financial markets. Political management of the power sector and state control (via the state banking system) of the allocation of China's extraordinary national savings rate of more than 40 percent of GDP remained the keystones of this policy. What generated the first period of reform was not so much crisis in the established electricity system as the desire in the 1980s to tap into capital formation from growth outside the state enterprise system and fears in the early 1990s of excessive inflation caused by state credit and wasteful SOE investment.

The more radical consequences of this first stage reform were the entrance of new actors into the sector and the development of a partially decentralized process of energy sector decision making to supply residual demand not satisfied by the national power system. Local and

---

[17] The $129.5 million and $350.2 million issues carried a three-year term at 11% and 8% annual interest rates, respectively. The first issue was paid back, and the second issue was first allowed to be traded on the Shanghai security exchange in May of 1999.

Table 3.6. *Capital construction financing (1996–2000)*

	$ billion	%
By Source		
Central government sources	31.4	44.6
Local government sources	13.6	19.4
Enterprise internal funds	9.2	13.1
Foreign investment	12.2	17.4
Other sources	4.0	5.6
Total capital construction	70.4	100.0
By Type		
Bank loans	29.5	42.0
Government special funds	9.6	13.7
Enterprise raised funds	9.2	13.1
Debt	0.8	1.1
Foreign investment	12.2	17.4
Unclassified source	9.1	12.9
Total capital construction	70.4	100.0

Source: Wang and Chai, 2001.

provincial governments made autonomous decisions about how much and what quality capacity additions they would construct; in doing so they tuned the power system to local needs and capabilities. New sources of finance outside the state banking system, including local credit unions, investment corporations (ITICs), offshore corporations and township and village enterprises were marshaled in this effort. In effect, Chinese electricity development after the first reforms had a strong core of centrally planned and integrated utilities and a periphery of more varied, usually smaller, operators.

In most important respects this dual system was simply a continuation of past practice. The core sector was planned, operated, and financed as it had been in the pre-reform period. In practice, the new entrants at the periphery merely fit into the existing structures. Peripheral plants that didn't have formal power purchase agreements (PPAs) found themselves negotiating on a recurring basis with provincial power utilities as well as government bodies overseeing planning and operations of the power system over dispatch and tariffs – what we call a "political merchant market." Foreign investors, who had required binding PPAs for their investments, soon found that their legal guarantees were not enforceable, and they were equally reduced to adapting to the political merchant market. In retrospect, the first stage of reform was only concerned with relieving capital constraints on capacity additions and marked no real shift toward competition or other elements of textbook reform for the electricity sector. Nevertheless, as proven during later phases of reform, its effective relocation of some policy decisions away from the center and the establishment of political and economic partnerships between local authorities and associated business units would produce an ability to contest and delay more extensive reforms.

Reforms to separate business from politics (1997–2002)

Until the late 1990s most SOEs, including those in the power sector, continued to be subject to pervasive political controls over their commercial decisions even as they seemingly acquired greater financial autonomy. Mounting losses and lack of innovation in state firms outside the power sector led the central government to launch economy-wide reforms in 1997 with the goal of separating government administration from business operations. Like all Chinese reform, this shift was not guided by a long-term strategy focused on clear goals. Rather, it was an exploration of the ill-defined territory that lay between competitive markets and state planning without clear rules of operation, an ordained agenda, or schedule for change. The actual course of the reforms was left to be determined by specific factors. In practice, the most important force affecting this new reform was a coincident shift in macroeconomic conditions which exposed the political and economic interests of the new actors – the provincial and local governments and private firms – that became important players in the sector as a result of the first reform period.

In the electricity industry this second reform, like the first, entailed dramatic organizational reshuffling. In 1998 the government eliminated the MEPI and assigned the bulk of the Ministry's stock of productive assets, including higher quality generation and all transmissions assets, as well as its business responsibilities, to the SPC.[18] The Ministry's administrative and policy-making functions were transferred to the newly established Electric Power Department of the SETC. A parallel separation was carried out in the organization and regulation of the electricity industry at each level of government. The SPC itself was reorganized from an administrative department into a (non-stock) corporation owned by the national government, with state-appointed executives and a state supervisory body along with a western-style (but state-appointed) corporate board. The government also created provincial subsidiaries within the SPC and attempted to give them more

---

[18] A dozen other industrial ministries were also abolished in the same year.

discretion in making business decisions, with the aim of rewarding efficient business operations.

Following these organizational reforms, in 1999 the SPC began to experiment with wholesale market competition between generators on a very limited basis in six provinces. The experiment was associated with the unexpected arrival of a power surplus caused mainly by slack demand after the Asian financial crisis. This macroeconomic reversal caused serious conflicts among different power producers – now owned by different levels of central, provincial and local governments, as well as private firms – and exposed brittleness in the long-standing Chinese practice of dispatching electric generators by political allocations (i.e., the political merchant market) instead of relative economic costs. When demand fell short of capacity starting as early as late 1997, dispatchers simply cut most power producers' generation quotas proportionally, although actual quotas were also affected by regional political alliances and side deals made among local governments to induce capital expansion. In a tight market this approach of adjusting dispatch proportionally was tolerable because there was a nearly insatiable need to dispatch power, but a slack market made glaring the system's economic and political flaws.

Six provinces (Liaoning, Jilin, Heilongjing, Zhejiang, Shanghai, and Shandong) were selected to experiment with market competition to lower cost and increase sales.[19] The experiment followed a very crude model of the England and Wales power pool. Each province adopted its own scheme. The province decided that certain power plants – including co-gen plants, hydropower, and a single unit with capacity less than 10 MW – would not participate in the experiment. The remaining power generators were twelve "independent" companies (recently spun off from the integrated provincial utility). For each, the total power capacity was divided into a contractual quantity (which would be allocated through the traditional proportional dispatch system) and a smaller quantity (typically 10 percent) that it was required to sell competitively. The contractual amount was dispatched as usual every day at the politically set price. The 10 percent beyond the contractual amount was bid into the grid at market price on a daily basis.

Simulation of the competition began in July 2000, with no actual financial settlements. The experiments in all six provinces were

---

[19] Electricity surplus was large in these provinces. Some provinces also had a more diversified ownership structure in the generation sub-sector. For example, the average operating hours of all power plants in Liaoning province dropped to below 4,500 hours, from more than 5,500 during the shortage years. By the province's account, there were 85 power plants which were not owned or controlled by the provincial power company.

suspended after two years for various reasons including unfair competition, an upturn in demand that extinguished excess capacity, and the announcement of prospective government policy initiatives that presaged still newer reform models (discussed later in the chapter). In all, the experiment of wholesale market competition was inconsequential.

Although the central government no longer aimed to control the operation of power plants, it retained its underlying commitment to state planning through siting of new capacity, fuel choices (and thus technology), and tariffs. As a result, instead of partially withdrawing from business, the national government merely switched its role from direct ministerial administration of integrated utilities to indirect controls over investment capital, project approval, and appointment of corporate management in the core electricity firms concentrated under the umbrella of the SPC. This ongoing politicization of the energy sector explains why SOEs, although now corporatized, still calculate financial viability and risks of their investments so differently than do organizations that pay market prices for capital and build political risks into (higher) required rates of return for projects.[20]

While the second stage of electricity reforms, like its predecessor, did not fundamentally restructure the power sector, it did alter some of the organizational incentives. State administration receded. The newly chartered SPC pursued policies to improve sectoral performance by decentralizing plant management. In response to macroeconomic declines that reduced demand and exposed inefficiencies in system operations, the central government fostered some competition at the margin, such as through the limited pool experiments. However, these experiments with competition were in part reactions to incipient political divisions of interests between firms owned by multiple levels of governments in a more diversified system. With ownership separated from policy and operational decisions, the central government was conscious of the tensions between the interests of local generators and SPC firms over whose power (and profits) would be put on line. As with new environmental reforms that targeted smaller and dirtier local power producers, the market reforms that would have disproportionately benefited more efficient, larger-scale SPC generators were resisted by more local governments. The second stage of power sector reforms

---

[20] For example, the Chinese oil industry SOEs would not hesitate to start to construct the long-distance West–East natural gas pipeline when neither future gas price nor offtake was understood. Similarly, state generation companies would not hesitate to import expensive gas turbines when they knew the regulated gas price and power market condition would make gas power noncompetitive. Their risks were insured politically by the government.

primarily consisted of pragmatic and piecemeal reactions to the twin goals of improved system efficiency in a weakened economy and protection of the economic position of the newly segregated central government assets.

Market reform to introduce competition (2002–present)

In December 2002, the central government announced its intent to create truly competitive power markets. This apparent rejection of the established government planning and control schemes that had persisted through the first two stages of organizational reforms had been heatedly debated among domestic policy makers since 2000 and was strongly recommended by international experts on the utility industry (Berrah, 2001; DRC, 2002). The de-integration and the competitive market model embraced the textbook alternative for more comprehensive reform, which at the same time fit the country's general effort to replace central planning with markets. The immediate decision to reduce state controls was a direct response to the failure of the SPC-led system in the late 1990s to cope with power market fluctuations.

The dispatching difficulty of Ertan Hydropower station, a large hydropower station in China, due to the SPC monopoly made the State Council determined to break up SPC and de-integrate the system. Ertan was built in the late 1990s to supply power to Sichuan province. However, since its commission it was only able to sell two-thirds of the contracted power and at the very low tariff of just above two cents. The reason was partly because the Provincial subsidiary of SPC, which owns transmission and distribution in Sichuan favored its own power plants in the slack market that followed the Asian financial crisis. This created great financial stress for Ertan (see *People's Daily*, July 10, 2000, for more details). More generally, in Beijing the motivating forces for this reform were tied to the desire to eliminate any residual monopoly powers of the provincial integrated utilities and to curtail the economic regionalism revealed in the second reform period. However, the evolution of these reforms that were imagined in the poor macroeconomic environment of the end of the century was quickly caught up in the return to rapid economic growth that took off in 2003. This growth restored the policy priority in favor of capacity expansion that marked the first reform period and transformed both the pace and character of the textbook agenda.

In its initial pursuit of more competitive markets, the central government dissolved the SPC at the end of 2002 and created five state-owned independent generation companies to hold the SPC's generation assets and a new State Grid Company to take over most of SPC's T&D assets across northern China. The SPC's T&D assets in three southern provinces (Guangxi, Yunnan, and Guizhou) were merged with the formerly independent Guangdong Provincial and Hainan Island grids to form the new China Southern Grid Company, a company jointly held by the central government and Guangdong Province. Other provincial subsidiaries of the SPC underwent a similar shuffling of assets. The generation assets of the SPC's provincial subsidiaries were reallocated to the five national state generation companies; T&D facilities were relabeled as provincial subsidiaries of the State Grid Company (in the north) and minority partners of the China Southern Grid Company (in the south). The Chinese electricity industry is now composed of two regional grid companies and five nationally competitive state-owned generation companies. Public and private independent power producers previously outside the SPC system continue to operate and, in principle, compete with the five state generation companies.

Although these state companies have fully "de-integrated" generation from T&D and the five generation companies are now called independent power producers (IPPs), all are legally owned and controlled by the same central government body – the state-owned Assets Supervision and Administration Commission of the State Council. In some cases these companies hold controlling stock interests in listed companies themselves established as IPPs in the 1990s. Still, their businesses remain subject to a five-year central planning process that is largely unchanged, notably in the central government's control over the allocation of capital. These generation companies are not "independent" in the traditional use of the IPP concept elsewhere in the world power industry, but are dual firms that combine the residual political connections from a state-administered economy with a substantial degree of managerial autonomy and formal corporate governance to have attributes of firms that operate in competitive markets. Dual firms seek to make money and also to cooperate with the state as instruments of government policies.

In addition, in March 2003 the government created an independent regulatory agency under the State Council, the State Electric Power Regulatory Commission (SERC), which is supposed to set rules for competitive electricity markets and to set standards for power quality. However, the commission is still in its infancy and lacks meaningful authority. Its investigations into appropriate market rules have been slowed by preoccupations with infrastructure growth. It is not yet possible to draw any conclusions about the degree of independence SERC will be able to exercise against the political influence of other government agencies or the dual firms created by the breakup of the SPC.

To this point, the third stage of reforms has largely repeated the experience of the second, by reorganizing enterprises in the core state system without actually implementing much redesign of the market. A potential first step toward competition in generation markets, the dissolution of the SPC into multiple state firms, has been subsumed by the rising tides of explosive economic growth, electricity shortage and easy finance through both expansive government credit and private profits. A frantic rush to invest in new capacity has also derailed further institutional reforms that were originally slated at the time of the SPC's de-integration. The central government (indeed government altogether) has lost control over the size and shape of the electricity industry, and market competition has been put off for now.

Although Chinese advocates of comprehensive electricity restructuring still hope to solve both efficiency and development problems of the power system through the discipline of markets, various factors cloud the future of the third-stage reforms. Of these clouding variables, the most general is the underlying nature of Chinese political and economic reform. As was the case in prior stages, the consensus long-range goal of change is only loosely located in that wide middle ground between markets and state planning. The embrace of the specific propositions of the textbook model was always more a response to the problems thrown up at the central government in prior reforms than a particular commitment to the predominance of market mechanisms. Despite professed interest in markets, the central government is still populated with strong currents that reinforce planning, state resource allocation, and economic intervention.

We have argued that Chinese pragmatism in reform leaves open space in which the specific speed and course of reform will be decided more by the macroeconomic context and the political interests of actors emerging from earlier changes than by textbooks reflecting principled commitments. This is especially the case in contemporary China, where analysts are mindful of the unhappy experiments in reform elsewhere in the world. Utility market reforms have proven more complicated than the textbook manuals would suggest. In most countries, political and institutional factors have confounded efforts to create well-functioning markets for electricity. Even the market reform designer, the National Development and Reform Commission (NDRC), has not indicated whether it will give up control over tariffs and administrative authority over power project approval.[21] This has led to worries among

---

[21] In fact, government planning is such an entrenched fixture in the Chinese economy that even reform experts believe that pricing, project design, and financing should continue to be authorized by the NDRC to maintain stability, and the function of the regulatory commission should mainly be designing rules of the game, and supervising the

researchers that the new regulatory commission will never attain independence but, instead, will become another "decoration" under continued government control.[22] What is already apparent is that China's reform strategy to move in the direction of market reform without abandoning state power will create a continuing uncertainty about the rules that apply to the electricity system.

Next, although there will be cyclical and temporary gluts of electric power, at present China faces a pressing short- and medium-term need to increase generation and T&D capacities. The Chinese record indicates that as long as overriding attention is paid to the need for infrastructure expansion, reforms that create uncertainty for investors will be on shaky ground. In the first reform period, when high growth prevailed, the problem was solved through substantial decentralization of administrative control over investment. This same response has also marked the years between 2003 and 2005, during which more than 100 GW of new power have been added by private and public investors (at all levels of government) through both authorized and unauthorized projects. The enormous pool of earnings retained by businesses and informal financial markets produced by national growth levels between 10 and 12 percent has made domestic capital available inexpensively to these various investors in a new wave of expansion of the electricity periphery.

In addition to effective decentralization, the particular character of power sector reform is shaped by the slow rate of reform in official capital markets. Financial markets in China remain only weakly liberalized and strongly politically influenced. The new state-controlled dual firms in the core power sector have selective access to credit from state banks (along with smaller amounts of capital from security listings). Under the expansive Chinese macroeconomic policy since 2000, liberal state bank credit has allowed state electric companies to avoid the discipline imposed by other finance sources such as local governments, foreign investors or competitive capital markets. Foreign investors have been largely inactive in the recent expansion after the repudiation and renegotiation of their PPAs during the power glut of the late 1990s. Still, easy access to cheap capital strengthens the market position of the new state-owned national generating firms and enhances the organizational advantages that those firms already possess in unstable, politicized markets. Ironically, with this combination of political and economic power,

---

implementation of NDRC authorized projects. See, for example, *International Financial News*, October 28, 2002.

[22] Liu Jipeng, *China Economic Daily*, September 16, 2002.

in the absence of any effective controls on oligopolistic behavior, an introduction of real competition in China could permit the same abuse of oligopolistic power by national generators that plagued California's failed effort to implement textbook reform of its own electric power.

Given the pragmatic nature of Chinese reform and the contingencies that affect its development, predicting the long-term outcomes of this third-stage reform will be highly speculative. However, the earlier efforts at reform suggest that substantial economic growth and the counter-vailing political interests of the new actors that have emerged on the periphery of the state system during the first stage of reform and at its core during the second and early third will strongly influence its progress. In the shorter term, rising demand will induce rapid capacity expansion in the national or core power sector. This expansion will be inexpensively financed by state bank credit and securities issued by the new national generating companies under the broad guidelines of central investment planning. The core sector infrastructure will be primarily coal fired, large-scale (600 MW), domestically manufactured plants, although some incremental gas-fired and nuclear capacity will be supported at the margins for reasons of energy security, environmental protection, and the business interests of powerful corporatized state firms in the oil and gas sector. In addition, the central government will maintain its political commitment to the economic development of interior regions through the centrally planned construction of large-scale hydro plants and dedicated transmission lines, supported by offtake mandates to transfer power to eastern load centers. Policy that sets the rate of T&D investment and the corporate choices of the two national grid companies about how far and fast to integrate what have until now been fragmented power networks will answer key questions about the scale and structure of the core sector. As noted above, although better integration would increase the potential for effective inter-regional competition, the substantial market and political power that could be brought to bear by the new state generating companies if the economy were to fall back into a power surplus could compromise the efficiency of emerging national markets.

Conclusion

The Chinese electricity industry has faced the challenge of large-scale system expansion since the 1950s. To power national development, the government organized electricity production and distribution as a state-owned, vertically integrated utility, structured and operated under central planning. Electricity was supplied on the basis of political priority instead of cost.

Since the mid-1980s, the Chinese government has experimented with sequential reforms that relaxed elements of the traditional central planning to encourage more investment. In particular, it relaxed its once exclusive control of capital investment through budgetary grants to allow other actors to raise money and build power plants. It increasingly recognized the need for higher tariffs to better reflect costs and the need for investors to earn a competitive rate of return for projects in the utility sector. Moreover, it has more recently tried to limit the central government's complete control over business decisions and to reorganize the sector to facilitate competition and accountability.

While many Chinese researchers attribute the success of capacity growth and access to a national commitment to market reform, we do not. This study has reached two conclusions. First, the capacity growth in the past twenty years was achieved in great part under continuing economic and political control of the electricity sector by the central government. Where the central government ran up against inefficient state bank lending and macroeconomic limits on state credit expansion, it allowed local governments and some foreign investors to develop a more diverse array of plants to supplement the state core. However, after two decades of reform efforts what has principally changed are the sources and forms of financing and the roster of players who sit at the table where wholesale tariffs and off take quotas are negotiated. Little occurred in the reform of operations, dispatch, corporate governance, environment, or end-user pricing. The resulting new organization remains more a political than an economic market.

Second, gains were achieved within the medium of a dynamic authoritarian governmental system. Although raising end-user electricity tariffs has proved to be the most sensitive problem in pluralist political systems, the Chinese central government has not been constrained by popular grievances in selectively increasing tariffs to support capacity growth. At the same time, the central government relaxed the scope of its administration to allow provincial and local governments measured autonomy to raise needed capital for capacity expansion to accommodate high growth with reduced reliance on excessive and inefficient state bank financing. Since 2003 the need for new infrastructure to match current growth rates favors continuing decentralization of policy decision making about the electricity portfolio. As before, when economic growth is high, commitment to power market reforms is far more a symbol than an effect.

As much as the central government-dominated system has up to now been flexible enough to cope with the needs of high growth, tougher challenges to systematic reform still lie ahead. The reforms announced in 2002 to institute competitive markets are beset with uncertainties. It will be politically difficult to restructure power markets because of concentrated market power among generators. The context for true competition – well-functioning financial markets, legal institutions, and independent sectoral regulators – is absent. Under these circumstances, it is likely that the government will opt to defer reform or limit the scope of competition to a small portion (perhaps 10–20 percent) of the wholesale market in order to maintain both system growth and political stability in a partially reformed power sector that encompasses the interests of the core national generators and the periphery of diverse local producers. China's electricity system has moved well away from its pre-reform command structure. But its transition away from a deeply political market foretells a yet lengthy process that is unlikely to resemble the textbook examples of power sector reform.

4   The political economy of Indian power sector reforms

Rahul Tongia

Introduction

India's power sector has grown tremendously since the country's independence in 1947, with installed capacity rising on average over 8 percent annually to 115,000 MW by 2005. Despite this, per capita consumption of electricity is still less than 500 kWh per annum – much lower than the world average of approximately 2,500 kWh. Indians often compare their performance with China, which had a lower level of development two decades ago, but today has roughly triple the per capita electricity consumption (and double the GDP) of India.

Most troublesome in the Indian power sector is the financial picture of a system that has been bureaucratic, inefficient, and riddled with theft. The state-owned enterprises (SOEs) that dominate the Indian power system collectively lose almost $5 billion per year (nearly 1 percent of GDP). The losses are only partially offset by direct state government subsidies of around $2.5 billion annually. Bureaucrats and politicians defend these losses (and the SOE system that creates them) because electricity is a vital public good; yet only half the population has access to electric service.

After independence the Indian economy followed a socialist path, with the state taking an ever-larger role in economic activity. In the power sector, the central government created State Electricity Boards (SEBs) that gradually assumed responsibility for nearly all power activities in the country. Like SOEs in other sectors of the economy, the SEBs survived on "soft budgets" – government transfers, rather than their own performance, dictated their financial health. Inevitably, the SEBs became bastions of political patronage rather than true business enterprises. By the 1970s, blackouts were widespread, and the system appeared headed for collapse. The central government responded to these failings by asserting greater control over power and created new state-owned corporations for generation and transmission intended to supplement the faltering SEBs that nonetheless remained the primary institutions for delivering power to final users. By the end of the 1980s state budgets could no longer offset the losses of the SEBs; in some states, SEBs had become the single largest drain on state finances and had eroded the states' ability to supply other social services such as health care and water infrastructure. The system was long ripe for change, as the increasingly soft fiscal constraints on the SEBs came against increasingly hard constraints faced by the states. The floodgates of reform opened when a new, reform-minded central government was elected in 1991. Reacting to a balance of payments crisis, they ushered sweeping economic liberalization into the power sector.

Electricity reforms, still ongoing, have proceeded in three phases. The 1991 reformers launched the first phase focused on increasing investment in power generation. The calculus was simple. The reformers aimed for 8 percent annual economic growth; historically, demand for electricity had risen at one and half times the rate of economic growth. This implied the need for billions of dollars of investment to sustain a 12 percent annual growth in the power system – money that Indian sources, alone, could not supply. At the same time, the reformist government embraced the slogan "India Means Business" and made a special effort to attract foreign investment, with electricity as a major focus area. Foreign investors and equipment suppliers were already building power plants in other countries, offering a model that Indian reformers sought to emulate. The result was a focus within the reformist government on creating rules to encourage Independent Power Producers (IPPs) with guaranteed rates of returns that were attractive to foreign investors. The government granted eight showcase projects "fast track" status, which included streamlined approval procedures and sovereign repayment guarantees. In hindsight, these IPP projects were very expensive, but the focus on generation at any cost is well-characterized by the often quoted statement from Homi Bhabha, architect of India's nuclear electricity program: "No power is as costly as no power." In practice, IPPs supplied only a tiny fraction of the new generation requirements, and the reforms left untouched the underlying fundamental weaknesses of the SEBs, which lost ever-larger sums with each kilowatt-hour (kWh) they bought from outside suppliers. End-user tariffs remained well below the actual cost of supply, and the gap was growing worse.

The 1991 reforms emanated from the central government, but the mindset of reform created the political space that allowed a second phase of reform as several states sought to restructure their SEB systems. At least one state (Uttar Pradesh) had attempted to restructure its power system earlier, but had been dissuaded by the central government. The unlikely front-runner for structural reform was Orissa, one of India's poorer states. There, the World Bank withdrew support for a pending hydropower project in 1991 and made further assistance for power projects conditional on structural reforms of the state's power sector. With funding from multilateral agencies and designs pushed by external consultants, Orissa unbundled its SEB starting in 1996, and by 1998 had created two generation companies, one transmission enterprise, and four distribution companies. Some of these new companies it then sold to Indian and foreign private investors. By the late 1990s several other states (Haryana, Andhra Pradesh, and Rajasthan among them) began their own reforms but none of these has gone so far as privatizing their distribution companies; rather, they intended to reorient the existing SOEs toward commercial goals, with the eventual intent of privatizing them. The wariness of privatization was animated in part by the early disappointing results from Orissa, where financial losses as well as theft and technical losses of electricity continued to swell even after the reforms. Reformers also faced political opposition from farmers, who had come to rely on enormous quantities of low-cost electricity for pumping water, and labor unions that represented electricity workers who feared losing their jobs if the bloated SEBs were subjected to the fiscal discipline of private ownership.

This second phase of reforms – structural – also included the establishment of independent electricity regulatory commissions (ERCs). Several states created ERCs in the mid 1990s as part of their broader electric reforms, and in 1998 the central government adopted the ERC Act that created a similar central regulatory commission and made it easier for the states to create ERCs without the rigmarole of enacting their own customized state-level legislation. A primary motivation for creating independent regulators was to slice through the Gordian knot of tariffs. Tariffs were controlled by the state governments (through the SEBs) and had become highly politicized. The voting masses (farmers and domestic consumers) secured low tariffs for themselves, which forced the SEBs to try to offset their losses by raising tariffs on industrial and commercial users. Whereas in China, Mexico, and most OECD countries, these large users have lower than average tariffs (reflecting in part the lower costs to supply them power and in part the political power of industrial users), in India the situation is reversed. One of the responses has been for these industrial and commercial users to reduce their grid purchases and build their own on-site or nearby ("captive") power—triggering a vicious cycle that further deteriorated SEB finances as the most lucrative customers exited the system. The ERCs, it was hoped, would vest independent technocrats with the authority to set tariffs – in turn, this scheme was supposed to yield a more rational tariff structure and an industry that was financially self-sufficient and an attractive venue for private investors. In all, the hallmark of this second phase of reforms was state-level action – the central government did little to direct the effort (though, unlike in the past, the central government usually did not block reforms), and there was no overarching national strategy for reform.

A third phase of reforms emerged at the end of the 1990s, as the central government attempted to coordinate a reform strategy for India as a whole. In addition to institutionalizing the reform process underway in several states, this third phase of reform sought to improve the distribution of electricity by stemming the losses from theft and poor delivery of power. The second phase of reforms had been inspired by grand ideas that proved impractical because investors remained aloof and state governments rarely had the resources to fund essential programs, such as installing meters and upgrading distribution systems. (Much of the electricity sold in India is still unmetered, especially in agricultural areas; low voltage distribution systems allow for easier theft and cause larger technical losses than higher voltage systems.) The states were stuck in a quagmire. The SEBs were too politicized to raise tariffs; if they raised tariffs then increased theft might offset the higher revenues from the few who actually paid their power bills; perpetual impoverishment made it impossible to invest in new systems that would be needed to tame the thieves and defaulters, who often included the governments themselves. This new third phase of reforms, underway at present, aims to break the quagmire with special central funding mechanisms that offset the cost of improvements that are prerequisites for long-term viability. All states are eligible for the grants and loans, and those with the best performance in reaching specific milestones earn extra rewards. A recent highlight of this phase has been the Electricity Act of 2003, which aims to foster competition in the power sector, but it is still premature to assess that Act's effectiveness.

We begin with a brief review of the history of the Indian power system and summarize its current statistics. We then focus the bulk of the chapter on the three phases of reform and their motivations. India is a vast country with a federal structure, and thus we use the experiences of several key states – notably, Orissa, Andhra Pradesh, and Delhi – to explore and illustrate the different reform processes.

This chapter makes four arguments that relate to the larger themes of this book. First, India's power sector reforms originated in a financial crisis that exposed the government's inability to continue financing the power sector as a state enterprise. Its solution to this problem was to create an enticing environment for independent power producers (IPPs), and thus most reform efforts at the federal level began with a focus on power generators even though the central problems with the Indian power sector lie with the dismal financial performance of the distribution companies.

Second, India's federal structure offers the opportunity to observe how different Indian states have developed and applied reform strategies, notably in the perennial loss-making distribution sector. Looking across the state experiences reveals that many of the standard elements of the standard "textbook" model for power sector reform do not work so neatly in practice. Privatization, limited in its realization, has failed to improve the performance of enterprises, especially where new private owners discovered that enterprise accounts were not accurate and where regulators have not been able to make credible promises. Across India, there has been wide variation in the influence and competence of regulators. The study shows that some of that variation is due to differences in the regulatory bodies themselves, but much of it reflects variation in the political commitment to reform and also in the institutions (including the courts) on which regulators depend for their authority.

Third, as in most of the countries examined in this book, Indian reformers have faced enormous political obstacles – notably those linked to the rise in user tariffs required to make solvent the utilities that distribute power. For politically powerful groups, notably farmers, tariffs are set far below the actual cost of service today; moreover, all new power sources are more expensive than the incumbents. The central government is still trying to find ways to realign the incentives in favor of reform, such as through the creation of special funds that award grants that are earmarked for reform along with additional resources for the best performing states.

Fourth, and finally, this chapter shows that the Indian reform process has not simply created a space for new private firms to own and operate parts of the Indian power system. Rather, firms with a special combination of modern management and political connections – what the introduction and conclusion to the book call "dual firms" – have emerged to occupy a space between the old state-owned system and a hypothetical 'textbook' power sector that is dominated by purely private firms. These dual firms – which include the National Thermal Power Corporation (NTPC) along with privately owned conglomerates Reliance and Tata – are able to combine the management systems needed to manage costs and performance along with the political connections needed to ensure access to markets and reliable payments from the loss-making utilities that purchase most power.

Origins of the state-dominated power sector

Electricity generation in India began under British rule with a demonstration of electric lighting in Calcutta on July 24, 1879, and in 1897 a 130 kW hydropower generator at Sidrapong in Darjeeling. In this same year the government of Bengal granted an exclusive twenty-one year license for electricity to illuminate and power the area of Calcutta (today, Kolkata) to the Calcutta Electric Supply Corporation (CESC) Limited, which was registered in London. In 1899 CESC commissioned its first power station (1,000 kW steam generator) and sold power at one rupee per kWh – the tariff set at parity with electricity in London at that time (CESC Limited, 2001). Electricity was quickly adopted for lighting, fans, and some commercial purposes. Bombay (now Mumbai) was the second city to electrify, and soon a number of private companies built urban power supply systems across India under franchises that allowed for reasonable rates of return and included regulatory oversight to prevent monopolistic abuse. India was at the frontier of electric technology; in 1902, the world's then longest transmission line was erected from Shivasamudram to the Kolar Gold Fields in Karnataka (Sankar and Ramachandra, 2000).

A handful of these companies continue today as private electricity suppliers for several major cities including Ahmedabad, Kolkata, and Mumbai. However, the vast majority of the private entities were amalgamated after independence into SOEs. The 1948 Electricity (Supply) Act, modeled on a similar British law from 1926, led to the creation of the SEBs[1] that were responsible for all new generation, transmission, and distribution (Choukroun, 2001). As in Brazil and Mexico, where SOEs were initially created to invest in new power supply, the SEBs also gradually assumed the existing privately owned services, often as their concessions lapsed (see chapter 2 by de Oliveira and chapter 5 by Carreon-Rodriguez, Jimenez and Rosellon, in this volume). India's constitution, which took force on January 26, 1950, created a federal government, and electricity was placed in the "concurrent list" – constitutionally assigned to both the central and state governments. In practice, especially under the dominating governments of Nehru and his successors, central authority overrode the states.

Consistent with their socialist ideology, India's new leaders established multitudes of SOEs to occupy the "commanding heights" of the economy. The intention was to advance employment and other social imperatives while ensuring that profits were invested back into growth

---

[1] Some utilities were termed Electricity Departments (EDs) but the distinction is largely semantic.

and development – not squandered by the elite. In the electricity sector, the newly created SEBs were interconnected as grids to enhance system reliability, allow economies of scale, and increase geographical coverage – in contrast to the earlier, isolated service areas. Legally, the SEBs were autonomous bodies and free to set their own tariffs. The regulatory oversight that was enshrined with the early licenses under British rule was disbanded – the SEBs, as extensions of the state, were assumed to be free of monopoly instincts. The dark side of this arrangement, however, was the complete interference by the state in management and operations. By statute the SEBs were required to generate a profit with a mandated 3 percent minimum rate of return on net asset value (NAV). Through a flawed accounting system that could be adjusted to deliver almost any result, the states were able to post the statutory returns for many years. In practice, however, the SEBs' internal accruals were insufficient for growth, and they sought assistance from the state in the form of grants, subsidies, soft loans, etc.

To assist the states, the central government sought to augment the SEBs by establishing a number of publicly owned companies that generated and transmitted power to more than one state. These were created in the 1960s and 1970s, a period of increased nationalization and central control driven by Prime Minister Indira Gandhi.[2] The central government established the National Hydroelectric Power Corporation (NHPC) in 1975 to build large hydropower projects. NHPC has not met its original aspirations partly because hydro projects – which are under the "concurrent" list of the constitution – require consultation with the states, which not only favor allocating water resources to their own hydropower projects but also face pressure for competing uses of water, such as irrigation and water supply.[3] In addition, building large hydro projects faces environmental and societal difficulties.[4] As of 2005, NHPC (and its joint ventures) had accumulated an installed capacity of 3,475 MW.

---

[2] Indira Gandhi's *Garibi Hatao* ("Remove Poverty") program was the rationale for much of the nationalization. However, this socialist agenda also masked a political one—many of the high taxes and trade controls were aimed at squeezing the business class, who were a pillar of the main opposition party at the time, the Swatantra Party (The Economist, 1997).

[3] Water allocation disputes between states in India are often very bitter, requiring central intervention at times. Hydropower projects are a special case where downstream beneficiaries are in direct conflict with those upstream whose lands will be submerged.

[4] The Sardar Sarovar Dam (Narmada Valley Project) is a visible example of such controversies, where activists have blocked an inter-state project and even sought abeyance from the Supreme Court.

Because of the failure of several successive monsoons (and delays in several SEB-led projects to build generators), the central government was keen to exploit India's coal reserves in large plants that could supply power to more than one state. The National Thermal Power Corporation was incorporated in 1975 and has grown into the world's sixth largest thermal power producer with a capacity of 23,749 MW as of March 2005 (NTPC, 2005). The government divested part of its ownership in October 2004, and 10.5 percent is now held by investors, banks, and some public institutions. NTPC is considered professional and efficient by world standards, and is expanding rapidly. Preliminary data for 2004–2005 show it nominally earned an 11.8 percent return on capital, which exceeds that of many world utilities. In 2004–2005 its after-tax net profit, on approximately $5.2 billion in revenues, was around $1.3 billion, or 24.8 percent (preliminary results from NTPC, inclusive of one-time settlements). NTPC's success with its original mission has led to aggressive expansion plans for hydropower, power trading, consultancy, and other operations. It has recently sought to obtain a controlling stake in the distribution business in the city of Kanpur,[5] and its subsidiary, NTPC Electricity Supply Corporation Ltd. (NESCL) is considering purchases in other cities as well. NTPC can use its size to bypass state enterprises and obtain fuel directly from national and international suppliers and the company is even taking steps to enter the coal production business.

By the 1960s, the Indian power system was set up with five regional synchronous grids, with their own Regional Electricity Boards and load dispatch centers.[6] Central SOEs like NTPC built their own transmission lines to feed into the state grids. To facilitate transmission of power from such non-SEB generators, and with the aim of eventually creating an integrated national grid, in the late 1980s the government created PowerGrid Corp of India Limited (PGCIL), which took over NTPC's transmission assets and assumed responsibility for all interstate power transfers. With over 50,000 km of transmission lines that link one-third of the nation's generating capacity to load, it carries some 40 percent of the country's power. Its 2004–2005 provisional profit of $181 million gave it a 26 percent profitability (net profit on gross revenues), very high for a transmission company.

---

[5] Kanpur's divestiture has languished for several years over valuation and risk mitigation issues – the generation company would be earning far higher returns than the proposed distribution company, for lower risk.

[6] Today, some power is transferred between these grids through small DC connections, but in essence the grids remain separate.

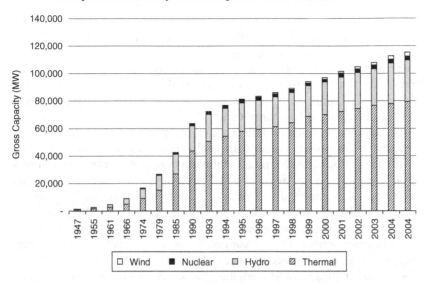

Figure 4.1. Growth of installed utility capacity excluding captive power
Sources: Ministry of Power, Ministry of Non-conventional Energy Sources and CEA

Until the reforms of the 1990s, most regulation was centered on technology and standards, and was in the hands of the Central Electricity Authority (CEA), a statutory body within the Ministry of Power. Even after reforms, CEA continued issuing techno-economic clearances for power plants, but the emergence of ERCs has scaled back its purview.

Generation and fuels

The earliest power projects in India used coal and hydro – two locally abundant prime movers – and today these two still dominate (figure 4.1).

Coal is king. At the 2003–2004 annual production rate (361 million tons, of which 259 went to the power sector), known coal reserves will last hundreds of years (Ministry of Coal, 2005). However, India's coal is geographically concentrated in the east, requiring long distance transportation. Railways, the only practical bulk carrier, are already stretched thin – 252 million tons of coal were moved by rail in 2003–2004, nearly half the weight of all freight (557 million tons) carried on Indian railroads (Ministry of Finance, 2005). Worse, typical coal grades for power production are of very poor quality, with more than 35 percent ash content in some cases, leading to environmental degradation from particulate pollution. Coal washing facilities, which remove the ash, are few; thus, much of the tonnage moved by the railways is essentially rock. Within the electricity planning and railroad tariff system, however, there are few incentives to improve on this bizarre practice – most compensation and planning metrics have been based on weight of coal transacted rather than energy content.

A proper accounting for low productivity in Indian mines and the high transport cost reveals that Indian coal is not cheap compared to other major coal producers. Many coastal plants are considering coal imports from places as far as Australia and South Africa – which are less costly despite Indian import duties of approximately 15 percent. Even today, in the midst of market-oriented reforms throughout the economy, central planners (and state authorities for a few transactions) sustain a de facto monopoly over coal supply. Thus, coal prices are not volatile, and most generators need not employ sophisticated financial instruments for managing and hedging fuel costs. A future shift to allow competition is expected to make prices more volatile and to create stronger incentives to import coal from abroad.

Other fuels play a smaller role (see table 4.1). Hydro accounts for a little over 25 percent of total capacity; government planners have long touted an "ideal" ratio for hydro-thermal mix of 40:60 (e.g., CEA, 1997; Ministry of Power, 2002). Although not rooted in any solid foundation, that benchmark has proved to be a durable fixture in the insulated world of state planning. Natural gas is a relatively new fuel but its use is rising rapidly. Private players have especially favored natural gas plants because of their rapid construction times as well as quirks in the tariff setting regime that could allow for slightly higher returns (Tongia and Banerjee, 1998). India's known gas reserves would last barely a dozen years if latent demand were satisfied. The prospects of rising gas prices and the fuel's superior economic performance (compared to many alternative fuels) are leading to incentives for private investors to explore for gas, with several new major discoveries as well as numerous projects for gas imports. Imports of liquefied natural gas (LNG) began in early 2004 and there are serious discussions underway for pipelines from West and Central Asia. India's ambitious nuclear power program has had limited success, in part because India's 1974 nuclear test isolated Indian nuclear power developers and in part because limited domestic availability of uranium has forced India to explore less conventional plutonium and thorium fuel cycles; still, there are fresh discussions of a nuclear renaissance in the country. Renewable power, notably wind and biogas generators, play a modest role despite

Table 4.1. *India's March 2004 electricity capacity from utilities in megawatts (excludes captive power)*

Ownership/Mode	Coal/Steam	Hydro	Gas	Diesel	Wind	Nuclear	Total
Integrated SEBs	20,445.00	11,049.72	1,614.50	286.81	29.61	–	33,425.64
Unbundled SEBs/ Other Public bodies (noncentral)	19,569.50	12,320.96	1,735.92	288.88	38.96	–	33,954.20
Central	20,700.00	5,230.00	4,329.00	–	–	2,720.00	32,979.00
Private	4,241.38	906.15	4,160.40	597.14	2,419.56	–	12,324.63
Total	64,955.88	29,506.83	11,839.82	1,172.83	2,488.13	2,720.00	112,683.47

Source: CEA (2005).

great government fanfare and the existence of a whole ministry devoted to nonconventional energy (perhaps the only such ministry in the world). The growth of windpower is notable – a result, in part, of special depreciation rules and high buyback rates for renewables. Most of the renewable capacity is connected to the grid, though planners aim to use off-grid technologies (both renewable and fossil-fuel based) for electrification of remote villages. The actual contribution of renewables to generation is lower than the capacities shown, as the capacity utilization factor is much lower. Fuel choices were often based on availability and mandates from central planners whose influence on the system persists until today. In this system, performance and cost of fuels rarely affected choice, since a cost-plus culture of electricity pricing merely passed fuel costs on to end-users. In practice, users paid only a fraction of total electricity costs, and thus the SEBs accumulated the liabilities. Equally importantly, operational decisions about load factors for plants (e.g., base-loading versus peak production) and other factors related to optimization and operation of the power supply system, which in turn affect fuel choice, have traditionally not been a large part of the planning process.

Planning targets have had little influence on the real strategy for development of the power sector. Unlike in China, where the Soviet-style planning mechanism is often gospel, in India actual plant constructions are typically about half the official target set by central planners, and in recent years the gap between Five-Year Plans[7] and reality has increased. In the early 1990s government expenditures for the electric power sector were 19 percent of the total Plan; by the end of the decade that had declined to 12.2 percent;[8] planners had hoped the arrival of private power producers would make up the difference, but those investors were scarce. Until the last decade, planners also allocated relatively low funding for transmission and distribution (T&D) and to renovation and modernization of the existing infrastructure, which perpetuated a power system characterized by high technical losses and suboptimal assets – in some areas, for example, over 10 percent of transformers burn out every year according to data compiled by regulatory commissions.

Part of the gap between Plan and reality reflects that the planning process has been slow to understand (at least formally) the effects of structural change in the Indian economy. As observed in nearly all

---

[7] Similar to the old Soviet model, government planning is based on official Five-Year Plans.

[8] Figure excludes Jharkhand State.

Table 4.2. *Relationship between electricity capacity and GDP* [a]

		Elasticity (Electricity capacity vs. GDP)
First Plan	1951–1956	3.14
Second Plan	1956–1961	3.38
Third Plan	1961–1966	5.04
Fourth Plan	1969–1974	1.85
Fifth Plan	1974–1979	1.88
Sixth Plan	1980–1985	1.39
Seventh Plan	1985–1990	1.50
Eighth Plan	1992–1997	0.97
Ninth Plan	1997–2002	0.75

Note: [a]These elasticities are for generation capacity available to utilities, which is the metric of greatest use to planners. Elasticities for actual power supply would be different because, in recent years, generation output has grown more rapidly than capacity, leading to slightly higher elasticities for power supplied versus GDP. In addition, captive power has grown at a higher rate than utility electric capacity.
Source: Author's calculations from Planning Commission and Ministry of Finance Economic Survey data

advancing economies, the elasticity between electricity capacity and GDP has declined as Indian incomes have risen and services (which are less energy-intensive than manufacturing) have occupied a larger share of GDP (table 4.2).

Indian planners have focused on 1.5 as a magical benchmark (the long-run average is 1.4), although the actual elasticity dropped below 1 in the 1990s. From their benchmark, planners sketch grand visions for construction. The current Five Year Plan (2002–2007), for example, envisions economic growth of 8 percent and thus implies the need for perhaps 60,000 MW of new generation capacity as well as complementary increases in T&D. Using a rule of thumb for coal-based power systems – about $1 billion per MW generation, plus $500 million for (T&D) – implies the need for $90 billion over five years, roughly 4 percent of the GDP. Unlike in China, where domestic savings are high and the government orders banks to finance favored projects, in India domestic financing alone is unable to satisfy the Plan targets (even if, as is more likely, only 20,000 to 30,000 MW are built over the five year period). Thus reformers have focused on attracting private (especially foreign) investors to the sector.

Although power generators and distributors faced little direct competition, "captive power" has offered at least one avenue for the partial entry of market forces – a backstop for large energy users against complete failure of the state-dominated system. Poor power quality and high tariffs for commercial and industrial users (discussed below) has led many consumers to opt for "captive" on-site generation. Captive generating capacity, excluded from most official statistics on national power generating capacity, has grown much faster than utility capacity and ranges from an additional 15 percent to 20 percent of total capacity in India.[9] Most of these captive plants are fired with diesel fuel, although some (especially the larger ones) burn coal or gas. Estimates of captive power capacity exclude the hundreds of thousands of smaller generators ("gensets"), usually diesel-fired, that are unregulated and difficult to count. One World Bank study indicates that 76 percent of Indian businesses rely on on-site primary or backup power units (CEA, 2005).

Consumption, access, and growth

Total consumption of electric power has risen on average at about 8.6 percent annually since 1950. However, Indian accounting of generation and sales of electricity are difficult to reconcile and, on close examination, reveal disturbing trends. The most troublesome fact is that a large fraction of power generated is lost enroute to the final customer (see table 4.3). In 2003–2004, for example, total power generation from utilities was approximately 565 billion kWh (row 1), but documented sales (row 2) were merely 361 billion kWh – a loss of 36 percent. Table 4.3 attempts to reconcile these numbers – rows 4 and 5 show the two factors that should explain the difference.

Auxiliary consumption (row 4) is the use of electricity for essential equipment at electric power plants; in most countries, generators report only net production (i.e., power available to the grid), which leads to some confusion in comparing Indian statistics with other countries. (A foreign IPP investor found a discrepancy in price projections that exceeded 5 percent simply due to this little appreciated detail.) T&D losses (row 5) are a residual, and thus they include not only technical losses but also theft. Strictly speaking, even agricultural consumption (included, as an estimate, in row 2) is unknown with any degree of certainty because most agricultural consumption is not metered (see table 4.4).

Lack of accurate accounting allows utilities to mask T&D (and theft) losses throughout the system by simply increasing their estimates for

[9] One official figure by the Central Electricity Authority (CEA, 2005) indicates 2003–2004 captive capacity, from units over 1 MW in size, to be 18,740 MW, or a little over 15% of "utility" capacity.

Table 4.3. *Accounting for generation and sales from utilities, excluding captive power*

	units	1950	1970	1974	1980	1985	1990	1995	2000	2003
(1) Gross Generation	Billion kWh	6.575	61.21	76.68	119.26	183.39	289.44	379.88	499.45	565
(2) Sales to Final Users[a]	Billion kWh	4.157	48.46	58.26	89.74	134.36	210.15	277.08	314.84	360.94
(3) Sales to Generation Ratio	Out of gross Generation	63.2%	79.2%	76.0%	75.2%	73.3%	72.6%	72.9%	63.0%	63.9%
(4) Reported Auxiliary Consumption	Out of gross Generation	n.a.	5.6%	6.3%	6.9%	8.1%	7.9%	7.2%	7.2%	7.0%
(5) Residual T&D Losses (incl. theft)	Out of *net* Generation	15.8%	16.1%	18.9%	19.2%	20.3%	21.2%	21.4%	32.1%	31.3%

Note: [a]Including government estimates for unmetered agriculture supply. The net consumption includes a very small amount of net imports of electricity from Bhutan and Nepal, 1.7 billion kWh in 2003–2004, which do not appear in the "generation" figures.

Table 4.4. *Key sectoral consumption shares (%)[a]*

Share of total consumption	1950	1970	1974	1980	1985	1990	1995	2000	2003
by Industry	62.6	70.8	65.8	61.7	59.1	50.1	38.0	30.5	34.5
by Agriculture	3.9	9.2%	13.3	16.1	17.5	23.9	30.9	29.1	24.1

Note: [a]2003–2004 source data follow different accounting and assumptions; it is unlikely agriculture's share fell as dramatically as the numbers above would imply.
Source: Calculated from Ministry of Power and Planning Commission data.

Table 4.5. *Power consumption by sector (2003–2004, utilities only)*[a]

	Consumption [billion kWh]	Share (%)
Domestic (Residential)	89,736	24.9
Commercial	28,201	7.8
Industry	124,573	34.5
Traction (Railways)	9,210	2.6
Agriculture	87,089	24.1
Other	22,128	6.1
Total	360,937	100.00

Note: [a]"Other" is a pliable category whose contents depend on the accounting method; variously, it has included municipal bodies, street lighting, sewage plants, and rural cooperatives. The official share of total power consumption by agriculture has declined somewhat compared to its peak of over 30% in the mid to late nineties, but such calculations are highly assumption-driven.
Source: CEA Annual Review, 2004–2005.

"agricultural" consumption, and thus nobody knows the true level of agricultural supply (Dixit and Sant, 1997).

In states where SEBs have undergone reforms – discussed in greater detail later in the chapter – information uncovered as firms have had an incentive to do proper accounting has resulted in upward revision of these loss statistics, which would suggest that the staggering losses estimated by aggregating official data (e.g., table 4.3) could still underestimate the true magnitude of the problem nationwide.

Thus, with a population of almost 1.1 billion people, the per capita consumption can only be estimated as 500 kWh, the lower end of official claims, when we factor in captive power and allow for theft to be considered as "consumption." Table 4.4 gives information on consumption trends, and table 4.5 shows details on the consumption pattern.

For decades, the planning process has been focused on the task of closing the gap between supply and demand. In electric power systems, of course, total power supplied must always equal total *serviced* demand (plus en route losses). However, official publications on power supply estimate a shortfall of about 11.3 percent – that is, demand not met due to power outages and forced load shedding (Bharadwaj, 2006).[10] True demand would be even higher if power were actually available round-the-clock to

---

[10] In comparison, the US recently had an average power downtime of 117 minutes only, or 0.02% (Brown and Marshall, 2001).

all consumers, and capacity would need to rise yet further if India had capacity reserve margins comparable to many other countries (~15 percent).

Supply in rural areas remains particularly limited. Most agricultural supply is throttled with time restrictions during which area consumption is curtailed.[11] Prime Minister Indira Gandhi's 20 point agenda in the 1970s included "Power For All," but achievement of that goal used to be measured at the village level – thus villages that had only a single access point were nonetheless classified as "electrified." By this metric, over 87 percent of villages were electrified by March, 2003 (Ministry of Power, 2003). At the household level a much bleaker picture emerges: only 70 percent of urban households have electricity, and rural areas fare much worse, at 43.5 percent (Ministry of Power, 2003).[12] A new policy measures village electrification with a stricter threshold (including having 10 percent of homes with electricity), and by this metric less than 80 percent of villages are electrified. Consumption is extremely low – three-fourths of electrified homes use, on average, less than 50 kWh/month.[13] Theft offsets these official statistics – probably by a significant margin in agricultural areas. For example, there are approximately 14.3 million electricity-based pumpsets in the country – out of an official total potential of nearly 20,000,00 pumps (per CEA estimates) – but another 1,000,000+ unsanctioned pumpsets hooked to illegal connections are probably also in operation.

Agriculture – The bane of India's power system

Agriculture consumes at least one fourth of the power in India, yet provides less than 5 percent of the revenues. Official estimates of the subsidy to agriculture (table 4.6) are based on the difference between the tariff charged and the average cost of supply for all users. The actual subsidy, although unknown, is probably much larger – agricultural loads are remote and infrequent, making them perhaps

---

[11] Some utilities are attempting to separate rural household supply from agricultural supply by phase, to try and provide rural homes with single-phase power for non-agricultural or industrial uses.

[12] Some official publications state rural access to be as low as 31% (Ministry of Power, 2001). Some of this discrepancy might be because of how households are computed, such as based on permanent home structures, which removes the homeless, transients, and extremely poor from the statistics. Regardless of the exact number, there are hundreds of millions of people who lack electricity.

[13] Part of this may be due to poor metering. Older, electromechanical meters have a threshold below which they fail to register consumption. Newer electronic meters only became available in the 1990s.

30 percent more expensive than other loads to serve (author's estimate). Low voltage systems used to distribute power for agricultural users are characterized by high technical losses (10 percent in some areas), in addition to typical transmission losses of 8 percent, and are prone to theft (Bharadwaj, 2006). For comparison, total T&D losses in the United States are around 8 percent and theft is near zero.

Agriculture's special grip on the Indian power system stems from its central role in society. It provides some one quarter of the GDP and sustains over two-thirds of the population. The dramatic famines in the 1950s and 1960s made agriculture a government priority. The central and state governments subsidize many inputs (water, power, finance, etc.) and control ("administer") food prices. In practice, much of the benefit from these policies flows to rich urban residents who consume subsidized food. Moreover, it costs several rupees in poorly targeted policies and inefficient administration to transfer just one rupee to the poor (Srinivasan, 2001).

India's agricultural development strategy has focused on lifting yields through the green revolution. Erratic monsoons, however, have required irrigation. Gravity-fed irrigation with surface water has been provided nearly for free – charges are often based on area and crops, rather than cost, and do not even cover operating expenses (Srinivasan, 2001). But surface water is limited and thus most irrigation comes from underground using electric pumpsets. Electricity is kept cheap, ostensibly, so that pumped water matches the artificially low price of surface water and so output food prices are low for poor consumers.

Despite national consensus against the practice, for example, pledges at the national gathering of Chief Ministers (the top political authorities of the state), some states offer free power to farmers, especially when elections are close – a trend set by the Congress party in the 1977 state elections in Andhra Pradesh (Dubash and Rajan, 2001). Across the nation, nearly all farmers are charged flat rates based on their reported pump capacity (horsepower) rather than actual power consumption, which has encouraged farmers to purchase the most inexpensive (and inefficient) pumpsets. Overuse of water, soil erosion, and water saturation have followed. Excessive power loads have lowered voltage levels and frequency, which burns out transformers as well as the pumpsets themselves – a further discouragement against any users who might be inclined to invest in better pumpsets. System managers have sought to control loads by cutting the supply to agricultural areas, which today are often served only for a few off-peak hours per day. Farmers respond by leaving their pumpsets on overnight – hoping that the power supply come which leads to overuse, waterlogging, salinity, and other problems. One study across several states suggests that as much as one-third of gross farm income is spent on electricity, of which the majority is due to the consequences of low quality power – such as burned out pumpsets and unreliable energy services (World Bank, 2001). In addition, the flat-rate pricing is regressive, assisting large landowners more than smaller farmers. There are indications that policy makers recognize this, but politicians cater to larger landowners as they are key swing voters, patriarchs who bring with them their entire community (Lal, 2003).

Fixing the problem will require installing meters and raising prices, which is politically challenging. (Nor is it logistically easy – given the more than 14 million electric pumpsets in the country.) Some larger farms have exited this vicious system by installing diesel-powered pumpsets, which indicates the high willingness to pay by some agricultural users for reliable energy services, at costs 50–100 percent higher on a percentage of production costs basis (World Bank, 2001).

Administered crop prices and cheap electricity have caused large changes in cropping patterns. Dry areas, like the Telangana Region of central Andhra Pradesh (around the capital Hyderabad), where coarse grain was the traditional crop, switched to water-intensive rice production. Large water withdrawals have also led to declining water tables – as much as several meters per year in some locations (Padmanaban and Totino, 2006) – which imposes a still greater need for lifting power.

Rural electrification has swayed in strong political winds. Election cycles often dictate rapid results – accomplished with long low voltage lines strung from substations to politically important areas. Such programs have smaller upfront capital costs than an optimized electrification program but yield higher technical line losses and are more vulnerable to theft. The central government is now working toward the goal of "Electricity for All." The targets include complete village electrification by 2007 and all households by 2012. While some additional funds have been earmarked for the purpose, it is unclear how the targets would be met, especially the latter.

Tariffs, finances, and budgeting: prime causes for reform

The principal problem for the Indian power system is its financial insolvency. For at least three decades tariffs for final users have been set

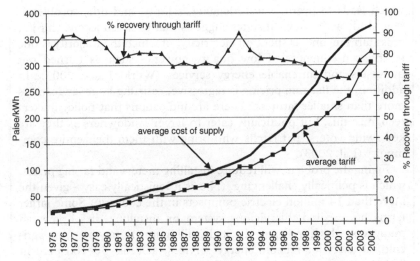

Figure 4.2. Cost of supply and average tariff, 1974–2004[a]
Note: [a]Data up to 2001–2002 are from the Indian Planning
Commission; revised estimates used for 2000–2001; data for 2001–
2002 are from the Annual Plan; the last two years are CEA estimates
based on less rigorous methodologies. Numbers are in nominal paise;
100 paise = 1 Rupee.

below the actual cost of supply. On the eve of the first wave of reforms in
1991 tariff recovery was barely 80 percent; today it is just about the
same (figure 4.2).

Tariffs have risen steadily in the last three decades – during the last
thirteen years, since reforms began, tariffs have increased over 9.9
percent per annum even as the wholesale price index has risen only 6.9
percent annually (Ministry of Finance, 2004). Yet the "average cost of
supply" – defined in official Indian statistics as the total expenditure by
the utilities divided by total kWh sold – has climbed even more rapidly
than tariffs (at 10.0 percent per year).[14] Since 1990 most new power has
come from generators other than SEBs – mainly the central generators
(notably NTPC) but also IPPs – and the long-run marginal cost of these
generators is much higher than the average cost of the incumbent
generators. Costs have also risen at SEBs that have unbundled their

---

[14] After 2002, due to data difficulties and other reasons, the Planning Commission has
ceased publishing the *Annual Report on the Working of State Electricity Boards and
Electricity Departments.* This makes transparent, granular data on tariffs difficult to
obtain without individually working through the many dozens of utilities in the country,
who often use different accounting systems.

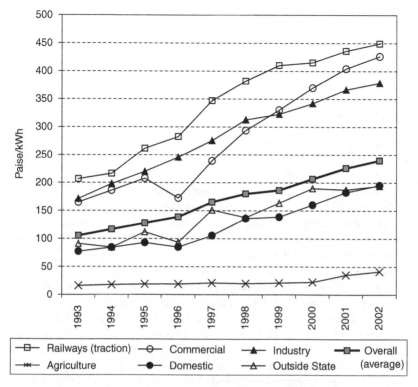

Figure 4.3. Average retail power tariffs by sector[a]
Note: [a]Actual tariffs vary widely across the states; data here are averages
for all of India. It is difficult to calculate an average all-India sector-wise
tariff as most consumption is tiered by amount of usage; e.g., large
residential consumers in some states can pay over Rs. 5/kWh at the
margin, even though the average tariff may be closer to Rs. 2.5, while
limited consumption households may pay under Rs. 2.

generation companies – unbundling has forced better accounting and has
also required each separate business unit to be individually profitable,
which has exposed the large internal subsidies to generators. These
unbundled utilities must now bear the total (average) costs of the formerly internal generators, not just the variable costs they bore before.
Based on estimates for the last few years, newly empowered regulatory
commissions have ordered steep rises in tariffs, but regulators are unlikely
to allow similar increases in the coming years; rather, they have mandated
utilities close the gap between cost and tariff by reducing system losses.

Consumer tariffs vary substantially across sectors (figure 4.3). Commercial and industrial users pay well above the average tariff even

though these large users are actually the least costly to supply. Households and especially agricultural users – both groups of political import – pay much lower rates. The result is that the industrial share of power consumption has declined steadily (though there has been a recent uptick), in part because of their shift to more reliable and (often) less costly captive power, and in part because under-priced agricultural consumption has skyrocketed (tables 4.4 and 4.5). On average, as of 2004, the SEBs lost roughly Rs. 0.70 rupees per kWh they delivered – their average cost of supply was approximately Rs. 3.75 /kWh, and the average tariff only Rs. 3.05/kWh (CEA, 2005).

The shortfall in revenues leads to both enormous losses as well as cross-subsidies by overcharging industrial and commercial consumers as well as explicit subsides of roughly 2.5 billion dollars by state governments.

Table 4.6 attempts to summarize the subsidy flows, starting from the eve of the first wave of reforms. The gross subsidies are based on the difference between the sectoral tariffs and the "average cost of supply" for each type of user. The net effect is a loss, which gives rise to the need for a gross subsidy. The improvement (line 7) seen in the last few years is mainly due to increased subventions from the states – pushed by the new regulatory commissions – and increased cross-subsidies from industrial and commercial users. The rate of return (line 8) also appears better only because of the larger net asset value (NAV) base upon which it is calculated; the larger denominator leads to a smaller ratio.

The states are obligated to provide budgetary subsidies to the SEBs to cover the losses due to under-charging users in particular sectors. In practice, state subsidies are rarely cash transactions but rather a host of other offsets such as foregone interest payments to the state, electricity duties, and other payments for which the SEBs would otherwise be liable. These practices vary widely across the states, but all have a common feature: the SEBs' lack of viability means that the states are left with a bill that has grown beyond what most states are willing to pay – the 111 billion rupees of direct subsidies (table 4.6, line 3), which is roughly 0.6 percent of the total Gross State Domestic Products, are sometimes carried forward. Uncovered subsidies have ballooned (table 4.6, line 6), which has forced the SEBs and states into elaborate accounting tricks. A favorite tactic is to divert funding from the state or central government intended for capital projects into operating needs. Another useful trick by the SEBs involves inventing accounting numbers that seem plausible – often involving agricultural consumption, where statistics are particularly malleable – and are advantageous in the subsidy shell game.

Table 4.6. *Financial status of the SEBs and privately owned utilities*

(Rs. billion)	1991–1992	1996–1997	2000–2001 (provisional as of 2003 reports)	2003–2004 (Provisional)
(1) Gross subsidy from SEBs by under-charging specific sectors:				
a. Agriculture	59.38	156.28	240.74	233.46
b. Domestic (households)	13.1	42.34	99.68	88.85
c. Inter-state sales	2.01	2.85	3.86	9.23
(2) *Total gross subsidy*	*74.49*	*201.47*	*344.28*	*331.54*
(3) Budgetary subsidy received from state governments	20.45	62.84	88.2	110.81
(4) Net subsidy	54.04	138.63	256.07	220.73
(5) Surplus from sales to other sectors (cross subsidy)	21.73	78.49	34.35	61.33
(6) *Uncovered Subsidy*	*32.31*	*60.14*	*221.72*	*159.41*
(7a) Commercial losses (excluding subsidies)	41.17	94.53	253.95	203.79
(7b) Commercial losses (including subsidies)	N.A.	N.A.	165.75	92.98
(8) Rate of Return (RoR) – on Net Asset Values	−12.7%	−17.2%	−41.8%	−28.3%

Source: Ministry of Finance Economic Surveys, 2002, 2004.

The SEBs are statutorily required to be profitable with a 3 percent return on Net Asset Values (NAV).[15] The SEBs have complied on paper with this rule by computing return on operating costs *after* the inclusion

---

[15] NAV is itself an archaic baseline – an artificial accounting concept that has become the benchmark for all planning and operations. Some of India's cleverest accountants are focused on the task of meeting the 3% NAV rule through manipulations in subsidies or waiver of interest payments, electricity duty, etc. High depreciation rates (roughly 10% per annum, despite the long life of many assets) lead to exceptionally low NAVs. Back-calculating from table 4.6, the total NAV is estimated at only $16 billion, an exceptionally low figure given that SEBs and successor SOE utilities host over 70,000 MW of assets as well as a large share of the nation's transmission assets, and almost all

Table 4.7. Balance sheet for the SEBs[a]

(Rs. billion)	1997	1998	1999	2000	2001
Total revenue	525.67	596.21	652.97	715.65	824.63
Total expenditure	445.08	532.51	619.65	721.91	827.94
Gross operating surplus	80.59	63.70	33.32	−6.26	−3.32
Depreciation	48.41	52.00	56.14	59.55	67.17
Net operating surplus	32.18	11.70	−22.82	−65.81	−70.48
Total interest payable	78.93	87.68	101.15	116.45	131.72
Net commercial profit (+)/loss (−)	−46.74	−75.98	−123.97	−182.26	−202.20

Note: [a]Gross operating accounts include state subsidies, and are revenues less operating costs such as fuel, salaries, etc. With what's left, institutional creditors are paid interest and then subordinate state loans are covered (Sankar, T. L., 2001). In practice, states would often waive interest charges to help the SEBs meet the 3% rule; in some cases, when a shortfall persists, states lift subsidies – or SEBs show a pending subsidy that is never actually paid from the state – to ensure compliance with the 3% mandate. (The table is not updated past 2001 because the Planning Commission has stopped publishing such statistics.)
Source: Planning Commission 2002.

of subsidies and by excluding most new capital expenditures. Yet returns are actually negative (table 4.6, line 8). Detailed profit and loss accounting reveals that the SEBs are no longer able to cover even their operating costs (table 4.7).

The poor cash flow from the SEBs stems, in part, from substantial defaults by end-users who are billed for services but then do not pay, sometimes for tens of percent of billables. In the State of Uttar Pradesh, for example, 40% percent of the SEB's accumulated unpaid billings were from the government itself (Sankar, 2001). The SEBs have addressed this problem of arrears by delaying payments to their own suppliers, such as generators or the state-owned Indian railways. In the past, SEBs could offset some of the rail freight charges against electricity charges, but with reforms and unbundling of many SEBs the generators have often become separate entities and no longer sell power directly to the railways. By 2001, total arrears to SOEs from the SEBs were 340 billion rupees, of which 110 billion was principal owed to NTPC alone (Ahluwalia, 2001).[16] In exchange for partial waiver of outstanding

the distribution infrastructure that delivers most of India's 115+ GWs of generating capacity.
[16] NTPC has been forced to increase its borrowings through short-term debt to cover some liquidity needs, hurting its return on capital. In addition, in a few cases it has

interest and surcharges, the central government pushed the SEBs to securitize their debts using special government instruments (typically special, tax-free bonds at 8.5 percent interest, totaling almost Rs. 290 billion (Ministry of Finance, 2004). Resultantly, arrears to central generators (notably NTPC) have dropped to nearly zero in the last few years.

As is clear from these numbers, accounting problems in the power sector were already manifest by the early 1990s; regretfully, comparable data are not available to reveal how these problems evolved prior to the waves of reforms. Indeed, the entire reform process has been hampered by the lack of proper accounting concepts, guidelines, or personnel.[17] Despite requirements of the Indian Companies Act of 1956, power utilities didn't adopt commercially based accounting rules until 1985 (Ruet, 2001). Perhaps the most serious ongoing problem is that electricity accounting has been geared to average costs, whereas project-oriented accounting should rather focus on the margin. The SEBs, until a few states sought to unbundle them, rarely knew either their average or marginal costs of generation.

When the SEBs sought to expand their generation capacity they had three financing options available – internal accruals, debt, or equity. Until the 1970s, internal accruals were large enough to fund most expanded capacity – especially when the SEBs could deploy creative accounting and the 3 percent rule. As that well ran dry the SEBs sought equity financing in the form of government grants – which proved to be quite limited, leaving no other option but debt. Backing from the states meant that SEBs could preserve a credit rating needed for borrowing; state governments don't default, since debt servicing is a prioritized item in the budgets (National Institute of Public Finance and Policy, 2001). (However, in a few cases governments found it impossible to avoid equity investments when they needed to strengthen the books of the SEBs – for example, by converting debt to equity and thus relieving the SEBs of the need to make interest payments.)

Some of the financing for expanding the power sector came from intermediaries created for special tasks and able to borrow on the strength of the central government's repayment guarantees. The Rural Electrification Corporation (REC) was established in 1969 after the famines of the 1960s, with a mission to "facilitate availability of electricity for accelerated growth and for enrichment of quality of life of rural and

assumed control over SEB assets in lieu of past dues (e.g., in 1995 obtaining the Talcher power plant in Orissa).

[17] Ruet (2001) found that Haryana SEB had only 10 chartered accountants, out of 50,000 employees. Most accounting was done by people with less formal or structured training.

semi-urban population." In practice, the REC funded many projects with only a tenuous link to rural electrification; it provides loans to utilities (not end-users) at or just below market rates. The Power Finance Corporation (PFC) was created in 1986 to augment expenditures on new power projects beyond the funding allocated through India's five-year plans. Its loans (historically below market rates, with a pool of capital it raises in part on the strength of the central government's balance sheet) are channeled to central, state, and municipal enterprises. Despite its strong performance, PFC can only meet a small fraction of the needs of the system.

The dire financial situation of the SEBs (and the states that back them) helps to explain why the center has attempted to exert control over the SEBs and power system, even though the SEBs are organs of the states and constitutionally electricity is a concurrent responsibility of the states and the center. When states are indebted to the center (which is always the case), Article 293 of the Constitution requires the states to obtain central government permission before borrowing from the domestic market (Rao and Singh, 1998). (Until the recent financial reforms of the 1990s, the states were barred altogether from borrowing on the international market.) The Center's control over financing is reinforced through its dominance of the banking system, enhanced after the nationalizations of 1969–1971.[18]

In principle, the center could impose a "hard" constraint on state budgets; in practice, the states have focused intense creative and political energy on finding ways to circumvent such controls, such as through diverting resources meant for capital projects and accruing arrears with central government enterprises (Srinivasan, 2001). In addition, political fragmentation in the 1990s has opened new spigots of financing from the central governments, leading to profligacy by the states.[19] In 1955–1956 the states financed 69 percent of their expenditures with in-state revenues; by 1993–1994 that had declined to

---

[18] Rules requiring a large portion of banks' funds to be set aside for "priority" or governmental lending, often below cost, effectively crowded out money for the private sector, while simultaneously buttressing the government's rising public sector deficits (Williamson and Zagha, 2002). Even then, banks were unable to support significant financing for the power sector.

[19] State and regional political parties have become increasingly important in the last decade, as many central governments are coalitions built between minority national parties and state/regional partners. This results in significant leverage for discretionary funding. This reduction in the political power of the Center has also allowed the states greater flexibility in policy and decision-making. In China, the abundant availability of central credit has been indicative of exactly the opposite outcome—when credit is loose the Chinese central government (which is an organ of the Communist Party, not a product of coalition forces) supplants all other financing sources and thus exerts de facto control over investment in the sector at the expense of the provinces. See Zhang (chapter 3 of this volume).

Table 4.8. *Governmental expenditure (state plus central) for various development sectors*

(Rs. billion)	1990–1991	2000–2001	2003–2004 (Revised estimate)
Total Expenditure	1,637	5,956	8,874
Education	171	670	808
Health	73	280	369
Electricity (Plan Outlays)	114	280	307
Direct electricity subsidies (by state govts.)	Less than 32[a]	88	111

Note: [a]Rs. 31.82 billion is the figure for 1992–1993; one can estimate that 1990–1991 was probably 20–25% lower.
Source: Ministry of Finance (2005); Planning Commission (2002) data.

55 percent (Rao and Singh, 1998). The center makes up the difference through a constitutional mechanism to devolve tax receipts and supply grants, Planning Commission funding for state-level development projects, and Ministry grants to respective state counterparts. This pattern became pronounced as the states invested heavily in physical infrastructure (power, ports, irrigation, etc.) and social infrastructure in the 1980s. The subsidy for such services is now estimated at about 7 percent of GDP (Williamson and Zagha, 2002). While these trends helped to exacerbate the financial crisis in 1991, today the fiscal situation is as bad as it was at that time. Looking at overall state budgets, the revenue deficit increased from Rs. 53.1 billion (0.99 percent of GDP) in 1990–2001 to Rs. 404.9 billion (2.30 percent of GDP) in 1998–1999 and an estimated 4.4 percent of GDP in 2003–2004 (this is excluding the central government deficit, which grew to over 5.5 percent recently but has since stabilized). The losses of the 19 major SEBs increased from 5 percent of the state revenue receipts in 1992–1993 to 6.5 percent in 1998–1999 (Ahluwalia and Bhatiani, 2000).

The relative magnitude of the state and central governments' expenditures propping up the electricity system can be seen by comparing it to expenditures on other social services (table 4.8).

The outlays for the power sector are amongst the largest segments in the Annual and Five-Year Plans, many times higher than for other infrastructure, and these exclude significant non-Plan expenditure such as retained earnings (especially available to generators or PowerGrid) or by private entities. Power sector direct subsidies (mainly for agriculture users) are a significant expenditure, and these figures exclude implicit subsidies that are comparable if not higher. Unfortunately, like much government expenditure aimed at helping the poor, power subsidies have proved to be an inefficient way to address poverty.

Electricity reforms

Reforms and policy – context of change

For decades after independence, India followed socialist policies and the government assumed many aspects of commercial activity—especially large projects that, over time, comprised a large but inefficient industrial complex. The system sustained itself financially and politically through a series of interlocking rents and vested interests that were locked into place through a myriad of institutions and legislation. Energy was typical, with the SEBs sharing responsibility with the central government and focusing, when possible, on large, visible projects such as dams. Nehru declared, "Dams are the temples of modern India."

Although politically expedient, over time this system took a heavy toll on the economy. Until the early 1980s economic growth averaged around 3.5 percent per year – barely above the rise in population and famously branded the "Hindu Rate of Growth." During the 1980s a series of policies to attract investment accelerated growth to around 5 percent, and Indian central planners adopted a target rate of 8 percent. This rapid rise in growth in the 1980s was built on a mounting debt that proved unsustainable and triggered a fiscal crisis. External debt, about $18.3 billion in 1980–1981, swelled to $71.1 billion on the eve of the macroeconomic crisis of 1990–1991; the gross fiscal deficit of the central and state governments had climbed to 9 percent of GDP. Adding the losses from nonfinancial state enterprises (including the SEBs), which are not included in the consolidated government accounts even though the government is liable for their losses, increased the public sector deficit to 10.9 percent of GDP in 1990–1991 (Srinivasan, 2001). More than one-third of the deficit was interest payments on already accumulated debts.

The fiscal crisis of the early nineties forced hard choices. In democratic India most politicians opted for the continuation of politically popular subsidies while transferring the task of financing capital-intensive projects such as infrastructure to the private sector (The Economist, 1997). Thus most political parties indicated their support for economic liberalization in the wake of the severe financial crisis yet abhorred the fiscal discipline that a full reform would imply.

The job of implementing economic reforms fell to a newly elected minority government, which faced the immediate task of managing the 1991 financial crisis. India's foreign exchange reserves had dwindled down to just days' worth of imports. Already inclined toward reform, the new government – led by Prime Minister P. V. Narasimha Rao and populated by distinguished economists, notably Finance Minister Manmohan Singh (now India's Prime Minister) and Finance Secretary Montek Singh Ahluwalia (now the head of the Planning Commission) – used the crisis to impose broad and dramatic reforms, including a sharp devaluation of the rupee and convertibility of the current account. Most important, the new government slowly began to unravel the numerous controls on private economic activity, dubbed the "license-permit-quota Raj" (Singh and Srinivasan, 2002). They sought to attract foreign investors throughout the economy – an aim that extended to the power sector as well.

Other concurrent trends aided and focused the efforts at reform. The early 1990s marked an uptick in foreign investment in developing countries generally; the period also saw the implosion of the Soviet Union (India's socialist idol) while the persistent rise of China offered an alternative to the classic socialist model of growth. (Indians have often argued that China's economic success stemmed from its lack of democracy, but the reformers knew that market forces and institutions, not totalitarianism, were the keys to the China miracle.)

In contrast with the "big bang" theory of reform that guided policy in much of Eastern Europe, India's followed a path of gradualism (Ahluwalia, 2001). Guided by broad reform goals, reformers fine-tuned the detailed steps required to unravel the old system through trial and error. A process of "reform by stealth" included tolerance of market-oriented enterprises that evaded laws, rather than the politically more difficult task of changing the web of interlocking legislation that had shackled the Indian economy (Bardhan, 2003). For example, some state governments conveniently ignored factory owners who diluted strict labor laws or firms that established their own (sometimes illegal) captive power stations to avoid the poor quality and expensive power from the state-dominated electric system.

Much of the gradual structural reform focused on SOEs as they accounted for a large fraction of economic activity and were particularly inefficient. In most sectors, SOEs (with the exception of oil and gas enterprises, NTPC and a few others) created huge losses for which the government was ultimately liable. From the mid-1980s – long before the financial crisis of 1991 – the central government had attempted to improve the efficiency of SOEs by giving them greater managerial autonomy and increasing their access to capital, with the hope that some SOEs would become more entrepreneurial. In 1991, a new tack was taken: the reformist government launched a period of "disinvestment," a term politically more acceptable than "privatization." The aim was to raise revenues, in part to satisfy the IMF, which had bankrolled India in its moment of crisis and demanded lower fiscal deficits in exchange. Most disinvestments, however, involved selling only small minority shares, which made the ventures less attractive to private investors. Whole-hearted privatization only began later, around 1997, with the sale of controlling shares. The nationalist BJP government, elected in 1998, actually institutionalized this process of privatization by creating a Ministry of Disinvestment – despite the fact that during the bitter election it had wrapped itself in nationalism and criticized globalization. A measure of the consensus supporting reform, and the lack of any viable alternative options, is the consistent march to a more liberal economy through diverse governments despite considerable public anxiety about the effect of reforms.[20]

In some quarters, efforts to block the gradual reform process were successful. Some industries, such as agriculture commodity trading and numerous small industries, were able to delay or exempt themselves from these reforms. Moreover, the reforms touched on controversial issues such as labor policy and were the subject of numerous public interest litigations (PILs) – most of which the courts dismissed, though typically after substantial litigious delays. A modest opposition gathered strength – animated by the claim that reform was tantamount to "privatizing profits and nationalizing losses" – but the reform process continued. The changes were most dramatic for the largest SOEs, of which electric power was the most visible example.

Generation and IPPs – the 1991 reforms

By the late 1980s the problems of the power sector were already overdue for remedy, but the central government had no strategy for reform and feared the political consequences of upsetting a delicate equilibrium of accounting transfers, shell games, and deception. The state of Uttar Pradesh had explored the possibility of unbundling and corporatizing its

---

[20] The current Congress party led coalition government has support from leftist parties who oppose many facets of privatization, and observers comment that some of the reforms process have slowed down in 2004–2005, in part due to such pressures.

SEB into profit centers, but the central government squashed the effort (Agrawala, 2003).[21]

The broader reforms launched under Prime Minister Rao in 1991 were animated by a fiscal crisis – and the remedies sought were immediate. Thus these reformers did not dwell on the structural inefficiencies of the SEBs – which would require many years of working with the states to rectify – but on the immediate problem of meeting the shortfall in generating capacity that had been perpetuated by the SEBs poor finances. The reform government also hoped, although with no actual experience in India or in most other developing countries to suggest that their theory was valid, that private investors would flood into the market and provide an efficient and inexpensive alternative to the SEBs. A focus on investment in new (i.e., "greenfield") power generators was also consistent with the reformist agenda of attracting foreign direct investment (FDI), which reformers assumed would flow more readily into separate greenfield investments than through privatizing the utilities themselves, which would have been politically more difficult as well.

It proved relatively easy to create the legal conditions needed to attract private investors for greenfield electricity generation. The Electricity Laws (Amendment) Act of 1991 changed the 1948 Electricity (Supply) Act to allow private generators to operate on a costs-plus model with their tariffs regulated by the CEA. Shortly after making that legislative change, a Government of India Resolution expanded that window to open up "electricity generation, supply and distribution" to the private sector (D'Sa, 2002), but the only real activity was in generation.

The central government set tariff rules that would be particularly attractive to investors, with a guaranteed 16 percent return on equity (after tax) and full repatriation of profits in dollars. (The indices used in computing return were often not updated and were vulnerable to accounting tricks; in many case, investors appear to have earned well above the 16 percent rate (See footnote 42 on page 163)).

To catalyze the process the government awarded "fast track" status to eight projects (many with foreign participation), promising rapid clearances and central government repayment guarantees – which were never offered again – that would help assuage investors who feared dealing with insolvent SEBs (the customers for most bulk power). The

[21] The plan was outlined in the Vasant Committee Report, which later provided key inputs for Orissa's reforms (per the author's interview with former Uttar Pradesh Power Secretary and Committee Secretary, Pankaj Agrawala).

program was limited to just these early investors, partly so that the government could limit its exposure. Articles 292 and 293 of the Constitution limit the volume of guarantees and counter-guarantees that the government can issue, though some exceptions have been allowed. Most of these projects – both those on fast track and the normal projects – included a power purchase agreement (PPA) between the operator and one SEB based on cost-plus methodologies. Some of the fast track projects were approved even without techno-economic clearance by CEA, evidence that the government put its highest priority on attracting these investments – almost at any cost.

So far, only three of the fast track projects have produced power – more than a decade after the fast track initiative – and many projects have been abandoned. Boxes below highlight the diverging experiences of two of these projects – one built by GVK Industries (which is operating successfully) and the other by Enron (which produced some power but was suspended in a financial and legal quagmire and awaited restructuring before restarting).[22] In many cases the government was unable to deliver on its promise of rapid approval as the projects became touchstones for antiglobalization lobbies who used protests and environmental PILs to slow approvals until investors withdrew. Cogentrix, the largest promoter in Mangalore Power Company, in Karnataka, finally left the project after years of opposition and PIL-induced legal wrangling. Enron's Dabhol project (see box) epitomized what was seen as flawed in the IPP policy and fast track projects in particular; secret PPAs and lack of competitive bidding burdened the Maharastra SEB with power that was much more expensive than alternatives and put the project under a cloud of suspicion.

Enron's Dabhol power company project

Enron's Dabhol Project was seeded in the early 1990s, shortly after the 1991 financial crisis, when Indian officials visited the United States seeking investors and met with Enron. Enron's response was bold: an integrated gas-based power plant (the largest in the world, in a country that had almost zero gas-fired capacity at the time). The Indian officials were attracted to the project – which promised to be the largest FDI project in Indian history – as a showcase for the new reforms and signed an MoU in 1992 for a series of units totaling more than 2,000 MW; the Maharashtra SEB was slated to acquire a 10

---

[22] The third project is the smallest of the three – Spectrum Power's 208 MW gas-based Kakinada Project, located in Andhra Pradesh and commissioned January 1998.

percent stake. Opponents within the Maharashtra government sought a World Bank opinion of the project, and a confidential 1993 report from the Bank claimed that project "is not economically viable, and thus could not be financed by the Bank" (Choukroun, 2001). Among the reservations was the concern that such large capacity could not be absorbed by the system and the very high cost of the power. CEA issued only provisional clearance on the project's technical and economic merits in November 1993, but in December that year Enron nonetheless concluded a 20-year PPA with the Maharashtra SEB.

A new Shiv Sena government elected in 1995 in Maharasthra filed suit to cancel the PPA on grounds of corruption and fraud. For reasons officially unknown but subject to speculation,[23] they renegotiated the contract, based on an eleven-day review by a committee headed by distinguished economist Kirit Parikh. Earlier, Parikh had expressed reservations about the deal, but he supported the project contingent upon some modifications (including price reductions and change in fuels). This renegotiated contract cut the tariff that Enron was allowed to charge from Rs. 1.89/kWh to Rs. 1.86[24] and in 1996 the Dabhol Power Corporation secured sovereign guarantees and a binding PPA for the plant's full capacity.

Having visibly promoted the plant, the central government reaffirmed its support throughout the controversy – Power Minister Salve, for example, stated that halting the project would be tantamount to an "anti-national act. Contracts have been signed and the price of canceling will be very high" (Choukroun, 2001). US Energy Secretary Hazel O'Leary echoed support for the project, warning in June 1995 that "failure to honor the agreements between the project partners and the various Indian governments will jeopardize not only the Dabhol project but also most, if not all, of the other private power projects proposed for international financing" (Bidwai, 2002).

Dabhol's first phase began in May 1999, with power that proved too costly for the Maharasthra SEB to bear.[25] The second phase

---

[23] Critics mention "special deals" as a reason, pointing out that on November 7, 1995, Enron Executive Rebecca Mark missed a scheduled appointment over Dabhol with the Maharashtra Chief Minister to instead meet with the politically powerful but non-elected (and nonaccountable) Bal Thackeray, who controls the Shiv Sena party. Enron also admits to spending $20 million to "educate" the public about its project.

[24] Many of the IPP projects had cost components pegged in U.S. dollars (and pass-through fuel costs). The 1997 Asian financial crisis raised the cost of the dollar to the rupee by almost 25% in a short period of time, which drove up expected tariffs from almost all IPPs dramatically (Gray and Schuster, 1998). This was an added nail in the coffin of IPPs, especially ones with foreign participation.

[25] The assumptions about fuel and operating costs and currency rates proved to be wildly optimistic; when real costs were passed through, Dabhol actually charged the

never began operations, and until recently the whole plant was mothballed as the stakeholders wrangled over contract violations and ownership – problems made worse by Enron's own bankruptcy. Since the Enron debacle, the Maharashtra SEB has obtained virtually no additional generation capacity, and power shortages have grown more acute. Following a restructuring that has brought NTPC and the state-owned gas company (GAIL) as part owners the Dabhol plant expects to begin full production in 2006, and the Maharashtra SEB has issued a target price cap of Rs. 2.30/kWh (which will be hard to meet at current high fuel costs).

Other IPP projects have resulted in more conversation than power. While there were hundreds of Letters of Intent (and even MoUs) signed in the early to mid-1990s, most yielded no serious investment. Most projects with foreign investors were established as joint ventures, with local partners chosen for their ability to aid in navigating the Indian "system."[26] According to one SEB official, this practice was the source of some of the problems, with nonprofessional parties joining forces with genuinely interested parties. By August 1995, MoUs or Letters of Intent existed for 189 projects that would have totaled 75,000 MW; only a handful cleared the next stages of approval (CEA techno-economic clearance, Ministry of Environment and Forests clearance, Foreign Investment Promotion Board clearance, Fuel Supply Linkage, Lending, and Financial Closure). Since IPPs were no longer able to obtain sovereign counter-guarantees, investors sought other instruments (e.g., escrow accounts) to mitigate some of their payment risks. At the same time, the financial situation of the SEBs was deteriorating. The issue remained that SEBs just did not have the finances to create the demanded escrow accounts (between one to two months worth of gross billables).

The fruits of this reform focused on private generation should have ripened during the second half of the 1990s; ironically, however, public sector capacity actually grew during that period at a rate double that of privately owned generators. In addition to the obvious failure to attract much actual investment in new capacity, this first wave of reforms yielded plants that were much more expensive than the incumbents'

Maharasthra SEB as much as Rs. 7.81/kWh with the plant running at part load; even at full load the actual tariff charged would have been more than Rs. 5/kWh (http://in.rediff.com/money/enron.htm).

[26] The JV system along with the desire to reduce exposure led to the extensive use of non-recourse project financing, typical of energy projects in developing countries.

and even more expensive than power from new plants built by state-owned enterprises. Take-or-pay clauses in the PPAs, high rates of return, and a contracting structure that offered large potential windfall earnings to investors while saddling the purchasers (SEBs) with fuel and currency risks were all the product of a "power at any cost" mentality.

GVK Industries' Jegurupadu gas-fired plant

While Enron has been analyzed extensively, including by Parikh (1996), the success of GVK's 235 MW Jegurupadu project is less well documented. According to interviews with GVK officers, the decision by GVK to finance the project by absorbing much of the risk itself (rather than through elaborate debt financing and complicated joint ventures) was key to this project's relatively rapid construction and successful operation.

Andhra Pradesh (AP) had found natural gas in the eighties, and the state's SEB had planned to build a 400 MW plant. After the central government adopted its IPP policy in 1991, AP Chief Minister M. Chenna Reddy encouraged G. V. Krishna Reddy to undertake the project himself despite his lack of any prior experience with power projects. A successful industrialist of Indian origin but living in the United States, Krishna Reddy established a special purpose vehicle for the power plant (GVK Industries), signed an MoU in 1992 and secured CEA clearance. Central government counter-guarantees and finally financial closure came only in 1997. Long before that, GVK had begun construction (using a loan from IDFC); even ABB, a European turbine vendor that later took a financial stake in the project, delivered the plant turbine before financial closure. This allowed the first turbine to begin operations by 1996.

Jegurupadu's levelized costs are pegged at Rs. 1.82/kWh, and its first year tariffs were Rs. 2.1/kWh. Among the factors in the plant's profitability is low-cost natural gas. GVK secured an allocation of gas from the AP government at Rs. 3,900/thousand cubic meters (about $2.45/MMBTU @ Rs. 45/US$), leading to variable costs of only Rs. 0.86/kWh. GVK's PPA allows it to reach a negotiated rate of return by delivering power at 68.5 percent of its maximum theoretical load – the so-called plant load factor (PLF). In fact, the plant operates at about 85 percent PLF and thus earns significant extra returns for its investors. Such returns have led to many criticisms of the use of low PLF requirements in PPAs.

Structural reform and independent regulation – a state-driven process

As the central government focused on attracting private generators through the IPP mechanism, several states in parallel sought to remedy the crux of the problem: the SEBs. Their goal was to make SEBs more efficient – ideally financially self-sustaining. The central government did not have a strategy for addressing the problems with the SEBs, and no single idea emerged to dominate the state-level reform efforts. In the vacuum of intellectual leadership, outside consultants, the World Bank, and "conventional wisdom" assumed a large role. A report prepared in mid-1996 for USAID by the consultancy Hagler Bailly offers a convenient snapshot of what were widely accepted by state level reformers as the three critical elements for state-level reforms (D'Sa, 2002):

Independent organizations

The SEBs would be reorganized to separate them (at least to arm's length) from the state; in addition, independent regulatory bodies would be created.

Unbundled functions

The previously vertically integrated utilities would be broken into generation, T&D entities.

Private ownership

Privately owned enterprises would be created where possible and would respond to commercial incentives to invest in growth of the sector.

Elsewhere in this book we call this vision the "textbook model" for reform (see chapter 1). We focus here on how these three central elements were put into practice.

State Experiences

The power sector, like most else in India, varies enormously across the country. Yet most statistics that are readily available on Indian electricity are national averages that obscure regional variations. System losses, for example, are much lower in many southern states than in the north – reflecting better technical management and more successful efforts to reduce theft. To capture some of these variations we examine the experiences in three states in detail. Subsequently, we focus on the special roles played by newly created ERCs.

Orissa: Restructuring with Privatization

State-level reforms began, by chance, in Orissa. Like all Indian states, Orissa's SEB was a money-losing venture that had become a drain on the state budget. In 1991, just at the moment that the central government became tolerant of electricity reforms, unrelated events forced the World Bank to withdraw support for a pending hydropower project in Orissa. The Bank made further assistance for power projects conditional on structural reforms in the state and faced no opposition from the reformist central government, which in an earlier era might have claimed that such conditionality was interference in its internal affairs. In most other states such reforms still might have been politically toxic because any serious reform would require tampering with agricultural tariffs; in Orissa, however, the agricultural load is relatively small.

To unlock the Bank's support, in 1995 the Orissa cabinet approved an agreement between the World Bank and Orissa SEB (OSEB) entailing (Rajan, 2000):

- Unbundling and corporatization of OSEB;
- Privatization (by competitive auction) of each of the newly unbundled enterprises;
- Establishment of a competitive market for generation;
- Creation of a separate regulatory body that would oversee the competitive market
- Reform of tariffs to allow suppliers to become financially solvent

The World Bank promised $350m, and the British bilateral assistance agency (DFID) offered $100m to help implement the plan; the blueprint and milestones for the reforms were drawn up based on the World Bank's Staff Appraisal Report (SAR). OSEB was first split in 1996 into one T&D company ("Gridco") and two generation companies (one thermal and one hydro). By 1998 Gridco was split into a transmission company (which retained the name "Gridco" and remained in the hands of the Orissa government) as well as four distribution companies whose controlling shares were sold the next year to private investors. BSES, the private utility that served parts of Mumbai, acquired three of four zones in 1999, with the remaining zone ultimately going to AES Transpower, the US firm whose strong interest in acquiring the distribution company was obtaining government approval for buying a 49 percent stake in the thermal generation company.

By the time these private owners took over, the financial situation of the enterprises had worsened. Gridco suffered from both liquidity and solvency crises, as the power it bought from the generating companies had risen in price but it could not fully pass the higher tariffs to the distribution companies. Through 2003, three of the four distribution companies performed much worse than expected (indeed, they lost money), although initial data for 2004 suggests that the distribution companies may now be approaching profitability. AES formally abandoned its distribution company in 2001, and the state took over operations, revoking AES's distribution license finally in April 2005; AES may also try to exit its generation assets as well. As the firm suffered losses worldwide, it shifted its focus to the immediate task of staying afloat and plugging financial drains in its operations. Supply of power to agriculture decreased from 6 percent in 1992–1993 to a very low 3 percent in 1999–1900 (Kanungo Committee, 2001), but it is unclear how much of this reduction was due to tighter accounting required under the reforms and what fraction reflects constrained supply. Nonetheless, many analysts warn that Orissa's experience is an indicator that rural penetration might not grow under reforms because private power companies push aggressively wish to minimize their exposure to unprofitable customers.

Part of Orissa's troubles stem from the lack of investor interest in purchasing the privatized distribution companies. Initially, BSES was the only eligible bidder for the 4 zones after the Indian firm Tata (which also ran distribution services in Mumbai) withdrew its bid for the central zone (Prayas, 2001). AES was already an investor in the state with its 500 MW IPP project in the Ib Valley. Under government pressure, it somewhat reluctantly submitted a bid for the central zone—thus preventing a single firm (BSES) from acquiring all distribution assets (Mahalingam, 1998). In part, Orissa's troubles also stemmed from inattention to the allocation of debts and liabilities. In a scenario that might unfold similarly in other states as they reform, Orissa's T&D companies found it difficult to remain profitable as regulators allowed generators to lift their wholesale tariffs in an effort to become profitable themselves; for example, in 1996 Orissa's newly instituted hydro company increased its power charges five-fold almost overnight.

The main reason for Orissa's troubles, however, was the lack of realistic expectations or accurate baseline information on the actual performance of the system, coupled with the failure of the state government to follow its original plan for reforms. Investors had developed their bids on the expectation that actual losses in the (T&D) system were 39.5 percent (as stated by OSEB), and the investors calculated that they could make money through improved operational efficiency and by reducing theft – for example, they had projected that losses would be cut to 22.7 percent by 2000–2001. When the new owners took control and applied proper accounting methods they found that actual T&D losses were 49.4 percent and did not decline as expected. Nor did the envisioned growth of industrial customers – the most lucrative purchasers of power – materialize. Importantly, the government did not supply the expected level of subsidy to offset losses – diverting, instead, the monies that had been earmarked for power sector subsidy to other purposes in the state budget. The state government even failed to pay its own power bill, some Rs. 1.5 billion. The government sought to slow the rise in tariffs through pleadings at Orissa's electricity regulatory commission (OERC) by arguing that the distribution companies could achieve profitability by reducing T&D losses, and the OERC heeded the government's instruction and awarded lower tariff increases for many consumers than had been envisaged in the original plans as per the World Bank Staff Appraisal Report.

Andhra Pradesh: restructuring without privatization
Only shortly after Orissa began its reforms, Andhra Pradesh (AP) – a forward looking state in India led from 1995 to 2004 by the reform-minded (and technologically savvy) Chief Minister, Chandrababu Naidu – also sought to improve the performance of its electricity board (the APSEB). As in Orissa, AP unbundled and corporatized the system (in stages from 1999 to 2000). Unlike Orissa, AP never privatized – rather, the government sought to improve efficiency through the adoption of more rational tariffs and performance incentives. As in Orissa, AP also created an independent electricity regulatory commission (APERC).

The first models for reforming APSEB into separate profit centers were explored by the 1995 Hiten Bhaya Committee commissioned by the government, which envisioned structural reforms that would avoid privatization and keep the SEB as a state-owned holding company. In reaction, the World Bank wrote a note highlighting options for fuller reform – that included full unbundling and privatization. The AP government has steadfastly maintained that the Bank was only an advisor, but in practice the reforms adopted map nearly perfectly on the Bank's advice (Reddy, 2000). The reform-minded government implemented the plan rapidly; the ruling party introduced a bill on April 27, 1998, suppressed opposition, and passed the final legislation within a day while the opposition parties walked out in protest (Reddy, 2000).

Key to the AP model is the concept of annual revenue requirements (ARR) – in essence, the cost of serving customers. APERC calculates the cost of serving customers as well as the difference between costs and tariff charged. The government is expected to pay any difference as a subsidy, in contrast with the traditional pricing model in which a series of cross-subsidies and accounting tricks supplied the subsidy. As in most states with a well-developed regulatory commission (Orissa is an exception), so far the AP government has been willing to pay the calculated subsidy. This system is still laden with some distortions – the transmission company, for example, varies its bulk supply tariffs to the four distribution companies based on customer mix and ability to pay.

Compared with other states, the power shortage in AP is relatively small – mainly because of governmental support for the reforms process and a pro-business environment that drew investments into IPPs such as GVK. Part of AP's success with IPPs (over 1,000 MW, more than any other state) was due to the availability of inexpensive natural gas.

The subsidy paid allows the distribution companies to become financially self-sufficient only if they meet performance goals for reducing losses. To aid in achieving these goals, the government passed a stringent antipilferage act under which thousands have been convicted (including hundreds of APSEB employees). By some estimates, the act alone has reduced theft by 2–3 percent.

Interestingly, politicians still exert considerable control over the power sector. In August 2002, the Chief Minister announced that AP had surplus power and that farmers would receive 9 hours of guaranteed supply daily, and rural homes would get 24-hour supply. While genuinely concerned for the rural masses, this move was likely timed for the 2004 elections, which he lost nonetheless. It has resulted in an annual additional loss of some Rs. 10 billion to meet the extra supply. (The newly elected government announced at its inauguration ceremony that it would give free power to all farmers.)

The AP experience is widely seen as one of the "best" of all the states and is a model for most others. The regulator has pushed hard for reduction of losses, and for 2005–2006 the goal is about 23 percent,[27] which is a very rate low by Indian standards. In the central government's rankings of states – discussed in more detail later – AP largely defines "best practice" for the country. In most states, as in AP, privatization has proved to be politically and logistically difficult; restructuring without privatization is much more feasible.

---

[27] This figure excludes losses outside the state, i.e., under PowerGrid's or alternative inter-state transmission lines.

Delhi: privatization with innovative incentives

The experience in Orissa seemed to confirm Indians' wariness of privatization. The experience was painful for investors and customers alike. Lessons learned in Orissa guided the reforms in Delhi, which offers an alternative model for restructuring with privatization.

Delhi established its regulatory commission in 1999 but was unable to impose much change in the performance of the state-controlled utility, Delhi Vidyut Board (DVB). Despite being an urban area with virtually no agriculture – factors that should have led to good performance – Delhi experienced T&D losses (including theft) as high as 40–45 percent and had a crumbling infrastructure that would require massive investment to upgrade. Privatization appeared to be the only solution; yet the Orissa experience sounded caution.

In the Delhi model, potential investors placed bids not on the value they assigned to the underlying assets but rather on a "concession" to operate each of these concession areas; the firm that promised the largest reduction in losses is the winning bidder. The winners would invest in and operate the distribution company, earning 16 percent on their equity if they met their bid; if operators surpassed their bid target then they would split the benefits with consumers.

Delhi's regulatory commission calculates the annual revenue requirements (ARR) for each distribution company on the basis of power costs, performance targets (i.e., losses), and return on equity. The distribution companies actually pay the transmission company (owned by the Delhi government) a lesser amount based on collections from customers. (The difference between ARR and payments to the transco is a subsidy for the distribution company; in turn, the transmission company is subsidized by the state budget.) Over five years collections are supposed to rise (eventually to ARR) as the operators improve performance and the regulatory commission lifts retail tariffs. This scheme, which pays the subsidy through the transmission company, is intended to reduce the exposure of the operators of distribution concessions to the risk that the government might renege on its subsidy commitments, as happened in Orissa.

In some respects, Delhi may have over-reacted to Orissa's problems. One of the chief failures in Orissa was the lack of accurate information about losses. In Delhi the Regulatory Commission pegged losses at 50.7 percent! Since performance goals are set against this loss benchmark, undue returns may flow to the private operators if they find windfall reductions or if the original estimate proves excessively high. As in Orissa, few investors initially showed interest; indeed, few Indian firms are probably technically, financially and politically able to operate a distribution company and few outsiders would even contemplate taking the risk (especially after the AES experience in Orissa). Foreign firms with relevant experience include Electricite de France, which has lost one billion dollars in the distribution business in Rio, Brazil, alone (see de Oliveira, chapter 2 of this volume). The global market, for the moment, is not rich with investors. Only Tata and BSES submitted final bids. Tata won the North West Delhi Distribution Company, while BSES (now a part of the conglomerate Reliance) took the South West and Central East Companies.[28]

Critics of the Delhi privatization process, including Montek Singh Ahluwalia, the former Finance Secretary and present head of the Planning Commission, have noted a lack of transparency. Some initial bids did not comply with the terms of the tender; new bids were based on negotiation rather than proper arm's length re-bidding. In addition, the terms are quite favorable to the investors, with most unserviceable debts remaining with the government and a very low valuation compared to estimates from independent consultants.

Independent regulation

Although much of the attention to the state-level restructuring has focused on unbundling and the controversies surrounding privatization, a key innovation was the creation and empowerment of independent regulators. One of the primary responsibilities of these new regulatory authorities is the rationalization of tariffs, making it possible for the electric power system to operate according to accurate price signals and (eventually) without the massive recurring losses. Individually, key states such as Orissa made the first moves to create independent regulators. Aware of the need for independent regulation and the plethora of potentially inconsistent state-led efforts, in 1996 the Ministry of Power convened a conference of Chief Ministers to reach a consensus on a national reform strategy. Among the many elements of their codified Action Plan – which included recommendations for streamlining approvals for power projects and increasing the autonomy of SEBs – was the key recommendation to create independent electricity regulatory commissions (ERCs). This led to the Electricity Regulatory Commissions Act (1998), which provided a legal basis for such commissions and eased the process of establishing ERCs in the states that

---

[28] In addition to the three newly created private distribution zones, Delhi continues to have two special niche power distributors, the New Delhi Municipal Corporation (NDMC) – a municipal corporation like in Mumbai, but with a small distribution zone, mainly catering to politically important government consumers – and Military Engineering Service (MES), which caters to the Army Cantonment area.

hadn't already independently created legislation for regulatory authorities. The same Act also created the Central ERC (CERC) with jurisdiction over inter-state electricity trade (leaving in-state matters to state ERCs). The state-led efforts and then this central response culminated in the creation of a new class of governmental entities that have aspired to meet several key attributes:

Independence

Most of the key entities in the electric sector are powerful governmental bodies, such as NTPC and the SEBs, which governments themselves have proved unable to regulate. True independence, such as job security for staff and independent financing, was intended to blunt political interference and to create a more predictable regulatory environment. However, the commissions were never intended to operate in a political vacuum – they are agents who implement policy that is set by central and state governments. "If there is any dispute on whether a directive relates to a matter of public interest, the legislation is clear about the decisions of governments being final" (Sankar and Ramachandra, 2000).

Jurisdiction and powers

The ERCs have been granted extensive authority over the power sector. Their rulings can be challenged only in the highest courts of the land (high courts in states, or the national supreme court). The core functions of ERCs include setting of tariffs, monitoring quality of service, adjudicating disputes, enforcing licensing conditions, monitoring compliance, and redressing grievances (Sankar and Ramachandra, 2000). In addition, they are also empowered to provide advisory services to the government or other entities within their jurisdiction.

Professionalism

The ERCs are meant to be professional bodies, and Members must be senior professionals from technical and other fields at least 55 years of age and are eligible to hold office for five years (or to age 65). SERCs (composed of 3 members), and the CERC (5 members) are selected by committee, and members may be removed only in exceptional circumstances with proceedings akin to impeachment.

In practice, the rules that govern the ERCs – enshrined in the 1998 Act – have made it difficult to attain these three aspirations. First, judicial review of decisions has been necessary to ensure that the ERCs are subject to some oversight, but it has also exposed the ERCs to the delays and uncertainties that are intrinsic to India's unpredictable and backlogged legal system. In interviews, officials in the regulatory commissions have commented that the legal framework bogs them down, with some of them spending half their time preparing for or in court. The Indian Courts are viewed as impartial (though often activist), and there is growing evidence that the courts ultimately affirm the independent, powerful role of the ERCs. The Supreme Court has vacated most stays issued by lower courts, and in a landmark October 2002 case the Indian Supreme Court overturned a West Bengal High Court ruling that had undermined a key state ERC tariff rule.[29] Judicial review is limited to jurisdiction and legislative authority; there is virtually no appeal process on the substance of the ERC decisions. Nonetheless, the courts are an attractive venue for stakeholders who seek delay. For example, NTPC recently took CERC to court over new guidelines that would reduce the charges that NTPC could pass through to its customers and also raised the required availability of NTPC's generators, which in effect cut NTPC's growth projections in half.[30] The Electricity Act passed in 2003 (discussed in more detail below) has created special tribunals that are likely to increase oversight of the regulatory commissions and also reduce uncertainty and delay from court proceedings.

In its attempts to populate the ERCs with "eminent professionals," the ERC Acts fall prey to the rigid Indian hierarchy of age. The minimum age is just enough to allow ERC positions to be considered a career climax job – a swansong for retirees from government service. Thus typical commission members have backgrounds in government and the SEBs, which limits the supply of new ideas and also predisposes the commissions against disruptive decisions.

ERCs also suffer from understaffing of specialist personnel. Low government salaries make ERCs unattractive postings for experts with other options; a rapid rotation of officials seconded from government

---

[29] The West Bengal case is important because it reaffirms the authority of the regulatory commissions. However, the particular ruling at stake in that case was bizarre – a mandate in the name of "tariff rationalization" to charge all consumers an identical tariff of Rs. 3.9/kWh. The intent of the regulatory commission seems to have been removal of rampant subsidies, but that objective is not achieved with identical tariffs – the cost of service varies across user classes and thus a subsidy-free tariff scheme should, also, allow for variation in tariff. To undo this strange mandate from the regulatory commission, the West Bengal state legislature had to devise legislation that would formally allow differentiated tariffs and cross-subsidies.

[30] CERC raised the required plant availability for NTPC from 70% to 80%, while simultaneously reducing the allowed depreciation rates from 7.84% to 3.6% and the allowed O&M escalation from 10% to 6%. As per the Ministry of Power, this will reduce NTPC's internal resources by Rs. 230 billion over 11 years, forcing them to reduce their 20,000 MW capacity addition program to only about 8,000 MW (Ministry of Power Annual Report, 2001–2002).

agencies such as CEA erodes institutional memory. To avoid loss in continuity, the 1998 ERC Act requires that a selection committee be in place about 6 months prior to the known retirement of a Commission member. Yet vacancies are still rampant at all levels in the ERCs. After the long anticipated retirement of CERC's founding Chairman (Dr. S. L. Rao) in January 2001, there was no replacement until April 2002, when Mr. A. K. Basu – himself on the selection committee – assumed the position upon retiring as Secretary, Ministry of Power.

The center consolidates reform (focusing first on distribution and, subsequently, competition)

The many states that engaged in reforms followed a myriad of different paths. Virtually all states that have pursued reform have started with creation of a regulatory commission and unbundling of the functions of the SEB into generation, transmission, and distribution. Some states such as Karnataka had created separate generation enterprises long before this wave of reform, but true unbundling did not begin until the middle 1990s with Orissa's reforms. The central government, along with many states, recognizes the successful examples of private distributors that operate in Mumbai and Ahmedabad,[31] but Orissa's troubles amplified the controversy over privatization, and most states have stopped short – they have created separate ("corporatized") distribution companies but continue to operate them as state enterprises. States that are not considered reform leaders have typically created a regulatory commission but not done much else. The state of Maharashtra, for example, has created a strong regulatory commission yet has not unbundled the MSEB. Tamil Nadu also has not unbundled, and its ERC is relatively new – yet prices for power in Tamil Nadu declined due to improvements in the SEB's operations. At this writing (2005) twenty-four states had begun the reforms process and had formed or planned to form regulatory commissions, nineteen of which have issued tariff orders. Thirteen states have unbundled or corporatized their SEBs. Notable laggards remain, such as Bihar, which has not yet constituted its ERC. In addition to structural changes, there was a growing recognition of the need to improve operations, especially distribution. Although the focus on distribution emerged from the states, the center rapidly assumed a dominant role. The difficult task is not to explain why the central government seized upon state-level reforms focused on

---

[31] The argument that private operators are profitable and thus superior is simplistic as the private operators that are profitable have urban or suburban jurisdictions.

distribution – indeed, the vast majority of independent analysis of the Indian power system showed that the biggest problems were at the state level, and failure to address the loss-making SEBs (in particular, theft-prone and under-priced distribution services) was exerting a drag on the whole Indian economy. Rather, the difficult question to answer is why the central government remained focused as long as it did on pushing increased supply as the solution, often with private investors; yet for most of the SEBs, a larger supply meant a larger loss.

Through its control over financing, the central government has considerable leverage on the behavior of the states. Throughout the 1990s the central government did not ignore the needed reforms at the state level – in particular in distribution – but its efforts proved ineffective. Often working through the regulatory commissions, it set broad and sweeping mandates such as universal metering and universal service, yet offered no strategy for achieving the exhortative goals. Starting in 2000, shortly after the Central Electricity Regulatory Commission commenced operations, the central government focused its goals on a series of measurable outcomes, and it backed the effort with a new funding mechanism in 2000–2001 – the Accelerated Power Development and Reform Program (APDRP)[32] – that funds infrastructure upgrades and provides additional rewards to the states that demonstrate superior performance. The prime mover behind APDRP was financial. Ever more strapped for cash, the SEBs found themselves unable to fund distribution upgrades from their own resources or to borrow from financial institutions; only the central government had the resources and incentive to fill the void.

Funding associated with APDRP is extremely high – over 2002–2007, the budgetary assistance to states will be 400 billion rupees (Ministry of Power, 2005). Half the investment amount for reforms and upgrades shall be from the central government (broken down into half as grants and the balance loans), and governmental or quasi-governmental financial institutions are expected to provide the remaining funds. The result has been a substantial flurry of activity by utilities, contractors, and consultants. APDRP transformed the political economy of reform, by removing the most severe financial obstacles while also offering visible carrots to actors within the states who have the strongest incentive to overcome political opposition to reform.

---

[32] This began in 2000 as the Accelerated Power Development Program (APDP). APDRP adds a focus on reforms. In addition, the Deepak Parekh Committee (2002) recommended improvements making APDRP more results (output) focused, and less organizationally burdensome in terms of projects.

By 2005, the central government had signed Memoranda of Understanding (MoUs) with all of India's twenty-eight states – in each, the state pledged to create a regulatory commission, to meter fully the electricity supplied to final distribution rings, to pay subsidies on time, and other key actions. In return, the central government pledged to increase output from central power stations, upgrade inter-state transmission lines and to provide sundry other benefits including enhanced financing. The central government has promised to match (with funds) any savings that the states realized through the reduction of theft, which offers a substantial windfall that can offset the political cost of cracking down on nonpaying users. In addition to this carrot for reforms, the states face the stick of the ERCs, that will set tariffs so that utilities that do not improve performance will suffer operating losses without the prospect of a financial bailout. (The credibility of this threat is unclear but probably low.) To help guide the way, APDRP has also targeted several dozen distribution segments as "models of excellence" with full metering of all users, energy audits aimed at optimizing the system, increased use of low-loss (high voltage) distribution lines, and other schemes for reducing losses (Ministry of Power, 2002).

The keystone to APDRP is measurement of indicators related to improvement in T&D, installation of meters, institutional reform, and steps towards commercial viability. Simple and transparent indicators, along with ranking of each state, are intended to make it easier to allocate resources according to true performance, thus creating a competition between states and strong incentives for innovation. Two independent ratings firms (ICRA and CRISIL) produced the first such ranking, published in 2003, and the third annual review was released in March 2005.[33] Over these three years, reform-minded Andhra Pradesh ranked first, second, and first, respectively; Orissa performed very poorly (23rd out of 29 in 2005) – if not for Orissa's independent regulatory commission the state would have scored even lower. The central government's restructuring program includes many other aspects, such as investments in energy conservation. The Energy Conservation Act 2001 includes standards and regulations for efficiency, and to oversee efforts at boosting efficiency the central government created a Bureau of Energy Efficiency. These efforts seem poised to achieve little; much of the effort is focused on auditing energy use, and there are no defined timetables or mechanisms (e.g., partnerships, challenge programs, or

---

[33] http://powermin.nic.in/report/Rating%20of%20State%20Power%20Sector-January%202003.pdf; http://powermin.nic.in/whats_new/pdf/Final_2005.pdf

financing schemes) that are probably needed to achieve demonstrable improvements in energy efficiency.

The style of this newer phase of reforms is markedly different from the central government's earlier attempts at reform. There are pervasive efforts to engage a wide range of stakeholders through public hearings, web posting of information, and media outreach campaigns, although the legislation for these reforms do not actually require such aggressive public participation (Ahluwalia and Bhatiani, 2000). Recently the central government even purchased full-page newspaper advertisements touting its power sector reforms and success, advocating "power for all" by 2012, and noting that it had held 2,100 road shows to sensitize the public to the need for power sector reform.

Despite the central government's enthusiastic embrace of reform, it proved difficult to achieve the central goal – to supplant the incremental reforms scattered across the states and central government with a comprehensive electricity reform strategy. The central government initiated such efforts in 2001 when it proposed a comprehensive Electricity Bill; stalled in Parliament, the bill passed only in 2003 (the "Electricity Act 2003"). Under this new framework, private investors will be encouraged in all aspects of the power system – generation, transmission, and distribution. Generators will be allowed to build facilities without a license (except for hydro facilities, as they use state-owned water resources). Transmission will operate under "open access" rules, which will allow (among other things) bulk purchasers of power to sell electricity directly to large users. The Act leaves many transitional issues ambiguous – to be resolved by the regulators. While it is premature to analyze the Act in detail or speculate on its impact, the Appendix summarizes and discusses key features. In the next section, we focus on the main issues that even this latest effort of reform fails to adequately address.

Unresolved issues

Even as reformers have established dramatically new frameworks for managing the Indian power system, the many central- and state-led initiatives have left several critical issues largely untouched. These are difficult to evaluate at this stage because the reforms themselves are young and have barely taken effect. Here we focus on four: (1) "cherry-picking" of good customers and service areas, leaving uneconomic service to the struggling state; (2) labor markets; (3) the financial design of the system, particularly tariffs; and (4) the "social contract" with the electric sector, notably the supply of electricity to low-income households. All four of these have figured in the reform effort already and are likely to be durable challenges.

Cherry picking and hybrid markets

The Indian power system has allowed some generators to be profitable – such as NTPC and the IPPs whose payments were prioritized – even when most power was purchased by insolvent entities (i.e., the SEBs).[34] Reform through unbundling will ultimately require each element in the chain – from generation to transmission to distribution – to achieve a profit. This fact raises questions about the structure of tariffs (which we address later) and will make some service functions and areas more attractive than others. "Cherry picking" of these potential profit centers could bifurcate the Indian power system and further erode the viability of service for most users. The risks arise in two areas.

First, nearly all the visions for restructuring the power system envision unbundled (in many cases, privately owned or managed) generators and distribution companies while transmission functions remain as a state-owned function, at least in the foreseeable future.[35] Yet transmission will be increasingly squeezed if firms upstream (generators) and downstream (distributors) alter their tariffs and payments to attain profitability.[36] In principle, this problem can be addressed by increasing subsidies for transmission, but it remains to be seen whether state governments will be able to sustain the political support needed to pay a subsidy that will flow to an entity that is not directly supplying electric services to the (voting) end-user. So far, a series of stop-gap measures have kept the subsidy shell game moving. For example, after the March 2001 conference of Chief Ministers there was a consensus on the need to resolve the problem of Rs. 410 billion outstanding dues owed by the SEBs to the various SOEs that provide fuels, power generation, and transmission. The Expert Group on Settlement of SEB Dues, chaired by

---

[34] Why the system evolved to have external generators able to prioritize payments, or, indeed, even reap profits of over a billion dollars (in NTPC's case) is unclear. NTPC was identified as a "jewel" in the central government's portfolio, and it likely had significant additional leverage with the states given that it supplies such a large fraction of the total power in the country.

[35] While the Electricity Act 2003 allows new entities to establish transmission systems, one cannot predict how competitive this segment will become.

[36] We see this playing out in New Delhi, where private distribution companies have assured minimum returns, and generators have profitable tariffs, but the TransCo is increasingly indebted and reliant on subsides. Delhi's rank in the annual ratings fell from first to third in the last year, largely because its score on progress towards commercial viability was zero; the TransCo has accumulated tens of billions of rupees of losses.

Montek Singh Ahluwalia, had recommended a one-time securitization of these outstanding dues through the Reserve Bank of India, with half the interest and other surcharges (about 40 percent of the total) to be written off (Ahluwalia, 2001). Such remedies, while useful, will not make the sector viable unless attention is put on solving the underlying problems rather than concentrating on the problems in one link of the chain, for example, the transmission system. If the managers of transmission entities respond to insolvency as did the managers of the SEBs – for example, by cutting maintenance and not investing in expansion – then transmission will become the weak link.

Second, cherry picking of assets and functions is already evident in retail services. Efforts to privatize distribution have focused on urban areas such as Chennai (formerly, Madras), Gwalior, Kanpur, and Noida (near Delhi – already privatized), following the logic that urban areas are more likely to be profitable and thus likely to attract private investors. At the same time, distribution areas have been carved into blocks, following the logic that smaller units would attract a larger number of potential bidders – the Orissa and Delhi experiences indicated a dearth of qualified and interested parties for distribution privatization. As was already evident when AES abandoned its concession in Orissa, investors are predisposed to navigate around the zones that prove unprofitable – leading, perhaps, to a geographical patchwork of vibrant investment zones amidst a sea of chronically under-funded networks. In addition to this tendency as the distribution system is restructured, cherry-picking is also under way through captive generation. Most state regulatory commissions set rules that discouraged widespread use of captive generation by restricting open access to the grid. The Ministry of Power has stated that open access to distribution networks will only occur after the elimination of cross-subsidies, unless the stakeholders are willing to pay an appropriate surcharge set by regulators (Ministry of Power, 2005). While the Electricity Act 2003 liberalizes captive power, it allows regulators to set (typically) high access and wheeling charges, where applicable. Despite these obstacles, captive power now represents over 15 percent of India's installed capacity and the new Act could accelerate the bifurcation of service into large lucrative entities (who supply themselves) and smaller residential and agricultural loads (who are stuck in an ailing state-dominated system).

Labor markets and human capital

Despite massive reforms to the economy over the last decade, labor in India remains highly regulated. Under the Constitution the federal government and the states share responsibility for labor matters and have adopted some 47 federal laws and over 170 state statutes in this area. Many labor rules are based on a century-old legislation, and a large number of key labor decisions are rooted in the Industrial Disputes Act of 1947, which, for example, requires all but the smallest companies to obtain (rarely granted) government permission prior to laying off employees or closing plants (Rao, 2000).

Over decades the SEBs have built up extremely large rosters of employees who view their jobs as permanent government entitlements. Prime Minister Rajiv Gandhi jokingly referred to SEBs as the State Employment Boards (Ruet, 2003). Labor productivity, despite doubling in the last decade, remains several times below international norms, and the low wages do not compensate enough for this. In Uttar Pradesh, for example, the SEB has slashed its workforce from 120,000 to 70,000 during the last decade – yet the US state of Connecticut serves an electric load of similar size with a staff of only a few thousand. Comparisons between the state-dominated power systems and those in private hands reveal the distance still to be covered. When BSES took over two of Delhi's distribution areas in 2002, it acquired 1.6 million customers and 13,000 employees. In comparison, in Mumbai, where BSES was the incumbent private operator, only 4,500 employees are needed to serve 2.2 million customers (approximate numbers as per personal communication).

Despite efforts to make the SEBs more efficient, personnel costs have risen sharply in the last few years – estimated today at more than 15 percent of the tariff (figure 4.4). Part of this rise stems from states implementing pay raises in the middle and late 1990s – to levels even higher than the recommendations of the Fifth Central Pay Commission, which recommended salary increases to avoid flight of key personnel to the private sector. However, the same government entities that lifted salaries ignored the Pay Commission's recommendation to reduce government employment by one-third over ten years (Srinivasan, 2001).

The lack of more pervasive labor reforms has hampered electricity reform in three ways. First, organized labor has responded to reforms as expected – with strikes and severe opposition. Invariably, labor's discontent has forced compromises in which newly corporatized (or even privatized) entities are required to guarantee job security for a period of time. In some countries the government has undertaken the politically sensitive task of firing surplus workers before privatization – in order to extract the maximum price from private bidders – but in India the governments have avoided this task. Not only does this legacy impose costs on new managers but it also hampers the ability of the new firms to innovate by applying new technology and work culture.

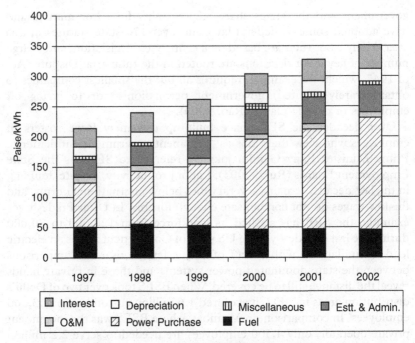

Figure 4.4. Cost of service: the SEBs' perspective[a]

Note: [a]Components of retail tariffs are drawn from statistics supplied by SEBs, which show detail for personnel ("Estt. and Admin.") and other costs incurred at the SEBs themselves. The category "Power Purchase" embeds all expenses passed on by non-SEB generators (i. e., fuel as well at O&M and personnel for the generation component). Because of such accounting, we cannot directly determine the cost of generation for electricity, or the total labor costs. Total generation costs are at least equal to Power Purchase plus Fuel, which is a starting point for the tariff exercise presented below. While labor costs have grown by over 50% in these 5 years (on a normalized basis of paise/kWh), the greatest increase has been for Power Purchases, which have grown by over 150% (while only increasing from 46% to 64% of net availability). Similar breakdowns for the last few years are not available, but we expect continued increase in almost all components of costs, and increasing costs for power purchase as generation becomes separated. Ultimately, as all generation is unbundled, the "fuel" costs will go to zero since distribution companies will be required to purchase all their bulk power.

Source: Planning Commission, 2002; Revised Estimate 2000–2001; Annual Plan 2001–2002.

Second, the dysfunctional nature of labor in the SEBs has been implicated in the rampant theft in the Indian power system. Under-employed, under-paid, and suffering from low morale, often it is employees of the SEB themselves that lead the rings that provide illegal connections and "ignore" nonpayment of bills. Several states have recently enacted legislation to impose severe punishments on such employees. In addition to theft, the rampant culture of dishonesty and side-dealing can lead to collusion in tendering for contracts and parts. While tendering offers the greatest image of propriety, it often leads to ignoring superior technology or operating procedures, further hampering change in the system.

Third, the reforms have not directly addressed issues of corporate governance, which is partly a question of human capital in top management. Not only do government decision-makers (bureaucrats) come from the Indian Administrative Services (IAS), even the most senior operational positions within the electric power enterprises also usually go to IAS officers or other civil servants, not career power professionals. The result is resentment in the ranks since good performance on the job is not a prerequisite for advancement to the highest positions within the enterprise. Moreover, the highly competitive and elite IAS operates within its own rules and cultures that might impede the development of a business culture in the power system; indeed, the IAS might be loath to "downsize itself" through reforms. The IAS system creates generalists who spend only brief stints in each job as they work their way up the IAS ranks.[37] Short-term appointments encourage projects that reap rewards within the brief tenure of the appointment and discourage long-term innovations and investments that can be undone easily by the next person in the job. Through reforms, a hybrid model of state and private ownership and control has emerged, which creates difficulties for a private firm that is vulnerable to government directives and whims[38] while competing against state-owned enterprises that are better connected politically. Even in states like Delhi, political pressure on private operators remains high. In the summer peak of 2005, consumers reacted violently to proposed hikes in retails tariffs and the Delhi government "persuaded" the regulators to roll back some of the hikes. They also

[37] There are indications the government wants to revamp the Indian Administrative Services, with specialization and tracks, but it would take many years to effect change in the operations of SOEs.
[38] This was seen in the telecom sector, where the telecom ministry, despite relinquishing operating control of the state-owned service provider VSNL to the Tata group of companies in 2001, continued to interfere with board decisions.

forced Reliance Energy (who absorbed BSES nationwide) to fire their operating company CEO for his failure to meet the needs of the people.

System design and tariffs

Popular discussions of power reform in India often fall prey to the common misconception that reform is yielding *deregulation* and *competition*. In reality, the reform process is about recasting the role (and functions) of regulation – not deregulation. Moreover, reforms have been most effective where they have induced better performance in the industry – such as through imposition of hard budget constraints, performance rewards (e.g., in Delhi), transparency of O&M costs, etc. – and little of that success has come through *competition* per se (Ahluwalia and Bhatiani, 2000).[39] Even where competition has occurred in partial ways – such as through auctions – the effect of competition itself has been limited and disappointing. In the two states that have privatized distribution the number of bidders has been very low. Even at the generation level – which in theory is the easiest to make competitive – competition has entered only through the IPP process, and many generators negotiated their power purchase agreements without competitive bidding. Only after 1995 did the Ministry of Power mandate competitive bids, but even that mandate applied only to plant construction agreements and not the wholesale market ("power pool") for electricity.[40] Even after government guidelines for competitive bulk supply issued in January 2005, tariffs from suppliers are likely to remain de-facto costs-plus recovery. The hybrid system that is emerging includes government and private participation, with elements of both competitive markets as well as a regulated system that is anchored (loosely) in the concepts of cost recovery regulation. The single-buyer model that has thus far emerged has a particularly vulnerable link: the transmission entities. In some areas these have tried to exploit their monopoly position.[41] The most likely outcome, however, is that these enterprises will

---

[39] Even with the Electricity Act 2003 – which aims to increase private participation and competition – issues of market power have not been addressed adequately, except by allowing new entrants to compete.

[40] Attempts to create a market, such as through the Power Trading Corporation (PTC) – the SOE established in 1999 to "correct the distortions in the market" – have been very modest in their impact (only a few percent of kilowatt-hours, at most, including a fraction from import of electricity). This will remain the case while supply lags demand, unless, of course, policies enable generators and consumers to bypass the current lossy system through trading.

[41] Many transmission companies charge a significant markup for transmitting power; e.g., in Andhra Pradesh, the markup is oin the order of 25% (compared to a U.S. markup ~10%). Some of this is structural, as many of the assets of the SEB migrate to the

get squeezed if the political process is unable to sustain the subsidy needed to make transmission viable.

The fundamental problem with the emerging hybrid single buyer model is that the rules that govern power transfers do not correspond with a normally functioning power system. The government sought to remedy the shortfall in power production not only by encouraging (private) investment in new generators but also boosting the low load factor for existing plants. It created a cost-plus regulatory system that allowed generators to recover their capital costs and pass through operational costs, and thus few had an incentive to focus on performance. New rules in 1992 set standards for plant load factor (PLF), which is the fraction of time that the plant is generating power, and created rewards for plants that beat the benchmark PLF.[42] The policy was quite successful in that regard – for all types of generators, including the SEBs.

Unfortunately, this "bonus" return on equity for high PLFs drove many generators to ignore despatch orders since the reward from boosting output was substantial. One major grid collapse affecting all of northern India was due to the over-frequency that occurs when power supply exceeds demand as generators do not back down as required. Strangely, some Indian planners appear to consider 100 percent PLF as a theoretical maximum goal, treating normal backing down[43] during off-peak periods as "unplanned outages."[44] In fact, there are limits to how

transmission company during the process of unbundling – for example, in the "unbundled" structure of Andhra Pradesh, the CEOs of the state-owned distribution companies report to the CEO of the transmission company.

[42] Generator tariffs were based on the K. P. Rao Committee (1990) which – trying to improve load factors – proposed measures to move towards what were termed performance-based ratemaking, consisting of a two-part tariff: fixed costs – recoverable if the generator performed at a normative load factor, and variable – as per actuals. They advocated returns (on equity) as Reserve Bank of India (Central Bank) rate plus 5%, then totaling 16%. However, despite falling bank rates, the allowed returns for generators and transmission companies have become fixed at the original 16%, and this figure has become embedded in decision-makers' plans and targets throughout the power sector, and only recently has been modified to 14%. In reality, this costs-plus model can lead to significantly higher legal returns – through leverage, flexible financing, etc. – witness the very high returns of PowerGrid and NTPC today, even though both enterprises operated (in principle) within a regulated rate of return context.

[43] Since electricity cannot be stored, during periods of low demand, some generators must back down (reduce output). Such operating decisions should normally be made by a dispatch authority.

[44] "The gap between the plant availability and PLF indicates that though the plants are available at 80% of the time, they are forced to back down in some of the states, particularly in eastern region, during the off-peak hours due to lower demand. Efforts need to be made to address this issue and utilize the plants optimally." Planning Commission (2002).

much PLF can rise, since there will always be off-peak periods when capacity is not required. In an optimized power dispatch system there are plants of various types – baseload, mid-load, and some peaking plants – and the PLFs should vary with the purpose of the plant. Unfortunately, the Indian system of the 1990s was designed as if every thermal generator would be operating at the same benchmark PLF, 68.5 percent (previously, 62.8 percent). India's planners don't properly utilize load-duration curves to help choose type of fuel or load factor when establishing contracts. (However, Indian load curves are artificially flatter – less peaky – than many other countries with large non-industrial loads because agricultural loads are typically cut when other loads are peaking such as morning and late afternoon, and supply overall is constrained during peak periods ("load-shedding"). There are also few tariff parameters for ancillary services (like reactive power, frequency control, etc.), and time-of-day tariffs are not common.

To decouple returns and actual generation, CERC has instituted Availability Based Tariffs (ABT) for bulk power from central generators. The system is similar to capacity payments that have been a central part of reforms in other countries, such as Argentina, and a primary objective (along with increasing plant availabilities) is to prevent the over-generation that occurs under PLF-centric tariffs. Under the ABT scheme, central generators and consuming utilities must commit, in advance, to certain levels of supply and demand to maintain grid discipline. While ABT has helped improve the grid frequency stability (including through limited guidelines for ancillary services), this new system is not ideal – generators have ways to game the system (as they did for PLF rules). Moreover, "availability" itself is not an ideal metric as most new plants have high availabilities – non-SEB generators such as NTPC show about 90 percent availability. Nonetheless, the government aims to extend ABT to the state level, with the goal of promoting economic dispatch and grid discipline (Ministry of Power, 2005).

While the impetus came from an ADB consultant in 1994, the ABT draft circulated for many years until January 4, 2000, when the ABT Order was issued. Still, many affected stakeholders (including NTPC) didn't comment on it until after the rule was adopted – and NTPC's commentary took the form of a lawsuit. ABT was created with operational efficiencies in mind, but it might provide a useful starting point for structural changes in the system. Firm day-ahead commitments for power needs might be the first step towards creating a market that follows the load curve and rewards suppliers accordingly.

At the intersection of system design and regulation of tariffs, numerous defenders of the old system have found it to their advantage to confuse average costs and marginal costs. Many experts, such as Sankar (2002), have argued that resources such as old hydropower plants should be dedicated for special users – a convenient argument for the defenders of low tariffs for farmers. These old plants have already paid their capital costs and operate with very low marginal costs. Failure to focus on long-run marginal costs in planning and pricing sends misleading signals to the consumers about the real cost of power, encouraging over-consumption and discouraging efficient investment in new, efficient end-use equipment. Data on average costs are pervasive in annual reports (the so-called "average Cost of Supply"); marginal costs receive little attention, even by regulators. Many observers assume that reform will cut costs and lead to lower tariffs. In fact, the fundamentals in the industry point to the opposite conclusion for at least two reasons. First, the SEBs are increasingly purchasing power from non-SEB generators, and these new power purchases are more costly than the incumbent SEB supply (figure 4.4) – in part because new fuels (especially gas and liquid fuels) are more costly than the predecessors and in part because the non-SEB suppliers demand (and obtain) a return on their investments whereas the SEBs, as we have amply shown, did not. (The bulk of this non-SEB power is from NTPC, but NHPC and other central generators like the Nuclear Power Corporation play a substantial role, and IPPs are increasingly important over the period. Even in-state generation companies have higher tariffs than the integrated utility faced prior to unbundling.)

Second, and closely related, is that greater transparency and unbundling of the functions of the electric power system will reveal fully the need to lift tariffs so that each link in the power chain (generation, transmission, and distribution) is viable. Generation can already be considered viable, and new central power plants (e.g., NTPC) and IPPs are probably viable and typically supply power at about Rs. 2.0 to 2.2/kWh.[45]

Calculating the final tariff is not as simple as figure 4.4 would imply, in part due to opaque and inconsistent accounting. In fact, the summary of the major expenses in the power system as seen in figure 4.5 is the first analysis of disaggregated accounting presented in literature; Indian data are not organized in a way that makes the costs at each link in the power chain transparent. The exact calculations for the pre-reforms (top

---

[45] This is a levelized estimate; typically, front-heavy tariffs that allow early recovery of capital costs are higher in the initial years. These generator costs are higher than in the United States (estimated at around Rs. 1.8/kWh at 2005 exchange rates), despite the higher environmental standards in the United States. Some of the difference stems from Indian policies and financial conditions, such as import duties and the higher cost of capital in India.

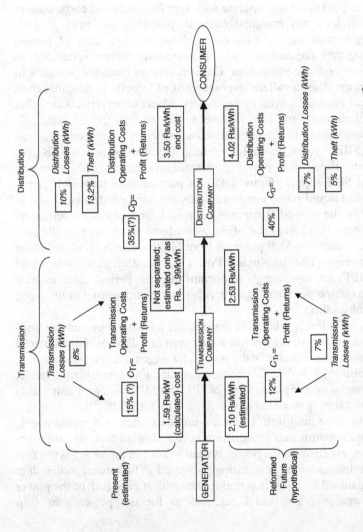

Figure 4.5. Pre-reform and post-reform cost of power: the consequences of unbundling[a]

Note: [a]For the pre-reform case, transparent accounts for all generators do not exist; our estimate of generation cost in 2001–2002. (Rs. 1.59) is based on calculating the in-state generation costs, and Rs. 3.50 was the average retail *cost* in 2001–2002. Future estimates, of course, are hypothetical – but the operating costs for T&D, as well as loss levels, are plausible (and actually lower than sometimes seen today in the case of C_{Tr}).

portion) breakdown between generation, transmission, and distribution and are highly complicated, subject to both assumptions and estimates.[46] The bottom portion of the figure shows a hypothetical future of major expenses, post-reform.

In this simple model, electricity from generators is transmitted to a distributor (with losses in transmission) and then to final customers (with additional losses in distribution). Figures adjacent to each arrow show the cost after that link in the system (e.g., Rs. 3.50 is the average cost of electricity that is supplied to final customers by the distributors for 2001–2002 – the average *tariff* was only Rs. 2.40/kWh). The percentage markups for transmission (C_{Tr}) and distribution (C_D) are estimated from the operating costs and required return on investment and are in addition to T&D losses.

Reforms will affect several points along the chain. On one hand, many regulators have insisted on a reduction of technical and commercial (theft) losses, and they have also demanded the state governments explicitly pay any subsidies beyond the allowed cross-subsidies. Through such efforts we anticipate a sharp reduction in distribution losses (from an estimated 23.2 percent total down to 7 percent technical losses and 5 percent theft), and even some decline in transmission losses (to 7 percent) due to more efficient utilization of assets. On the other hand, the generation prices increase, sometimes dramatically, due to the imposition of hard budget constraints, full cost accounting, and returns for investors. Thus we estimate generator tariffs at Rs. 2.1/kWh. The distribution companies also must attain profitability, which will raise costs; while government companies have only targeted "modest returns" in the short term, private operators have asked for returns on

---

[46] The average tariff in 2001–2002 for purchase of bulk power was estimated by the Planning Commission (2002) as 194 paise/kWh (100 paise = 1 rupee), higher than the 185 paise net share shown in figure 4.5. This is because roughly 35.6% of power was internal (in-state), and a little under one-third of the generation is lost along the way, which is why these purchases became an effective, average cost component of 185 paise per total kWh *sold*. Using these figures and the gross charges paid for purchased power, we can back-calculate that internal generation explicitly came to only 86 paise/kWh, based on using average numbers for the whole of India.

This result is low because in-state generation explicitly shows only fuel as the cost component. We add only some estimated additional variable costs (10 paise/kWh) to the calculated 86 paise/kWh for the pre-reforms value, as the noninclusion of lack of including capital costs is a hallmark of the pre-reforms scenario.

To this we add some variable costs only, leading to estimated total in-state costs of about 96 paise/kWh. This implies that the average net generator tariff per kWh was only 159 paise/kWh. As we know the total losses, retail sales, and final tariffs, we can then estimate the total markups required by the SEB for the transmission and distribution of the power. Subjectively, we can apportion the losses and the markup between transmission and distribution.

the order of 16 percent, which represents a significant increase. The exact magnitude of the increase will depend on the valuations and also on the extent to which private operators can wring efficiency gains from the system. Nonetheless, the estimate is that the distribution markup will need to increase by 5 percent, compared to a small decline for the transmission markup. Thus, even if reforms yield a sharp reduction in losses, the total cost of electricity will rise by almost 15 percent, from Rs. 3.5 to over Rs. 4 per kWh. These prices would be high by world standards (9.14 ¢/kWh at 2005 exchange rates) and are much higher than current retail tariffs; the average US retail price in 2004 was 7.57 ¢/kWh, (EIA, 2005).[47]

"Social Contract"

Each chapter in this book is examining the impact of the electricity reform process on the "social contract" – the relationship between the electric power system and protection of the environment, investment in innovation, and provision of modern power services to low-income users.

Environmental considerations have not played a major part of Indian reforms, although the net effect of reforms has probably been positive for the environment. Reform is probably reducing losses in the power system, which will lower emissions per unit of energy actually delivered. In generation, reform is probably encouraging the construction of more efficient plants. Critics have complained about the environmental consequences of IPP projects – even filing lawsuits to halt IPPs – but these modern plants are better designed and have lower emissions than vintage plants. A major improvement for the environment is found in the rise of natural gas – a trend that is due to many factors largely unrelated to reform, such as new gas finds and exogenous improvements in gas-fired generation technologies. Incentives for IPPs have, to some extent, accelerated the shift to gas as private investors favor the lower capital costs and more rapid recovery of investment that is typical of gas-fired plants. A disproportionately large fraction of Indian IPPs is gas-fired.

The reforms also have limited focus on technological innovation. Worldwide, there are concerns that deregulation limits the ability of utilities to invest in R&D as the costs can no longer be passed on to ratepayers as before. In India, of the major electric utilities only NTPC

---

[47] In contrast to India, where residential users are subsidized, the US average price for 2004 of 7.57 cents/kWh was based on industry paying 5.11 ¢/kWh, residential 8.94 ¢/kWh, and commercial 8.17 ¢/kWh (excluding end-user taxes).

has a significant outlay for R&D; in addition to its own in-house research it is a member of international research consortia such as the US-based Electric Power Research Institute (EPRI). The SEBs have virtually zero R&D budget. This is detrimental not only to long-term operational efficiency but it even hampers rapid uptake of complementary technologies in the short term, such as high voltage distribution lines, low-loss transformers, etc. The SEBs have virtually no experience at the frontier of technology. The central government created the Central Power Research Institute (CPRI) in 1960 to undertake R&D for the power sector, but this body receives little direction from the power utilities. CPRI's limited budget leads it to focus much of its research effort on transmission and a few other tasks, and much of its role is focused on equipment testing and certification.

Low power quality – A hidden cost for consumers

Power quality in India is abysmal, and even the norms are somewhat lax – based on the Indian Electricity Rules of 1956. For low-voltage (retail) consumers, voltage is allowed to deviate by 6 percent while the frequency is allowed to deviate by 3 percent – normal operating ranges have been from 48.5 Hz to 51.5 Hz, although the new Grid Code (2002) implores operators to *try* to stay within 49 Hz to 50.5 Hz.[a] Although these deviations seem small, they wreak havoc with electrical equipment such as motors – indeed, agricultural pumpsets have failure rates as high as one or more times per year, imposing high implicit costs on farmers (who in turn impose high costs on the SEBs through over-use of under-priced power). In practice, voltage drops at the end of long rural feeder lines can be more than 20 percent, and frequency can dip by more than 4 percent. Consumers have responded to these problems with massive investment in power stabilizing and correcting equipment, especially for modern electrical and electronic equipment – another costly imposition of the power system on Indian society.

Note: [a]In contrast, US norms are to maintain frequency within 0.02 Hz, and UK norms are for 0.2 Hz deviation.

The reform has not directly addressed access to power, but the issues have attracted attention contemporaneous with the reform process. Extending electricity to all villages by 2007 and all households by 2012 is a daunting target, and while the former can be achieved through off-grid technologies, the latter will mandate new financing schemes amongst other solutions. Upgraded infrastructure and schemes like *Kutir Jyoti* – free power connections for subsistence users who are projected to draw the power of just a single light bulb – have thus far provided over 500,000 connections.[48]

These bold visions appear to be disconnected from the effort to assure financial solvency through SEB reform; indeed, there are few indications of how such goals could be realized without further worsening the finances of the utilities or enormous government outlay. Accepting the latter, the central government recently approved a Rs. 50 billion outlay over two years for Rural Electricity Infrastructure and Household Electrification that will subsidize the cost of rural electrification 90 percent and provide a full subsidy for households below the poverty line (Ministry of Power, 2005).

As Orissa has shown, some reforms might hamper efforts to increase rural access because private investors have little interest in serving loss-making customers. At the root of India's electrification woes is limited ability (or willingness) to pay.

Conclusion

The Indian power system has undergone widespread reform since 1991 as many factors converged. Not only was there a worldwide trend towards restructuring power markets to encourage private participation, India's shortfall in capacity could not be met by governmental expenditure. Initial attempts at increasing capacity without reforming the underlying SEB structure proved to be a failure, necessitating reforms to disassemble the SEBs and empower independent regulators. The states were given free rein to choose their modes of reform – with some choosing to privatize distribution, some simply unbundling the SEBs, and others keeping the SEBs intact while adopting organizational reforms aimed at improving economic efficiency. There has been a large variation in the performance of the states and reforms alone do not indicate success in terms of loss reduction or efficiency. For example, the state of Tamil Nadu implemented few structural reforms to its SEB until recently, yet has been successful in bringing down tariffs while also reducing losses. The main factor in explaining outcomes is the ability of the state governments to implement reform plans, the strength of their

---

[48] In most states, if a consumer needs a new connection, they have to pay non-trivial connection fees if the lines need to be extended; such charges vary by state. Under APDRP and new initiatives, the central government has announced financial assistance for states to help household electrification.

institutions, and their ability to achieve operational improvements, with or without reforms per se. Governments with weak institutions have performed poorly even when they had ambitious reform plans – as in Orissa. Governments with strong institutions and sustained commitment to reform (e.g., Andhra Pradesh and Delhi) have fared much better.

Early reforms focused on IPPs, but through the 1990s the main supplier of new electricity has been NTPC, which is nearly wholly owned by the central government. Indeed, throughout the reforms the role of the state did not diminish significantly; rather, the main change in the state's role was in separating key functions (e.g., setting tariffs) from the politicized ministries and SEBs and empowering regulators to perform these functions. The role of the private sector remains relatively limited; in general, performance in the country's power system has improved (dramatically in some states and segments), but most of the improvements stem from transparency and rationalization of charges and incentives rather than actual privatization. In part, private operators have been hobbled in their efforts to introduce more dramatic improvements in operations by political deals that are struck at the time of privatization, such as commitments to keep bloated workforces. Most improvements have come from the state enterprises themselves. Privatization of distribution has been quite limited (to two states and a few urban areas only).

Unfortunately, the reforms fail to address fundamental issues. The average tariff remains far lower than the average cost to the utility, and no amount of theft reduction will overcome the fundamental need to raise tariffs – not simply for the industrial and commercial users who have been the financial lifeline for the SEBs. In recent years, regulators have resisted continued large increases for such users, and the new Electricity Act (2003) makes it easier for them to "exit" the system through greater use of captive power and eventually direct purchases of power from generators. Central and state regulators operate with a clear mandate to rationalize tariffs, but political interference, system inefficiency, and consumer inability to pay hamper their efforts.

To date, reforms have increased the average costs at the SEBs at a rate comparable to or higher than the increase in revenues, primarily because reforms have forced a shift to greater reliance on non-SEB generators whose costs include commercial rates of return. Regulators have allowed fairly sharp increases in tariffs in recent years, especially for some consumer segments (while capping some tariffs on industrial and commercial users), but pressure against further rises in tariffs is mounting. We estimate that reforms in distribution and transmission (regardless of whether these functions are privatized) will also force a sharp rise in final tariffs, even if better operators yield steep cuts in losses. The coming years will be a period of enormous political challenges with the continued need to raise final tariffs and sustain the subsidies needed to keep the system solvent.

Appendix – Electricity Act 2003

The Indian government passed the Electricity Act 2003 to supplant many existing laws with an aim towards greater private sector (competitive) participation. The Act does not directly establish a power market; rather, it encourages regulators to come up with markets for power trading (Section §66). It also doesn't give details on how this is to be achieved (e.g., roles for Independent System Operators). It removes licensing requirements for generation (except hydropower) and requires transmission companies to provide nondiscriminatory access to their system. It allows captive and standalone power, including dedicated transmission lines, especially for rural areas (§9). In a further attempt to improve service in rural areas, the Act removes licensing requirements and encourages creation of cooperatives, nonprofit societies, user associations, and other rural distribution entities who will be allowed to buy bulk power (thus bypassing the SEBs).

Regulators would set many of the tariffs, but the policies would be set by the Central Government, in consultation with state governments and regulatory authorities. A long-term National Electricity Plan – as per the National Electricity Policy – would be issued once in 5 years (§3).

Regulatory commissions would be allowed to license transmission, distribution and electricity trading for periods up to twenty-five years – in an attempt to empower regulators to create the conditions for a market. The bill seeks to limit monopoly powers, in part by requiring advance approval for sales, mergers, and takeovers of entities within the same jurisdiction (state) and in part by stating no licenses would be exclusive within a region. Of course, the bill allows grandfather licensing for existing SOEs.

At an operational level, the Act supports the existing Regional Load Despatch Centers (RLDCs), but envisages a national LDC. However, the actual implementation of orders would take place through lower level State Despatch Centers, still to be established – the operational relationship between the many levels of dispatch is uncertain and could prove quite troublesome.

The regulatory bodies remain in charge of tariff decisions (bulk and retail) and have a firm mandate to reduce the required subsidies and cross-subsidies and various special surcharges that are pervasive in the power system today. However, the Act recognizes that these cannot be removed overnight, and empowers the ERCs to make decisions on appropriate surcharges and fees for wheeling and captive power transmission. The Act, perhaps to encourage private generation, allows liberal use of electricity cooperatives and associations that can transfer electricity as "captive power" instead of paying the often-higher wheeling charges (which can be set at rates to cover cross-subsidies as allowed by the regulators). This might hasten the exit of bulk consumers from the system, i.e., the commercial and industrial users. If the government wants to explicitly subsidize a class of consumers, it would have to pay the licensee in advance – a strong disincentive to subsidize. In the case of power shortages, the Regulators may fix a maximum and minimum ceiling of tariff between generators and licensees.

Regulators are given increased financial independence through the creation of special central and state Regulatory Commission Funds. At a policy level, the act recognizes the supremacy of the state or central government over the regulator, especially when it comes to matters of policy and "public interest" (§108). To streamline and ease review of regulatory decisions, the Act creates an Appellate Tribunal to hear appeals against orders of adjudicating officers or the respective Regulatory Commission. This is similar to what was done for the telecom industry, and clarifies how Commission orders should be challenged without channeling all these cases to the Supreme or High Court. The Tribunal will have the powers of a Civil Court and will be guided by the principles of natural justice rather than the procedures laid down by the Code of Civil Procedure (1908).

To handle cases of theft and the like, the state governments may set up Special Courts (§153), to provide speedy trials. Theft is treated quite seriously, and is punishable by up to three years imprisonment and/or fine. There are dramatic powers given to "authorized personnel" from the states to inspect and seize any properties or goods related to such theft or abuse, as per Code of Criminal Procedure, 1973. Unfortunately, the fine for noncompliance with Commission orders is very low, set at Rs. 100,000 – a trivial amount for large utilities who may, say, draw more power from PowerGrid than they are entitled to.

The Act aims to make it easier for private participation in the power sector, which, ultimately, should lead to competition. Under the Act, the older CEA techno-economic clearance for generators has been done away with, and process as to facilitate financial closure of IPPs have been established, including an "Inter Institutional Group (IIG)" and "Green Channel" clearances (Ministry of Power, 2005). However, reduction of red-tape is only a necessary but not sufficient condition for improving private participation – finances matter.

The Act leaves several important questions unanswered, including many already described in this chapter. While the Act may *permit* increased competition through new entrants, having new distribution companies lay parallel infrastructure appears cost-ineffective and unlikely to occur in scale, except for delivery of power to select consumers (further cherry-picking). The Act does not specify structural separation or open access over wires by a distribution licensee (especially during the coming years when cross-subsidies will persist). The Act also does not address the issue of valuation, a key question in privatization, more so because many licensees seek a guaranteed Rate of Return. Finally, the Indian system has not come to grips that given its cost structure (high and growing charges for generation, high losses, high operating costs, etc.), the end-price will necessarily be high. In a supply-constrained world, any "efficient" market would lead to yet higher prices.

5 The Mexican Electricity Sector: economic, legal and political issues

Víctor G. Carreón-Rodríguez, Armando Jiménez, and Juan Rosellón

Introduction

This chapter aims to explain the motivations and strategies for reform in the Mexican Electricity Sector. Our focus is on the effects of politically organized interests, such as unions and parties, on the process of reform. We show how particular forms of institutions – notably, the state-owned enterprises (SOEs) within the power sector as well as the state firm that supplies most fuels for electricity generation – shape the possibilities and pace of reform. The tight integration of these SOEs with the political elite, opaque systems for cost accounting, and various schemes for siphoning state resources explain why these institutions have survived and the actual progress of reform has been so slow. Where private investors have been allowed into the market it has been only at the margin through the independent power producer (IPP) scheme, an oxymoron since the purchase agreements and dispatch rules that determine payment to these IPPs are dominated by the state.

In its origins in the late nineteenth century, the Mexican power system grew as a series of privately owned, vertically integrated regional monopolies. Investors, mainly from firms based in foreign countries, built power systems in areas where they thought they could earn a profit – mainly mining and textile industrial areas as well as the largest cities – while leaving aside most rural areas. The Mexican Revolution period (1910–1917), and the political consolidation of the country (which included the assassination of President Álvaro Obregón) caused foreign private investment to trickle. By the late 1920s, two things were clear. First, electricity supply was (and still is) strongly associated with the concepts of "nationalism" and "sovereignty."[1] Second, private investment in the sector was declining and electricity demand was rising. Therefore, there was an urge for the government to step in and assume control of the power system. During the 1930's the industry was swept up in a broader process of reorganization as the *Partido Revolucionario Institucional (PRI)* consolidated its grip on power and unified the far-flung Mexican states into an integrated federal country. As a result of this consolidation, Mexico had the *Código Nacional Eléctrico* (National Electric Code), and a newly created state-owned and state-financed enterprise – *Comisión Federal de Electricidad* (CFE) – which came to dominate all investment in new capacity. At the same time, worker unions were developed. Given that electricity was a key sector for the Mexican government (and mainly to the party in power), the Electricity Worker Union quickly gained political power. Since then, the strong correlation between the evolution of the electricity sector and the political environment has become stronger. Throughout the 1940s and 1950s, installed power-generating capacity continued to rise as the government and a few private generators invested heavily in the sector.

In 1960, a constitutional amendment to Article 27 nationalized the electricity industry, formally giving the government "exclusive responsibility" for generating, transmitting, transforming, and distributing electricity. Private participation in generation ended and new challenges emerged. Political issues, lack of credible data on the true cost of electricity, among other difficulties, raised barriers for setting economically efficient tariffs. Also during this decade, the government created the *Compañía de Luz y Fuerza del Centro* (LFC) to supply electricity to Mexico City and the neighboring states. Reinforced by these changes in the power sector, populist ideas claiming sovereignty and state autonomy as the government's primary goals became more important than efficiency and economic growth. As was the case in many countries during the 1960s and 1970s, Mexico alienated private investors and insulated the power system from market forces, allowing it to grow without much consideration for the economics of the business. Moreover, the "soft budget" of state financing allowed these enterprises,

---

[1] The modern Mexican nation was built around the idea of sovereignty as a key element to keep the country united against external forces. To understand the importance of that concept it is necessary to recall that Mexico lost half of its territory in the nineteenth century to the United States. Since then Mexican leaders have used the discourse of nationalism and sovereignty as persuasive and unifying elements to protect Mexico's borders and maintain the country's independence. Although its territorial sovereignty is no longer in danger, several decades of indoctrination can persist even if international conditions have changed. Today, privatization and foreign private investment are rejected because some groups perceive them as new forms of colonialism.

CFE and LFC, to operate (albeit inefficiently) and to wield growing political power. Nonetheless, a steady supply of new technologies (developed mainly abroad) as well as the economies of scale in building ever-larger power systems made it possible to sustain low tariffs for end-users without causing these firms to become a huge drain on the state budget. Although these improvements were largely exhausted by the 1970s, the surges in oil prices at that time delivered a windfall to oil-rich Mexico, much of which was directed to subsidies for electricity generation. On the other hand, when oil prices crashed in the early 1980s, a deep financial problem created both the urgent need and the political opportunity for reforms that would make the power sector more efficient while reducing the burden on the state to supply all new capacity. Even though those reforms started slowly and cautiously, successive financing crises have created additional pressure for reform.

In the late 1980s and early 1990s, the Mexican government implemented swift market reforms in various economic sectors (including banking and pension systems) and started to open its markets to international free trade. These included foreign investment agreements allowing participation in several sectors (including electricity) and the creation of new economic institutions that were required to implement those reforms. The *Comisión Federal de Competencia* (Antitrust Federal Commission, CFC), *the Comisión Federal de Telecomunicaciones* (Telecommunications Federal Commission, COFETEL) and the *Comisión Reguladora de Energía* (Energy Regulatory Commission, CRE) were created to regulate markets in order to get the desired social outcomes. More specifically, the CRE was created in 1993 to help build an electricity market. During the late 1990s, former President Zedillo attempted a comprehensive reform of the electricity sector, which included amending the Mexican Constitution, but he faced strong political resistance. Finally, in year 2000, for the first time in modern Mexico's history, a candidate from the opposition – the *Partido Accion Nacional*, PAN – won the Presidential election. The new government made a new reform attempt; but in a divided Congress its proposal did not achieve the required majority support. At the same time, both major parties in the opposition, PRI and *Partido de la Revolución Democrática* (PRD), presented their own proposals. Most of these proposals are presently being debated.

This chapter proceeds as follows. The following section recounts the history of the electric industry in Mexico to explain the structure of the SOEs that dominated during most of the twentieth century and are now the subject of reforms. We analyze the performance of the system, to the best possible extent given the limited data, by looking at patterns of investment and tariffs. We also examine the spread of electrification to the rural poor, regulation of the environmental impact of electricity generation and other social dimensions of the power system. In the next section we examine motivations and outcomes from the various attempts to reform this state-dominated system, starting with the financial crisis in the early 1980s. We analyze the changes introduced in 1992 and the reform proposed by former President Zedillo in 1999. The main political actors – consumers, parties, government, unions, etc. – are also introduced. This is very important since the Mexican electric system (as any other system in the world) should not be seen separately from the political and economical standpoint since both have shaped the power sector. While there has been some progress in the process of reform, fundamental issues remain unsettled due to a combination of economical, political, and legal factors: the composition of both chambers (deputies and senators), the judicial decisions about the legality of the present regulatory schemes, the role of public opinion, especially on issues of nationalism and sovereignty, the new role of the CRE, the evolution of tariffs in the near future, etc. We summarize those in the next section, where we discuss the evolving agenda. In the final section conclusions are stated.

History of the Mexican Power Sector

1880–1979: Mexico's political consolidation and power sector growth

The origins of the Mexican Power System can be traced back to the late nineteenth century when private investors built and operated electric networks that would provide traction, lighting and machine motors for industry (mainly textile and mining) and lighting in the major cities. The first plants deployed whatever source of primary energy was readily available – coal for thermoelectric plants and, where appropriate rivers were available, the power of running water. The first thermoelectric generation plant started operation in 1879, mainly to supply a textile mill at León in the state of Guanajuato; the first hydro plant produced electricity a decade later for the mining industry at Batopilas in Chihuahua. In parallel, governments sold lucrative concessions for electrification of cities – the first of these, in 1881, awarded electric service for Mexico City to the privately held *Compañía Mexicana de Gas y Luz Eléctrica* (Rodríguez y Rodríguez, 1994). Through these vertically integrated monopolies, installed capacity grew at nearly 20 percent per year by the first decade of the twentieth century (Rodríguez y Rodríguez, 1994). Private investors were drawn only to the wealthiest and most industrialized areas. However, investment concentrated in the center of the country, around Mexico City. Low prices and generous terms for the concessions, along with the demographic growth of Mexico in the early 1900s, attracted investors – most from firms based in Canada, France, Germany, and the United States, with only a small share from Mexican investors. This private model of electrification was followed in all five of the countries examined in this book. It included few requirements to invest in activities that the private investors themselves would not find profitable, such as "universal access" to electricity or rural electrification. Moreover, this administrative law instrument (i.e., a concession) was laden with ambiguities that, usually, were interpreted in ways that benefited the investors, and there was no authority with clearly articulated competence for setting policy and enforcing the terms of the concessions (Rodríguez y Rodríguez, 1994).

Mindful of the increasing social, political, and economic relevance of electricity, the government tried to tame the monopolistic tendencies of the electricity companies. But the task was daunting. The central government was weak and the industry itself was in the midst of a massive reorganization that would produce even larger monopolies that, by design, would not compete or even complement each other. The most important firms became holding companies by absorbing the many small retail companies – interestingly, this consolidation occurred at roughly the same time that Samuel Insull, in the United States, was creating a vast holding company by acquiring the assets of smaller isolated firms. The *Mexican Light and Power Company* adopted a single 50 Hz system across its entire network, but *Impulsora de Empresas Eléctricas* operated at eight local frequencies – from 25 to 58 Hz – and did not attempt to seize the economic advantage of full interconnection. These two firms, together with a much smaller one, *Nueva Compañía Hidroeléctrica Chapala*, dominated the market. In a few jurisdictions, local government regulators had discovered their ability to wield influence and, in most cases, demanded low tariffs set without regard to costs. Wary of such pricing schedules that, in effect, expropriated monopoly profits, private firms reduced their investments in new capacity. The result was, arguably, the worst of the two worlds. Monopolistic pricing flourished where regulators were weak, but in the heart of the industrializing nation, Mexico City, arbitrary tariff rules set the stage for perpetual under-investment in the power sector.

In 1926 the federal government adopted a policy strategy that would cast a long shadow over the century. The *Código Nacional Eléctrico* changed the Constitution and declared electricity a public service and conferred to Congress the authority to legislate in related matters. In the short term, this constitutional move had little impact because the federal government remained weak – financing and regulation of local electric monopolies, for example, was controlled by state and city governments and the large industrial users of electricity. Congress adopted rules that demanded rural electrification, a politically popular mandate, but the private companies ignored new mandates that made no business sense. However, the *Código* did require homogenization of the frequency standards over the complete system – and on that score it had great effect since it supplied the public good of coordination and required only two of the dominating firms (*Impulsora* and *Chapala*) to align their practices with the third.

As it is the case in other countries examined in this book – such as Brazil and South Africa – the Mexican government tried to circumvent the difficulties of sustaining private investment by assuming the function of supplying electricity itself. The seeds of this effort are found in the creation, in 1934, of the *Comisión Federal de Electricidad* (CFE), with a modest initial budget (50,000 pesos, about $14,000 at the time), a tiny staff of twenty employees and two main objectives: 1) to operate as a regulatory agency and liaison between foreign companies and government, and 2) to supply electric service to those areas considered as unprofitable by private power companies. With its loose mandate and tiny budget it was hardly clear at the time that CFE would emerge as the dominant force in the entire Mexican electric power system.

At the same time, President Lázaro Cárdenas consolidated power around his Party, PRI. Although PRI had a strong influence on peasants, its key strength rested in Unions, the best organized of which were those in the largest industries – mining and electricity. Indicative of the growing power of these unions was the *Sindicato Mexicano de Electricistas* (SME) (Mexican Electric Workers Union), which struck *Impulsora de Empresas Eléctricas* and its seven subsidiaries in 1936. The oldest and strongest union in Mexico, SME became a critical piece in President Cárdenas' policy that became known as "Mexican Corporatism" – strong central government ruling in collaboration with organized labor unions. By the late 1930s the PRI was firmly in control. Land reform and nationalization of economic resources became symbols of Mexican national sovereignty and key planks in PRI's policy platform. The 1938 Electricity Public Service Act, issued just as PRI was completing its consolidation of political power, required strong federal regulation of electric services, including tariffs.

Foreign firms, already finding their investments squeezed by low mandated tariffs in a few key jurisdictions, reduced their investments still further. In most cases, they maintained their existing capacity but invested little in expansion (for these firms, World War II was an additional discouragement to invest abroad). From 1937 to 1943 private investment grew less than 1 percent. Wartime President Manuel Avila Camacho sought to nationalize the power system but feared a backlash if he simply appropriated the assets of powerful foreign investors. Rather, he launched a rolling process of nationalization. CFE was instructed to buy (at depressed prices) existing electric assets, and, with state resources, also oversaw the construction of new generation, transmission, and distribution services.

Prior to the 1940s, private firms supplied all investment in new capacity (*Mexican*, *Impulsora* and *Chapala*). But then private investment flagged. Nationalization began in 1944 when CFE acquired *Chapala* (the third largest of the private electric companies) and built CFE's first generating facility (Ixtapantongo). During the 1940s and 1950s, CFE acquired and consolidated hundreds of regional electricity monopolies into a single firm – linking all with common technical standards and taking advantage of the ever-larger economies of scale offered by new generation equipment. From 1939 to 1950, 52 percent of the total investment in the power system came from public resources and 30 percent from contracted credits by the government – essentially all of this within the growing CFE system. Only 18 percent was private investment from firms that remained outside CFE's network (Bastarrachea and Aguilar,1994). By 1959, total installed capacity had reached 2,739 MW, of which CFE controlled about half and the remaining private networks accounted for smaller shares: the *Mexican Light and Power Company* with 21 percent and *Impulsora de Empresas Eléctricas* with 8 percent. (see figure 5.1 for the increase in new capacity during this process of nationalization and consolidation of the system. Almost all new capacity came from additions from CFE while the other firms kept the same installed capacity.)

Consolidation was largely complete in 1960 when the Federal Government bought 95 percent of the common shares in *Impulsora* and also acquired a majority stake in *Mexican*. These new acquisitions also allowed for a reorganization of the sector. Control was given to CFE over all segments and regions of the power system except for the central states of Mexico, Morelos, Puebla, Hidalgo, and Distrito Federal, which became the service area of a new SOE, *Compañía de Luz y Fuerza del Centro* (LFC). This division of geographical responsibility between two state enterprises remains today. By the time nationalization reached the

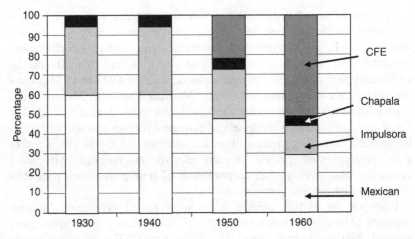

Figure 5.1. Percentage of total capacity by firm, 1930–1960 (CFE and Nafinsa)

nation's capital, a politically well-organized and (at the time) efficient power company already existed; fearful of being rolled into CFE, the incumbents in the center carved LFC out of the remnants of *Mexican* and implored the Mexican President to establish their service as a separate enterprise.

Having largely completed its nationalization, in 1960 the government formalized the arrangement with a constitutional amendment (Article 27, paragraph 6) declaring: "It is the exclusive responsibility of the Nation to generate, transmit, transform, distribute and supply electricity that is intended for public service use (from Breceda, 2000)." As in most Latin American countries in the 1960s and 1970s, nationalization along with an import substitution strategy were part of the government's effort to control economic development – to accelerate the rate of growth and to spread the benefits widely. During the decades that followed, the power system controlled by the government connected millions to the grid, achieving nearly universal coverage, which is one of the reasons why the population at large – particularly the poor and marginalized – support state control of utilities in Mexico. Along the way, the notion of social justice was expanded to include a wide array of subsidies for urban and agricultural consumers – as in many countries (e.g., India) electricity tariffs were constructed with an eye to political benefits rather than economic cost, and over time they led to mounting losses.

Under this new legal framework, CFE continued to grow by acquiring the few regional companies that remained in private hands, buying the last, *Compañía de Servicios Públicos de Nogales*, in 1972. New functions added to the national electricity system built around these two SOEs. In 1974 President Luis Echeverría Álvarez sponsored yet another amendment to Article 27, this time to grant the state the exclusive right to use radioactive materials and nuclear fuel for generation of energy, as well as Article 73 that reserved for Congress the right to legislate on nuclear energy matters. The process of nationalization and consolidation of control into the hands of the state was finalized legally in 1975 with the *Ley del Servicio Público de Energía Eléctrica* (LSPEE) which declared CFE and LFC as public suppliers of electricity. State-controlled monopoly, it was thought, was essential for ensuring the real-time management of electric power. Only a state enterprise could be trusted with a technology that had large economies of scale and thus natural tendencies to monopoly. Furthermore, private generators sought only profitable markets, leaving a large part of the population without electricity, and it was assumed that only a SOE could deliver electric service more equitably.

As in most of the SOEs studied in this book – with the possible exception of Eskom in South Africa – CFE and LFC were managed like government offices rather than private, competitive firms. Relying heavily on the public budget for financing, they were (and still are) a source of political patronage for senior appointments. Among the strongest of the nation's unions these enterprises also host key elements of the PRI power base. In addition to these generic features of SOEs, management of these firms has been complicated by frequent changes in policy as well as by the difficulty of drawing a line between state and enterprise.

We now turn to the task of evaluating the system that emerged from this historical context, with particular attention to factors that have affected the choice of fuels, the setting of tariffs, and the financial performance of the state-dominated system. We also examine the system's performance on several politically important dimensions (beyond financial) – notably, its ability to connect people to the grid. The analysis of successes and failures sets the context for the goals that reform efforts, begun in the wake of a financial crisis in the early 1980s, sought to achieve.

This system, controlled and financed completely by the state, appears to have performed adequately during the 1970s. Demand grew rapidly, but so did installed capacity. However, as in many state-dominated systems, over-building was commonplace – reserve margins were greater than 30 percent throughout the period from 1970 to 2002, as shown in figure 5.2.

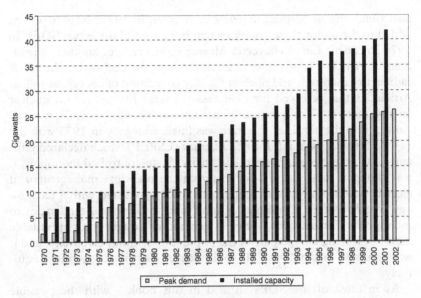

Figure 5.2. Growth in demand and generation capacity (Secretaria de Energia and comision Federal de Electricidad)

As the power system expanded over the twentieth century the need for primary fuel quickly outstripped the availability of high quality coal and generators turned to other locally available options: water and oil resources (see table 5.1).Rivers were tapped from the earliest decades of electrification, but Mexico's water resources in the north are scarce and the load factors on hydroelectric plant factors rarely exceed 30 percent. That left fuel oil from petroleum as the main fuel, particularly as Mexico became one of the top ten world oil producers in the 1970s and growing concerns about environmental pollution favored oil over coal. Since the 1980s, with the availability of cost-effective gas turbines, oil fell out of favor as more costly than gas alternatives – much of the history of reform in the power sector, to which we turn to in the next section, is intertwined with efforts to secure a larger share for gas in the power sector.

Within the political and organizational calculus of CFE and LFC, the preference for fuel oil is easy to understand.

First, even though Mexico is rich in natural gas, the state-owned *Petróleos Mexicanos* (PEMEX) that is responsible for hydrocarbon production did not consider gas as part of its core business throughout most of this period and thus could not guarantee a gas supply to the power sector. Even today, gas is a poor second cousin to oil extraction at

Table 5.1. *Total installed capacity by type of generation of plants in operation*

	Hydro	Steam	Combined Cycle	Turbo Gas	Internal Combustion	Geothermal	Dual	Coal	Nuclear	Wind	Total
1879		1.8									1.8
1900	14	4									18
1910	99	0									99
1920	192	0									192
1930											475
1940	355	40			72			12			680
1950	559	171			174			12			1234
1960	1249	839			205	3		12			3021
1970	3228	2353			271			37			7414
1980	5992	6616	540	1190	137	150					16862
1990	7805	11367	1687	1779	86	700		1200	675		26267
2000	9619	14282	2914	2360	116	855	2100	2600	1365	2	36213
2001	9619	14283	5188	2381	143	838	2100	2600	1365	2	38519
2002	9608	14283	7343	2890	144	843	2100	2600	1365	2	41177
2003	9608	14283	10604	2890	143	960	2100	2600	1365	2	44554

Source: SENER-CFE.

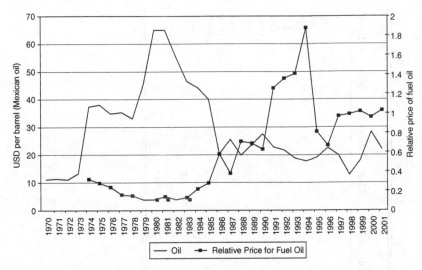

Figure 5.3. World oil price and relative price for fuel oil in Mexico

PEMEX. Second, Mexico does not have coal with the quality needed to generate electricity. Third, the logic of "dependency" and the strategy of import substitution animated a self-sufficiency policy under which imports of technology and fuels would be minimized. Coal and gas plants typically require greater purchases of equipment overseas, whereas oil-fired facilities would be relatively easy to construct and supply with fuel from an oil-rich nation. Crucially for CFE and LFC in their internal decision making, during the 1970s and 1980s PEMEX sold fuel oil to the power sector at around 30 percent of its opportunity cost (see figure 5.3).[2]

From the perspective of managers within CFE and LFC, allocation of investment towards oil was actually efficient. Viewed from the vantage of the country as a whole, this strategy was extremely costly – the under-pricing of fuel oil amounted to a massive implicit subsidy to the power sector that averaged about $1.5 billion dollars a year.[3] When world oil prices soared so did the subsidy; ironically, however, the subsidy proved easiest to sustain when oil was dear and thus large

[2] Until the early 1990s fuel oil prices were regulated in Mexico at a level far below the true opportunity cost. World oil prices (left scale in figure 5.3) is the average cost of acquisition of Mexican heavy crude by US refiners; the relative price of fuel oil (right scale in figure 5.3) is the ratio of price charged for fuel oil in Mexico (available only since 1974) vs. a similar product in the United States (residual fuel oil #6, 3% sulfur, Gulf Coast average).

[3] From 1974 to 1989, in 2001 constant dollars.

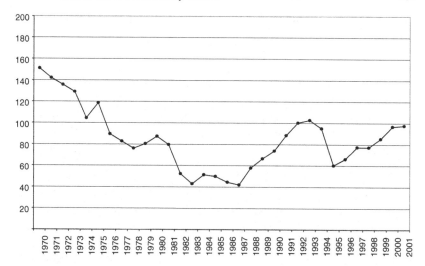

Figure 5.4. Mexican electricity tariffs as a % of US tariffs (CFE – SENER)

windfalls flowed to the state budget from Pemex oil sales overseas. Even when oil prices plummeted in the late 1980s the price charged to CFE and LFC for fuel oil was only 70 percent of its true opportunity cost. The philosophy of import substitution and "Mexican sovereignty" had been built into every aspect of the Mexican power system; even today, a reliable political strategy for opposing reform of state-dominated enterprises is to hype the threat to Mexican sovereignty.

While low fuel prices allowed for tariffs set far below their opportunity cost, the exact relationship between tariffs and costs is difficult to assess because, even today, there are no credible statistics on the true cost of electricity production in Mexico. We attempt to compare tariffs with costs by comparing Mexican tariffs with those in the United States (see figure 5.4). Mindful that there are many differences between the systems, such a comparison is nonetheless a useful place to begin in assessing Mexican tariffs.

In most jurisdictions in the United States tariffs were set "in the public interest" by independent regulators and implemented by privately owned utilities whose stockholders demanded that the enterprise cover its cost and make a predictable profit. In Mexico, the function of regulating tariffs was (and still is) played by the *Secretaría de Hacienda* (Ministry of Finance) and is an extension of the development strategy that the government pursues at any given moment. Often, the agenda at *Secretaría de Hacienda* has not been compatible with the needs of a financially self-sustaining power sector – as in all the other countries examined in this book, such mismatches would not necessarily cause turmoil in the sector so long as the government was also willing to cover the difference (usually indirectly through its financing of new projects). *Secretaría de Hacienda* consistently set tariffs for public purposes (e.g., street lighting), for agriculture and for residential service at levels below those of the United States – a reflection of the importance of rural agricultural and low/middle income class voters to the PRI, and the tendency not to draw a strong line between core public functions and the full cost of services supplied by SOEs. In many respects, the integrated state budget was a gigantic shell game.

In general, tariffs for the other classes remained well above US levels, which we conjecture is the result of at least two forces. First, the state-owned power system in Mexico was less efficient than the US power system – payrolls were larger, the aversion to outside equipment meant that technical losses (although not known) were probably larger, and quality of service was lower.[4] Second was the ability of *Secretaría de Hacienda* to extract higher rents from commercial and industrial consumers, which are not a power base for PRI.

Overall, the Mexican power sector's tariff policy seems to have been broadly reflecting costs until 1973. Electricity prices were a bit higher than in the United States but it was probably due to the oil-intensive and somewhat inefficient Mexican system. After 1973, there is a clear shift in the tariff policy that appears to mirror the shift in the country's general economic policy – an inward policy that allowed *Hacienda* to lower tariffs with the help of oil money. Lower tariffs were used as an inflation control policy followed by the government during that time. The late 1970s through the 1980s marked a peak period for state control and budgetary shell games, thanks to the lubrication of oil revenues. This is evident in figure 5.4, which reveals that the Mexican tariff level has followed the availability of oil subsidies, with a delay of about two years for the normal cycle of state budgets. Tariffs declined sharply in 1981 (after the oil price windfall created by 1979 Iranian revolution) and then climbed in the late 1980s as the cost of subsidy mounted and oil prices softened.

---

[4] Efficiency measures are against CFE and LFC. First, the energy sold per worker is only about 1.85 GWh/worker in CFE and 1.6 GWh/worker in LFC, compared to about 4.5 GWh/worker in Australia. Second, the power interruption per user is 230 and 331 minutes, in CFE and LFC, respectively. In France and the United States, it is 115 and 120 minutes, respectively.

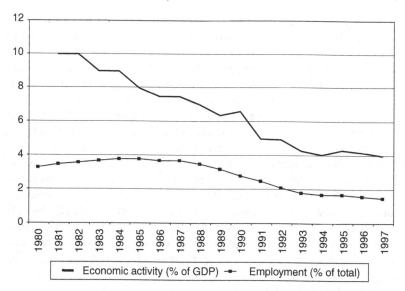

Figure 5.5. Role of state-owned enterprises in the Mexican economy

Shifting the State-Dominated Economy: 1982–2003

1980–1989: The lack of resources to increase infrastructure

Starting in the early 1980s the Mexican government's framework shifted from a situation in which, in the words of former President José Lopez Portillo (who ruled from 1976 to 1982), "Mexico has to learn to manage its wealth" to a scenario with spiraling public debt and hyperinflation. By 1980 the Mexican Government was operating with a total deficit of 7.5 percent of GDP, and the electricity sector alone ran a deficit at almost 2.4 percent of GDP – all financed by extraordinary oil revenues. Despite oil prices that remained high in the early 1980s, shortly before Miguel de la Madrid assumed the presidency in 1982 Mexico defaulted on its external debt. The shock of this financial crisis created a window of opportunities for reformers who imposed tight fiscal controls, dismantled the import substitution strategy, integrated Mexico into the world economy, and reduced the role of the state in the local economy. Ever since, the role of SOEs in the economy has declined steadily – first as a fraction of GDP and then, after delays, in the aggregate workforce (figure 5.5).

Moreover, we can observe that the share of employment rose as the share of GDP fell in early 1980s as a consequence of the financial crisis, which generated economy-wide unemployment. Among the few industries that escaped privatization in the two decades of reform that followed were the two areas with the greatest implications for the state budget – electricity as a drain, and oil as a source of revenue. The failure to disengage the electric sector is evidence of key political and constitutional factors at work – to those factors we now turn.

One of *Secretaría de Hacienda's* immediate responses to the crisis was to adjust prices with the twin (and often incompatible) goals of reducing financial losses caused by low tariffs while at the same time taming hyperinflation. *Secretaría de Hacienda* increased the price of fuel oil burned for electricity and also reformed commercial and industrial tariffs, which in 1983 had reached a historical low while keeping flat the more politically sensitive residential and agricultural tariffs (figure 5.4). On the assumption that industry could pay a stiffer rate, the cross-subsidy from industrial and commercial users to the others grew over the following years. These modest reforms on fuel prices and tariffs bought time, but they did not fix the structural problems within the state-owned power sector.

1990–2000: Structural reforms towards building a new market architecture

During the 1990s, Mexico shifted from a country that avoided foreign direct investment to one that actively sought it, especially in export-oriented industries. Through expanded access to markets offered through trade agreements – notably NAFTA (1992) and the World Trade Organization (1994) – the value of Mexico's exports almost quadrupled from 1990 to 2000. These investor and trade friendly reforms also created buffers for the Mexican economy that, in contrast with the 1982 crisis, have made it easier for Mexico to weather subsequent macroeconomic shocks. Nonetheless, each financial crisis since 1982 has brought stern limits on public debt, which in turn has limited the ability of CFE, a public company, to raise the capital needed to build new plants at the pace of rising demand. In contrast with the 1970s (see figure 5.2), during the era of crises – from 1982 through the 1990s (and perhaps to the present) – the growth in supply and demand was more unpredictable; reserve margins varied widely because of a lack of investment in capacity as demand was steadily growing.

A new financial crisis in 1994–1995 proved to be the breaking point. Politically, this crisis induced a strong change in the electorate preferences that allowed for a new composition of the Mexican Congress

Table 5.2. *Political control of congress: the percentage of deputies and senators*

	Deputies (lower house)				Senators (upper house)			
	PRI	PAN	PRD	Others	PRI	PAN	PRD	Others
1964	83	10	0	7	100	0	0	0
1967	83	9	0	8	100	0	0	0
1970	84	9	0	7	100	0	0	0
1973	82	11	0	7	100	0	0	0
1976	82	8	0	10	100	0	0	0
1979	74	11	0	15	100	0	0	0
1982	75	13	0	12	100	0	0	0
1985	72	10	0	18	100	0	0	0
1988	52	20	0	38	94	0	6	0
1991	64	18	8	10	95	2	3	0
1994	60	24	14	2	74	20	6	0
1997	48	24	25	3	60	26	12	2
2000	42	42	10	6	47	36	12	5
2003	45	31	19	5	47	36	12	5

after the midterm elections in 1997. After more than sixty-five years of control, the ruling party (PRI) lost its majority in Congress (see table 5.2).

The absolute majority enjoyed by PRI in both houses of Congress had long been a crucial asset for the PRI-controlled presidency. Any policy that the President (and PRI) sought to implement – such as import substitution in the earlier era, and shifting from the state-dominated economy along with free trade agreements during the era of reforms – could be assured a working majority. Any significant opposition came from within the establishment itself and could be addressed within the PRI apparatus.

Economically, this crisis also had a series of seismic effects because the government's negotiated settlement with its creditors included a prohibition against SOEs incurring additional debt. For the power sector, this did not seem a substantial concession – the economy was expected to tip into recession and thus demand for power would be sluggish, and a considerable excess capacity was available from the years of over-building. Reality proved to be quite different. Integration with the United States fueled rapid growth in Mexico and power demand rose at a much higher rate than expected. The government found relief in Amendments to Mexico's *Ley del Servicio Publico de Energía Eléctrica* (LSPEE), which was altered in 1992 to allow private participation under

Table 5.3. *Activities considered for private participation*

Scheme	Description
Self-supply	Generation of electricity to meet an industrial facility's own energy needs. Refers to power plants owned and operated by private companies
Cogeneration	Refers to electricity generated simultaneously with steam or other types of secondary thermal energy to be used in an industrial process, or the generation of electricity from the surplus of thermal energy of an industrial process
Independent Power Production	Refers to power plants with installed capacity larger then 30 MW, built and operated by private companies. All generated power must be sold to CFE under a power purchase agreement
Imports and Exports	Exports refer to electricity produced under cogeneration, IPP or small scale generation categories. Imports refer to electricity exclusively used for self-supply purposes.
Small-scale generation	Refers to power plants with an installed capacity no larger than 30 MW built and operated by private companies. This electricity is to be sold solely to CFE.

different schemes such as Independent Power Production (IPP) Cogeneration and Self-Supply (see table 5.3).

These legal reforms had been undertaken to comply with the energy chapter of NAFTA, which was artfully constructed to permit continued state control of the oil and electricity sectors (as enshrined in Articles 27 and 28 of the Mexican Constitution) while at the same time allowing for private participation in the power sector. As shown in figure 5.6, an interlocking array of constitutional, international and national laws then applied in the power sector; as we will see, the interaction between these laws has strongly shaped the outcomes.

With the LSPEE already on the books, though not yet implemented, the government jumpstarted the IPP program to alleviate the looming crisis in power supply caused by CFE's inability to contract debt. The first tender (Merida III, a combined cycle gas-fired plant) was awarded in January 1997. In practice, IPPs on their own were not a miracle solution because generators still had to sell their power through one of the state-owned distributors – LFC or CFE – and the power purchase agreements (PPAs) that underpinned IPP investments were, in essence, a form of long-term debt-like commitment that the post-1995 settlement would seem to have forbidden.

The proposed solution was a shell game established on December 21, 1995 when the Mexican Congress approved reforms to the Public Debt

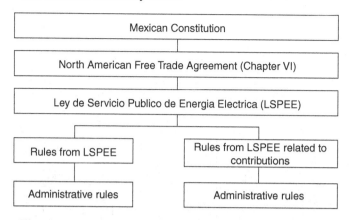

Figure 5.6. Legal framework for the Mexican power sector

and the Budget Laws that created a new scheme for the development of long-term infrastructure projects, currently known as PIDIREGAS.[5] Under this scheme, tailor-made for IPPs, only the capacity payments of a PPA of the starting and the following year are accounted for as liabilities. Future payments are considered as contingent liabilities but are not included in the government's yearly budget. Since IPPs work under long-term PPA contracts, it would seem normal that the capacity payments were not considered as liabilities. However, since the Mexican power sector is operated as a vertically integrated publicly owned monopoly, every single IPP project that is operating or under construction has sought and received explicit government guarantees. These guarantees are in essence contingent liabilities, which must be handled more like normal liabilities. As of June 2005, PIDIREGAS debt for CFE alone amounts to $4.47 billion, with payments distributed over the following ten years. So far, there has never been a default on any of the PIDIREGAS liabilities; even as investors in power plants have lost vast sums in many other developing countries, all of the contracted IPPs are rewarding investors more or less as expected. For investors and government managers the scheme is attractive; however, since PIDIR-EGAS backs PPAs denominated in 2003-dollars there remains a substantial devaluation risk – a constant feature of Mexican financing for the last three decades that might prove to be a major problem for power sector investors.

---

[5] These schemes were designed to hide and shift accruing debts in areas such as airlines and PEMEX.

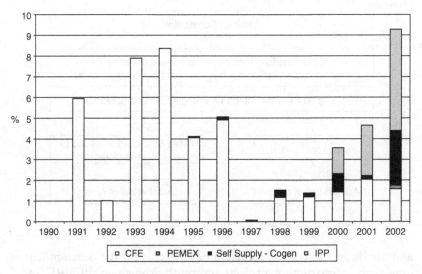

Figure 5.7. Growth in new generating capacity

Merida III entered into service in 2000. Since then 3495 MW of capacity have been added through IPPs, which has contributed considerably to restoring the sector's reserve margin.

As shown in figure 5.7, from 2000 to 2002 about half of new capacity came from IPPs. In 2002, one-third of the new capacity came from self-generation and cogeneration facilities – that is, power plants that are located at industrial sites outside the direct control of CFE and LFC. Barely one-third of the new capacity from 2000 to 2002 came from the traditional CFE and LFC-dominated model of power plant construction. Despite this new surge in investment, IPPs alone were not enough to meet the growth in demand, and there are several indicators of the chronic underinvestment due to the continuing severe restrictions on public debt. First, reserve margins have slipped – to just 1 percent in summer 2002 – and have been maintained in part by delaying the retirement of old plants, especially plants that burn high cost fuel oil. Second, the government has slashed the authorized budgets for maintenance and repair – typically, as shown in table 5.4, to levels that are 30 percent lower on average than the level desired by CFE executives. These short-term measures helped to preserve resources for capital investment and helped to avert crisis in the power sector, but they were merely stopgap measures.

Even more worrisome than these problems with current investment are the inconsistencies laden in CFE's official planning forecast for the

Table 5.4. *Solicited and authorized budgets for maintenance and repair at CFE*

	1995	1996	1997	1998	1999	2000	2001
Solicited Budget (Millions of Pesos)	2924	3128	3403	2610	2514	2844	3150
Authorized Budget (Millions of Pesos)	1904	2011	2502	2045	2002	2045	1937
Proportion	65.1	64.3	73.5	78.4	79.6	71.9	61.5

Source: CFE.

next ten years: a 25,000 MW increase in net installed capacity through the addition of 28,000 MW of new plants; with planned retirements amounting to only around 4,100 MW, about half the level expected (Secretaría de Energia, 2002).[6] From both a financial and technical perspective, the power sector appears to be in serious trouble. The Mexican State will be unable to meet these growth targets because it has no financial resources itself for investment in the required new capacity.[7] IPPs can meet some of the shortfall, but the confidence of IPP investors may wane as the latest scheme to defer crisis – the PIDIREGAS mechanism – becomes exhausted.

Two conclusions can be drawn from the experience so far with the IPP program. First, it has resulted in almost no change in the market architecture of the sector. Although a leap for private investors, IPPs are a stopgap measure. By design, they exist inside the LFC and CFE-dominated system and require minimal adjustment of that structure. They solve an immediate problem – surging demand but stagnant supply and aging incumbent plants – at considerable cost that is largely not transparent in current state accounts. Second, IPPs have had a dramatic effect on the technology available in the sector in ways that are probably quite beneficial for Mexico. All the IPP projects have been built by foreign companies using state-of-the art combined cycle gas-fired technology – with gas purchased from the United States or from PEMEX. In other countries examined in this book the introduction of gas has been difficult because fuel costs in a gas system are higher than the incumbent coal (China, India, South Africa) or hydro (Brazil). In

[6] Considering a life plant of about thirty years (for thermal plants), and Mexico's thermal installed capacity of around 30,000 MW (excluding cogeneration and self-supply) one would expect in the period from 2002 to 2011 retirements of around 8,300 MW – suggesting the need for constructing about 32,000 MW in new power plants, which is almost 15% higher than official figures.

[7] As of June 2003, total debt – excluding contingent debt like social security debt, highway and sugar industries debt – was around $236 billion (around 36% of GDP). Moreover, the debt service in the first semester of 2003 amounted for 60% of the income and valued added taxes collected by government in the same period.

Table 5.5. *Mexican electricity tariff/cost ratios*

Consumer class	1995	1996	1997	1998	1999	2000	2001	2002	2003
Residential	0.47	0.42	0.40	0.38	0.37	0.36	0.38	0.46	0.42
Commercial	1.31	1.16	1.13	0.96	0.96	0.87	0.86	0.83	0.84
Public service	0.88	0.79	0.81	0.91	0.90	0.86	0.85	0.89	0.83
Agricultural	0.33	0.28	0.28	0.29	0.29	0.28	0.29	0.30	0.28
Medium industrial	0.88	0.84	0.91	0.83	0.83	0.80	0.77	0.80	0.81
Large industrial	0.81	0.83	0.91	0.87	0.87	0.83	0.81	0.85	0.84
Average	0.71	0.70	0.74	0.65	0.65	0.63	0.62	0.65	0.64

Source: Secretaría de Energia

Mexico, the incumbent fuel is expensive and gas plants not only have lower capital cost but also are less costly to operate – in addition to being much cleaner.

Even as the creation of the IPP and the PIDIREGAS schemes offered new tools to avert crisis, *Secretaría de Hacienda* continued to reform fuel prices and tariffs with the aim of restoring some sustainability to the sector. Nonetheless, tariffs appear still to be at a level below cost – especially as the cost basis of the oil-intensive Mexican power sector is much higher than in the United States, where low-cost coal is the dominant primary energy source. According to the Ministry of Energy, Mexican electricity tariff/cost ratios are as shown in table 5.5.[8] Despite these increases in tariffs, the sector still loses vast sums of money.

Official figures estimate a net subsidy of $8.3 billion for 2003 (see figure 5.8), principally because residential and agricultural tariffs are set far below cost – the residential subsidy alone is more than 50 percent of the total subsidy. (The distributional effects of this subsidy are enormous; total tax collection outside the oil sector is around 10 percent of GDP.) In 2003, residential consumers received 61 percent of the total subsidy; the industrial sector, 22 percent; the agriculture sector, 9 percent; and the commercial sector, 5 percent. As a consequence of this policy, residential consumers face a tariff that is among the lowest in the world; but it relies on a regressive scheme as shown by López-Calva and Rosellón (2002). A new thirty-six-category tariff scheme marks a further step at rationalization; still, residential tariffs remain below cost – implying a subsidy for 98 percent of users.

[8] We reiterate that exact costs of generation, transmission and distribution are unknown. Data should be treated with caution because of the indiscriminate use of financial costs and long-run marginal costs to calculate final tariffs.

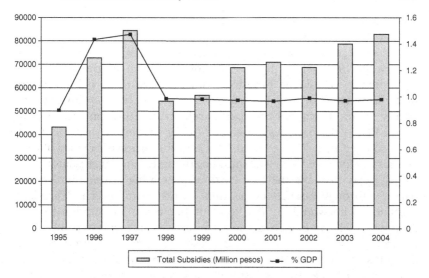

Figure 5.8. Evolution of total subsidies to the power sector (million peros).

Politically it has proved extremely difficult, if not impossible, to raise residential and agricultural tariffs. Most analysts conclude that the only practical way to make the sector financially sound is to reduce costs. Yet that, too, is politically challenging as it requires confronting the powerful unions that are embedded in CFE and, especially, LFC. These unions – *Sindicato Mexicano de Electricistas* at LFC in a cross alliance with the leftist Party PRD, the leftist wing of PRI, and some other social organizations and unions and the *Sindicato Único de Trabajadores Eléctricos de la República Mexicana* (SUTERM) at CFE (which has a mixed position on the reform issue) – have led a broad coalition to block any attempt to allow private investment into the sector or to modify significantly the market architecture (e.g., tariff reform) in ways that could hurt their interests. Since the SME and the SUTERM are well-organized interest groups with the ability to mobilize votes, no political party has been willing to face the political cost of supporting a modification of the electricity subsidy policies or a substantial modification in the market architecture to allow for the implementation of competitive fares.[9] If both consumers and unions oppose changes, then it becomes a risky

---

[9] As an example we should remember that President Fox implemented some changes in the subsidy policy (reduction of subsidy for some classes of residential consumers) and then overturned it in the northern states because it faced very strong opposition from those consumers.

business to pass a bill, which eventually could cost votes or popular support for the involved parties.

The strongest of the referred political opposition to reform became evident in 1999 when the first profound reform of the sector was attempted by President Ernesto Zedillo. Before then, policy makers under President Carlos Salinas, mindful of the political sensitivity of the energy sector, attempted only partial reform. In 1992, amendments to the LSPEE – the basic legal architecture for the power sector that had been codified in 1975 – allowed IPPs into the sector (discussed above) and also empowered a new institution, the independent regulator. The strategy was to make the true costs of generating power more transparent – through market competition – and to empower independent regulators who would be able to scrutinize costs. In addition to promising the delivery of electric service at lower cost, a shift to competitive electricity markets would make it possible to remove key operational decisions in the sector from the grip of unions. Markets built around transparent rules as well as tariffs set at levels that ensured recovery of costs would attract private investment into new generating capacity and would also allow CFE and LFC to direct their scarce resources towards dire needs such as repair and maintenance of existing assets. Moreover, they could implement better management of the system to reduce theft of electricity, a rising problem that threatens to further undermine the financial soundness of the system. Indeed, the experience in telecommunications, highways, the pension system, and the banking system, seemed to confirm that privatization and the introduction of market forces would lead to an influx of private capital that could constrain the government's ability to torque tariffs to its macroeconomic and political agendas.[10] Today, the political case for privatization and market reforms is thus extremely difficult to make – indeed, policy makers often engage in verbal and legal contortions to argue that the proposed reforms do *not* involve privatization and unfettered markets.

---

[10] In the years since, sober assessments of the privatization process have revealed a more subtle story. In highways and banking, privatization spawned corruption that required reassertion of control by the government; in telecommunications, the process of privatization was not accompanied by the creation of an adequate regulatory authority, with the result that competition and tariffs have delivered only a fraction of the potential benefits from privatization. A private monopoly, *Telefonos de Mexico* (TELMEX), has become the focal point for claims that privatization and liberalization yield changes that benefit only a few. Mc Kinsey and Mookherjee (2003) analyze the distributive impact of privatizations in several Latin American countries, including Mexico. They find positive welfare effects that do not support the generalized bad public opinion towards privatization that exists in the region.

The Regulator in the Power Sector

The 1992 Amendments to the LSPEE did not alter the Mexican Constitution, and thus the state still held the exclusive right to generate, transport, and supply electricity for public service. Reforms required careful balance to preserve the constitutionally assured role for the central government, as we have seen with the emergence of IPPs. The creation of an independent regulator presented a new frontier in this balancing act; although formally part of the government, the regulator would have an arm's length relationship with the traditional entities of government precisely to preserve the political control of electricity that was originally envisioned in Article 27 of the Constitution. In 1993 the government created by decree the CRE as an advisory body on gas and electricity issues. In October 1995, the *Ley de la Comisión Reguladora de Energía* (Energy Regulatory Commission Act, LCRE) transformed CRE into an autonomous agency in charge of regulating the natural gas and electricity industries. The CRE has its own budget (which is allocated via the Energy Ministry with few strings attached) and has technical and operational autonomy. It consolidates functions that had previously been scattered among several agencies, and pursuant to its enabling Act, in the electric sector CRE is empowered to perform several key tasks:[11]

(a) Participation in the setting of tariffs for wholesale and final sale of electricity;
(b) Issuance of permits to generate electricity under the schemes allowed by the LSPEE;
(c) Review and approval of the criteria for determining fees related to public electricity service;
(d) Verification that entities responsible for the public electricity service purchase electricity at the lowest cost and also offer optimum stability, quality, and safety of electric service;
(e) Approval of the methodologies for calculating payments for the purchase of electricity used in public service; and
(f) Approval of the methodologies for calculating payments for electricity transmission, transformation and delivery services.

In addition to these functions, CRE also performs similar functions in the gas sector, including the issuance of building and operating permits for gas infrastructures. By 2003 CRE had granted 218 permits in all schemes accounting for investment commitments of over \$12.2 billion

[11] See www.cre.gob.

for the construction and operation of nearly 20,000 MW of capacity. Nonetheless, CRE's authority and power are not clearly specified in many areas, and its influence is hobbled in key areas – such as in tariffs, where the operations of LFC and CFE are far from transparent and thus rational tariff setting is essentially impossible. CRE approves the methodologies for calculating payments for electricity transmission and distribution, but does not have the authority to establish tariffs.

Despite reforms to create an independents regulator and allow the entry of IPPs, the fundamental barrier to competition and private participation remained – Articles 27 and 28 of the Constitution. In February 1999, near the end of his tenure, President Zedillo proposed structural reforms that would have modified the Constitution, but these never passed the Congress. Many factions inside PRI opposed reform that could erode a traditional power base – the unions in CFE and LFC – and they relied on a public that remembered the failed promises of earlier privatizations.[12] In addition to opposition within his own party, Zedillo's earlier political reforms meant that he didn't have a working majority in the Congress (see table 5.2), which required him to negotiate with many different parties to achieve the support needed for passage of his proposals. In order to amend the Constitution a majority vote of two-thirds of each House and 51 percent of Local Congresses are needed. February 1999 proved to be a difficult time for such negotiations as few were willing to compromise with the July 2000 Presidential elections on the doorstep. In addition to these political factors there existed a lack of general awareness about the problems in the sector. To the casual observer, everything appeared to be working well – costs and quality were not out of line with the experience of most Mexicans.

Zedillo's plan sought a comprehensive reform that would introduce competition in generation, distribution, and marketing of electricity. The proposal followed closely the UK model, although studies have shown that alternative systems – such as the Australian system with a regulated market for capacity reserves – would be more appropriate in the Mexican context (Carreón Rodríguez and Rosellón, 2002a). Under the Zedillo plan, nuclear generation, some hydro generation (mainly in the south of the country), and the system operator would remain in the hands of the state – nuclear for reasons of security, and large hydro because the state manages the nation's water supplies for multiple purposes, including agriculture. The independent regulator, CRE,

---

[12] Using evidence from other Latin American countries, Mc Kinsey and Mookherjee (2003) show that this public perception contrasts with actual empirical evidence. There is no clear pattern in prices – in half the cases, reform brings lower prices – and the impact on payrolls is not large, while the fiscal effects of reform are favorable.

would oversee the aspects of the system that were prone to monopoly, such as transmission and distribution. Regulators would also ensure that generation and marketing would remain contestable activities, through monitoring of market power, barriers to entry and other factors that would undermine a competitive market.

The Zedillo plan envisioned three stages of effort. First, the government would implement basic organizational changes. CFE and LFC would be partially unbundled into several generation, transmission, and distribution companies kept at arm's length; a government-controlled system operator would be created. Separate state enterprises would be created to hold nuclear and hydro assets. And basic rules for a competitive electricity market (and its regulatory framework) would be debated. Despite the failure to implement the Zedillo plan, some progress on this first stage was already accomplished when CFE created a "shadow market" in which generators compete for service at 1,400 nodes through the use of a power flow model. Since September 2000, CFE's "shadow market" has sought to emulate a truly open, competitive market; it uses a merit order rule for dispatching generators and includes a one-day-ahead market as well as a "real-time" balancing market. In the one-day-ahead market, bids for hourly slots are submitted to CFE's system operator by thermal plants that are administratively separated so that they plan their strategy, to some degree, as different power producers.[13] Payments to generators include a "capacity" payment intended to foster the development of generation capacity reserves. In this shadow market, distribution companies are also divided into several units; a MW–Mile method is used to set transmission tariffs.[14]

The second stage of Zedillo's proposal envisioned opening the sector to private investment and the creation of a wholesale electricity market that included both short-term and long-term markets as well as competition for contracts with distributors and large users. In the final stage, the arm's-length entities would be separated fully and privatized.

---

[13] Non "programmable" generators are small producers that only supply power according to a previously set energy delivery schedule. Hydro generators also make available all their generation capacity, and face production constraints in the one-day-ahead market. Both types of generators then have zero variable costs.

[14] Through this method, charges for transmission services for 69kV and higher tension lines are calculated as the higher of "fixed plus variable costs" and "operation and maintenance costs". To this amount, fixed administrative costs are added. Fixed costs are set at the long-run incremental cost of the transmission network and allocated among consumers of the current grid and consumers of the future expanded grid according to the impact that each has on congestion in the complete network.

In addition to political obstacles, the Zedillo plan faced technical problems. It sought to balance state-of-the-art economic theory with the practical realities in the context of the Mexican power sector. One of the main omissions was the lack of a mechanism for creating incentives to expand transmission capacity. The plan envisioned that the State would neither bear risks nor provide guarantees to private investors; yet it vested transmission planning solely within the Ministry of Energy and potentially created risks that most private investors would avoid unless given a state guarantee similar to the PPA that IPP generators required. Related to this problem was the lack of incentives to address problems of short-run congestion, which in turn could create bottlenecks for new generators (Rosellón, 2005). Nor was there clarity in the incentives that would govern the system operator. Finally, it was not clear how the IPPs would be incorporated into the reform – the state would retain strategic control of the sector, but it was unclear how to square that vision with investors' requirements for predictable returns on their projects. These flaws and the many possible remedies were never given serious consideration – the upcoming election and the fragmentation of political power scuttled the Zedillo plan before the government ever had a chance to build a political coalition for its passage.

Electricity and the social contract

Although key choices about fuels and tariffs made during the 1970s would later undermine the financial sustainability of the power sector, that decade was a period of substantial progress in delivering benefits from electricity more widely to the society – what the editors call in the introduction to this book the "social contract." We focus on three dimensions: electrification of rural and poor populations, protection of the environment, and investment in long-term research and development. On all three, the accomplishments rooted in the 1970s were notable, and ironically these achievements (especially that of electrification) have reinforced public support for a state-controlled power system.

The greatest success in these three dimensions of the social contract is evident with electrification. Access to electricity more than doubled from 1970 to 1990 (see figure 5.9).Residential and agricultural tariffs declined in the 1970s, which aided electrification, but the progress in electrification has continued even through the flat and rising tariffs of the 1980s. Even as the sector has experienced enormous financial difficulties in the 1990s, electrification continued apace. By 1997, 94.7 percent of the Mexican population had access to electric power. At this writing (2003), penetration has reached 96 percent, despite the

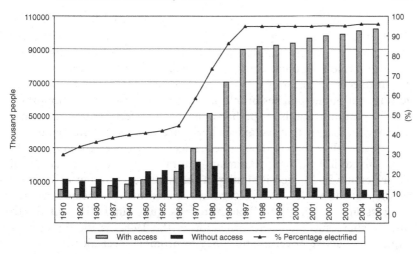

Figure 5.9. Population with access to electricity (CFE)

Table 5.6. *Correlation coefficients for the Mexican economy*

	State GDP	Urbanization	Residential Electrification	Water Services	Access to Telecommunications
State GDP	1.00	0.81	0.81	0.80	0.68
Urbanization		1.00	0.99	0.98	0.42
Residential Electrification			1.00	0.99	0.36
Water services				1.00	0.34
Access to telecommunications					1.00

country's complicated geography and remoteness of small settlements in diverse rural areas. Despite this achievement on a national level, however some states have lagged markedly – notably, Oaxaca, Chiapas, and San Luis Potosi where there is a high percentage of indigenous communities living in remote rural areas where the cost of service is high.

Many factors could explain the pattern of electrification. In table 5.6 we report simple correlations using basic demographic and economic statistics from all states between 1970 and 2000 (one observation per state per decade).[15] The correlation with electrification is highest for

---

[15] Coefficients calculated with single-year estimates for 1970, 1990, and 2000 (1980 is incomplete) reported by the government.

GDP ($R^2 = 0.81$) and urbanization ($R^2 = 0.99$). A multivariate regression confirms these simple results – urbanization has been the main driving force for electrification, and there is little residual value that might indicate a role for policy. Similar results are evident for water services, but in telecommunications the correlations are much less robust, suggesting that public policies promoting access have been more important for telecommunications or, perhaps, the cost of telecommunications has declined so sharply that factors such as urban access and income have a less intense effect than in the public services – such as electricity – where costly fixed infrastructures remain central. The story of successful electrification in Mexico is similar in many respects to that of China – factors outside the electric sector have spilled over to create dramatic progress in electrification. This history is quite unlike that of South Africa, where success in electrification in the 1990s is the direct consequence of active government policy to promote electrification.

Second, on environment, the sector is subjected to increasingly strict regulation concerning siting and effluents. The relevant norms are under renewed consideration at the present as Mexico considers the possibility for even stricter rules based on improved state-of-the-art technology. The government is in the midst of designing a credit trading system for regulating large sources of sulfur dioxide, including power plants as well as the many facilities of PEMEX. Progress on environmental issues depends heavily on the rate of technological change in the electricity sector. As in the United States, most environmental laws in Mexico "grandfather" existing facilities with weaker regulations, and thus the difficulties in the power sector that have resulted in slowing the retirement of old plants have had negative consequences for the environment. The greatest news – and good news at that – is the arrival of gas in the sector, which is mainly a function of technological improvements (gas turbines) that occurred outside Mexico as well as decisions on IPP tenders that were taken in part because gas is cheaper than the oil alternatives. The environmental benefits are a windfall.

Third, on investment in innovation, two institutions support long-run research and development in the power sector: the *Instituto de Investigaciones Eléctricas* (Electric Research Institute, IIE) and the *Instituto Nacional de Investigaciones Nucleares* (National Institute for Nuclear Research, ININ).[16] The IIE was created by Presidential Decree in December, 1975 as a public decentralized entity with legal personality

---

[16] The *Instituto Mexicano del Petróleo* (Mexican Petroleum Institute, IMP) is in charge of research on issues related to the oil industry. In this sense it is important for the power sector because of its relationship with natural gas and fuel oil.

and own patrimony, with scientific and technological character. The origin of the ININ goes back to 1956 when the Nuclear Energy Commission was created as the Institution in charge of research and regulation in nuclear issues. Later, in 1979, the National Commission on Nuclear Security and the National Institute for Nuclear Research were created to separate those activities. Since then the ININ is in charge of basic and applied research and technological development on nuclear and related matters.

The evolving agenda

Under the current legal framework for the electricity industry, private investment co-exists with the state in key areas, such as power generation. Nonetheless, the reforms implemented so far are stopgap measures – they include minor reforms in tariffs and fuel pricing implemented from 1982 to 1990, the IPP scheme created in 1992, the empowerment of CRE in the 1990s, and a new tariff schedule adopted in 2000. Each of these measures pushed crisis a bit further into the future, but the sector remains financially unsustainable. Indeed, the engine for partial reforms is now running out of steam as the gap between expected demand and supply grows and the financial needs of the sector multiply. Yet the need for reform has not commanded adequate political support, and the fragmentation of political authority has made it even harder for government to assemble viable reforms. Serious reforms will require institutions such as a truly independent regulator with substantial powers and information – all conditions that are difficult to satisfy in the current context. Moreover, serious legal problems remain as long as reformers have attempted to navigate around the constitutional restrictions on private participation in the sector. The Mexican Supreme Court ruled in 2002 that the 1992 law – the cornerstone to the IPPs and CRE's authority – might be unconstitutional, which has cast a shadow over investors. A myriad of proposals has induced madness in the public opinion on these topics as consumers (and some key actors) do not know with certainty what is going on in the sector and what to expect in the near future. Meanwhile, time is running out and Mexico is getting closer to a critical situation in its power sector. We examine each of the referred issues in turn – the need for new investment to close the gap between demand and supply, the financial sustainability of the sector, the constitutional challenge and the role of the Supreme Court, the authority and role for CRE, tariffs, public opinion, and the main current proposals for reform.

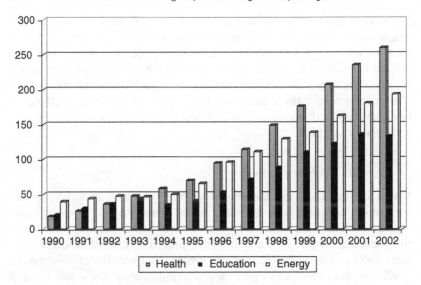

Figure 5.10. Public spending (billion pesos)

Demand, supply, and gas

The government expects that from 2001–2011 electricity demand will rise 5.6 percent per year. At present, most of the total capacity (about 44.5 GW in 2003) is supplied by hydroelectric and conventional steam plants fired mainly with oil (22 and 32 percent of the total, respectively). Combined cycle generation accounts for 24 percent, although these plants are the newest. About 44 percent of the generating power plants are at least 30 years old. If the power sector expands as expected, about $25 billion in investment will be required through 2006; from 2003–2011, the expected investment cost will exceed $50 billion, with about 40 percent for generation, 24 percent for transmission, and 21 percent for distribution. Of this total, the Ministry of Energy envisions that various private sector investment schemes, notably IPPs, will contribute $39 billion, about four-fifths of the total. Nonetheless, the (smaller) requirements in the public sector will impose an extraordinary strain on the budget and could divert resources from other social priorities such as education, social security, and poverty relief. (figure 5.10 shows public spending from 1990 to 2002.)

To serve the growing demand for power a variety of fuels is available, but one (by far) is the most attractive: gas, especially gas burned in combined cycle baseload plants. About 90 percent of the 18,700 MW of new capacity scheduled to open by 2006 is gas-fired combined cycle. By

2011, half of Mexico's expected total generating capacity of 64,000 MW will be gas fired (Secretaria de Energía, 2002b). Demand for gas will rise accordingly – about 7.4 percent per year over the next decade.[17] By 2010, perhaps 60 percent of all gas sold in Mexico will be burned for electricity generation.

This shift to gas is good news for the environment and also promises to lower tariffs. However, it is not clear how such a massive shift will be achieved. Close to the end of the Zedillo's administration, the Ministry of Energy and PEMEX announced an ambitious program, *Plan Estrategico de Gas Natural* (Strategic Plan for Natural Gas, PEG) that outlines a vision for meeting this demand, calling for PEMEX to double its natural gas production from 2002 to 2006. However, actual progress at PEMEX has been lackluster – the PEMEX budget is set by *Secretaría de Hacienda*, and as with CFE it has not received all that it requests. In tough times, PEMEX focuses on its core business, oil, and shunts gas aside. PEMEX lacks not just the capital but also the expertise to develop new gas fields, so it has turned to *Contratos de Servicios Multiples (Multiple Service Contracts, CSM)* – a scheme to allow private participation in natural gas extraction in the Burgos fields (in the northeast of Mexico) without actually conferring ownership of the fields to the non-PEMEX operators (which would contravene the Mexican Constitution, which assigns sole authority over hydrocarbons to the state). The CSMs, however, have come under a similar cloud that threatens the constitutionality of reforms in the electric sector, and most foreign operators remain wary of participation under those terms. Nonetheless, the first CSM was granted to the Spanish Oil firm Repsol-YPF during the fall of 2003.

The monopoly position of PEMEX includes not just control over fields but also pricing and retailing of gas. The current regime sets gas prices on a "netback" basis to Texas markets, which made sense when most gas was imported from Texas but yields undue windfalls to gas suppliers (i.e., PEMEX) as large indigenous supplies are envisioned. It also creates difficulties for gas-on-gas competition as LNG terminals are built and will compete for contracts with local natural gas supplies. CRE has directed PEMEX not to discriminate in its pricing and marketing of gas, but the problems are structural. Gas is used in IPPs by private investors who are stuck between a monopsony (CFE) and a monopoly (PEMEX). This situation is a damper for competition as fuel accounts

---

[17] Demand for gas in electricity generation is expected to rise rapidly (10.2% per year), but that rate will be offset by sluggish growth in self-consumption of gas in the oil sector.

for approximately 60 percent of the total costs of gas-fired electricity. The pervasive problem of competition in the gas sector extends even to the siting of power plants, which, in effect, is determined by PEMEX and its decisions about location of the gas transportation infrastructure.

Constitutional integrity: The supreme court decision and beyond

The keystone to sustaining investment in the power sector, in the context of the very limited reforms that have been implemented so far, is the 1992 amendment to the LSPEE, which created the framework for IPPs. In May 2001, President Vicente Fox proposed further reforms to Articles 126 and 135 of the LSPEE which would have modified the terms and limits of the self-generation and co-generation schemes to make them more attractive to private investors. Banking on success of this proposal, the Fox administration was already projecting that by the year 2011, about half of the country's generation would take place under the self-generation and cogeneration schemes. However, on July 4, 2001, the Mexican Congress filed a petition before the Supreme Court for review of the proposal and argued that the proposed articles envisioned giving the Executive Branch (which would control tendering and operation of these projects) more power than allowed under the Constitution.

The Supreme Court ruled in favor of Congress, but the Court did not restrict itself just to the immediate issue of separation of powers. It also speculated about the consistency of the entire LSPEE framework for private generators with Article 27 of the Constitution. The Court implied in its decision that, if asked, it would rule against the IPP scheme that had become the bedrock of efforts to expand the power system. Important investors – such as *Electricité de France*, the largest private investor in the Mexican power sector – announced that they would not participate further in the IPP scheme until further reforms that clarified their constitutional position had taken place. The Supreme Court decision illustrates that reformers must not focus on just the key legislative and regulatory actions, but must finally achieve a reform in the Constitution itself.

The Supreme Court decision has introduced yet another uncertainty into an already contentious and fractious debate. Long ago – with the Zedillo proposal of 1999 – the subject of electricity reform left the technical arena and has almost totally evolved in the political arena. Participation of the labor unions as well as the multi-dimensional negotiations between political parties are the main determinants of reform proposal success. Proposals under consideration in late 2003 ranged from PAN and President Fox's vision, for a liberalization of the sector that builds on the Zedillo proposal while rectifying important flaws, to the proposals of the PRI and the PRD (the main Parties in opposition to Fox's Party), which foresee tinkering at the margins of a system that would remain vertically integrated and organized much as it is today.[18] According to the negotiations taking place in late 2003, the proposal that is most likely to be discussed in the Congress is the one presented in the last column. This proposal was negotiated by PAN and some fractions of PRI. However, a common factor in all these proposals is the lack of technical discussion on the specifics of the electricity sector. Even the Fox proposal seems to be totally unaware of the highly complicated task of designing an electricity market under the presence of a vertically and horizontally integrated incumbent state firm. It is not clear how under such conditions there could exist a leveled playing field for entering private generators that would have to compete with generators that belong to a state holding company that is able to deliver subsidies across its different subsidiaries.

Evolution of tariffs in the near future

The direction of tariff reform remains difficult to predict, yet continued alignment of tariffs with costs is essential. We attempt to develop different scenarios for future tariffs by looking at each of the major contributors to final tariffs. At present, costs are allocated for low-voltage supply with about 35 percent for generation, 5 percent for transmission, 50 percent for distribution, and 10 percent for marketing. For residential customers, who account for 24.4 percent of the total load, the gains from distribution and marketing could only arrive via efficiency gains given the proposals. So in order to discuss some possible scenarios we assume that this 60 percent of the current cost will remain unchanged.

With respect to transmission, all the current proposals under consideration envision that the government will retain control. Therefore, any reduction in this tariff will come from efficiency gains rather than outright competition. Lower tariffs from efficiency, however, will be offset with the creation of proper incentives to invest in transmission assets. Even large changes – positive or negative – will have little effect on the final.

---

[18] For a more complete discussion, see de Rosenzweig and Femat, 2003.

Generation costs are likely to have a much larger impact on the total final tariff. Improved efficiency through competition should lower tariffs, although generation tariffs are already artificially low due to underpricing of fuel oil. Gas fueled power plants should increase efficiency, but the difficulties of attracting investors for indigenous gas production, and the rising gas price trend in North America, has given rise to the need for imports of LNG. The first such facilities are slated to open soon at Ensenada, Baja California, Altamira, Tamaulipas and Lázaro Cárdenas, Michoacán, with delivered costs of perhaps 30 percent to 50 percent higher than the price of domestic gas. However, it is important to note that LNG terminals make economic sense with prices of LNG above $4.00 per MMBtu. Although new plants should replace costly old oil-fired facilities, already those old plants, through CFE's "shadow market", are being dispatched only during peak periods, and an increased load in the future – with ever-larger residential demand – may actually result in a higher cost for peak power, which reforms will attempt to pass on to final users. The most likely effect of all these forces, we estimate, is a higher cost of generation.

Finally, one must consider the fate of subsidy policy in a reformed environment. While there will be pressure to maintain the current subsidies, we doubt that the high cost of this program – though offset a bit, perhaps, through efficiency improvements – will allow for continuation at current levels, which amount to around 50 percent of the true cost for residential consumers and 70 percent for agricultural users. Only in the case that investors mistakenly over-invest and produce a glut of low-cost baseload power is it likely that tariffs could be kept low while subsidies are also reduced.

New role of CRE

Although the creation of an independent regulatory authority in the mid-1990s was an enormous accomplishment, the powers and authority of CRE require further clarification – especially as key functions that are performed by regulators in other countries, such as setting tariffs, are actually controlled by *Secretaría de Hacienda* as an extension of government policy. Indeed, the Fox proposal for continued reform includes a further specification of CRE's role, including its role in overseeing a transparent tariff policy. A consensus is emerging that CRE should be vested with independent authority to define the rules for market operations, set tariffs, and regulate natural monopolies.

The Greatest challenge to reform: Public opinion

The fragmentation of politics in Mexico has exacted a considerable toll on the process of reform. Not only has debate over reform left the technical arena and become a completely politicized issue, but the constant debate and the lack of control by any single party in the Chamber (see table 5.2) has undercut any continuity in the reform strategy and made it difficult for critical investors to anticipate outcomes.

Moreover, available data shows that public opinion opposes privatization as well as even private investment in the energy sector. Mexicans who are even aware of the existence of reform proposals (a small minority of the public) believe that the essence of the most comprehensive reform – proposed by the Fox government – is a privatization that will undermine Mexico's sovereignty. This view is the result of a carefully manufactured public opinion by interest groups such as unions that fear (probably correctly) that reform will harm their narrow interests. Detractors have found fertile soil for sowing discontent. The 1995 financial crisis, which cost Mexico 7 percent of GDP, has led many to believe that neoliberal reforms are the cause of economic malaise. Opposition parties to the then-PRI-led government, especially the PRD, have found success in bashing technocrats as the cause of social problems and injustice in Mexico. Once the PRI lost the presidency in the year 2000 and PRI as a party has fragmented, the core of "anti-neoliberals" has swelled in number. In many other Latin American countries, the decade of liberal reforms has yielded a similar (and powerful) coalition of illiberal crusaders.[19] These voices have found it particularly easy to be heard in countries, such as Mexico, where the 1990s liberal reforms were ridden with corruption.

These observations are illustrated in a recent poll conducted in 2002 by *Coordinacion de Estudios de Opinion* (CEO). According to the poll, 36 percent of those who know about President Fox's reform bill think it is about privatizing the power sector, while only 5 percent mention attracting private investment. In that same poll, 35 percent of the population opposed private investment and only 17 percent supported a strategy of attracting new private funds in the industry. Citizens appear to fear private money almost as much as they loathe privatization. About half (49 percent) of Mexicans believe the country has electricity problems, a figure far from being overwhelming. One-third of those who think that electricity is poor cited high prices as the main problem in the

---

[19] See McKinsey and Mookherjee (2003).

sector. Of the whole sample, only 14 percent said that the quality of electric service was bad, while 33 percent said that service quality is good.

Additionally, according to the CEO survey, only 29 percent believe private investment would guarantee electricity supply in the decades to come; 28 percent believe poor and rural communities would be electrified, while 30 percent do not believe that would happen; surprisingly, only 24 percent believe the government would channel more resources to social spending, while 36 percent says that promise is false. In the same vein, only 23 percent think service would improve as a result of private investment. Moreover, the survey suggests that the public sees many dangers in reform; 60 percent believe worker rights would not be respected, and a majority believes that private investors will force higher tariffs.

Thus reformers face a problem of credibility with the public. Their mission of reform is viewed by many as unnecessary and harmful. Why should people believe that this time benefits will be fairly distributed among the population? Why should they believe that corruption will be absent? Why will reform yield better service and lower tariffs when similar (unfulfilled) promises were made for reform of, for example, the banking system?

Thus, old-fashioned popular politics, not economics or technical design, has become the most important factor explaining the failure of power reform in Mexico. One strategy for fixing this problem would be a massive campaign to alter public opinion by explaining the benefits of reform (improved service and a chance of reduced tariffs in the long run, as discussed above) and the current hidden costs to the status quo, such as subsidies that could be redirected to other social purposes. However, available data suggests that such an effort would not be very effective as citizens distrust the ability and honesty of the government to reallocate one peso saved in electricity to other worthy goals. A second strategy would entail waiting for a more favorable composition of reformers in the Chamber of Deputies and the Senate. However, this strategy depends on political variables that are outside the control of energy reformers. Moreover, the tide is turning against reform. Elections for the period 2003–2006 of the Lower House have left the PRI with a greater number of representatives, and none of the three major political parties (PRI, PAN, and PRD) have absolute domain. The Senate will face new elections only in 2006 – for this strategy, a large measure of patience and luck would be needed. A third strategy might entail striking a bargain with PRI to assure that it would not pay an electoral cost for its support of a reform bill. Despite the preferences of public opinion against energy reform, this is not a main issue in the minds of the electorate – polls show that voters care much more about employment and public security. At this writing, some efforts appear to be under way on this front. Indeed, with public opinion generally focused elsewhere, PRI may be over estimating the electoral cost, which is suggested to be minor. Although PRI may be over-estimating the cost for supporting reform, it is still unclear whether PRI would see a benefit from reform (especially if PAN, which would be most visibly identified with reform, were to reap most of the political gain if reforms were successful).

Creating a winning political coalition for reform will be especially important because many unions in the electric sector have amplified their political power by forming alliances with other unions to block reform. Even if PRI's leadership could be convinced to support reform, the party's relationship with many unions would strain. The only group with a strong interest in mobilizing in favor of reform is industrial users. They clearly face costs under the status quo and would enjoy substantial benefits from better service and more competitive tariffs.[20] To date, however, industrial consumers have been ineffective at influencing members of Congress and public opinion despite some lobbying and communication efforts. Moreover, with provisions for cogeneration and self-supply already on the books (and under lesser constitutional threat than for IPPs), the largest industrial users may actually find it cost-effective to create their own power systems and exit, largely, from the public system – as is already evident in India.

Conclusions

Many outside analysts are surprised at how much quarrel and opposition arises from attempts to reform the power sector in Mexico. To some the rhetoric and populist claims of lost sovereignty – at the expense of economic efficiency and growth – are difficult to comprehend in the modern era of open economies. A close look, however, reveals that behind the rhetoric a set of powerful economic and political incentives are at work. In contrast to the late 1980s and early 1990s, when the Mexican government implemented swift market reforms in

[20] However, industrial consumers in Mexico have had contradictory traditional positions. The price of natural gas is a clear example of this, and of the lack of credibility of the Fox government in engaging in truly efficient reforms (based on technical criterion and not on political pressures by industrial consumers). The famous story of the 4 by 3 PEMEX gas contracts is one case. Under such contracts the government offered a deal to sell one million Btus for $4 during three years. This contract was offered when this price was over $6 to $8. Industrial consumers accepted the deal; but, when prices went below $4 they rejected the contract and asked for market prices.

various economic sectors, today new reforms seem unlikely as many forces have emerged to blame market reforms as the cause of poverty, inequality and stagnation. For five decades the power sector has been dominated by consolidated, state-owned utilities that have entrenched themselves in the organization of the Mexican economy and the Mexican constitution – their position has, ironically, proved difficult to unravel now that reforms are implemented in the context of political fragmentation. These incumbents have also entrenched their position by touting important achievements such as 96 percent power access coverage – although we have shown that success on that front probably stems mainly from urbanization and economic growth. Power service appears to have improved and, more importantly, the public (in general) believes that the power system is functioning well. In the last decade, niches for private investors have been created, but the broader judicial reforms have brought even these under a cloud of constitutional contention. Without any party holding a working majority in any of the chambers, further reforms have become gridlocked. The greatest challenges that remain in the sector are complex and not visible to average citizens. They include large and inefficient subsidies in tariffs, which have made it difficult for the government to contract additional debt and have skewed government spending on a wide array of other programs. We have suggested that further power sector reform is essential as the high growth in demand for electricity is narrowing the gap with available supply, and the various stopgap measures adopted to attract investment (and delay closure of old plants) are running out of steam. Even budgets to maintain old plants have been slashed. Although it is difficult to assess, the competitiveness of the country is probably harmed – perhaps substantially – by this continued gridlock. Yet absent massive apparent difficulties, such as widespread blackouts (themselves a possibility as reserve margins recently dipped to just 1 percent), the needed consensus for reform remains elusive.

6 The political economy of power sector reform in South Africa

Anton Eberhard

Introduction

The dominant trend in the evolution of the power sector in South Africa over much of the last century was the growth and consolidation of a large and powerful state-owned, vertically integrated monopoly, Eskom. Most of the early private power producers were gradually taken over by Eskom, which became responsible for new supply. The main drivers for the increased concentration and public ownership of the industry were potential economies of scale in power plants, the requirement for large amounts of capital that could be facilitated by government guarantees, and the fact that electricity was seen as an essential ingredient of the government's industrialization strategy. At the same time, the state was also assuming a dominant role in other key infrastructure industries, including rail, air, and sea transport, telecommunications, water, coal-based synthetic fuels, nuclear energy, and also the iron and steel industry. Competition and private ownership in these sectors were thought to be non-optimal; the state viewed these industries as key instruments for industrialization, employment creation, and economic development.

However, by the 1980s poor economic performance of state-owned enterprises (SOEs), combined with broader economic and political pressures on the apartheid state, caused government to look at reforming these institutions. The management of Eskom was not fully accountable but could plan and finance excessive generation capacity. Poor investment decisions were made. The result was massive costs to the economy and, initially, to the consumer as well. At the same time, the vast majority of disenfranchised South Africans remained without electricity.

Following the democratic revolution of 1994, emphasis was given to electrification, improvements in the electricity distribution industry (EDI), the creation of an independent regulator, and the corporatization of Eskom (in parallel with reforms in other SOEs). Eskom's governance was overhauled and new commercial principles were embedded in the operation of the utility. Productivity was improved and the financial guarantees of government were removed.

The reform process has been slow and modest. Eskom remains in state ownership and there appears to be no political urgency to fully unbundle the utility. Yet Eskom has played an important role in bringing electricity to more people.

Prices are currently low (amongst the lowest in the world) because there has been no need for investment in new capacity for many years, and the cost of the older plants has mostly been amortized. But South Africa is living on borrowed time. Prices will have to rise to fund the next wave of new capacity, expected to begin in 2007. Some analysts have predicted rolling blackouts will visit South Africa without the new peak supply.

Analysts have pointed out opportunities for creating a more competitive and efficient environment for new investment decisions. However, these arguments are still not widely accepted or understood by most stakeholders. An Energy Policy White Paper and subsequent Cabinet decisions laid out a path of managed liberalization. Yet the urgency of securing new generation capacity has delayed the restructuring of Eskom. The government continues to rely on Eskom as the supplier of last resort, while at the same time opening up space for new independent power producers (IPPs).

In the first section of this chapter, we trace the historical development of the power sector and describe its key features. Next, we outline political-economic issues and the main drivers of reform. The bulk of the chapter is a section that focuses on the reforms in the Electric Supply Industry (ESI) itself. The discussion is broken down into broadly chronological key episodes where the rationale for reform, the interests of the different stakeholders, the reform models, and the outcomes of reform are analyzed. Finally, a concluding section summarizes the key linkages between the reforms and the broader political economy.

History of the electricity supply industry in South Africa

The new electrical lights and machines developed in the late nineteenth century spread rapidly around the world and South Africa was amongst the first countries to adopt these revolutionary technologies. The first electric lights in South Africa were installed at the railway station in Cape Town in the Cape Colony, barely two years after Thomas Edison invented the incandescent lamp in 1879. In 1882, the same year that the world's first central power station began operating in New York, the mining city of Kimberly in the Cape installed the first electrical street-lights in South Africa, well ahead of London which was still using gaslights. The electricity industry expanded quickly, spurred by the capital being invested in gold mining in the Transvaal Republic in the interior (Christie, 1984 and NER, 2001).

The first commercial central power station was built in 1897 by the Rand Central Electric Works and supplied electricity mainly to the gold mining industry around Johannesburg. Over the next two decades many of the mines built their own power stations and some also supplied electricity to neighboring towns. In 1906 the Victoria Falls Power Company was established, but its plans to harness hydroelectric power were soon abandoned in favor of cheaper coal-fired generation.[1] After the union of South Africa in 1910 (combining the British colonies of the Cape and Natal, with the conquered Boer Republics of the Transvaal and the Orange Free State), the pattern of power development continued to be a mixture of municipal and private utilities. The utilities had different technical standards and were governed by a diversity of provincial and municipal bylaws. An example was the Transvaal Power Act of 1910 that provided for the establishment of a Power Undertakings Board with power to license generators and distributors of electricity in a specific area (NER, 2001 p. 91).

By 1920 the concept of connecting individual power stations into a single network began to be considered, as well as the electrification of the railways and adjacent towns. The government was also promoting the development of coal and iron industries and the availability of cheap and abundant electricity was seen as essential for industrialization. The Electricity Act, No 42 of 1922, created the Electricity Supply Commission (ESCOM). Commissioners appointed by the Minister controlled ESCOM. It was given statutory powers to establish generation and distribution undertakings to supply electricity at the lowest possible cost. It had to raise capital though the issuing of bonds (although it did receive interest-bearing loans from the government in the early years[2]). ESCOM was not allowed to make a profit or a loss and was exempt from corporate income tax.

The Electricity Act of 1922 also provided for the establishment of the Electricity Control Board (ECB) to regulate electricity supply undertakings. The ECB licensed the operations of private generators and ESCOM and approved their tariffs. Municipal undertakings did not

---

[1] Typical power station sizes at this time were 40–60 MW.
[2] ESCOM received government loans only in the years 1923–1928, but by 1934 these had been fully repaid (Electricity Supply Commission Annual Reports 1923–1935).

require a license from the ECB. However, they required approval from the Provincial Administrator who, in turn, had to seek the opinion of ESCOM on whether it could not supply electricity more cheaply and efficiently. Through this mechanism, ESCOM became involved in power supply in Durban, Cape Town, and many other cities and towns. ESCOM also objected to the granting of further licenses to private producers such as the Victoria Falls Power (VFP) Company, and a compromise was reached whereby ESCOM would finance and own new power stations and the VFP Company would build and operate them (Steyn, 2001). The ECB did not resist this concentration of ownership.

The general pattern of power sector development in South Africa was not very different from that in many other countries in the early decades of the twentieth century. Large power companies integrated the full value chain from generation plants to transmission lines to retail distribution. They extinguished competition by taking over smaller companies. As the scale of investments and the opportunities for interconnection grew the state became increasingly involved, progressively advancing to a monopoly position in the sector.

ESCOM set about exploiting South Africa's huge deposits of inexpensive, low-grade coal. By 1930, electricity produced at its 100 MW Witbank station was amongst the cheapest in the world (NER, 2001). The prime minister of the time, General Smuts, stated that electricity in South Africa was

as cheap as anywhere in the world, because wasteful competition had been eliminated ... There will always be a very large field for private capital to operate in, but there are certain industries which experience has taught us can be driven better by Government without loss through wasteful competition.(Steyn, 2001, p. 67)

In 1948 ESCOM purchased the largest private producer, the VFP Company. Apart from a few industrial and mining sector self-generators, and a few small municipal generators, ESCOM now controlled most of the power stations, as well as the high voltage transmission lines. By 1973 the transmission grid was interconnected and nationally controlled. Growth in demand was rapid. New power stations were built immediately adjacent to coal mines, mostly concentrated in the north-east of the country. The coal mines were privately owned and entered into long-term supply contracts with ESCOM. Increasingly, economies of scale were sought with typical power station capacities increasing from 440 MW in the 1950s to 3,600 MW in the 1980s. While efficiencies did improve, there were also unexpected costs: longer lead-times for the construction of new generation plant ensued as well as

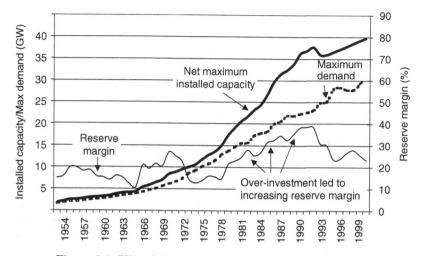

Figure 6.1. Historical growth in maximum demand and capacity at Eskom

Sources: Eskom Annual Reports, 1980–2002; Eskom Statistical Yearbooks, 1985–1996

greater interest burdens and less flexibility in the face of uncertain demand growth.

With the oil shocks of the 1970s, the economy increasingly turned to electricity. Unprecedented growth resulted in reserve margins as low as 11 percent in 1975. Annual growth in peak demand between 1972 and 1982 ranged between 6 and 16 percent. There were also initial technical problems in the scale-up of boiler designs and the use of low-grade coal. ESCOM engineers and planners were concerned that there would be power shortages and they ordered even more power stations. By the end of 1983, ESCOM had 22,260 MW of generating capacity on order, double the capacity than being operated (Steyn, 2001 p. 75; see figure 6.1).

These capacity expansions were funded through commercial debt and the issuing of bonds on the local and international capital markets. The government guaranteed these bonds and also provided foreign exchange cover through the Reserve Bank.[3] However, South Africa was experiencing a capital shortage and the cost of finance was increasing. The Electricity Act was amended in 1971 to allow ESCOM to retain substantially more earnings to build up a Capital Development Fund,

---

[3] Government guarantees for Eskom's International Bonds were only withdrawn in 1995. Personal communication: interview with Eskom Treasury Department, January 27, 2003.

subject to the approval of the state President. The consequence was large price increases disquiet amongst stakeholders who thought ESCOM's management was arrogant and unaccountable – leading, eventually, to a government inquiry in 1983. The De Villiers Commission criticized ESCOM's governance, management, electricity forecasting methods, investment decisions, and accounting.

The Commission's recommendations led to changes in the Electricity Act in 1985 and to new Eskom and Electricity Acts in 1987. ESCOM was renamed Eskom and was reconfigured with a new two-tier governance structure, modeled broadly on the German corporate governance system. A full-time executive management board now reported to an Electricity Council comprised of representatives of major electricity consumers, municipal distributors, and government representatives, all appointed by the Minister. The Capital Development Fund was abolished and Eskom's old fund accounting system replaced with standard business accounting conventions. The principle of operating at "neither a profit nor a loss" was replaced by the need to "provide the system by which the electricity needs of the consumer may be satisfied in the most cost-effective manner, subject to resource constraints and the national interest"(Eskom Act, 1987).

The principle effect of the actions that followed the De Villiers Commission was to improve the financial and commercial performance of Eskom. The changes did not, however, make Eskom any less powerful. The drafters of the new Act, who included members of ESCOM's legal department, managed to insert a clause that exempted Eskom from the requirement to have a license issued by the ECB and thus from having its prices regulated. The ECB now regulated neither Eskom nor the municipalities and was concerned simply with a few private producers on the periphery of the industry.

In principle, the new Act shifted responsibility for regulating tariffs from the ECB to Eskom's consumer-dominated Electricity Council, subject to government review and approval. In practice, consumer interests were never strongly represented on Eskom's Electricity Council. Under the influence of the strong personality of its new chairman (an influential industrialist) the Council acted more like a Board of Directors concerned chiefly with the financial health of a commercially run company. Nevertheless, Eskom's new leadership was careful to develop and retain a strategic relationship with government. A pricing compact was concluded that set out a broad price path for future years. The compact helped sustain a more arms-length relationship between government and the utility.

Table 6.1. *Dates of commissioning of major Eskom power stations*

Name of power station	Date of commercial service First–Last unit	Net maximum capacity MW
Komati	1961–1966	906
Camden	1966–1969	1520
Grootvlei	1969–1977	1130
Hendrina	1970–1977	1900
Arnot	1971–1975	1980
Kriel	1976–1979	2850
Koeberg	1976–1985	1840
Matla	1979–1983	3450
Duvha	1980–1984	3450
Tutuka	1985–1990	3510
Lethabo	1985–1990	3558
Matimba	1987–1991	3690
Kendal	1988–1993	3840
Majuba	1992–2001	3843

Source: Eskom Statistical Yearbook, 1995.

In an attempt to limit the extent of surplus capacity that was looming as a result of overplanning, construction of generation sets was delayed and plans for new stations were canceled. Older plants were decommissioned or mothballed. Previous demand growth projections of 7 percent were scaled back. Nevertheless, maximum generating capacity still exceeded peak demand by nearly 40 percent in 1992. Eskom began to promote load growth through low-cost electricity contracts to energy-intensive users, including new export-oriented minerals-beneficiation investments in aluminum and ferro-chrome. No new power stations have been ordered since the early 1980s, although the go-ahead for constructing the *last* three units of the last power station, Majuba, was delayed until 1995 and the last unit was only completed in 2001. The dates of commissioning of the major coal-fired and nuclear powered stations are shown in table 6.1. Komati, Camden, and Grootvlei were mothballed temporarily during the period of surplus capacity but are now in the process of being re-commissioned.

This pattern of overinvestment and subsequent contraction is not dissimilar to that experienced by many vertically integrated power company monopolies during the 1970s and 1980s. When economic growth was forecast to be rapid, shortages in power supply seemed imminent and vast, new expansion projects would be undertaken, mostly within a context of investors or SOE managers assuming little risk, as the costs would be passed through to electricity consumers and debt guaranteed by the state. But the investments were lumpy and

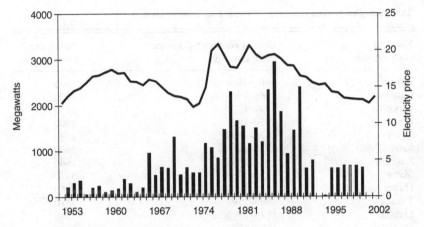

Figure 6.2. Eskom capacity expansion in MW (*bar*) and electricity price in SA cents/kWh (*line*), 1950–2000
Sources: Eskom Annual Reports, 1980–2002; Eskom Statistical Yearbooks, 1985–1996.

had long lead-times. Expected growth rates were often not realized and the inevitable consequence was wasteful overcapacity. Planning of new plants and further investment would then stop until a new potential crisis in meeting future demand would arise. The impact on prices was profound, as shown in figure 6.2. Prices rose sharply in the late 1970s and 1980s, and although they declined steadily during the 1990s, the current price is no lower than it was in 1950 or 1970, despite the apparent economies of scale that were envisaged with the larger coal-fired generation investments.

South Africa, along with many other developing countries, now faces renewed calls for capacity investment. Electricity customers have become used to cheap power from the previous generation of plant expansion whose underlying capital is largely depreciated. New capacity will inevitably require higher prices and possibly more stringent environmental standards. It was inevitable that new investment frameworks would begin to be explored.

In 1988, the first Eskom privatization study was undertaken. It was commissioned by government but managed and led by Eskom, assisted by a committee of government and industry stakeholders. The study was initiated at a time when the state was reviewing the performance of its SOEs. There was a need to attract foreign direct investment. The study review suggested that Eskom be privatized in its entirety – there were no recommendations for the introduction of competition. However, the proposals coincided with the beginnings of the secret dialogues with the African National Congress (ANC) on South Africa's political future, and were quietly dropped (Morgan, 2003).

Eskom faced a very different environment in the 1990s. The democratic revolution of 1994 unexpectedly resulted in further liberalization of the economy. The state-centered orientation of the National Party government, and also of the ANC during the years of the liberation struggle, gave way to a more market-oriented policy, which included conservative fiscal management. The state would still play a responsible role, but this would be more transparent and predictable through improved governance and regulatory frameworks and institutions. State-owned enterprises were corporatized and subject to shareholder performance contracts. Some were even privatized. Eventually the focus would turn once again to Eskom. At the same time, some stakeholders were becoming aware that a revolution was sweeping though the electricity industry worldwide. The old traditional model of a publicly owned, vertically integrated ESI was being superseded by unbundled, competitive, and mostly privately owned industries. Similar proposals were made for the reform of the South African power sector but, as we shall show later, these did not materialize.

Overview of the electricity industry in South Africa

The South African ESI remains dominated by the state-owned and vertically integrated utility, Eskom, which ranks seventh in the world in terms of size and electricity sales (Eskom, 2000). It generates about 96 percent of South Africa's electricity and more than half of the electricity generated on the African continent. Eskom owns and controls the high voltage transmission grid and it supplies about 60 percent of electricity directly to customers. The remainder of electricity distribution is undertaken by 177 local authorities that buy bulk-supplies of electricity from Eskom, while some also generate small amounts for sale in their areas of jurisdiction. A few industries have private generation facilities for their own use (see figures 6.2 and 6.3).

Of the electricity generated 91 percent is from coal, nuclear energy accounts for 6.5 percent, and bagasse, hydro, and emergency gas turbines make up the remaining 2.5 percent. Total licensed operational generating capacity in 2003 was 43GW, of which Eskom owned 39.8 GW. Some capacity is mothballed and total net Eskom operating capacity amounted to 36.2 GW. Peak demand on the system reached nearly 32 GW in 2003.

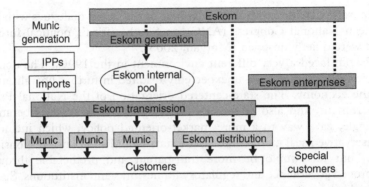

Figure 6.3. Structure of the electricity supply industry in South Africa

Eskom has twenty-four power stations: ten large coal fired stations dominate – most of them situated on coal mines in the northeast of the country. Nine of these stations have long-term coal contracts.[4] Six of these long-term coal contracts are "cost-plus" and three are "fixed price." In the cost-plus contracts, Eskom and the coal supplier jointly provide capital for the establishment of the colliery. Eskom pays all the costs of operation of the colliery and the supplier is paid a net income by Eskom on the basis of a return on the capital invested (ROI) by the coal supplier in the colliery. The ROI is divided into two components, a fixed and a variable portion. The fixed portion is a set ROI, payable irrespective of tonnages of coal supplied and the variable portion is based upon tonnages supplied to Eskom. The ROI is generally escalated for half of the duration of the contract and is typically between 15 and 25 percent. In the fixed price contract, coal is supplied at a predetermined price (i.e. a base price which is escalated by means of an agreed escalation formula). There are no early termination provisions in the contracts. Coal costs in South Africa are regarded amongst the cheapest in the world. Although it is Eskom's stated intention to reduce its reliance upon long-term coal supply contracts, more than 90 percent of Eskom's coal is still procured in this way.

Africa's only nuclear station is at Koeberg, 30 kilometers north of Cape Town, and is also owned and operated by Eskom. There is modest hydro capacity on the Orange River (located on two dams) and there are two pumped storage schemes, which play a critical role in meeting peak

---

[4] The tenth largest coal-fired power station, Majuba, operates at variable output on a small medium-term coal contract.

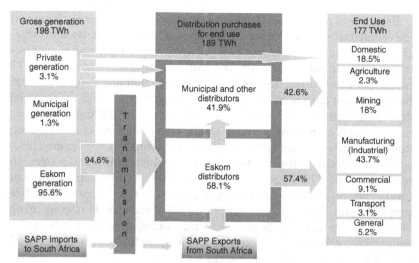

Figure 6.4. Energy flows in the electricity supply industry in South Africa, 2000
Source: National Electricity Regulator.

demand, as well as in system balancing and control. Municipalities own twenty-two small power stations and back-up gas turbines, but these total only 5 percent of national generation capacity and generally run at low load factors. Private generators comprise the remaining 2 percent of capacity (Eskom, 2001 and NER, 2001a).

South Africa sells electricity to neighboring countries (Botswana, Lesotho, Mozambique, Namibia, Swaziland, and Zimbabwe) representing about 3 percent of total net energy produced. Contractually it is bound to take electricity from Mozambique's Cahora Bassa hydroelectric station on the Zambesi. Eskom also imports some power from the Democratic Republic of Congo and from Zambia – mainly for peak load management.

Eskom operates an internal pool, which generates an optimal dispatch schedule. The system operator and the procurement of auxiliary services are part of Eskom. Eskom owns the national, integrated transmission grid (with the exception of the Motraco line which is jointly owned with the utilities in Swaziland and Mozambique). The national grid comprises 27,000 km of high voltage lines, the bulk of it at 400 and 275 kV. Transmission energy losses are less than 4 percent. There are an additional 330,000 km of low-voltage lines owned by Eskom and local authorities.

Eskom sells most of its electricity as bulk power to its large mining and industrial customers and municipalities. These three customer categories account for 82 percent of its revenue and 89 percent of its electricity sales. In addition to the 3.4 million customers serviced by 177 municipal distributors, Eskom itself operates retail distribution services for 3.1 million customers. The average selling price in 2003 to industrial customers was about 2 cents/kWh and for residential customers was 5.5 cents/kWh. Eskom average tariffs cover average costs (Eskom, 2003).[5] Tariffs for rural and low-income residential customers are cross-subsidized from industrial tariffs and surpluses earned on sales to municipalities. The large municipalities, in turn, make an additional profit from reselling Eskom electricity, which enables them to subsidize property rates and to finance other municipal services. However, many of the smaller municipalities face debt, nonpayment by a substantial proportion of their low-income consumers, inefficient operations and lack of technical and managerial capacity.

Nationally, there has been an impressive electrification drive and the proportion of households with access to electricity has risen from one-third in 1993 to nearly 70 percent in 2004. In the years 1994–2001, 3.5 million households were electrified. About two-thirds of these connections were accomplished by Eskom and the remainder by local authorities. Until the late 1990s – when restructuring of the industry forced a reassessment by Eskom (discussed in more detail later) – the capital costs for these connections had been provided by Eskom and amounted to a direct subsidy to new low-income households on the order of $1.5 billion (R 9.88 billion in nominal values), with an average cost of connection of about $450 (NER, 2001). The electrification program has resulted in significant increases in peak demand in the morning and early evenings with profound implications for future generation plant mix. The next requirement for capacity addition will be for peaking plants, such as gas turbines or pumped storage schemes. The need for demand-side management programs is also becoming more apparent.

Eskom has grown a significant R&D capacity over the years. Research emerged from its engineering division and still focuses mainly on "sweating assets," that is, incremental improvements that lower costs and increase efficiencies in its main generation, transmission, and distribution businesses. However, Eskom has also devoted R&D resources to environmental issues, end-use technologies, and alternative and future energy technologies, including the development of a new generation

[5] Assuming an exchange rate of 1 US$ = R6.5.

"pebble-bed" nuclear reactor. R&D expenditure increased rapidly in the 1990s and amounted to about 0.8 percent of total revenue (Hofmaenner, 2002).

Political and economic context in the 1990s

The reforms in the electricity industry in South Africa over the past decade – to which we turn in the next section – have taken place within a context of radical transformation of the political, economic, and social institutions in the country. After decades of institutionalized racial segregation and discrimination, the minority white government in the late 1980s faced overwhelming opposition from the majority of South Africans and sustained international pressure, including selective economic sanctions. International lenders refused to roll over outstanding loans. Internal resistance was intensifying. Choices were becoming narrower. Either the leaders of the apartheid state would take South Africa down a path of increasing political violence and diminished wealth, cut-off from the international community, or they could begin to negotiate a new democratic future. Responding to these pressures, in 1990 the government removed the ban on the ANC and freed Nelson Mandela from prison.

The ANC won the first democratic elections in 1994 with 63 percent of the vote, and for the first few years there was a Government of National Unity with representatives of the other major parties in the Cabinet. The new government in 1994 represented an overwhelming majority of South Africans, and its style of governance was to make policy debates and decisions much more visible – in sharp contrast to the closed, elitist system of apartheid governments that had concentrated economic and social opportunities in the hands the white minority.

The ANC's economic philosophy in exile had been broadly socialist. Indeed, the first ANC-led government adopted the Reconstruction and Development Program (RDP) – an integrated policy platform that set out a Marshall Plan-like program for social and economic advancement centered on the development of infrastructure in poor communities. The RDP promised to redistribute land; promote affirmative action; create employment; provide houses, electricity and water, and attack poverty and deprivation (Marquard and Eberhard, 2000).

While the RDP did deliver some important benefits, for example in areas such as electricity and water provision, the new government soon faced macroeconomic constraints. Under the previous National Party government, the budget deficit before borrowing had soared to an unsustainable 7 percent of GDP. The RDP was superseded by the Growth, Employment and Redistribution (GEAR) policy, essentially a conservative, macroeconomic plan that aimed to reduce the budget deficit, increase growth rates, lower inflation, reduce trade tariffs, stabilize the currency, and create jobs. Some of GEAR's critics have labeled it as a self-imposed structural adjustment program.

The shift to GEAR was symptomatic of a re-alignment of priorities from social to macroeconomic challenges. The budget deficit has since declined to around 2 percent of GDP. Industry and agriculture have become much more competitive. Economic growth, although steady at about 3 to 4 percent per year, is far below the 6 or 7 percent that would be needed to cause a significant decline in unemployment (currently in excess of 30 percent).

The trade union alliance partners of the ANC have been particularly critical of the fiscal conservatism of the government and its policy of economic liberalization. They have argued that privatization of state enterprises will harm the provision of services to the poor. They also fear further job losses. The government has had to factor these concerns to its reform agenda, but it has not radically changed its policies, nor is that likely. The government argues that its policies have avoided the economic shocks and recessions being experienced by many other emerging economies. Public debt is relatively low and the interest burden is declining, thus allowing more scope for social expenditure.

The main challenges for the economy are now increasing the level of private investment, lifting growth rates, creating employment, and building the capacity to increase the rate and quality of delivery of services for the poor. The state is also pushing hard to increase the ownership and participation of blacks in the economy. Currently, the value of majority-owned black companies comprises less than 5 percent on the Johannesburg Securities Exchange. Targets have been set in the minerals and petroleum industry of at least 25 percent ownership by 2010, and attention is being given to opportunities in the electricity industry.

There has been a plethora of legislation since 1994 that has sought to restructure and reform the economy and society to address the inequities and injustices of the past, and to advance the principles of justice and development enshrined in the constitution. The political negotiations leading to democracy led to a new progressive Constitution and Bill of Rights, internationally admired for its protection of first generation rights (such as protection of individual liberty, property and freedom of expression), combined with second and third generation development-oriented rights which place obligations on the state to advance individuals' and communities' access to healthcare, shelter, a clean environment, etc. One of the important revisions has been the rewriting of labour law to provide the kinds of protection afforded employees in mature social democracies.

The above shifts in the political economy of South Africa in the 1990s help to explain the context for reform of the electricity sector. The ANC inherited an economy with large SOEs, not only in the electricity sector, but also in telecommunications and transportation. It is committed to utilizing these SOEs to fulfill national and social goals. For example, Eskom and Telkom have been tasked with the accelerated rollout of services for the poor. But at the same time, the thrust of its GEAR policies is to improve economic efficiency. This has translated into a process of gradual reform and restructuring of the SOEs. The trend has been towards further liberalization of markets, increased competition and even privatization, although the latter policy has been tempered by the fact that government is not desperate for privatization revenues as public debt is within manageable bounds.

Drivers of electricity sector reform

Most analysts identify three or four broad drivers for power sector reform internationally. First, there is the desire to improve investment and operational efficiencies that blight the performance of monopoly utilities – especially SOEs that are not accountable to shareholders. Second, the need for massive new capacity expansion places increased demands for finance not readily available from public sources, which calls for greater reliance on private sector involvement. Third, restructuring and privatization create the opportunity for redistributing the rents and assets of the electric power system and for unlocking economic value or reducing government debt. Some have identified other country-specific drivers, such as the felt need to follow the wave of reform that is now so powerfully sweeping through nearly all power sectors around the world.

It is probably true to say that none of these drivers are experienced strongly in South Africa. Most stakeholders believe that Eskom operates reasonably efficiently. South Africa has a well-functioning bond market and Eskom has had no serious problem financing expansion through raising private capital. Public finances are well managed and the National Treasury does not have a desperate need for privatization receipts. And the impacts of international trends in power sector reform are not widely appreciated locally. Eskom would prefer to stay as it is and will delay reforms as long as it is able.

Yet, the electricity sector in South Africa has undergone a number of changes during the 1990s and it is possible to identify specific factors that have influenced these reforms. In the period leading to the democratic revolution in 1994, attention was given to the fact that apartheid policies had resulted in a highly fragmented local government system with poorly performing service delivery departments. At the same time, there was a massive backlog in electricity connections to black households. The need was for consolidation of electricity distributors in order to improve financial viability and technical performance, and to position them for more effective service delivery.

A second reform driver emerged in the mid-1990s within the context of government economic policy that sought to improve efficiencies in the SOEs. Although Eskom was generally regarded as being better managed than other SOEs, there was a new focus on the corporatization of these entities through re-defining the relationship of the state as shareholder, clarifying tax obligations and putting in place performance contracts.

A third reason for reforming the electricity industry was expressed in a new comprehensive energy policy in the mid- to late- 1990s. Policy analysts pointed out the need to avoid the mistakes of the past when Eskom heavily overinvested in capacity expansion, and to create an industry structure that allocates risk in a manner that encourages investment efficiency (Business Map, 2001). The need for new generation capacity has raised the question of whether Eskom should build the next power station and what the appropriate industry and market structure is to encourage private investment.

A fourth driver for reform has become more apparent in recent years. There are discernable pressures for an accelerated process of black economic empowerment, including calls for the state to divest generation assets into private ownership. The effect of this reform driver is to reinforce the need to restructure the industry so that privatization does not simply create a private monopoly, but is accompanied by moves to achieve a more competitive electricity industry structure.

Inefficiencies in the distribution industry and responding to electrification backlogs

At the beginning of the 1990s the issue of overriding concern was the financial problems of the electricity distributors and the low levels of access to electricity. There were simply too many small, poorly run municipal distributors that were not financially viable and that were not in a position to provide expanded services to existing customers, as well as to those still not connected.

Many of these problems are the legacy of the apartheid era and the creation of separate local black municipalities. The electricity departments in these areas struggle with lack of technical capacity, a paucity of income-generating industrial customers, and a huge backlog in new connections for low-income consumers. Some of these smaller municipal distributors have already been amalgamated into larger entities, but most of them still lack viability. Nonpayment from customers has compounded the problem of accumulating debts to Eskom (the supplier of bulk power). Many distributors have also curtailed spending on essential maintenance needed to assure security and reliability of supply.

The fragmentation of the industry means that tariffs for the same customer categories vary widely between distributors. It has proved impossible to regulate the large number of distribution entities effectively. Reporting has been inadequate and it has been difficult to obtain accurate information on costs. Given all these problems and uncertainties, it has also been difficult to attract and retain skilled, motivated and adequately paid employees and managers in the industry (Mlambo-Ngcuka, 2001 and DME, 2001).

Rationalization and consolidation of the EDI is essential to create a sustainable platform for the delivery of reliable and affordable electricity services to existing customers as well as for supporting electrification for those who still remain without access to electricity.

Restructuring of state-owned enterprises

A second driver of reform in the electricity supply industry originated in the "self-imposed" structural adjustment program initiated in the mid-1990s. Having re-established macroeconomic stability, the emphasis moved to microeconomic reforms, including a new focus on improved efficiencies in government-owned entities. In August of 2000, DPE published "A Policy Framework: An Accelerated Agenda towards the Restructuring of State Owned Enterprises." Because of union pressure and also concerns within its own political constituency, the government has been careful to avoid the "P word" (privatization) and described its restructuring agenda thus:

Government's policy with regard to State Owned Enterprises is more properly referred to as a *restructuring* program, and not in the more simplistic terms of privatization. The program was and remains designed around a multiple array of strategies, or mixes of options, that are designed to ensure the maximization of shareholder interests defined in economic, social and development terms. Thus restructuring refers to the matrix of options that include the redesign of business management principles within enterprises, the attraction of strategic equity partnerships, the divestment of equity either in whole or in part where appropriate, and the employment of various immediate, turnaround initiatives.

At the enterprise and sector level, restructuring involves improving the efficiency and effectiveness of the entity, accessing globally competitive technologies where appropriate, mobilizing private sector capital and expertise, and assisting the creation of effective market structures in sectors currently dominated by the SOEs. At a broader, macroeconomic level, restructuring initiatives aim to attract private direct investment, to contribute to the reduction in the public borrowing requirement, and to assist the development of an economic context that promotes industrial competitiveness and finances growth. Social imperatives include the need to ensure growth in employment, particularly in new areas of endeavor, and to rationalize or develop new skills within the labor force and their deployment throughout the country.

The government decided to focus its restructuring efforts on the four largest SOEs, one of which was Eskom. Although created through statute, Eskom's ownership status had never been formally defined. It paid no taxes and there was no formally expressed set of performance expectations or obligations. The government wished to clarify its relationship with the utility and to formalize a performance contract.

Investment in the electricity supply industry

At first glance, Eskom appears to have performed well. It supplies electricity at among the lowest prices in the world; the average cost of electricity generated is below 1.5 cents/kWh. In recent years, it has consistently made a positive return on assets. Reliability and quality of supply are good. Average energy availability from its power stations has increased from 76 percent in 1991 to 92 percent in 2000.[6] Labor productivity has increased and employee numbers have dropped from over 66,000 in 1985 to 46,600 in 1991 and to 31,900 in 2003. Eskom is now commercially run with no recourse to the national fiscus. It raises finance through commercial debt, mostly through issuing bonds, which are well supported by local and international capital markets.

Eskom's recent low prices and exemplary electrification performance have left the impression that it is highly efficient and that there is no need for reform. Many would simply equate low prices with high efficiency. However, this is not necessarily the case. There may be specific factors that account for Eskom's low prices compared to other international utilities and there may be little hard evidence of superior efficiency (Steyn, 2001; Davis and Steyn, 1998).

---

[6] Availability is defined as capacity hours available × 100/total capacity hours in year.

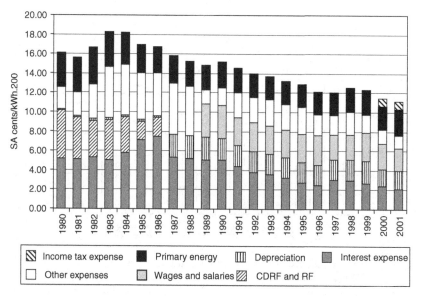

Figure 6.5. Cost trends at Eskom
Notes: [a]The Capital Development Fund was abolished after 1986;
wages and salaries were not reported separately before 1989.
Source: Eskom Annual Reports.[a]

A close examination of the South African ESI shows that low prices
and the ability to fund electrification have emanated, in part, from very
low coal prices (by international standards) and, until recently,
exemption from taxation and dividends (Steyn, 2000). Nevertheless, if
long-term price trends are examined (see figure 6.2, above) it will be
noted that, in real terms, prices today are no lower than in 1950 and
1970. This would seem to indicate that Eskom has not improved its
performance as much as would have been hoped.

Low Eskom prices today stem primarily from the fact that consumers
have largely amortized the debt, which funded the large investment
program of the 1980s that has provided the generation capacity currently
being used. Eskom has not had to invest significantly in new generation
capacity for some years and the largest contribution to lower overall costs
(and prices) has been lower debt and financing costs. Eskom's debt to
equity ratio fell from 2.93 in 1986 to 0.09 in 2003 (Eskom, 2003).

While operational efficiencies are important, investment efficiencies
often have a much more profound and long-lasting impact. Choices of
fuel-type, technology, financing, investment-timing, and construction
lead-times determine the primary cost structure of the generation plant.

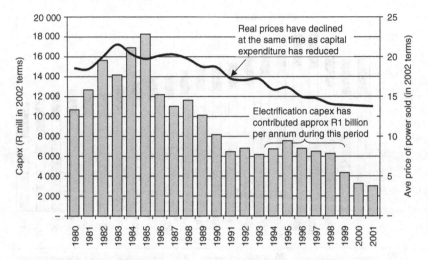

Figure 6.6. Eskom capital expenditure and price trends
Source: Econ, 2002.

The difference that can be made by good investment decisions is often larger than the incremental productivity improvements that can be made in plant operations. Figure 6.5 shows the extent to which changes in financing charges affect overall costs and hence prices.

This analysis of Eskom's investment record is not widely shared in South Africa. Most equate low prices with efficient performance. Few recall the debacle of Eskom in the late 1970s and early 1980s, the high price hikes, and the criticisms of Eskom's governance and management. Few understand the consequences of the massive overinvestment. Tariff reductions in the 1990s have erased memories; the overall standing and image of Eskom in the 1990s was much improved.[7] However, Eskom is now keen to see prices rise to levels that can support the new investment that is now necessary (see figure 6.6). Gradually, more stakeholders are coming to understand that current prices are economically unsustainable (Econ, 2002).

The National Electricity Regulator's Integrated Resource Plan suggests that by 2025 total maximum demand could rise to 60 GW. New peaking capacity might be needed on line as soon as 2007 – perhaps earlier – and additional base load capacity is probably necessary by

---

[7] Through a series of pricing compacts with the government, Eskom committed itself to a price decrease of 20% between 1992 and 1996, and a 15% reduction between 1994 and 2000. Actual price reductions were a little less than this.

2012. Options being considered are demand-side management, re-commissioning the mothballed coal-fired stations, gas turbines, pumped storage and new coal-fired power stations. Important investment decisions will have to be made soon. The primary policy challenge is to design an industry structure that provides the incentives to optimize investment efficiencies in the future (NER, 2002). The government is beginning to open up spaces for private sector investors in new generation capacity.

Black economic empowerment

One driver for reform being articulated in the political domain is the need to accelerate black economic empowerment. Eskom's assets are seen as attractive and a portion could be offered on a preferential basis to black South Africans, thereby widening economic ownership. However, it does not make economic sense to privatize a monopoly industry. If new private players are introduced, then the industry should be restructured to encourage competition (DME/DPE, 2000). This implies an unbundling of Eskom, through separating out the potentially competitive components of the industry (generation and retail) from the natural monopoly components (transmission and distribution). Thus the imperative of Black Economic Empowerment might become a key driver for the reform and restructuring of the electricity sector in the future. For now, however, these aspirations are frustrated by the government's renewed commitment to keep Eskom in state ownership.

Key achievements in the reform of the electricity sector since 1990

Despite these motivations for reform, the process has often been slow and uncertain. One reason is that there has never been a single, powerful champion for reform, either in government or amongs stakeholders. There has also been a lack of continuity in key personnel in government departments. Institutional memory and capacity have often been lost and have then had to be rebuilt.

Nevertheless, some key milestones have been reached. The 1990s saw the launch of a major electrification program with structured subsidies. A new National Electricity Regulator (NER) was established to protect the interests of consumers and to promote efficiency within the ESI. And a decision was reached on rationalizing distribution industry. These three milestones were greatly facilitated by the formation of a National Electrification Forum, a body that had wide representation of all interested stakeholders in the industry, and that mirrored a multitude of parallel negotiating processes in South Africa's move to democracy. A new national energy policy was finalized, including broad policy objectives and restructuring principles for the electricity sector. Eskom was corporatized and an industry restructuring plan was developed. However, plans to unbundle Eskom and to introduce a competitive electricity market have been put on hold. Eskom will remain for the time being under state ownership while private independent power producers (IPPs) are being introduced on the margin of the electricity market.

The section below highlights the key achievements in the reform of the electricity industry, the motivations and rationalization behind each reform episode, and the competing stakeholder interests that shaped the reforms.

Serving the poor: an accelerated national electrification program

The first significant change in the electricity industry was the recognition that urgent attention had to be given to providing electricity to the majority of South Africans. With the exception of some studies in the 1980s that highlighted the inequity of electricity provision, little data existed documenting the demand from un-served households.[8] Nearly all white South Africans, including remote farms, had electricity connections; few black households had access. Some researchers began to map out what a national electrification program might look like and argued that it would be important to restructure the inefficient distribution industry (e.g. Dingly, 1990; Theron et al., 1992). The changes in the political landscape in South Africa after 1990 lent some urgency to these calls for action.

Eskom, in anticipation of the shift to political democracy, and sitting with excess electricity generating capacity, announced in 1991 the target of electrifying 700,000 new households by 1997 (Eskom, 2001). The program was backed by a new call from its CEO, Dr. Ian McCrae, for "electricity for all." There were some high-profile initiatives in Elandskraal, Orange Farm and Soweto, which in hindsight can be seen as an attempt to position Eskom favorably in relation to a possible new black majority government – and the ANC in particular. But overall progress

---

[8] One such study is Eberhard (1984). Energy and poverty in urban and peri-urban areas around Cape Town. Second Carnegie inquiry into poverty and development in Southern Africa. Conference Paper No 155, University of Cape Town. When Eberhard asked municipal electrical engineers for maps and plans of areas that had access to electricity and those that did not, they were unable to produce any coherent or integrated picture. Planning for those who were unserved was simply nonexistent.

was slow. The Energy and Development Research Centre (EDRC) at the University of Cape Town argued for an accelerated program of electrification that would peak at 500,000 connections per annum and would electrify 85–90 percent of South Africans by 2010. The proposals were supported by detailed modeling and included recommendations for financing and institutional change (Eberhard and van Horen, 1995).

In February 1992, EDRC convened a national meeting on electrification on behalf of the un-banned African National Congress (Theron, 1992). The seminar brought together members of the industry with political parties, trade unions and civic organizations. From that meeting emerged the idea for a national conference on electrification and the creation of a negotiating forum involving all stakeholders. After two national conferences, involving more than seventy organizations, the National Electrification Forum (NELF) was launched in May 1993 (NER, 2001, p. 70).[9] It established working groups and initiated a number of studies, including the National Electrification Economic Study (NEES, 1993), which further developed a range of scenarios and assessed their economic impact. All stakeholders supported an accelerated electrification program.

The ANC's Reconstruction and Development Program, influenced by the above work, formalized the goal of electrifying 2.5 million new homes between 1994 and 1999, a goal that was exceeded by the new democratically elected government (ANC, 1994; see table 6.2 and figure 6.7).

Until the year 2000 the entire electrification program was funded by Eskom, either through internal subsidies (garnered mainly from higher-than-cost electricity charges to large industrial and mining customers), or through transfers to an electrification fund that the NER allocated to municipalities. The average annual capital expenditure on this program has been around $ 175 million.

Since the mid-1990s it has been national policy that a portion of the capital cost of connections should be subsidized (DME, 1998, p. 37). In practice, the subsidy has extended to the entire cost of connection plus a portion of the operating costs. Actual consumption of electricity in low-income homes has been much lower than forecast – thus revenues from

---

[9] The Management Committee of NELF consisted of representatives of the Association of Municipal Undertakings, the African National Congress, the Chamber of Mines, the Department of Mineral and Energy Affairs, the Development Bank of Southern Africa, Eskom, the National Union of Metal Workers, the National Union of Mine Workers, the South African Agricultural Union, the South African National Civic Organization, and the United Municipal Executive.

Table 6.2. Number of new connections to low-income households since 1991

Year	1991	1992	1993	1994	1995	1996	1997	1998	1999	2000	2001	TOTAL
Eskom	31035	145522	208801	254383	313179	307047	274345	280977	293006	250801	206103	2565199
LA's	51435	74335	107034	164535	150454	137534	213768	136074	144043	139780	127255	1446247
Farm workers	12698	16074	16838	15134	9414	11198	10375	6241	6438	3560	107970
Total	82470	232555	331909	435756	478767	453995	499311	427426	443290	397019	336918	4119416

Source: NER, 2001.

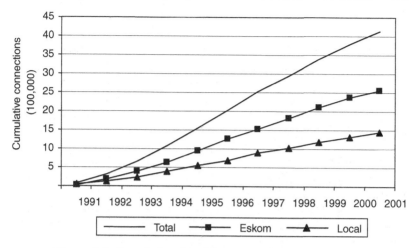

Figure 6.7. Cumulative electricity connections 1991–2001

electrification have also fallen short of plan. At the beginning of the program it was estimated that the average monthly consumption of newly connected, low-income households would be 350 kWh per month (compared with an average of 750 kWh per month for a middle-income family in South Africa). However, actual average monthly consumption has been less than a third of these estimates. The government has granted 50 kWh per month free to poor consumers.

Nearly all of these new connections have used pre-payment technology – customers buy tokens or add electricity credits to electronic cards to activate their electricity dispenser. The costs of the electricity supply and use were to be recovered through a flat energy unit charge. Many connections involve informal houses (shacks) and use pre-wired "ready boards" – typically with a few lights and plug points.

As the government begins to reform the power sector, it has moved to secure the national electrification program through establishing a separate National Electrification Fund in the Department of Minerals and Energy, funded by the National Treasury. Eskom now pays taxes and has stated that it will no longer subsidize the electrification program from internal income.

This experience is important as it demonstrates that the meeting of social goals and public benefits can be independent of industry structure. Electrification was carried out by the old vertically integrated, publicly owned utility, Eskom, and by local government distributors. The electrification program will continue despite restructuring of the electricity market in South Africa. Explicit policy and regulatory instruments have been put in place to ensure the continued commitment to move to universal access to electricity in South Africa.[10]

In addition to the grid electrification program, there has been an active off-grid program using photovoltaic technology. Between 1994 and 2000, 1350 schools were electrified with off-grid systems. Many rural health clinics have been equipped with solar systems. In addition, the government has awarded subsidy concessions to private industry service providers in five geographic areas to supply solar home systems – consisting usually of a 50W photovoltaic panel and a battery, wired for low voltage DC service – as well as supplementary fuels such as liquid petroleum gas for high energy tasks (notably cooking). These are not geographically exclusive concessions; other companies may also operate in the areas. However, the concessionaire in each geographic area receives an exclusive subsidy of around $ 500 per installation. The rationale is to assist service providers in building up adequate service infrastructure and to move towards financial sustainability. Supply targets and service standards have been set and performance will be monitored. The basic consumption subsidy for low-income users is also being made available.

The concession system has suffered teething problems and its future is uncertain. The tender process was far from perfect – for example, firms have bid on factors such as service quality (which is hard to measure) but not on the level of subsidy. Entrants have been few. Opportunities to encourage efficiency and cost competition have not been tapped fully. Nevertheless, there has been considerable innovation in the business models and vending technologies. Most suppliers have adopted a fee-for-service approach rather than the out rightsale of solar home systems, although the best approach is still a subject of vigorous debate.

The electrification program in South Africa is remarkable in a number of respects. Doubling access to electricity from one-third to two-thirds of the population in a matter of years is probably without international

---

[10] The claim that the success of public benefit programs, such as widened access to affordable electricity by the poor, is largely independent of the structure and ownership form of the electricity industry, is often contested. However, it is possible to provide examples of vertically integrated, publicly owned utilities doing either an impressive job of electrification (e.g., Eskom in South Africa) or, in contrast, a disastrous job (e.g., the majority of utilities in Africa). Equally it is possible to provide examples of electrification being advanced by privately owned, competitive utilities (e.g., in Chile) or where privatization has slowed electrification. The point is that the most important variable for the success of public benefit programs is not industry structure or ownership form, but rather the existence or lack of explicit public policies, regulatory instruments, dedicated implementing institutions, and funding to achieve desired social goals.

precedent. The program was clearly driven by the unique challenges that South Africa faced in overcoming the legacy of apartheid inequity. Yet there are lessons from this program that have more universal relevance. The South African experience demonstrates that it is possible to make substantial progress in widening access to electricity services for the poor, even as electricity industries are restructured. Although Eskom has not yet been unbundled or privatized, it has faced pressures to operate on a sound commercial basis, and has discontinued internal subsidies for new electricity connections. The electrification program was driven by the advent of democracy and a political commitment to provide services for the poor. It was made possible by an electricity industry that was technically competent and financially strong. And it has been put on a sustainable basis through explicit policy and regulatory instruments that will give expression to the government's social goals, even when the electricity industry is unbundled and possibly privatized.

A new electricity regulator

A second major element of reform was improved protection of electricity customers through the establishment of an independent regulator with control over the entire electricity industry. Eskom and municipalities would need to be brought under the jurisdiction of a regulator that would operate within a clear and transparent legal mandate to license *all* electricity suppliers, approve their tariffs, monitor the quality of supply and settle disputes. The Electricity Control Board (ECB), established in 1922, was hobbled by its lack of direct control over municipal electricity undertakings. The Electricity Act of 1987 also exempted Eskom from having to obtain a license.

One of the key recommendations to emerge from the NELF in 1993/4 was that the ECB should be replaced by an NER with wider powers to regulate the electricity supply industry. In October 1994, the Cabinet approved the NELF recommendations for the establishment of the NER. By 1995 NER was constituted legally as an independent institution. The only significant exemption to its authority over the industry was for persons selling less than 5 GWh of electricity per annum and self-generators with capacities of 500 kW or less. All others – Eskom, state departments, and local distributors – fell under NER's authority.

In hindsight it is curious that the one concrete accomplishment of NELF was the establishment of an independent regulator with jurisdiction over the entire electricity supply industry. Its original focus was on reforming the debt-laden distributors and on accelerating the electrification of all households. Yet there were some constituencies within

NELF and its working groups, mainly researchers/analysts and some senior Eskom staff, who recognized that it was an anomaly for Eskom, with its virtual monopoly in generation and transmission, and for local authorities, with their distribution area monopolies, to be exempt from regulation. Some had traveled to look at electricity sector reform in other countries and one had attended the first National Association of Regulatory Utility Regulators (NARUC) training course in the United States. Perhaps there was the desire to create a more predictable and transparent operating environment for the electricity industry during a period of political and institutional uncertainty.

Many of the initial staff in the NER were ex-Eskom employees. Over time, the NER has built its own staff and emerged as one of the more respected independent regulatory institutions in the African continent and its mandate has been extended to include also gas and petroleum pipelines. Nevertheless the NER still faces huge challenges in terms of building sufficient capacity to regulate Eskom and the many municipal distributors, as well as preparing for a new, competitive market in the future. Indeed, the creation of new, stable, and competent institutions in developing countries and emerging economies is a formidable task, particularly when there is little tradition and experience of independent regulation.

Restructuring the electricity distributors

One of the key concerns of most of the stakeholders represented in NELF was the restructuring of the EDI to improve efficiencies, make distribution financially viable, and to ensure that the EDI would be able to meet the ambitious tasks of the national electrification program. These concerns were not always shared by the large metropolitan governments who had gained surplus income from the sale of electricity and feared loss of that revenue. Local government, as represented by the South African Local Government Association (SALGA) and through the Association of Municipal Electrical Undertakings (AMEU) has been ambivalent in their support for the need for restructruing. Eskom was an early supporter of EDI restructuring in principle, although in practice it has often resisted reforms that would strip it of its distribution services (Eskom, 1990). The unions, on the other hand, have strongly advocated distribution reforms that would create one single, publicly owned national distributor.

After the elections of 1994, many of the negotiating forums that had been set up during the transition period to democracy were dissolved. In February 1995 NELF was disbanded. In the meantime, the NER had been established and was a potential vehicle for furthering reform. Its

Board considered whether restructuring the distribution industry could be forced through the licensing process (which it controlled) or whether further legislation from government would be required. It decided on the latter option and requested permission to convene an Electricity Working Group (EWG) to further develop proposals to restructure the EDI. The EWG comprised representatives from the NER, government, Eskom, and the municipalities, but excluded unions and civic organizations. They evaluated the work of NELF and submitted a report to the government with specific options for restructuring the industry. The government then set up an internal Electricity Restructuring Inter-departmental Committee (ERIC), which made recommendations to the Cabinet. After a long and convoluted process the Cabinet approved in principle, in May 1997, the consolidation of the EDI into the maximum number of financially viable and independent Regional Electricity Distributors (REDs). In June 1999, the Cabinet agreed that there should be six REDs. A new national, publicly owned EDI Holdings Company would be established to manage the rationalization and consolidation process.

The central problem for creating the REDs was drawing the boundaries. To be viable, each RED would require the right balance of below-cost (low-income residential) and above-cost (commercial and industrial) users. In early 2000 the government appointed a consortium, led by consultants PriceWaterhouseCoopers (PwC), to undertake detailed modeling and also the detailed planning to rationalize the REDs. They produced working papers on subjects such as the REDs' boundaries, ownership, asset valuation, regulation and human resources. Those papers became the basis for workshops and, in turn, led PwC to produce a synthesis paper in June 2000. The Government's Electricity Distribution Industry Restructuring Committee (EDIRC) – comprising relevant government departments, Eskom, local government, and the NER – oversaw the process and produced its own "Blueprint for EDI Reform" (DME, 2001).

As the EDI restructuring proposals were presented to the Cabinet Committee for the Economic and Social Sectors – starting in November 2000 – it was clear that all relevant Ministers had not been properly briefed, and some had not engaged in the process at all. The Cabinet's review led to a decision in January 2001 and reconfirmed in May of the same year – to adopt EDRIC's blueprint and rationalize distribution into six REDs, with an EDI Holdings Company to manage the transition. However, the Cabinet also recommended further consultation.

Elements of local government have remained ambivalent or hostile to the proposal and have threatened to challenge the plan in the

Constitutional Court. The ruling African National Congress has split on the matter – ANC's leadership asserts the importance of a national solution to the problems of electricity distribution, but those involved at local government fear losing their influence. With so many divided loyalties, no political champion for EDI reform has emerged, and thus implementation of EDI reform has slowed.

Discussion on reforming the distribution industry has meandered for a decade and there have been many lost political opportunities. Often new leadership has joined the debates without the benefit of previously reached understandings and agreements. Even after a definitive Cabinet decision, more than a year passed before establishment of the EDI Holding Company – the key first step to starting the restructuring process. The first RED has now been registered in the Western Cape, although the difficult process of managing a voluntary merger of all distribution entities is ongoing.

While conflicting interests have slowed the reform process, it is also probably true that one of the original reasons for reform (namely, the need to strengthen the capability of distributors to extend access to electricity to the majority of the population) was obviated by Eskom simply getting on with the job. However, the other reasons for distribution reform are beginning to receive more public attention: local government finances are in a parlous state and industry is now greatly concerned with the lack of investment and the deterioration of system reliability. Concerns around the quality and reliability of supply are likely to re-ignite moves to restructure the industry.

Eskom corporatization

An important milestone in power sector reform has been the formal corporatization of Eskom, which involved the conversion of the enterprise into a company with defined shareholding (wholly government) and subject to the payment of taxes and dividends. The move has strengthened the commercial focus of Eskom. In the standard model of power sector reform, corporatization is often the first step in electricity market reform. However, in the case of South Africa, the impetus for corporatization did not come from policy developments in energy and electricity but from the Department of Public Enterprises (DPE). Restructuring of Eskom was part of a broader process of restructuring of SOEs (Radebe, 2000).

The DPE policy document published in 2000, "A Policy Framework: An Accelerated Agenda towards the Restructuring of State Owned Enterprises," was explicit about the restructuring of the four largest

SOEs. It stated that:

- Eskom will be corporatized, with transmission, distribution and generation each forming a separate corporate entity.
- Different generating companies will be formed to promote internal competition prior to the introduction of private sector participation in generation, in conjunction with new power requirements.

The report thus understood the importance of not simply privatizing a monopoly, but creating a competitive industry structure before privatization. The report also suggests that transmission would probably remain in the hands of the state and would likely to take the form of a separate independent company.

The Eskom Conversion Act of 2001 replaced the old Eskom Act of 1987 and subsequent amendments. There was strong opposition to this bill from organized labor. It argued that government had not followed the procedures agreed on in the National Framework Agreement (NFA) whereby representatives of government and unions would negotiate the restructuring of individual SOEs. In May and June 2001, Cosatu (Congress of South African Trade Unions) made a submission on the Eskom Conversion Bill to the Public Enterprise Parliamentary Portfolio Committee. Its opposition centered on three main concerns: the Bill would pave the way for the privatization of Eskom; taxation of Eskom would impinge on its developmental role; and taxation would result in upward pressure on electricity prices. Agreement was reached in principle that new clauses would be included in the Bill regarding the developmental role of Eskom and the protection of employees. However, they did not win the argument about Eskom paying taxes and dividends (Tinto, 2002).[11]

A paradigm shift in energy and electricity policy

In the mid- and late 1990s two further strands of activity came together, providing both a framework for reform and the main political impetus for change. One was the articulation of a new energy policy – including electricity policy. The other was the "black empowerment" movement

---

[11] Labor has become increasingly alienated from government. Gwede Mantashe, the general-secretary of the National Union of Mineworkers, warned at a rally in Johannesburg that the ANC should not take the support of workers for granted. "It must listen to the working class and get their support, or it should listen to big capital and lose their support." Cosatu embarked on a political strike on August 30 and 31, 2001 and marched to Parliament in protest against the government's plans to privatize state assets. There have been a number of protests and threatened strikes since.

that aimed to privatize into the hands of black business leaders a portion of SOEs.

A new energy policy emerged from the process culminating in a Cabinet approved White Paper on Energy Policy released in December 1998. This new policy framework was consistent with the government's macroeconomic policy in that it emphasized the need to attract private investment into the energy sector and the promotion of efficiency through competition. It was a sharp break from the earlier apartheid-era energy policy, which had emphasized state provision of energy services and security of supply at any cost – epitomized in the state-controlled programs for nuclear power, the synthetic fuels program, and Eskom's costly overbuilding of the power system (Marquard and Eberhard, 2000 and Eberhard and van Horen, 1995).

While not all aspects of the White Paper have been implemented, it has become the reference point for policy in the sector. The overall policy objectives were seen to be improvements in social equity, economic competitiveness and environmental sustainability, as well as in energy sector governance and energy security. Remarkably, it emphasizes the importance of:

- "Giving customers the right to choose their electricity supplier;
- Introducing competition into the industry, especially the generation sector;
- Permitting open nondiscriminatory access to the transmission system; and
- Encouraging private sector participation in the industry" (DME, 1998)

These bold statements originated not from any commissioned studies, nor did they emerge from a formal consultative process with industry members. They were the result of the convictions of a small group of analysts and government officials who were observing international trends in power sector reform and were beginning to be concerned with the potential problems of monopoly power.

The White Paper states that the government believes that Eskom will have to be restructured into separate generation and transmission companies and that the government intends separating power stations into a number of companies. The White Paper also affirms the importance of independent regulation.

Thus the model of power sector reform laid out in the White Paper mirrors the standard or ideal model being followed internationally: vertical and horizontal unbundling in order to separate out the potentially competitive components of the industry (generation and retail supply) from the natural monopoly components (transmission and distribution wires), the introduction of competition through new private players, nondiscriminatory, open access to transmission, and independent regulation.

The main supporters of the White Paper were industrial electricity users who wished to contain future rises in electricity prices. Initially, Eskom also supported the White Paper process despite its traditional uneasiness in engaging with policy processes in the public eye. Eskom has supported competition in principle, but in practice it resists any proposals that it should divest more than 30 percent of its generation stations. At times it has also suggested the introduction of a private strategic equity partner in the Eskom Holding company, which would have the effect of slowing down or making more difficult a subsequent unbundling of Eskom. It has also attempted to delay the separation of transmission services from Eskom's other lines of business. At times, it has argued that placing transmission into a subsidiary company within the Eskom group would yield sufficient unbundling. It has also presented alternative models for distribution that would preserve a more prominent role for the firm as a vertically integrated monopoly.

Major opposition to the proposals in the White Paper were presented to Parliament by Cosatu, the union federation. In essence, they opposed privatization and argued that Eskom should remain a vertically integrated, publicly owned utility and should be used as an agent of government to provide low-cost electricity services to all, especially the poor. They supported restructuring the distribution industry, but wanted it as a single national distributor (Tinto, 2002).

The evolving reform agenda

Since the publication of the Energy Policy White paper in 1998, momentum has increased for industry unbundling and the introduction of competition. However, as we explain below, the reform process has since stalled and a different industry model is emerging.

In one of the rare occasions of its involvement in South Africa, the World Bank sponsored a Ministerial Workshop on Electricity Supply Industry Reform held from April 3–5, 2000 in Midrand. The Minister of Minerals and Energy stated at the workshop that government's main objectives of reform are to:

- increase economic efficiency in investment decisions and operation so that costs and prices are as low as possible;
- maximize financial and economic returns to government from the ESI;

- increase the opportunity for black economic empowerment; and
- protect public benefits such as widened access to the poor, energy efficiency, ongoing R&D, and environmental sustainability (Mlambo-Ncguka, 2000).

The World Bank-sponsored seminar brought to South Africa a number of experts with detailed knowledge of the reform experience in their own countries. There was no single ideologically inspired message or proposed model. Yet all advocated the merits of competition, but warned of the importance of careful design of the electricity market. At the end of the workshop senior government officials, including representatives from Eskom and the NER, agreed to a draft policy paper on restructuring the ESI (DME, 2000).

Eskom's top leadership was alarmed at the extent of the reform proposals, particularly the recommendation to reduce Eskom's market share of generation to 35%. It lobbied at the very highest levels in government, drawing on its reputation for delivering low prices and for supporting the government's RDP goals and its growing vision of an African renaissance, embodied in early versions of the New Partnership for African Development (NEPAD).

In May 2001, the Cabinet approved proposals for the reform of the ESI through a "managed liberalization" process. The elements of this are summarized here (Mlambo-Ngcuka, 2001):

Structure of the generation industry. Eskom is expected to retain no less than 70 percent of the existing electricity generation market, with privatization of the remainder, with the initial aim of transferring 10 percent to black economic ownership not later than 2003;

Vertical unbundling. To ensure nondiscriminatory and open access to the transmission lines, a separate state-owned Transmission Company will be established, independent of generation and retail businesses, with ring-fenced transmission system operation and market operation functions. Initially this transmission company would be a subsidiary of Eskom holdings and would be established as a separate state-owned transmission company before any new investments are made in generation capacity;

Market structure. Over time a multi-market model electricity market framework will ensure that transactions between electricity generators, traders, and power purchasers may take place on a variety of platforms, including bilateral contracts, a power exchange, and a balancing mechanism. The market design should facilitate both physical and financial hedging. A transparent and independent governance mechanism would be developed for the power exchange; and

Regulation: A regulatory framework will be put in place that ensures the participation of IPPs and the diversification of primary energy sources.

In an agreement, which originated at the Farm Inn Summit in October 2001, and was signed on March 15, 2002, the Department of Minerals and Energy (DME), the Department of Public Enterprises (DPE), the SALGA, the NER and Eskom reached broad consensus on the next steps in reform.[12] An ESI restructuring committee, chaired by DPE, would be established. Eskom would ring-fence its generation stations into clusters or portfolios for internal competition. Eskom Transmission would ring-fence its operations into wires and system operations. The agreement further envisaged that Eskom Holdings would establish subsidiary companies for Eskom Generation and Eskom Transmission (although this was later contested by Eskom). The internal Eskom generation pool would be converted into an independent market operation company (power exchange).

The DPE subsequently established an ESI restructuring office and detailed studies were undertaken by government-led, interdepartmental and stakeholder committees, with the support of consultants, on the clustering of Eskom generation plant and the creation of an electricity market, including a voluntary power exchange with a day-ahead market, a balancing mechanism, and a market for ancillary services and a range of other electricity trading platforms, including bilateral contracts and financial hedging instruments. However, it appeared that the middle-level bureaucrats and consultants were far ahead of their principals, and when the cabinet memos were prepared to take the market design through to implementation, senior government officials and ministers were unenthusiastic.

A follow-up Farm-Inn summit in March 2004, comprising DME, DPE, SALGA, the NER and Eskom, plus additional government departments (National Treasury, the Department of Trade and Industry, the Department of Provincial and Local Government, the Competition Commission and EDI Holdings), confirmed the reform steps, but agreed to significantly delayed target dates. For example, a portion of Eskom's generation assets should have been divested in 2003. The target date was shifted to 2007.

Although there have been general briefings to the Parliamentary Portfolio Committees and workshops have been held with industry stakeholders on the proposed market design, few details of the Farm-Inn agreement and the reform timetable have been made public. Organized

---

[12] A strategy for the implementation of restructuring of the South African electricity industry. An agreement between DME, DPE, Eskom and the NER, March 2002.

labor (Cosatu) remains opposed to any proposals to restructure the electricity industry. In 2002 they embarked on a national political strike and protested against the possible privatization of Eskom and other utilities and the effects that this could have on the poor. The strike caused a prominent and acrimonious interchange between Cosatu and the government, with the latter insisting that it would not be deflected from its restructuring agenda.

Figure 6.8 shows the structure of the ESI in South Africa as envisaged in the May 2001 Cabinet decision.

The government's stated reason for reserving a dominant share (70 percent) of the generation market is not well understood. DME and DPE suggested to Cabinet that, "In order to meet Government's developmental objectives, Eskom will retain no less that 70 percent of the existing electricity generating market" (Mlambo-Ngcuka, 2001). If the reference to "development" means electrification, then it does not make sense as Eskom will no longer be involved directly after the creation of the REDs. If it refers to affirmative procurement practices, these conditions could be included in any future privatization deal. If it refers to supporting the NEPAD then there is no reason why any future South African power companies could now become involved. Investors argue that there is no logic to this policy and that Eskom's share of the generation market could and should be reduced to below 35 percent.

The slow progress in electricity market reform has created a great deal of uncertainty. In early 2004, the NER conducted a survey of electricity stakeholder perceptions of the risks facing the industry. Most stakeholders asserted that the quality and reliability of supply were deteriorating and rated the risk of electricity service failure as likely and serious. They expressed concern about the capacity of the government to lead the reforms and argued that policy uncertainty was having the effect of inhibiting investment in distribution systems as well as new generation capacity.

The government responded to the latter concern by appointing a technical advisor to assist in designing a tender for new generation capacity. Given the time necessary to complete environmental impact assessments and the likely construction times, it became apparent that this tender would not solve the looming supply crisis in time. The inevitable consequence is that Eskom is once again regarded as the supplier of last resort. The government has now agreed that it should resurrect old, inefficient coal-fired plants, and also make new investments. Eskom, by delaying the reform proposals embedded in the Energy Policy White Paper has managed to maintain market dominance. The impact of these developments on the future competitiveness of the electricity sector in South Africa will be profound.

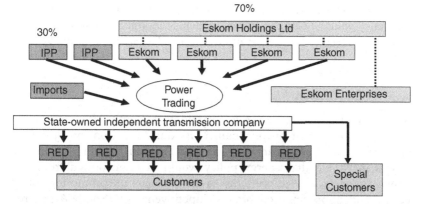

Figure 6.8. Possible future ESI model for South Africa electricity supply industry

By default, an alternative industry market model is evolving. Instead of a wholesale generation market, new generation investments will be undertaken either by Eskom or by IPPs with long-term contracts with Eskom. The renewed reliance on Eskom mirrors a broader shift in government policy. After a decade of market-friendly reforms, the government is concerned about inadequate economic growth and job creation, and persistent poverty among a significant proportion of the population. It sees the state playing a more significant role in infrastructure investment and development. State utilities in energy and transport are a key element of this strategy. Within this context, reform and regulation of SOEs will continue in order to improve efficiencies and performance – but probably without introducing full competition or privatization.

The South African government has yet to repudiate the Energy Policy White Paper of 1998 or to formally articulate a new electricity policy. However, it is clear that one is emerging. Security of electricity supply is paramount. Private, IPPs are being invited to bid for new capacity. There may be some limited competition *for* the market, but a competitive wholesale electricity market with electricity trading now looks unlikely in the short-term. The Minister of Minerals and Energy stated in parliament on June 22, 2004 that "the state has to put security of supply above all and above competition especially."

The one issue that might sustain the momentum for reform in the future is black economic empowerment. There is continued pressure to divest attractive state assets as one mechanism to broaden economic ownership. The partial sale of Eskom generation plants is one area that might receive attention again. There is a strong argument that divestiture should take place within a competitive market structure if efficiency gains are to be realized. Black economic empowerment may thus be the trigger for further reform of the electricity industry in South Africa.

Conclusion

There are elements of power sector reform in South Africa which are peculiar to its recent history, namely its transformation into a democratic state after many years of apartheid repression. Within this context, it was inevitable that energy policy would be transformed from the constrictions of a siege economy to a new focus on promoting social equity and improving economic competitiveness as South Africa reintegrated with the global economy. The Energy Policy White paper gave expression to this policy shift, but it was already evident in the launch of an impressive electrification program that sought to tackle the huge backlog of the previously disenfranchised's demand for affordable access to electricity. There was also the intent to consolidate and reform the highly fragmented and inefficient electricity distribution sector that originated in the separate development policies of the previous apartheid government. The urgency of promoting social equity and extending improved infrastructural services to the majority forced Eskom and the large municipalities to respond to the challenge of electrification, while the reform of the overall ESI lagged behind. Surplus and cheap electricity was available as a result of overinvestment in the previous decades, and a strong, large industrial consumer base enabled the ESI to cross-subsidize the electrification program without the necessity of imposing unaffordable price hikes.

The process of reform of the distribution sector has been slow and frustrated by the complex web of political interests at the local level and the fear of loss of control of an important infrastructure service and large income streams. Nevertheless, the process of restructuring continues and the government is intent on creating a more efficient industry in the form of new, commercially run public corporations.

The emphasis on corporatization reflects a general commitment to reassess the government's role in the economy, particularly the SOEs in the infrastructure sector. The government began to examine the governance and performance of these enterprises. As a consequence, the government also reformed Eskom's governance, withdrew currency guarantees and other implicit subsidies, and placed Eskom's operations on a more commercial footing. Eskom, along with other state-owned enterprises, was corporatized, had to pay taxes and dividends, and was subject to a shareholder performance contract. At the same time, the relationship of the state to the sector was clarified through the creation of an independent electricity regulator, which approves prices without political interference.

Although the liberalization and restructuring of the ESI in South Africa is not very advanced, the reform process continues, informed, in general, by government's commitment to increase the competitiveness of the economy and also to broaden economic participation and ownership for black South Africans. The momentum for reform has been set by the broad direction of economic policy. It has also been influenced by the work of analysts who brought international experience of power sector reform to bear on the Energy Policy White Paper, and who argue that South Africa is living on borrowed time in terms of low electricity prices. Arguments are now being made that a vertically integrated, state-owned monopoly industry, even if it is corporatized, is unlikely to make efficient investment decisions. The current low electricity prices are primarily a result of investment curtailment after a previous period of wasteful over-investment. The key challenge for the ESI is to create a competitive structure where investors bear a more equitable share of the risk, thus creating an environment for more efficient allocation of a resource, which is more attractive to private investors. the government has made a broad commitment to manage the liberalization of the ESI. Independent power producers are beginning to be introduced.

However, the government still experiences ambivalence and doubts about embarking on a path of full unbundling, competition, and privatization. Eskom is still seen as an important instrument of government policy, an apparently well-performing infrastructure industry that supports government's economic and social program. Current low prices create a false complacency. And the government faces serious resistance from organized labor, which has picked issues around Eskom reform as the battleground against privatization. In the next years, it could be the interests of the new black economic elite, interested in a share of privatization rents that maintains the momentum for reform. Other industry participants are also becoming concerned with the absence of investment that accompanies policy uncertainty. As power quality and reliability deteriorate and a supply crisis looms, power sector reform will gain greater political urgency. Ultimately, the overall context of economic liberalization (managed and regulated where appropriate) will sharpen the imperative of being competitive and efficient, and could sustain the path of reform of the electricity industry in South Africa.

7 Major conclusions: the political economy of power sector reform in five developing countries

David G. Victor and Thomas C. Heller

From 1990 to today many of the world's electric power systems have undergone dramatic institutional transformations. Where state-owned electric enterprises (SOEs) had historically prevailed, governments have sought to promote investment and better management by encouraging private enterprise and market competition. The studies in this book have examined that transformation in five key developing countries – Brazil, China, India, Mexico and South Africa. These countries are amongst the most sizeable and populous of the emerging economies. They offer a diversity of experiences with fuels, technologies, and institutions.

In all five of these countries, as in most of the world, electric power systems originated in the late nineteenth century as privately operated networks that supplied services to large industrial users, wealthy homes, and for some public purposes such as street lighting. Even in settings where the state owned and operated parts of these early power networks, the private sector dominated. Fears that private owners would monopolize their position were largely dormant – in part because these early private systems were often governed loosely as franchises and mainly because electricity was a boutique product that faced many competitors, such as the sun and town gas for lighting and water mills and steam engines for industrial torque.

From the 1930s through the 1950s the state assumed control over the power sector in all five of these countries.[1] There were few outright nationalizations. Rather, governments typically squeezed out the private sector through restrictions on market access, license conditions and

[1] In a few cases, such as Rio's city distributor Light and some Mexican utilities, the process of state assumption of control extended to the 1970s. In rare instances, such as distributors in Mumbai and Kolkata, both Indian metropolises, private ownership prevailed through today.

tariff orders that made additional investment by private firms unattractive. At the same time, governments and multilateral banks often also channeled state-controlled funds into newly created state enterprises. The timescales for change varied with the exact method and strategy. In Brazil, Mexico and South Africa the state worked mainly by constraining the private incumbents and channeling funds to new state entrants. As the for-profit business became increasingly unattractive, the state was able to purchase the remaining private firms, usually at discount prices. In these countries it took about one turnover of the capital stock (approximately three decades) for control to shift from predominately private firms to SOEs. In China and India, the shift to public control unfolded more rapidly when governments combined a squeezing of private enterprise with partial nationalizations in the 1940s.

The governments in all five countries used similar arguments to explain their actions. They branded competition as wasteful and dangerous. They argued that electricity had evolved from a boutique energy service to become an essential catalyst for modern industrial affluence. Electricity was too important, they claimed, to leave in the hands of profiteers outside state control. They saw government monopoly as the best way to improve service through economies of scale and scope, a logic that reinforced itself as technological progress gave further advantage to central power stations and demand for electricity increased with ever-declining costs and prices. Politicians also realized that state control would allow them to exploit the growing political benefits of the electricity sector, such as inexpensive electric service and the jobs that came from large construction projects (for example, dams). These factors – the essential role of electricity, concerns about private monopoly, and the desire to reap the political benefits offered by the power sector – resonated with development policies in fashion at the time that emphasized state control of the economy more broadly. Only a few countries in the world, notably the United States, left the power sector largely in private hands. Even in those instances, the state attempted to thwart profiteering by adopting rules that fragmented ownership, vesting special regulatory commissions to oversee the market, and creating special state-owned companies such as the Tennessee Valley Authority (TVA) that would compete with and supplant private enterprise.

The five case studies in this book focus on how the state-dominated system that prevailed from the middle of the century became viewed as inadequate and how reformers responded. In the 1990s reformers in all five of these countries – as in most of the developing world – initiated processes of reform in which the ultimate stated goal was a fully competitive market. This ultimate goal, what we labeled in chapter one the "textbook model" for reform, was framed by experiences in England & Wales and a few other markets, which demonstrated the potential benefits from privatization of state enterprises and the use of market competition to allocate investments and determine prices. According to the textbook, integrated state electric enterprises would be unbundled into separate generation, transmission, distribution and marketing companies, followed by privatization. And marketers would compete to provide power delivery and billing services. This standard textbook model also envisioned that generation and marketing of power would be re-crafted as competitive activities. Generators could compete to sell their power into a common pool or directly to final users. The parts of the system that remained natural monopolies – notably, the grid of high voltage transmission wires and the network of lower voltage wires that carry current to the final point of delivery – would be held as state enterprises or sold to regulated private firms. Independent professional regulators would oversee the entire system to ensure its competitiveness and to regulate those aspects of power systems that were natural monopolies. A cadre of experts from the World Bank and private consulting companies, along with market-oriented political leaders, spread this textbook vision throughout the world, including in all five of the countries we examine.

In this book we have asked how those reforms fared and why, in particular, the "textbook" is not observed in any of the countries in our sample. In this final chapter we summarize across the four major issues, introduced in chapter one, that each case study has addressed.

First, we examine the forces that explain why these countries sought to reform their power sectors. Why did all these nations begin to pursue market-based reforms from the early 1990s and not much earlier when the inefficiencies of the state-dominated system were already becoming evident? The studies show that market reform was not simply a trend or fad. Rather, in nearly every case, power sector reforms arose in the context of an investment crisis of similar origins. In most of the countries, politically-connected users had come to expect declining retail tariffs from the electric power system. For a time, the economies of scale and scope had kept costs in line with declining tariffs, but that process reached the point of diminishing returns in the 1970s for a variety of reasons – partly because the technologies of central power stations were reaching their limits for improvement, partly because the state run system accreted economic inefficiencies and rigidities, and partly because the oil shocks raised the cost of fuel. To close the financial gap, every country invented its own scheme to subsidize the power sector, and some (notably India) failed to keep up with rising demand.

Financial crises from the 1980s to early 1990s, themselves partly due to the mounting cost of subsidy for the electric sector, disrupted this political ecosystem and allowed reformers to impose change. Reformers sought new systems of industrial organization because the state, which traditionally had orchestrated funding for the sector, was unable to supply the capital needed for new capacity.

Second, we compare these countries' reform processes and strategies. By design, we selected a sample of countries that varied in the reform strategies they have pursued. Some initiated reforms in power generation while others started with distribution. Yet the outcomes, we will suggest, are striking for their similarity. We will argue that reform strategy has a large impact on the formal organizational structure of the power system – determining, for example, whether there are large numbers of privately-owned distributors or small numbers of integrated state enterprises that are responsible for distributing power – but it does not often have much impact on the actual functioning of the power sector. In part, this result simply reflects that reforms taken in the context of an investment crisis usually emphasize the need to attract private investment. Instead of a full blown reordering of the power sector, reformers have focused on the politically and technically easier task of attracting private investors to so-called independent power projects (IPPs). These electric power generators sell bulk electricity with long-term power purchase agreements (PPAs) often backed by state guarantees that allowed investors to believe that guaranteed contracts were less risky. (By contrast, private investors – especially foreigners – assumed that investments in the rest of the power sector were much riskier.) In our sample, Brazil is the only country that began reforms by privatizing distribution companies. Even in that case, however, distribution reform was animated by the desire to make the power sector financially solvent so that the country could attract IPPs. The studies show that, in practice, IPPs have been much riskier than investors had originally assumed, regardless of their PPAs, because their financial performance depends on broader reform of the power system (Woodhouse, 2005). In some countries, early successful efforts to attract IPPs made it especially difficult to reform the rest of the power sector because the host governments usually offered special provisions such as attractive PPAs and subsidies to entice private investors. Ironically, those arrangements made investors less eager for reform because further adjustments in the rules could upset their special deals and subsequent investors always saw an unrealistic and unsustainable benchmark.

In part, the striking unimportance of reform strategy reflects that other factors, notably financial solvency of the sector, are much more important than reform strategy in determining outcomes. The studies in this book have given particular attention to the role of government subsidies. For power systems where tariffs for final users do not cover the full costs of generating and delivering electricity – which is true for all but China in our sample of five countries – we argue that governments have been successful in shifting functions from state enterprises to the private sector only where they have made credible promises to deliver the subsidy needed to keep the system solvent. We find that the particular mechanism matters a lot less than its existence. Closely related to the problem of subsidy is that most governments have found it extremely difficult to remove themselves from the process of setting tariffs. Yet one of the central premises in market reform is that the market itself, or an independent regulator, will set tariffs. We find governments engaged in a seemingly endless array of schemes to adjust power prices – usually to keep power prices low, which is politically popular, even when the government has announced the need for higher prices to attract private investors. A particularly popular scheme is to distinguish "old" power from "new" power, where the former represents the output from existing amortized (and thus inexpensive) sources while the latter is much more costly. In a system designed by economists all power users would see the real marginal (i.e., "new") cost of power because electricity is fungible on the grid. In politically managed systems, however, the segmentation of power allows the award of inexpensive ("old") power to favored groups while other users must either scramble for subsidy or pay full ("new") prices. When grid-connected power, whether "new" or otherwise burdened, becomes costly or inconvenient, then these users may even exit the grid-connected system and generate electricity on their own. That outcome is especially evident in India as large industrial users and wealthy housing tracts rely increasingly on power from their own generators.[2]

Third, this study has examined how electricity reform has been affected by the broader institutional context that governs the allocation of capital in the economy, the enforcement of property rights and contracts, and the functioning of markets. This context consists of a wide array of interlocking rules and institutions, such as controls on how state enterprises invest, the operation of capital markets, and the provisions for an independent judiciary. Moreover, the context, itself, has been in flux in all these countries as they pursue a broader agenda for

---

[2] Research conducted in parallel with this study has focused on reforms in two Indian states, with particular attention to the exit of high-tariff customers through the building of on-site "captive power plants." See Shukla et al. (2004).

liberal reform across the entire economy – shifting from direct state control toward greater reliance on markets to allocate capital and guide operational decisions.[3] We find that financial reforms have been particularly important in forcing public enterprises to comply with hard budget constraints that expose the power sector to the true cost of capital. Judicial reforms – themselves often based on new arrangements in a nation's constitution – have been essential to giving regulators the authority to issue enforceable orders. We suggest that the field of experts on power sector reform has devoted excessive attention to the many aspects of power sector reform itself rather than those elements outside the power sector that are much more important.

Fourth, we have explored how reorganization of the power sector has affected provision of public services and goods – in particular, the supply of electricity for the poor, investment in innovation and protection of the environment. As governments have embraced markets, many analysts have warned that markets will not automatically supply these public benefits. We find that such fears generally have not been realized in practice – in part because not much full reform has actually occurred and in part because governments have adopted complementary policies along with their market reforms. For example, governments have created special obligations for privately owned distributors to service low-income families, with the additional cost paid either with special funding mechanisms or through cross-subsidy by more lucrative customers. Market reforms have had either neutral or positive effects on the investment in innovation. Some countries have created special innovation funds that did not exist previously. In addition, power sector reform has generally coincided with trade reforms that have made it easier to import foreign electrical equipment, which has spurred competition among indigenous equipment manufacturers and also made it easier to acquire more advanced power generation, transmission, distribution, and metering hardware. Such improvements have also generally been good news for the environment since they have led to a power sector that delivers energy more efficiently. Reform has also generally favored natural gas, which is intrinsically cleaner than the coal and oil burning

---

[3] Although our study was not designed to make such comparisons, it appears that market reform in the power sector is often much less advanced than reforms elsewhere in the economy. The reasons may be rooted in the political difficulty of adopting reforms that raise prices for politically salient goods (i.e., electricity), whereas reforms in telecommunications have usually led to lower prices due to the coincident technological revolutions in telecommunication services; [RT} such services were often even profitable, on the average. Moreover, power sector reforms are technically more complex, with more direct citizen interaction, than reforms that lead to privatization of ports and many other areas traditionally dominated by state enterprises.

equipment that dominates the power sectors in all of these countries except Brazil (where hydro reigns), because gas plants require lower capital outlay than most alternatives and can be constructed more rapidly – attributes that private investors value.[4]

In addition to examining these four common issues, we also proffer a theory to explain why none of these five countries has implemented the textbook power sector reform, although all five articulated a vision for reform that originally corresponded closely with this textbook. Much of the existing literature, which we reviewed in chapter 1, claims that this gap between vision and practice reflects the lack of political will and other factors that policy makers could adjust. It assumes that the various institutional barriers can be cleared if reformers made a fuller effort and obtained a deeper political commitment. We argue that hobbled reforms are structural. Not only is it politically difficult to shift an electric system to the textbook reform, but the process of reform creates new organizations and political interests that favor an alternative equilibrium – a type of "dual market" that combines elements of a state-centered and a market-centered electric power system. In this conclusion we suggest why this arrangement emerges and offer some predictions for how such a system will evolve.

We argue that this hybrid "dual market" form of industrial organization is not a brief waypoint on the road to some Shangri-la textbook market organization. Rather, the political and organizational equilibrium that defines a dual market appears to be remarkably stable. Achieving full reform is difficult not simply because it requires unpopular tasks such as raising tariffs but, rather, because it spawns a special type of enterprises – what we call "dual firms" – that have strong incentives to propagate the partial insolvency and regulatory uncertainty that characterize most power systems that are in the midst of transition. Such conditions make normal privately owned firms wary, but dual firms thrive in that environment.

Dual firms are marked by their ability to perform two quite distinct (even conflicting) tasks simultaneously. On the one hand, these firms are able to muster the political connections needed to get things done that are essential to their commercial viability – such as securing fuel supplies that are allocated through politicized planning mechanisms, the siting of new plants, and especially the regular payment of subsidies from the government and tariffs from government-controlled enterprises that

---

[4] In some cases, the higher operating costs of gas-based plants were completely mitigated by the ability to pass through fuel costs to consumers, such as in India.

purchase electricity. These political resources allow dual firms to operate in settings where normal private firms would be unable to manage the risks – for example, they can profitably run highly subsidized distribution companies even when the government is unable to make a credible promise to sustain the subsidy because the dual firm is uniquely able to muster the political connections needed to keep the subsidy flowing. At the same time, these firms are not entirely political animals; they are sufficiently well managed, in a manner akin to efficient private enterprise, that they do not become mired in uneconomic projects or bloated with excessive payrolls. What marks these firms is their combination of these skills, not the firm's ownership. Some dual firms identified in this book, discussed in much greater detail later in this conclusion, are privately owned (for example, India's Reliance or Tata Groups). Some are fully owned by the government (for example, South Africa's Eskom[5]). Many are state-controlled but have private minority shareholders (for example, India's National Thermal Power Corporation[6] or Brazil's Petrobrás), which has created conflicts in corporate governance because the interests of different shareholders vary. Some have segmented ownership in which a public enterprise's most market-oriented assets, which are those that are most attractive to minority private owners, are placed in subsidiaries that are listed on stock markets even as the rest of its assent are retained by the state (e.g., China's Huaneng power group). Mexico's relative stasis on power sector reform may reflect that no dual firm has emerged in that country, which is populated by one large, highly inefficient state-owned enterprise (the Comisión Federal de Electricidad, or CFE) and several entirely private IPPs. The space in the middle, combining both attributes, is empty. As we will show, most dual firms are rooted in a particular country because political assets are linked closely to particular settings and foreign firms, especially, have a hard time commanding patronage that is controlled by local governments.

We do not claim that this outcome is the most desirable in terms of economic efficiency or good governance. Rather, we suggest it is a likely (perhaps the most likely) outcome of efforts to reform power sectors in countries where market institutions are weak. We also outline some dangers to governments and firms if these hybrid dual markets persist. We also suggest that similar forms of industrial organization may exist in

---

[5] Eskom has changed names during its history; for simplicity, here we use just the current name.

[6] NTPC only recently divested full government ownership. Private owners were enticed by its remarkable profitability – a shining example of a dual firm – and the government was interested in raising funds rather than effecting structural changes in the company.

other capital-intensive, politicized area of semi-commercial activity, such as ports or the media. To gain an accurate prognosis for reform – for the entry of private investors, and the prospects for real market competition – analysts and reformers alike should give more careful attention to the types of enterprises that dominate the sector and the political forces that allow them to remain entrenched.

Finally, we close by drawing some specific conclusions for policy. Among them is the central importance of imposing hard budget constraints on the power sector; absent such constraints no amount of formal reform has much effect on the actual operations of electric enterprises. In addition, we argue that the process of regulatory reform has been widely misunderstood because regulators in these five countries – and perhaps all other countries where market institutions are weak – do not perform the same functions as regulators in the advanced industrialized nations. These regulators do not oversee the operations of ideal firms that are imagined in the textbook theory of power market reform. The authority of these regulators is often highly limited – if not formally, then at least implicitly since regulators often find their powers stripped when they make inconvenient decisions. Even where they do have powers of decision, these regulators often lack the mechanisms to discover and utilize the complex information that is needed, for example, to determine fair tariff levels. Most of the efforts to "train" regulators and to build up their capacities are rooted in the experiences of regulators in the advanced industrialized world. Those efforts, it appears, have been largely misplaced.

Forces for reform

In the advanced industrialized countries the impetus for power sector reform has come from the desire for economic efficiency. The most visible metric for successful reforms has been a decline in tariffs. Across the five developing countries in our study, however, the necessary condition for reform was not the desire for economic efficiency. Moreover, where reformers have been most successful, tariffs (especially at the retail end) have generally risen. These differences reflect the fact that most of the reform efforts observed in this study have been rooted in the need to overcome the financial insolvency of the power sector. The state system was unable to mobilize sufficient resources to invest in new power capacity; that state enterprises were often inefficient in their operations was only a secondary concern. Without reforms, it was thought, the lights would literally go out and economic growth would drag to a halt.

Each country study in this book recounts an idiosyncratic story, but many key elements are common. Rapid industrialization, especially since the 1960s, had produced the expectation demand for power would grow even more quickly than economic output. Governments – what we broadly call "the state" – had financed the power systems needed to keep pace with the industrial economy through a variety of mechanisms such as allocating capital grants, allowing state enterprises to operate with soft budget constraints, providing guarantees that eased the task of raising capital on international markets, and using state control over the banking system to channel loans into favored projects. State enterprises received this capital at favorable rates – in many cases, essentially free of charge – which along with bullish estimates for economic growth (and power consumption) encouraged over-building.[7] The exact mix of financing varied, and in some cases international financial institutions and development assistance played major roles, but the element in common was state control over the raising and allocation of capital.

State control over financing coincided with declining costs of generating and delivering electricity. Worldwide, the economies of scale and scope generally afforded a decline in the marginal cost of service through the early 1970s (EPRI, 2004).[8] Each kilowatt-hour (kWh) sold cost less than the last. Declining marginal costs of supply and over-building created a windfall of surplus power that was under state control and open to political appropriation. In all five countries the state set differentiated retail tariffs to benefit politically powerful groups. Several Indian state governments awarded practically free electricity to farmers from the early 1970s. South Africa kept low tariffs for white farmers and mining operations. China favored certain state industrial activities. Mexico's tariff structure broadly favored classes of industries and households that were also supportive of the ruling PRI party. Enormous investments arose around these tariff systems, which in turn have impeded later attempts to align tariffs with real costs. For example,

---

[7] Of the five countries, only India never overbuilt. That's because India's power shortages appeared earlier than those in any of the other countries – spurred partly by early politics to give away discounted power – and thus even when demand slackened supply never caught up.

[8] The exact timing for the exhaustion of the economies of scale and scope varied by fuel, technology, and the legacy of prior policies. For countries that had limits on imported technology, state enterprises operated a few steps back from the frontier and thus the prospects for declining marginal costs extended to the 1980s and in some cases the early 1990s. In China and India, for example, until the early 1990s the best new power plants were far smaller than the standard set in the industrialized world and thus somewhat more costly to build and operate. Today, all five countries in the sample contemplate investments in new power plants that are largely approaching the size and efficiency of the world standard.

today there are 14 to 16 million electric pumpsets in India for lifting groundwater to fields, which has distorted the choice of crops and exacerbated improper pricing of water throughout the Indian agricultural system. Cheap electricity in South Africa encouraged heavy investment in highly energy-intensive minerals industries. Users of cheap power, already a powerful political constituency, became strong advocates for preserving the state-centered electric system.[9]

For Brazil and Mexico the macroeconomic shocks in the 1970s through the early 1980s posed the first big tests for the state-dominated system. As the cost of capital rose in foreign and local markets and as the price of hydrocarbon fuel climbed, governments insulated the power sector with special payments that preserved a tariff structure that increasingly did not reflect true cost. In Mexico, for example, power generators were awarded fuel oil contracts (from the state-owned oil company) at prices far below world levels – a subsidy in the form of lost potential export earnings. As such subsidies grew they magnified distortions across the economy. Broader macroeconomic troubles that hit these economies in the 1980s caused massive disruptions to the patterns of finance in all state sectors. For the moment the electricity sector could sustain operations because macroeconomic crisis, itself, dampened the economy and depressed demand for electric power even as still more new generators, ordered in the 1970s by officials who expected soaring demand, came online. The surplus enhanced the political temptation to give electricity away for political reasons. But, when that glut was worked off and demand for electricity was expected to rise with freshening economic growth in the 1990s, state financing for the next round of building was not available on the old state-controlled development models. Yet the most powerful end users had come to expect inexpensive electric power.

The storylines in China and South Africa are variations on this theme. In China's case, exposure to world capital markets was minimal, and the impetus for electricity reform arose in 1979 with a systematic opening of the Chinese economy. Those efforts began in other sectors, but by the middle 1980s they included electric power. Reformers sought to decentralize control over investment because the central government

---

[9] The rhetoric of tariff-setting often distinguished between "old" power that was inexpensive and viewed as the legacy of public investment and "new" power that is more costly and often privately supplied. Economically, the distinction between these two types of power is meaningless as power should be priced to reflect the long-run marginal cost of new supply. Politically, however, the distinction gained traction as politically connected groups competed to claim that their preferential tariffs reflected allocations of the public's "old" power. (Only Mexico is the partial exception, where "old" power is fired with oil and may be more expensive than "new" gas-fired power.)

simply could not keep up with the planning and capital requirements of a system growing close to ten percent per year, without risking runaway inflation that would be created from unfettered supply of credit from state banks. A watchful macroeconomic policy along with soaring demand for power led the central government to invite investment from private firms and state and local governments to fill the gap. In South Africa exactly the opposite occurred. Eskom, the South African utility, had maintained a strong balance sheet and government guarantees of its borrowings allowed the enterprise to raise capital with relative ease through private markets. Thus in the 1970s – like many other state owned or regulated utilities – Eskom enormously overbuilt the South African power system. It had over-estimated demand, which slackened as the world economy went into prolonged recession through much of the 1970s and 1980s – a factor worsened by the increasing isolation of South Africa's apartheid state. Costs rose with the debt service; plants were delayed or cancelled and some of South Africa's power capacity was mothballed. When Eskom raised prices to service its debt, industrialists especially in core electricity-intensive sectors like aluminum, clamored for change. The government formed a commission to try and fix the country's power woes through improvements in commercial management and corporate governance.

The crisis in state-controlled financing for new power capacity explains much of the variation in the timing of market-inspired reforms. It explains why Brazil, China and India were the first in our sample to initiate electricity reform – their economic prospects were threatened by major bottlenecks in power supply by the late 1980s and their power sector reforms coincided with a severe shortage of capital in the sector. Crises in financing also partly explain which state distributors were first privatized in Brazil. The Brazilian government started with those in states with the worst financial troubles, where reformers had the greatest leverage precisely because they could tie the infusion of capital to overcome the financial crisis to structural reform. It explains why South Africa – whose economy slowed through the 1990s in the death throes of apartheid – had barely begun to put in place mechanisms for reforming the power sector by 2005, and was the last to attempt to introduce market forces. South Africa's state utility had the strongest credit rating of all the countries in our sample and thus was able to raise capital and over-invest the most. Its legacy of over-investing in the 1970s lasted the longest because South Africa's sluggish economic growth meant that demand for power increased the least in our sample. Only now, with regular brownouts during peak winter months have South Africa's politicians and regulators seriously focused on reform.

The role of finance also helps to explain why the first attempt to introduce a textbook market-based system examined in this book – in 1996 in the Indian state of Orissa – arose in an institutional context that was weakest and where the prospects for success with reform were probably the worst. There, the World Bank made a loan for essential new power supply conditional upon the adoption of key elements of the standard textbook reform – the privatization of generators and distributors and the creation of separate distribution areas. Orissa, one of India's poorest states, had no other options because it needed the World Bank's money. The Bank had recently adopted a new lending policy that reversed its decades-long practice of lending to state power institutions while not intruding on a country's internal organization and, instead, made market reforms a condition for future lending. The reform-minded Indian central government was inclined to allow the experiment to go ahead. (The results were disastrous because few bidders sought Orissa's assets and none of the complementary institutions – such as sound accounting systems and a proper regulatory framework – were in place before the experiment began.)

Many changes in economic policy arise because orthodoxy shifts with the arrival of trendy new ideas. However, none of the cases suggests that reform was merely a trend – an idea that had taken hold, spread by elite policy experts and ephemeral in fashion. Rather, the financial crisis in the power sector created an urgent need for new ideas as a political opportunity for reformers to implement them. And the suppliers of capital – such as the World Bank, as well as private investors – all appeared to demand reform as a condition for essential further funds. In all five countries the strongest internal champions for electricity reform were politicians who, at the same time, pursued broader agendas for market reforms. The absence of a viable alternative to market-oriented funding mechanisms explains why even when political leadership has changed to parties that have been more hostile to markets, most of the initial changes imposed by reformers have nonetheless survived.

Reform strategy

We selected a sample of countries that illustrated a wide variation in reform experiences (see table 1.2 in the introduction chapter of this book). In Brazil, reform began with the privatization of distribution companies and a tariff reform aimed at making the distributors profitable. In turn, it was hoped that solvent distributors would attract private investors to buy existing and build new generators. In China, India and Mexico reform efforts concentrated on private investment in generators.

Only recently have Indian reformers made sustained efforts to reform the other aspects of their ailing power network, notably the insolvent distribution companies that supply the majority of final users. In China efforts at reform have put only a small fraction of power generators in private hands; in Mexico, however, nearly all new power generators are built and operated by private companies. Neither China nor Mexico have made any significant effort to reform the distributors of electric power. South Africa has attempted some reforms of distributors and is just now seeking private investment in generators.

Despite this wide variation in strategy, very little of the variation in outcomes – measured, for example, as the cost of providing power supply or the extent to which the actual power system deployed deviates from a theoretical optimum – can be attributed to reform strategy. In Brazil, the private distribution companies that were the keystone to reform efforts are not able to operate much more efficiently than the public distributors. The reason is that the most critical function for efficient operations is the policing of theft, which is a highly political activity. Private companies have found it more difficult than state enterprises to enforce their billings. Brazil's privately owned generators display a wide variation in performance, very little of which is explained by ownership. Privately owned dams generate reliable (often high) returns for their owners because the country's power dispatch system is tailored to benefit dam owners by allocating risks away from dams to thermal plants (notably those fired by gas and oil). Publicly owned dams have the same financial benefit and perform similarly. Privately owned thermal plants have generally fared very poorly except in the few cases where private owners are able to sell the power to each other for example, when a private distribution company buys power from a generator that is owned by the same parent company. The best performing thermal plants are those that were conceived with a close relationship to Petrobrás, the state-owned gas company. The ownership of the plant matters much less than Petrobrás' fuel supply contracts.

In India, the most efficient producers – measured by their capital and operating costs – are usually central public sector plants, although some privately built plants have excelled as well. The best performing public sector company – the generation company, National Thermal Power Corporation (NTPC), which until recently was 100% owned by the central Indian government – is able to achieve high economic efficiencies by combining good management with favorable tariff rules and political connections that allow it to get paid even when other plants (notably privately owned plants) must struggle to earn an adequate return. NTPC plants compare favorably with the best in the world, and their profitability is perhaps one of the highest in the world. Plants owned by Indian state governments, by contrast, generally perform poorly.

In Mexico, privately owned plants have the lowest costs in the country. Yet a close look reveals that the good performance of these gas-fired plants is mainly due to the fact that the Mexican government absorbs all currency and regulatory risk through a payment scheme that makes these private investments among the least risky power plants in the world. By contrast, state plants are much older and nearly all are fired with oil, which is costlier. Those differences – absorption of risk and choice of fuel – explain most of Mexico's positive experience with private ownership. In all countries, especially China, it is very difficult to compare private and public assets because accounting standards are different.

We did find that reform appears to be correlated with an overall improvement in the performance of the power sector. But the standard reasons proffered for that improvement – private enterprise and competition within the electricity sector – do not appear to explain the outcome. Other factors must be at work, and to those we now turn.

The Institutional context: from states to markets

Each case study has examined not only the power sector, but also the broader institutional context within which reformers sought to change the power sector. A shift from state control to markets implies not just a discrete change in ownership but also a much wider array of changes in the organization of the state and its functions, which we outlined in chapter one. They include finance, governance, industrial organization, and policy-making. We described ideal types of "state-centered" and "market-centered" systems and asked each author to describe how the process of reform has shifted the functions of the government. Here we identify four main findings about these interconnections between institutional changes in the broader economy and the particular behavior within the power sector.

Financing: hard budgets and the cost of capital

In the introduction chapter of this book we identified the hypothesis, based on the experiences with broader economic reforms in the former centrally planned nations of central and eastern Europe, that the reform process depends critically on the control of financial resources. Specifically, we focused on the role of hard budget constraints and whether enterprises in the power sector were forced to pay the real cost of capital.

The studies are broadly supportive of this hypothesis. Where governments have applied hard budget constraints on the state agencies and enterprises that controlled the electric power business, improvements in management have usually followed quickly. In Brazil, the financial crisis of the late 1980s forced the most indebted state governments to cover gaping holes in their balance sheets, which partly required the sale of local generators and distributors to private owners. That privatization forced the state governments, generators and distributors to observe hard budget caps that, previously, did not exist. It also forced the enterprises that remained under public management to meet budget limits similar to those applied by private managers. By contrast, Brazil's least well-performing enterprises in the power sector are those that required large amounts of capital that was committed by governments without any stringent obligation for repayment. Two large dams built in the Amazon between the 1970s and 1990s, for example, do not even cover their costs by normal accounting standards. By contrast, projects built at roughly the same time but organized as separate vehicles with their own external financing and accountability – notably Brazil's Itaipú dam on the border with Paraguay – have had much better financial performance. The Amazon dams sold their power at reduced rates through the regional grid mainly to politically well-connected aluminum smelters and mines. Itaipú, by contrast, was forced to cover its costs and thus required the country to impose a special tariff on power users that better reflected the real cost of electric service.

In most of these five countries, state-directed capital has flowed via many complicated channels rather than simply as direct allocations from public budgets. One of the most demanding tasks for reformers has been to untangle this web of soft finance. Brazil partly shut off the flow of subsidized capital to its power industry because Brazil's power industry reforms began in the context of broader reforms triggered by a severe crisis in public finance, during which reformers gained a firm grip on the public purse.[10] Of the five countries we studied, South Africa has done the most to impose a hard budget constraint on its power system

---

[10] However, practically none of Brazil's power sector faces the true open market cost of capital. Rather, essentially all large power projects are financed with allocation from the state development bank (BNDES) at rates far below those available from private banks. Thus, in effect, capital planning in the power sector depends heavily on the decisions of BNDES and its political masters. A legacy of inflation and capital controls in the economy, along with varied regulation in the power sector, have made private banks wary of investments in the power sector.

because it had the least to do – it removed public debt guarantees for Eskom in the eighties and since then Eskom has conveniently demanded little investment. (Nonetheless, some South African distributors remain subsidized.)

In practice, though, it has proved extremely difficult to tame soft financing because subsidy that is removed from one part of the power system often metastasizes elsewhere. For example, some countries imposed hard budget constraints on generators because they believed that it would be easy to separate generators from the rest of the power system and to measure performance against known benchmarks. However, aligning generation tariffs with actual costs (usually at levels higher than in the past) merely shifted the point of subsidy and insolvency in the power system – usually to the point where it is politically easiest to sustain the loss. At the extreme, the Indian example suggests that if subsidies were removed from agricultural power supply (some 30% of consumption), food itself would need to be subsidized. Within the power sector, the cases suggest that the entities most likely to harbor insolvency are distribution companies – they are closest to the final customer and thus most prone to succumb to political pressure to under-charge for their service. But the exact patterns vary as governments invent new schemes that pretend to work around the fundamental problem of charging less for a product than the cost of supply. In India, recent accounting rules adopted in some states have attempted to concentrate insolvency (and thus subsidy) in state-owned transmission companies, for example, in Delhi. In all the countries we have studied, foreign-owned enterprises appear to have been particularly vulnerable to being forced to charge less than their long-run marginal cost, a phenomenon that we examine in more detail later.

The problem of insolvency shell games is most famous in India, where virtually all of the State Electricity Boards would be bankrupt if forced to comply with proper accounting practices. In the complex and opaque Indian system of government financial accounting, many states have historically been able to pass on their budget deficits to the central government – in effect, a soft budget constraint – thereby making the resolution of electricity reforms dependent in part on the future of Indian budgetary reforms. However, of the five countries we examined, Mexico – not India – appears to be the most extreme example. Most new capacity in the recent decade has been built as foreign-owned IPPs that are privately financed stand-alone companies that must operate under hard budget constraints. To meet those payments, the Mexican government and CFE moved three levers. One is the PIDIREGAS scheme that, in essence, lowers the cost of borrowing capital by backing long-term power supply contracts with the federal government's balance sheet. A second takes the form of direct subsidies from the federal government mainly to the state utility CFE that allow it to pay higher prices for the power it purchases and delivers than the tariffs charged to retail consumers. A third is the cross-subsidy built in to the tariff structure; indeed, in all five countries tariffs are lower for low-income users with a larger burden usually falling on (increasingly less content) industrial and commercial consumers.[11]

Judicial reform and independent regulation

A second area where the success of electricity reforms depends on the broader institutional context is the judiciary. Nearly all the literature on power sector reform has especially stressed the importance of creating independent regulators with the authority to make decisions within policy criteria set by government. In the integrated state-centered system, all relevant decisions about power supply were made by government agents that, by assumption, acted according to public interest and thus required no independent oversight. In the market-centered system, by contrast, an independent regulator is essential as private investors seek protection from the whims of the state and consumers must be sheltered from the whims of monopolists.

Whether regulators have been able to exercise their delegated powers has depended, in part, on the efficiency, independence, and attitudes of the courts. Of these five countries, the one that has done least well in creating an independent regulator is the one that has also done least well in establishing an authoritative judiciary – China.[12] The country where regulators have carved out the largest powers for themselves is the one where the judiciary has the greatest reputation for independence – India. In the middle – Brazil, Mexico, and South Africa – are countries where regulators' powers have been circumscribed and judicial authority contested, or where (in South Africa) the regulator so far has not made many difficult decisions.[13]

---

[11] Tariff structures are highly complex and reflect many local forces and rent-seeking strategies that are difficult to generalize. In Mexico, for example, despite a tariff schedule that appears to confer advantage to low-income users the effect of all subsidies in the electricity system is regressive (López-Calva and Rosellón, 2001).

[12] Such problems are, not surprisingly, pervasive in the Chinese legal system since they are a function of widespread lack of legal reform. For example, the rulings of China's securities regulator are routinely left un-enforced by courts protecting local industries.

[13] At this writing, South Africa is tendering its first new power plants in more than two decades, and with that decision the jockeying for regulatory independence is now beginning in earnest. Previously, the South African regulator has struggled just to create

Where the judiciary has not provided the rock-solid support needed for a truly independent regulator, regulatory bodies have nonetheless sometimes been able to function effectively – usually when the government itself replaced the judiciary in endowing the regulator's authority. In Brazil and Mexico, reform-minded politicians in the federal government made the creation of independent regulatory bodies a high priority and granted substantial powers to them. Pro-reform politicians and civil servants enlisted entrepreneurial heads for these new regulatory agencies and gave them the resources to hire competent staff and constitute independent and well-qualified boards.[14] So long as pro-reform governments backed the regulator, the regulator could pretend to be truly independent. When circumstances changed, regulators fell into disarray, as illustrated by the fragility of the authorities vested in Brazil's energy regulator. In Brazil's electric power crisis in 2001 – brought on by drought and poor management of the country's dam network – the government found it convenient to shift blame and suspend the regulatory authority's powers. Two years later, a new government with quite different ideological orientation visibly reinforced the need for regulatory "independence" when it was convenient. However, the new government again suspended key powers when the regulator tried to impose a politically unpopular rise in tariffs. The courts have interpreted these decisions as matters of government prerogative and largely refused to intervene despite the regulator's powers enshrined in statute. Nor have the courts – especially lower courts that are usually less independent and less technically competent – upheld contracts between power suppliers and users that are the backbone of the country's effort to shift toward markets for power. Contracts between private generators and distribution companies that have proved to be expensive – for example, deals negotiated during the country's power crisis of 2001 when the government and distributors were desperate to assure new power supplies – have been dragged through the

its own independent staff and to form a management board that has sufficient gravitas that its decisions are sound and respected. So far, the regulator has been through three boards and two corruption scandals in less than a decade.

[14] In neither Brazil nor Mexico was it clear how the courts would rule if they had been fully empowered to review regulatory decisions. In Mexico, especially, an independent judiciary was just testing its autonomy in the late 1990s after decades of suppression, and several high profile cases suggested that key judges were actually hostile to electricity reform, which they viewed as a violation of the Constitutional requirement that electric power be organized as a public service and be owned by public institutions. (Similarly, in the Mexican telecom sector the judiciary routinely forestalled regulators' decisions on formalistic grounds such as inadequate explicit delegation.) The creation of an independent judiciary, as the Mexican experience shows, does not automatically reinforce the authority of regulators.

courts after the power crisis subsided and these deals looked expensive when compared with the rain-refilled dams that have essentially zero operating cost.

Even in India, the case among our five countries where the foundations for regulatory independence are strongest because the Indian courts have the longest tradition of independence and competence, there has been substantial variation in experiences across the individual Indian states. A special law on regulatory commissions in 1998 created the legislative basis for a central regulatory commission, and some states constituted state commissions even earlier. Still, organized interest groups that felt disadvantaged by regulatory decisions could delay implementation by challenging them in court, where access was easy and the legal basis for regulatory delegation had not been tested. Regulatory commissions already suffering due to thin staffing found themselves tied up in legal proceedings and unable to issue credible orders. Only a 2002 Supreme Court case firmly established the authorities of regulators, and a new electricity law in 2003 has further clarified the wide scope of authority delegated to regulators. In the Indian states where governments have been most keen to advance reform, officials boosted the powers of state regulators by agreeing to honor any decisions. The regulatory commission in Andhra Pradesh, for example, earned a reputation for competence and authority because it antiseptically applied agreed rules to politically sensitive issues such as computation of subsidies, and a supportive state government complied with all of the regulator's main decisions. But that experience is not proof of regulatory independence because the interests of government happened to coincide with the powers of the regulator. In May 2004 a coalition of new parties – more populist in orientation and more wary of market reforms – took power in Andhra Pradesh. Its first act was delivery on a campaign promise to give free power to farmers, which will exacerbate the cost of subsidy and strain the regulator's authority. How the system will survive this test from the change in government is still unknown.

Factor markets

All five case studies also explored the ways that changes in factor markets outside of capital – such as labor and fuel – affected the reform process. We did not know what to expect at the outset of this study, so we simply asked each author to describe these relationships. The studies suggest that these markets have had a large effect on the outcome of reforms not simply because they account for a large share of the costs in the electric power sector but also because these markets can be highly politicized. Stakeholders in these factor markets, such as labor unions and fuel suppliers, have many levers at their disposal – some internal to the power sector, where these stakeholders may have little control if reformers are setting the agenda, but many others external.

For integrated utilities in the countries that we studied, labor is one of the largest expenses, and in nearly every case the electricity sector had been managed as a substrate for public employment and job patronage. Managers of reformed enterprises forced to meet a hard budget constraint have demanded the ability to limit labor costs, which has often required a change in legislation and politically accepted practice. While some managers have made significant progress toward solvency by cutting the labor force, this route to economic efficiency is often self-limiting. During the 1990s in India no utility cut its staff by more than half, which itself was hard fought and only in some states, and pacts made during the process of reform have averted further cuts. Even as most stories about Indian power reform today focus on theft of electricity and the very low tariffs charged to farmers – both of which are severe (and intertwined) problems – few places in India have yet to make much headway on excessive employment, and the potential leverage on profitability through better management of labor is rising as the share of tariff going to labor costs has increased with time. In Brazil, the labor force was cut by roughly half without much formal labor reform. A shift in expectations about the role of power utilities as social employers made Brazilian cuts feasible, and the actual instruments used were those that had been available all along, such as early retirement.

Fuel markets are also important. We selected the sample of five countries for diversity in primary fuels because we thought that the politics of reform would vary with the technical and organizational aspects of the different fuels. While that expectation has been borne out – as we elaborated in chapter one – all the cases share in common the characteristic that the primary fuel has embedded itself in the electric power system through a complicated series of interlocking payments, patronage, and tax arrangements. In Mexico, fuel oil was sold by the state petroleum corporation (Pemex) to the state electric generators at below-market prices, shifting resources from the state (which otherwise could have sold the oil on the world market) to the politically connected users of electricity. In turn, that arrangement allowed both the oil and electric monopolies to reinforce each others' economic and political positions. In Brazil, water laws adopted in 1930s conferred authority over falling water to the state and allowed the government to build up a vast enterprise of hydroelectric dams that it operated as a single organism – dams downstream on a cascade were dispatched in tandem with those upstream, making it difficult for generators such as gas-fired thermal plants operating outside that political ecosystem to gain a foothold. Even when the individual dams were privatized the hydro dispatch system has continued to function as one and special payment rules, in effect, have continued to impede entry of non-hydro sources to the market. In China, India and South Africa local coal is king because it is an inexpensive source of primary energy, and competitors face many barriers.[15]

Barriers to entry and distortions in the incumbent fuel markets partly explain the fuel and technology choices made by private investors. Private investors in Brazil have disproportionately favored hydro generators because the dispatch system favors those who produce within the hydro paradigm. Those that have invested outside that paradigm – notably in gas – have generally lost money. In China, most new power capacity in the last decade – whether built by state enterprises or by private investors – is fired with coal because that is the economically safest option.

Choices outside the dominant fuel paradigm deserve close scrutiny and explanation. Well-connected private investors in India have built power plants fired with pipeline gas because they could secure gas allocations from government and the state-owned pipeline company, GAIL. In Gujarat, local private generators (and the State Electricity Board) have selected gas because gas is locally available whereas India's coal fields are physically distant, creating exposure to India's notoriously unreliable rail-bound supplies of hard coal. They have selected gas for some plants (though always with dual firing capabilities, allowing the use of oil in case gas is unavailable or relatively expensive), and they have also chosen locally available lignite for some plants. Mexico is a

---

[15] Even where it is cost-effective to import coal, political currents often flow against economic logic. In parts of southern China and western India, for example, imported coal is less costly (adjusted for quality) than locally available sources, but the levels of imports are still much less than would be suggested by a straight economic analysis. In some areas, artificially low internal transportation tariffs have given local coal an advantage and also explain why few coal users bother to seek pre-washed coal. (Washing removes most ash and thus eases the task of transportation – in the low-quality coals that are prevalent in both China and India, ash can account for 25% to 40% of the total volume of the coal moved.) In India, coal freight tariffs are profitable for the railroads but used to cross-subsidize the politically visible services of passenger transport, with the result that the railroads overall are not financially viable. The resulting poor service makes rail an unreliable means of delivering coal to consumers, and coal plants are only to stockpile low volumes of coal onsite, sometimes as low as a few days worth. As the impoverished Indian railroads falter in their payments to the electric generators who supply the electrons for traction, the generators, in turn, delay payment to the coal mines. Such cycles of nonpayment binds all units together into a community of debt whose political fates are intertwined.

particularly interesting case because the systemic preferences for fuels changed at approximately the same time (early 1990s) that the country shifted to rely on private investment for most new power supply. Thus old plants are disproportionately fueled with oil and owned by the state. New Mexican plants, however, are mainly built by private investors who all select gas because fuel supply provisions in IPP contracts systematically favor gas. Gas was cheap through the 1990s because it was priced through an index in the US gas market. Now that gas prices have risen sharply, the Mexican government is imposing new gas price arrangements that have introduced fresh uncertainties for IPP investors.

Public accounts

As we have just recounted, factors outside the sector often have a larger effect than the particular reforms adopted within the power sector. Hard budget constraints and the imposition of market costs of capital are particularly important. Judicial reform and factor markets, in varied ways, have also been powerfully explanatory in some countries. In addition to these external factors, the studies also suggest another factor that we did not anticipate would be so important.

Power sector reform depends critically on the ability to elicit accurate information from enterprises that either do not have systematic accounts of their activities or have strong incentives to provide inaccurate information. In most of the countries examined in this book the function of regulation – whether performed by agents of government or by nominally independent regulators – includes the task of reviewing tariffs and payments to ascertain fair rates of return.[16] The tasks involved are not novel; indeed, much ink has been spilled over the question of how armslength regulators can elicit information needed to set rules that are sufficiently generous that they encourage investment, while not so generous that an improper share of rents flows to the investor rather than for public benefit.

In all five of these countries, however, the problems of asymmetrical information are much more severe than those confronted by regulators from the industrialized world. The underlying problem is that the electric power system in each country is dominated by state enterprise monopolies that emerged in an era marked by strong incentives to keep accounting systems closed to external scrutiny. The internal operations

---

[16] In four of the countries there is a regulatory authority with some review powers that actually attempts to exercise such powers. In China, while a regulatory body has been established recently essentially all the functions of regulation are still performed by planners in the center and the provinces.

of state enterprises were a jumble of politically useful duties, soft budgets, uncollected accounts, cross-subsidies, and padded payrolls and expenses. No one demanded real accounts, and political choices were often easier to manage in these shadows. Such problems of accountability have existed even when state enterprises have faced formal requirements to post accounts and attain financial benchmarks. In India, government utilities must earn a declared rate of return. Thus nearly all of the State Electricity Boards (the state-level enterprises that control most of India's power distribution system) post an official three percent return on their net assets even though all are actually severely bankrupt. Official books are meaningless. In Mexico, even if the regulatory authority had the power to set tariffs it would be unable to perform the task objectively – for example, by computing the tariff needed to obtain a certain rate of return – since the main state enterprise responsible for power services (CFE) does not have an audited record of expenditure. Many politicians' careers would end if such a record existed. In none of our cases do independent regulators have either the expert tools or powers to pry open such long shuttered organizations to reconstruct costs and compare them with sensible alternatives. Attempts at systematization and transparency are often extension of old accounting practices, such as the Annual Revenue Requirement (ARR) metric in India.

The lack of transparency helps to explain why regulators have often encouraged private investment in IPPs. Not only are regulatory institutions usually created within the paradigm of competitive markets and thus organizationally inclined to favor private enterprise for efficiency, but regulators also believe that private firms will supply a benchmark for judging performance of the state system. (A similar desire for regulatory benchmarks led the U.S. federal government to do the opposite by building state-owned utilities – such as the Tennessee Valley Authority – in the 1930s.) The wildly inaccurate information available about the actual performance of state enterprises was revealed during the privatization in Orissa, when the state government (with expert advice from the World Bank) made assumptions about levels of losses, theft and costs that were far wide of the actual values discovered when the new owners took control and applied more objective accounting standards.

The social contract

In the advanced industrialized world, plans for the restructuring of power markets have spawned opposition from advocacy groups and analysts who have warned that market reforms could erode the ability of the power system to provide certain public benefits. We focus on three elements: service to low-income households, protection of the environment and long-term investments in new technologies. These public provisions of the power system constitute what we call the "social contract" – a set of arrangements and expectations that have arisen over time and reflect what the public expects from electric power systems that operate in the public interest. Many have feared that private owners responding to market forces – concerned about their own near-term profitability rather than broad and distant goals – will not automatically satisfy these expectations of the social contract. To the extent that such concerns have merit, should reformers take pause?[17]

In these five countries, we find that restructuring has had little impact on the social contract. In some part, this finding simply reflects that few governments have achieved much restructuring and none has implemented the textbook model for reform. But, in larger part, it is rooted in the fact that the social contract has not been ignored during the restructuring process. We look at each element – the poor, the environment, and technology – in turn. Critics would also point out that the previous system performed poorly towards the social contract, especially rural electrification, and so reforms would be hard pressed to make things worse.

In all five countries, the process of restructuring has coincided with (but generally not caused) a significant increase in the availability of electric services for low-income households. In Brazil and Mexico, the fraction of the population with access to electricity has continued to rise since restructuring efforts began around 1990. To be sure, the rise was less dramatic than in the 1970s when there were many more households without electricity and lower incomes made electricity less affordable. Today's overt efforts to electrify the poor struggle at the margin of diminishing returns because of past successes, not because private firms control parts of the power sector.

In all five countries, the creation of special funds and tariffs that promote electrification have accompanied (or often predated) attempts at reform. In several, however, factors largely unrelated to the industrial structure of the power system may explain most variation in actual patterns of electrification. In China, perhaps 650 million people have gained access to the power grid since the middle 1980s when restructuring

---

[17] For a full-length exploration of the social contract, based partly on the results of this study, see Victor (2005).

began – the most dramatic story (based on numbers of people connected) in our sample of five countries. Today, more than ninety-six percent of Chinese have access to electricity. The case study on China suggests that most electrification has been a consequence of economic growth, urbanization, and decentralization of control over the power system. Special funds from the central government have also played a role, but the availability of those funds has been unrelated to broader power sector reforms. The relaxation of central control over investment, which allowed provincial and local governments along with quasi-private enterprises to build their own power systems, played an instrumental role in dotting the countryside with tens of thousands of small hydro and thermal plants and spreading the benefits of electrification alongside the rapid industrialization of the economy.

In some settings, overt electrification policies have played an important role, but we find no evidence that market-oriented reforms have undercut such policies. In South Africa, when the new African National Congress (ANC) government took control in 1994 its platform included aggressive electrification to reverse the long-standing pattern of using electric services to benefit mainly white households and white-owned heavy industry. Since then, about 300,000 low-income households per year have been connected to the power system, mainly to the grid and to a lesser degree with off-grid renewable power supplies. The proportion of households with access to electricity increased from one third to more than two thirds within seven years, and at this writing the central government is introducing a free tariff for the first 50 kWh per household and several provincial governments are adopting their own preferential tariffs. Eskom initially funded the program to connect poor households through internal cross-subsidies. Later, when Eskom was established under company law and was subject to the payment of taxes and dividends, the central government created a special fund to support electrification. In the coming few years the government has set even more aggressive targets for electrification, and there is ample evidence that adequate resources will be supplied regardless of South Africa's attempts to restructure its power system.

In India, the government created specialized government agencies, the Rural Electrification Corporation (REC) and the Ministry of Non-Conventional Energy Sources (MNCES) to promote investment in electric service, especially in low-income rural areas or remote locations that are not grid-connected. Nearly all Indian villages have some access to power, but electrification at the household level is still only about 56% and below 44% in rural areas. Exactly in parallel with the effort to accelerate private investment and to impose hard budget constraints on state utilities, the Indian government promoted an "Electricity for All" campaign that has visibly set a goal of full electrification by 2012, with concomitant investment in rural programs. Although India's track record is much less impressive than China's, the varied performance is mainly due to slower economic growth and not of failures to focus on low-income electrification as part of restructuring.

Regarding protection of the environment, the studies yield conflicting evidence and suggest that environmental issues have not played a significant role in the restructuring debate. On the one hand, the Chinese case suggests that restructuring can cause significant environmental harm. During periods of extremely rapid growth, the Chinese practice of allowing small power plants (less than \$30M investment) to be built without central government approval has populated the countryside with relatively inefficient and inexpensive power supplies that burned heavy fuel oil and coal, causing high emissions of sulfur and particulates. If the central government had maintained its established monopoly on financing and construction of power plants then this capacity might have been added in a more environmentally efficient fashion (notably with coal-fired central stations), but such a hypothetical scenario is implausible since China's macroeconomic problems required that state banks reduce the volume of their lending and the rapid rates of growth made it impossible for the center to keep pace with soaring demand for power. Local governments, charged simultaneously with building capacity and enforcing environmental law, have made their priorities for growth abundantly clear.

Elsewhere, restructuring has been excellent news for the environment, mainly because restructuring has coincided with (and partly caused) a shift toward natural gas – the cleanest fossil fuel. The capital cost of gas plants is the lowest of all major generation options, which is why private investors tend to favor such plants when gas is reliably available at manageable costs. In Brazil, India, and Mexico a significant fraction of new capacity is actually fired with gas (in Mexico, the fraction is nearly 100%).[18] In China, the central government and some provinces are leading installation of the infrastructure needed to utilize gas for a variety of purposes (including power generation), setting the stage for a potentially rapid shift to gas in Beijing, Shanghai, Guangzhou, and several other major cities. In South Africa, the government is considering the choice of gas for new baseload capacity. A new gas

---

[18] Brazil's shift to gas, while tentative, yields a contested environmental record since the alternative is hydro, which is emission free but causes its own environmental damages.

pipeline from Mozambique is initially earmarked for industrial uses, but could be easily expanded to supply gas for electric power generation as well. Although South Africa is just beginning the planning of new baseload capacity, if abundant and inexpensive coal is its choice for new power, the government has already made clear that the plant must include advanced controls to regulate sulfur and NOx pollution – unlike all the current installed capacity.[19] Where gas displaces alternative coal generators it is cleaner; where it displaces oil it is usually cleaner. When gas displaces hydroelectric supply (i.e., in Brazil) whether gas is cleaner than water depends on the relative weight that one places on carbon and NOx emissions (from gas combustion) versus the ecological debit of submerged ecosystems and the environmental costs of alternative (or no) power in dry years. Even without the shift to gas, newer thermal capacity (especially from larger private investors) has often been cleaner and more efficient than the incumbent generators because the technologies have become better with time and experience.

Some countries have also put a premium on energy efficiency in tandem with exposing the electricity sector to market forces. A system benefit charge of one percent on transmission is used to fund energy efficiency investments and R&D in Brazil. Brazil's "PRO-INFA" program also emerged as part of the reform process and, as its first step, is subsidizing 3000 MW of power capacity for wind, biomass, and mini-hydro. In South Africa the regulator has adopted a policy of allowing Eskom and distributors to pass the costs of energy efficiency projects to final users so that there is no disincentive for such investments, and tight power supplies have redoubled the government's and Eskom's interest in such projects.

Regarding investment in the public good of novel technologies, the studies reveal no pattern. Mainly, this neutral result reflects the fact that few of these countries had any concerted effort in place to invest in new energy technologies prior to launching their restructuring. India and Mexico had invested in modest programs to advance new technologies, but those programs generally operated far from the technical frontier. The general opening of economies that has usually occurred at the time of restructuring has forced national champions to become more competitive – for example, cuts in import tariffs forced India's equipment supplier Bharat Heavy Electricals Limited (BHEL) to compete directly with international vendors such as Alstom, GE and Siemens. A similar

[19] Capacity additions at this point are limited to four incremental peaking plants (open cycle gas turbines to run on light fuel oil). Two of these plants will be bid to private IPPs; the others will be constructed by state-owned Eskom, which remains the dominant player in the South African power sector.

story appears to apply to China. In these cases, improved incentives to adopt technologies with better performance have probably boosted the overall investment in novel technology. In South Africa, the state-owned utility Eskom is a member of the leading international consortium that invests in advanced electric technology (EPRI), and it runs its own technology laboratories that are among the world leaders in handling the low-quality coals that are typically burned in South Africa (and many other countries). India's NTPC, several Chinese firms, Brazil's nuclear program and some foreign-owned generators in Mexico also participate in EPRI. NTPC is also boosting its investment in its own in-house R &D laboratories. These patterns suggest that a shift to market forces can spur investment in innovation. On the other hand, some of the greatest investments in new technology in the five countries we examine have been initiated by large, integrated state enterprises that might not have pursued such ideas if they had been forced to focus on near-term profitability. Long-term investments by Eskom has made South Africa a leader in cooling systems for thermal plants that are specially adapted for South Africa's dry climate and applicable in many similar settings such as the arid zones of China. Eskom has also spearheaded an international consortium to extend development of a "pebble bed" nuclear reactor that would be intrinsically safe, small and modular and thus highly cost-effective.[20] Chinese firms, heavily backed by the Chinese government, are building a pebble bed nuclear reactor of their own. These two programs raise the possibility that one of the most innovative new designs for new nuclear power could be built to demonstration scale, tested and commercialized entirely within the developing world – a first for a new class of electric technologies.

Broadly we can conclude that there is no inevitable or predictable impact on public interest or public benefit programs when countries reform their power sectors. It is not inevitable that widened access to affordable electricity for the poor, investments in energy efficiency or R&D will necessarily suffer. On the contrary, these studies suggest that the reform process may bring these issues into sharper focus and lead to fuller provision of the services. The impetus for reform may also create new opportunities for protecting and enhancing the "social contract" if specific policies, regulatory instruments, financing mechanisms and implementing agencies are established alongside restructured markets. All five cases suggest that such special programs will, indeed, be established because of the enormous political support to assuring the

---

[20] South Africa also led development and use of coal-conversion technologies, to gas or liquid fuels, in part because of restrictions on fuel imports during the Apartheid era.

social contract – especially the provision of electric services to low-income households.

The dual market for electric services

None of the five countries in our study has implemented the standard textbook model for reform of their power sector. Rather, each has pursued a reform trajectory that is yielding part market and part state – a hybrid system that fits within neither ideal category of "state-oriented" or "market-oriented" that we outlined in the introduction to this volume. In general, the sphere in which market-based rules are dominant includes new generators and new fuels (usually fired with natural gas); the sphere of the state includes incumbent generators and most distributors who collect tariffs from final users. In most of the countries that we examined the sphere of state control also includes the apparatus that extracts and delivers the incumbent fuel – coal in China and India; oil in Mexico; water in Brazil. (In China and India, coal services are slowly and partially migrating to private providers, and in South Africa they are largely private. In all, however, the collieries' largest customers are state enterprises, and the state often plays a lynchpin role for transportation, such as via rail.)

In this section, we explore the dynamics and industrial organization of this dual system, with particular attention to the emulsion between the two spheres – the places of intersection between the parts of the system that are governed mainly by the laws of market economics and those that are governed mainly by the rules of political organization.

In the broadest terms, the sketch in figure 7.1 shows the dynamic process that has created and sustained this dual system. At the far left is the integrated, state-owned system before attempts at reform. Declining marginal costs from the economies of scale and scope – along with inexpensive allocations of capital and other subsidies – created strong incentives for these state-owned enterprises to expand their customer base. Grid service was offered at a price and convenience that beat the alternatives (including self-supply) for nearly all users, except those in unusual circumstances such as very poor or extremely remote households. All users were connected to the same grid and obtained comparable levels of service from the integrated system.

Reformers sought to disentangle the various parts of the integrated system and impose hard budgets and real costs of capital on the different units. That process has proceeded much more slowly than reformers had originally anticipated for reasons that we documented earlier in this conclusion.

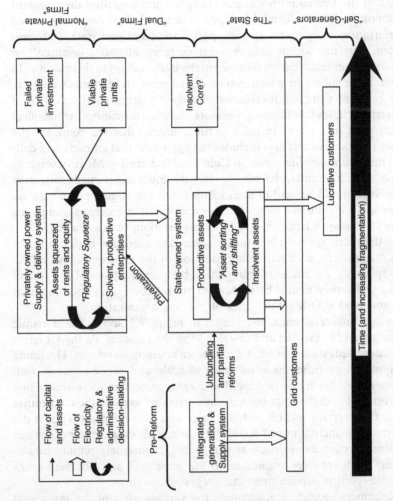

Figure 7.1. Power sector reform and the emergence of dual firms

Facing severe political and institutional difficulties, reformers first pursued the easier tasks, which has led them especially to encourage privately owned IPPs. In all countries that pursued IPPs, generating capacity was becoming scarce and reformers were required to demonstrate progress toward assuring new supply within the period of a typical term in office. Reformers also imagined that IPPs would ease the later steps in reform of the sector by providing benchmarks for regulators that would demonstrate best practices for economic efficiency. In contrast with distribution reforms, which would require confronting massive political challenges, IPPs were relatively easy to encourage.

In practice, however, both reformers and investors generally have been disappointed by the IPP experience because it has proved difficult to disentangle IPPs from the rest of the state-dominated power system. Few IPP investors have been willing to accept the risk of supplying wholesale power in merchant markets, not least because such markets rarely existed in the five countries we examined.[21] Rather, typical IPPs have contracted to sell their electricity wholesale under long-term power purchase agreements (PPAs) that offer a predictable quantity of their product (electrons) at a predictable price. Typically those contracts last for fifteen to twenty years; in Mexico some of them extend for thirty years. In Brazil, a new auction system proposed by the government in 2004 with the goal of attracting additional investment would award guaranteed long-term contracts up to thirty five years for greenfield projects.

The PPA model has created troubles for investors and hosts alike. For the hosts, PPAs have generally been more costly than expected because private investors demand risk premia and choose technologies and fuels that are substantially more expensive than the (usually subsidized and fully amortized) cost of incumbents. In addition to risk premia, some PPAs passed on risks to the buyers, such as fuel costs or even foreign exchange variability. This fact has made PPAs vulnerable to politicization as users jockey to avoid being stuck with the cost of "new" power. These high prices have not only created disruptive political risks and liabilities – most famously in Enron's Dabhol plant built in the Indian state of Maharasthra, where the original contract was nearly four times the cost of existing wholesale power – but they also erased the value of IPPs as benchmarks. Special technologies and conditions required for private investors – notably foreign investors – make IPPs one-of-a-kind

---

[21] China initiated some highly limited market experiments in some provinces at times when excess supply was available, but those experiments have been highly orchestrated and curtailed when inconvenient, such as when demand surged and provincial authorities needed all generators spinning.

entities that have reduced their value as metrics for assessing performance in the rest of the state-dominated power system. They were also often different in their size and fuel than many SOE units.

For private investors, especially foreigners, it has proved difficult to enforce PPA contracts. Having sunk capital in a project, investors found themselves vulnerable to forced changes in tariffs or other maneuvers that, in effect, squeezed the revenue stream from the committed project. This "squeeze," shown on figure 7.1, applies not only to IPPs but to any capital-intensive brownfield or greenfield investment. Investors have long known about the contractual risks, and thus they have pursued at least two strategies. One has been to demand strong contracts, with particular legal attributes such as offshore arbitration and special institutional arrangements such as assurances that professional regulators will ensure that contracts are honored. Indeed, a cottage industry of lawyers and deal-makers has arisen to hawk services in crafting "bombproof" PPAs. But this approach of managing risk through contracts has usually failed because politicians are unable to tie their hands credibly. Even when the setting of tariffs (and other decisions that are prone to politicization) is delegated, regulators have often proven unable to hold their technocratic ground.[22]

A second strategy for the investor has been to acquire political connectors so that he can navigate shifting political currents with political guidance of his own – a task that is often easy for insider investors (if they exist), but especially difficult for foreigners. For outside investors the most common approach is a joint venture, where the local partner provides political connections and cover for the deal. Such joint ventures have been consummated as equity deals (i.e., co-investors, although local partners often contribute little or no financial capital) or through debt (i.e., borrowing from well-connected local banks who will mobilize to avoid losing their commitment to the project). Absent standard mechanisms for assuring proper governance, such arrangements have been extremely difficult to sustain. In essence, the outside investor (who lacks the political capital to enforce a deal on his own) trades enforcement risk for corporate governance risk. He does not know perfectly the interests of his partner, and it can be difficult to

---

[22] For more on the enforceability and adjustment of PPAs, see research, done in parallel with this study, on the experiences with IPPs (Woodhouse, 2005). That additional research shows that the "squeeze" process concentrates on equity investors (whose assets are relatively easy to expropriate) but bank loans tend to be repaid, partly because governments are particularly wary of harming their reputation with banks and also because (in some settings) bank loans are backed with guarantees that leverage the enforcement powers of the lenders.

protect himself against changes in those interests, pilfering and other drawbacks in unaccountable governance systems. Foreign investors Alliant and El Paso have taken their local partners to court in Brazil, arguing that the local firm made decisions that harmed Alliant's share of their joint investment in the generator Cataguazes. Enron, GE and Bechtel have pursued a similar suit against their local partners in the failed Dabhol power plant in India, and many other examples proliferate.

As reformers sought to expand the role of private investment in the electricity sector, they found that it was difficult to distinguish parts of the system that could be made solvent (and thus attractive to private investors) from those that were more likely to remain unprofitable. In most of the countries we examined, a process of "asset shifting" has unfolded – through which potentially profitable units have been discovered and sorted from the insolvent assets. Government policy makers have often sought to counteract this process, such as by bundling insolvent and productive assets together in an effort to make even the unprofitable elements attractive for privatization. Reformers in Orissa, for example, sought to attract bidders for distribution services by linking those concessions to the potential for future investment in profitable power generators. But well-positioned enterprises have proved adept at avoiding the least attractive units; instead, they have imposed them on the state or unwitting investors. Through this process of asset shifting, productive assets migrated from the state-dominated core and, along with greenfield IPPs, constituted the privately owned part of the reformed power system, shown at the top of figure 7.1.

The problem for retail customers in this system is that the insolvent core consisted mainly of distribution companies – the customer's point of contact with the power system. Distribution companies have been particularly prone to insolvency because they provide politically valuable services whose cost and performance are prominently visible to key constituencies. Indeed, local and regional governments tend to be particularly keen to keep this function within their orbit – as evident in their opposition to the merging of municipal entities into six regional electricity distribution companies in South Africa or the opposition in Brazil and India to the sale of distribution companies. Most sales of distribution companies have been the result of pressure from outside reform-minded actors – Eskom, the government and the regulator in South Africa, the central government in Brazil, and the World Bank in Orissa.

Even in the cases where distribution companies have been sold to private managers they have not, in general, proved to be profitable. The same structural forces that make electricity a politicized good make it extremely difficult for a private operator of a distribution company to turn a profit. In Brazil, private owners of distribution companies have lost vast amounts of money; in Orissa the distributors have also lost handsomely. In the five countries that we have studied, only in India have a few private distributors actually illustrated a financially sustainable business model. Whereas Orissa was one of the poorest states with a large load of nonpaying or subsidized users and limited industrial/commercial growth, in some of the large cities private distributors have flourished because the load is dominated by higher income users. In effect, these private distributors represent a type of cherry-picking that hives off potentially profitable elements in a power system from the structural problems of the dual system more broadly. The best example of India's privately run distribution networks is in parts of Mumbai, one of the country's very few distributors that was never owned by the state. In Delhi, the state-owned distribution network is now being managed (and party owned) by private operators. However, it is notable that only two large Indian conglomerates – Tata and Reliance – participated in the bidding to partially buy Delhi's distributors. Making Delhi's distribution profitable will require actions that only well-connected firms can perform – ensuring that the government continues to pay the subsidies needed to make the system profitable and attractive for further investment and improving collection rates. (Delhi's power system is plagued by institutional theft, notably by the government itself.) Very few private firms have the clout needed to perform these highly politicized tasks.

Faced with unreliable and often costly power from insolvent distributors, customers have looked for alternatives and exited the system partly or fully. Initially the largest and wealthiest customers exercised this option by building their own power plants. As technological change has made small plants more viable economically and has eased the task of creating private power grids, smaller customers could join the ranks as well. Exit has been greatest in India and in China, where the grid system is most unreliable and expensive for industrial customers. Mexico is following in that pattern as grid electricity rises in price and declines in quality. The Mexican IPP law passed in the middle 1990s makes it relatively easy for large power users to build their own captive power plants and private networks. In India, about one-fifth of total installed capacity is actually private generation facilities located mainly on industrial sites.[23] A new law passed in 2003 will make it easier to build

---

[23] In the U.S., for comparison, the fraction of on-site power is about 12%. However, in the U.S. those facilities are backup plants at hospitals, schools, server farms and other

such sites and to link them together into private power grids. In China, the industrial landscape is dotted with privately owned small power plants. In Brazil and South Africa, by contrast, grid electricity is much less costly and generally more reliable; the incentives to exit in those two countries have been fewer. Yet even in Brazil, exit is increasingly evident as reforms have allowed large users to contract directly for power or in some cases build their own plants. This exit is shown at the bottom of the sketch in figure 7.1.

In sum, the power system that has emerged is neither state- nor market-dominated. Rather, financially viable units (generally privately owned) and insolvent systems (generally state-owned) can co-exist, along with a few profitable state assets, such as generation units. Islands of profitability have arisen within seas of insolvency. Around the profitable islands, hard budget constraints and standard efficient management for accountability prevail. The rest of the system is characterized by opaque budgets, and units are solvent only when they can obtain politically controlled allocations of subsidies, soft loans and other special payment and financing arrangements.

The line between the private and state systems is elastic and shifts through an endogenous process of asset-shifting and tariff-squeezing. The system, left to itself, will discover the profitable assets and move them into dual firms (whether privately owned or relatively independent state controlled firms) while the dysfunctional elements are shed and, in most cases, end up held in insolvent state enterprises (or unlucky private investors, at least until they shed such nonperforming assests). The system does not dissolve completely only because the grid itself requires interconnection, although the exit of valued customers may mark the beginning of the system unraveling. This elastic line creates enormous strategic challenges for regulators and policy makers. On the one hand, market-oriented policy makers are keen to encourage private ownership as a beachhead for broader competition and discipline through market forces. Reformers who follow this strategy welcome the fragmentation and pockets of profitability as harbingers of better futures for the entire power system. On the other hand, reformers must fear that success in their actions will cause fragmentation in the power system that unfolds more rapidly than the benefits from market competition accrue. Local equilibria may arise as investors and customers concentrate their resources on profitable and functional parts of the system, which in turn can make it hard to achieve a functional, fully integrated system in the

critical users who rarely run their equipment. In India, the majority of on-site power plants run regularly.

future. Thus some of the most ardent champions for reform have also aggressively fought to prevent fragmentation and exit. In India's Andhra Pradesh state, for example, the regulatory commission has seen its job as imposing discipline on final tariffs so as to make the entire system solvent – a goal they have furthered, in their view, by raising prohibitively high wheeling charges that have impeded the development of private power markets that would bypass the state utilities entirely.

This system has created a complex industrial organization in which four distinct types of enterprises account for the supply of electric services. At the top of figure 7.1 are normal private investors in grid-connected services. These enterprises are attracted to the business where they think they can obtain relatively predictable returns – that is, where regulators are truly independent and powerful and able to make credible decisions, such as to assure payments under long-term PPAs. We contend that this group is small, and after the disappointing experiences with IPPs in recent years this group seems likely to remain small. At the bottom of 7.1 are self-suppliers. These, too, are purely private enterprises that generate for themselves or for exclusive clients. Self-suppliers do not rely on the grid system for service or payment, although usually their clients are also connected to the grid so that they can select between grid and private supply. This group is also small, but may be poised to grow as technological change favors distributed generation and the dysfunctions of poorly managed grid systems create larger niches for private power.

In the middle are enterprises that depend heavily on state resources for survival. They include the state itself, which we posit will hold and operate an increasingly insolvent collection of mainly distribution assets as well as special generators that are too large or too costly to shift into private hands.

Alongside these classic state enterprises is a novel form of industrial organization – what we call "dual firms." We suggest that market-inspired reform has encouraged the emergence of a whole class of such firms, and the key to their existence is their ability to combine modern management (the private sphere) with political connections (the state sphere). Unlike traditional state-controlled firms they are nimble and efficient and thus able to identify and master control of potentially productive parts of the formerly state-owned system. But unlike classical private firms, these enterprises have political connections needed for their business model to function. The dual firm is the master of orchestrating the process of asset shifting, since political decisions lie at the center of choices about where to draw boundaries around assets to be disposed of from the integrated state system into private hands. Once the dual firm has sunk its capital it is able to use political connections to get its plants dispatched, to keep its tariffs unsqueezed, and to assure payments of subsidies from the state that are needed to justify the operation of otherwise dysfunctional assets. Because partially reformed systems continue to include islands of bankruptcy, subsidized tariffs and politicized regulation, enterprises that can manage instability will excel – such a context favors dual firms over classical private firms.

Already a host of dual firms has emerged. They include the privately owned firms of Reliance and Tata in India – both operators of private power grid systems whose connections allow them to thrive in the Byzantine world of Indian politics. India's state owned National Thermal Power Corporation (NTPC) has emerged from the state sector to become another dominant player in the Indian power system. Special rules ensure that NTPC gets paid even though most of its power is sold to bankrupt state utilities. At the same time, NTPC's plants are among the best managed in the country, and NTPC has become the largest single investor in new capacity. In Brazil, the leading example is probably Petrobrás – an oil company that is playing an increasing role in Brazil's power sector through its control of natural gas supplies. (Another gas supplier, Repsol-YPF, is also emerging as a key player in Latin America's power markets due to its ability to deliver gas for power.) In Mexico, there is no domestic firm that has emerged as a successful dual player – which may partly explain why Mexico has been so slow to de-integrate its power system – but the Spanish firm Iberdrola has such a commanding presence in Mexico's IPP market that it is probably the best candidate. Iberdrola combines access to foreign capital with intimate knowledge and contacts in Mexico (and throughout Latin America).

In China it is difficult to determine which enterprises will play this role, but entities such as the Huaneng Power Group are emerging as the likely winners from the periodic reform efforts. The Huaneng Group is composed of both former assets of the State Power Corporation (SPC) it received when the SPC was dissolved and those it built and acquired in its years as a pioneer state-owned IPP. Huaneng now lists minority stakes in those subsidiaries within its conglomerate that abide by conventional rules for the operation of publicly traded firms, such as the rules of the US Securities and Exchange Commission. At the same time, it hides many nonperforming assets behind veils of obscurity in unlisted business units, and it shifts assets between the veiled and public units as convenient and profitable. Some outsiders are also emerging as talented dual players in China. China Light and Power – a Hong Kong based utility – has the best track record as a foreign investor in power projects in China, as it is able to assure that its plants can compete with incumbent state-controlled generators, though even that firm has pulled back a bit. Electricité de France (EDF) is the largest western investor in China's power sector and may yet emerge with a special position in China – despite early losses, EDF's ability to muster capital from its regulated core market in France has allowed it to be a patient (some say irresponsible) investor overseas.

That is a brief description of outcomes from the process of reform in the power sector, which we offer in the spirit of suggesting new general theories of reform rather than as a fully tested scheme of taut hypotheses. Now we turn to a remaining question. Is the dual market system a stable and desirable outcome?

Are dual markets stable?

Is this dual market merely a transition to a fully reformed market or something else? In the broadest sense, these studies do not suggest that this outcome is permanently stable for one simple reason: the dual market concentrates in the hands of the state the parts of the system that are least viable financially. So long as these components – mainly distribution and final marketing of power – are insolvent then the electric power system as a whole will not be financially sustainable. In the short-run, our studies have uncovered four coping strategies that might suggest that dual markets may persist and allow a variety of "dual firms," foreign and domestic, private or autonomous public, to prosper within them. None of these coping mechanisms is itself stable, and the continuing turmoil is likely to favor dual firms that are better able than traditional private firms to manage the recurring uncertainties. Indeed, dual firms find that persistent uncertainties work to their advantage, with the result that they might actually encourage turmoil and block further comprehensive reforms.

First, current systems could persist through ongoing subsidy. So long as distributors take in lower revenues than it costs to deliver services, then some additional subsidy is needed. Some of the political systems studied in this book have demonstrated a willingness to pay extremely high subsidies to the power sector precisely to avoid the political difficulties of reform. In Mexico, total subsidies to the power sector approach five percent of GDP, which makes Mexico the least sustainable (financially) of all the power systems studied in this book. In India, one of the central tasks of the state regulatory commissions is to compute the subsidy that is required to make the system financially whole. This has been a key step in divorcing the various activities of the state electricity boards from the shell game accounting that has propagated financial harm to every other activity that has become interwoven with the function of supplying electric services. In Andhra Pradesh every subsidy calculated by the regulatory commission has been paid by the state government. Thus the system now balances its books and the dual market has attained stability. (If Andhra Pradesh had actually fully privatized all elements of its power system the state government might have been less inclined to pay the required subsidy, as has happened to Brazil's private distributors. It is politically easier to shift costs to an external, private actor – and thus squeeze his profits – than for government to ignore the need to subsidize its own operations.) However, this coping strategy will be difficult to sustain in the face of widespread decreasing tolerance for public budget deficits and the still rising costs of the incremental power capacity.

Second, the dual market outcome – although seemingly inefficient as an economic enterprise – could be sustainable if the system is able to cover its costs and power users do not mobilize to oppose this inefficient outcome. In two of the countries studied here – China and South Africa – final tariffs, on average, recover nearly the full costs of the present system.[24] In China, power is therefore relatively expensive. There is mounting resistance to tariff increases in China as users already paying high prices see the demand for still higher tariffs as evidence of inefficient corruption marbled through the electric power system. In South Africa, low tariffs yield cost recovery because the existing stock is already amortized owing to the long history of over-investment in the sector. Current tariffs are probably half the level required to make investments in new power plants viable, but tariffs in South Africa are on the rise and the total revenues of the power system are not substantially different from total costs. (Whether the much higher tariffs needed to finance investment in new capacity will be politically achievable remains to be seen. New plants are allowed, by law, to pass their costs through to users; however, previously South Africa's regulatory commission has scaled back proposals from Eskom to increase tariffs.)

Third, governments could adopt policies that make it feasible to reduce glaring costs and to make the system financially more sustainable without much altering its structure. Through labor reform it has proved possible to cut some payrolls in state enterprises. Through reforms in fuel markets – itself partly a function of labor policy – it might prove

---

[24] In China, some subsidy does exist – stemming from the relatively low cost of capital for some projects that are favored by the central government – but the rise in tariff needed to sustain the system remains much lower than typical rates of economic growth.

possible to reduce the cost of primary fuels. In Mexico, shifting from the current primary fuel (oil) to gas has cut fuel costs.[25] (In the other four countries the shift to gas will certainly raise average costs.) In power networks that are run inefficiently, various technical reforms could reduce costs. India's transmission and distribution system runs on relatively low voltages, and reforms to raise voltage and improve grid management would cut line losses and also make it harder to pilfer from the system. Such reductions in costs can help, although in most cases the plausible trimming of expense seems unlikely to offset fully the need for higher tariffs to finance expansion of the system to meet growing demand.

Fourth, the grid-based system could be allowed to deteriorate. Users that need high quality power could continue to exit, and a series of technological innovations in small generators and high power electronics is making that option easier to pursue. In the extreme case – partly evident in portions of India – the power system could return to its fragmented origins where lucrative customers supply their own power and the rest struggle. The integrated grid-connected system could barely limp along even as users willing to pay for self-supply get what they need. This outcome need not necessarily imply that only wealthy businesses and a few families would obtain reliable power. In many rural areas, systems of self-supply have emerged that cover their costs and, in some cases, are more reliable than grid services. This fragmentation of integrated power systems is likely to continue, but we do not foresee that a complete dissolution of the public power system – stranded with users who can't or won't pay adequate tariffs and readily accept lower quality service – is politically sustainable.

All four of these coping strategies are plausible and amply evident in the case studies presented in this book. Although none is likely to be permanently viable, the dual market offers local equilibria that could prove to be persistent. Moreover, the dual firms that bridge the gaps between the public and the private, and between competitive markets and political allocation, are most likely to prevail in the sector because they have substantial abilities to preserve the uncertain and unstable environment where they can best apply their skills at managing political and regulatory risks. Once embedded, such firms will protect and prolong the uncertainties that give rise to their comparative advantage.

---

[25] The exact effect of shifting to gas is difficult to quantify because fuel oil is subsidized unless gas has been priced with reference to the US market. Moreover, the high sulfur content of fuel oil used in power plants cuts the value of the oil for alternative uses.

Regulatory uncertainties are likely to persist for reasons detailed elsewhere in this volume. First, electricity has been generally treated as a political more than a commercial good. Certain groups perceive they are entitled to low cost and universal provision. Where these perceptions correspond with political power the result has been pervasive subsidies whose reduction or elimination is extremely difficult. Second, infrastructure markets in general are broadly seen as cultures of corruption. They are prodigious users of capital and suppliers of jobs; key decisions, such as the siting of power plants, are influenced heavily by political choices. If prices rise the expectable cry is that illegal payoffs must be at fault. Especially where privatization is an aspect of reform, it is often assumed that public assets are being transferred below cost in return for bribes and undercover privileges. Third, there are extreme asymmetries of knowledge between regulators and market actors that make it difficult for public officials to assess true operating costs and fair returns on investment – especially for new entrants that use novel technologies. These asymmetries accentuate the tendencies of regulators to hold down tariffs because they lack the experience or the analytical capacity to evaluate the true marginal costs of incremental power. Finally, regulators remain politically linked to the state enterprises from which they have only recently been separated. Reform away from integrated state utilities creates a formal divorce between policy-makers (regulators and ministry officials) and the partly privatized state firms that can emerge as dual firms. However, the re-apportionment or secondment of familiar personnel among these restructured organizations does not eliminate the personal ties or shared sense of joint purpose that has historically linked political goals (such as subsidy to important voting blocs or privilege for incumbent fuels) and the decisions that affect investment and operation. Regulators pressured from multiple sides in pursuit of multiple goals with limited access to reliable information are highly unlikely to produce stable or predictable rules. Rather, the rules are likely to be anchored in the incumbent system with periodic forays as reforming ideas gain hold or experiments are tried.

The volatile business cycles that arise in fast-developing nations are also likely to yield uncertainty in regulatory decision and confer advantages to dual firms. During periods of high demand, we have suggested that the government adopts policies that favor entry of investors, such as IPPs, that build needed capacity. When the rise in demand slows near the trough of the business cycle, lucrative time on the grid must be rationed among power suppliers. Dual firms fare best in that process while the equity returns of more peripheral, less politically connected, generators get squeezed. This squeeze on hours dispatched may even be orchestrated in the name of market-friendly reform because state-associated dual firms are likely to have a portfolio of large-scale, amortized, and reasonably efficient plants that would dominate merit order dispatch rules based on short-run marginal costs. New power from IPPs – financed on a project basis with hard capital and high risk premia, and fuel (usually gas) that is more costly than the incumbent fuel – have much higher marginal cost and are less able to adjust to flexible dispatch that can be tolerated by the incumbents.

In these nations undergoing broader economic reforms, the effects of business cycle swings are often exaggerated. Politicians anxious to legitimize their reform programs promise rapid increases in economic growth, implying the need for dramatic expansion in power capacity, only to find a glut later when the business cycle turns. As power demand races then stagnates, the combined market and political power of dual firms leaves them as the actors that are capable of surviving and growing through the cycles.

Studies of partial reform in other settings have arrived at similar conclusions (Hellman, 1998). Fundamental economic and political instabilities of partially reformed systems prevent regulators from finding a single equilibrium on which they can construct a credible set of rules of the game that can long withstand expectable political pressures. Certain firms – what we have identified as dual firms – possess organizational advantages that result in their ability to influence the ongoing unstable flow of regulation in their favor and to consolidate their status against potential competitors. What might happen if reformers observe these outcomes and, rightly, fear for their economic efficiency? We suggest three (not exclusive) responses may follow. First, reformers could redouble their efforts to de-integrate and privatize the power system. These efforts are likely to encounter severe opposition as the loci of insolvency are brought into focus and political groups mobilize in opposition. In all five countries tariffs have been most favorable for the groups that are most well-organized politically around the issue of electricity prices – exactly as any mainstream theory of political action would expect – and in every instance those groups obtain electricity that is less costly than the long-run marginal cost of new supply. In the four democracies those groups have tended to be populist in orientation, such as India's farmers and South Africa's poor urban households. In China they have been well-organized industrial users.

Second, a new wave of reformers burned by the dual market could attempt to re-assemble the power system into something resembling its original state. These efforts will require undoing the privileges that have accumulated for dual firms, which may prove more difficult as time passes. And re-integration will require facing the problems of inadequate investment and poor operations that inspired reform in the first place. The new integrationists might attempt SOE reforms such as through the imposition of hard budget constraints, transparent accounting, and stricter systems for governance. They might succeed, if they can also raise average tariffs to cover the cost of new supply. So far, this option has not been pursued in any of the five countries that we studied.

Third, the dual firms themselves might encounter problems that impede their ability to function in this hybrid role. The political assets of a dual firm are highly specialized to a country and perhaps even within particular jurisdictions inside a country. For firms that seek growth, this model can quickly become self-limiting. Moreover, dual firms may make poor partners for outside investors, such as multinational energy companies that are wary of local partners whose very political assets give them characteristics that make their governance opaque. If the dual firms falter, then reformers may need to look more closely at the first or second options. While we can rule out categorically none of these responses, the most likely outcome is stable uncertainty and domination by those new firms best adapted to such pervasive ambiguities.

Policy implications

We are mindful that a large body of policy advice about the design of power markets already exists and often is animated by the assumptions of the standard textbook model of unbundling, corporatization, privatization and market competition. Most real countries, as suggested by our sample of five, have made little progress toward that goal. Thus we focus here on the special policy implications that arise in the dual markets that actually exist and appear likely to persist.

The need to focus on distribution reforms

In periods of crisis and when brief moments of political opportunity arise, policy makers have reached for the textbooks that have been available on their shelves. The studies show that there have been partial successes in reforming wholesale supplies – notably with the introduction of IPPs – but little progress in reforming distribution services. The most serious problem is that distributors have been left liable for covering the difference between their costs and politically mandated final tariffs. In all four of the democracies examined in this book, average tariffs for retail customers are set below the full cost of new supplies, and in each case transmission and distribution enterprises have been left to bear most of the shortfall. This has given the state strong control over distribution companies that depend entirely on the state for subsidy. It has also impeded the ability of governments to mobilize financing for more costly new capacity since investors are especially wary of building power plants for customers that are insolvent with uncertain ability to honor contracts.

Governments have not ignored these problems in the enterprises that distribute electricity. However, they have found that these problems are much harder to solve because solutions require progress on the many other reforms mentioned earlier, such as the ability to impose hard budget constraints on state enterprises that supply highly politicized and under-priced electric service and the creation of independent courts and regulators. Even something as simple as cutting off nonpaying customers has required special legal reforms. In Brazil, the new private owners of distribution companies had their efforts to install tamper-proof metering systems in low-income areas challenged in court and government. In India, Andhra Pradesh and other states that have done well in reducing theft from the distribution system have passed special laws to increase the penalty for convicted electricity pilferers. Taming costs has required labor reforms that have been severely resisted – to the point, in Mexico, that labor unions at CFE control sufficient votes that they can block legislation that is needed to reform the power sector.

For outsiders who have advocated reform – like the World Bank and the many independent experts – a commonly suggested remedy is to privatize distributors. Private firms would face hard budget constraints and have the built-in incentive to cut costs. In practice, however, this has not been easy to do for two broad reasons. First, the government itself has often not wanted to get out of the distribution business, even when it loses money, because distribution of electricity is a visible public function that confers benefits. In South Africa, money-losing municipalities have strongly resisted the redrawing of lines around the regional electricity distributors (REDs) in an effort to make the REDs financially more viable by including in each RED a proper balance of higher paying industrial and wealthy residential customers along with low-income users whose tariffs do not fully cover the cost of providing services. Municipalities have coveted this service not just because it is a visible function of government but also because the ability to cut electric services has been a weapon that they have used to force users to pay their bills for other municipal services, including water. In India, government control over distribution has made it possible to promise nearly free electricity to farmers – a politically powerful group. In China, although tariffs exceed the cost of new supply, state-dominated utilities display the normal dysfunctions of state-dominated enterprises, such as management that focuses on employment and political tasks rather than efficient allocation of investment and fiscal solvency. Reform could raise efficiency, but these utilities are politically valuable channels for patronage – in the Chinese system such patronage lifts tariffs and shifts resources from diffuse and powerless customers to politically-connected suppliers, while in the democracies the patronage in electric utilities tends to shift resources (via subsidy) from the state itself.

Second, even if the government wanted to remove itself from the function of distribution it would need to convince private actors to purchase the system and assume the task. Few private investors would want the job unless the other reforms – such as labor reform, the creation of independent regulators, and judicial reform – had already been undertaken.[26] The empowerment of regulators has been particularly important. Where distributors have been in private hands – such as in the U.S., where most electricity is distributed by for-profit firms – regulators have seen their task as protecting consumers against the monopolistic tendencies of the distributors. In contrast, in most of the countries examined in this book the key challenge for regulators has been to muster the authority needed to protect the distribution companies against the monopsonistic tendencies of politically organized consumers.

In the five countries studied here, only two have actually attempted any privatization of distributors. In India, a few cities were already served by private distributors (notably Mumbai), and two states actually privatized distributors. In Orissa the privatization was a disaster – precisely because the other reforms were not already in place. In Delhi, the bidding for privatization was based on commitments to reduce losses rather than simply the price to be paid for the assets. This scheme, though still young, appears to be successful precisely because much of the logic of private ownership is not being followed. Private operators of the Delhi distribution system are improving collections and billings not merely because they own the system but because their tariffs are explicitly designed to reward them for meeting performance goals, principally system efficiency and collections. Moreover, both companies that operate Delhi's distribution networks are dual firms. Neither would be

---

[26] Indeed, on this point most conventional wisdom has settled – politically difficult reforms (including raising tariffs) should be implemented prior to privatization (Argentina, notably, followed this advice). This emerging consensus is reflected in a recent World Bank policy report on restructuring infrastructure. Ioannis N. Kessides, *Reforming Infrastructure: Privatization, Regulation, and Competition*, World Bank Policy Research Report (Washington, D.C., 2004).

profitable without their capacity to mobilize the political decisions to extend the subsidies after the formally established period when the subsidies, paid to TransCo who supplies the distributors with bulk power below cost, are supposed to be phased out.

The other country in our sample to experiment with privatization is Brazil – there, the government adopted tariffs that made privatization look attractive, until an unexpected currency devaluation in 1999 and a sharp decline in power consumption in 2001 revealed the full risks for private investors after they had sunk their money. The Brazil experience – and a similar experience in Argentina, where all elements of the power sector found their tariff renegotiated in the wake of the 2002 financial crisis – should make private investors in distribution especially wary. Two instances of outright privatization (in Brazil and in Orissa) have rested on regulatory rules that, in effect, allowed private investors to delude themselves about real risks when purchasing distributors – in Orissa because private investors did not know what they were purchasing, and in Brazil because a new economic context motivated a change in the original deal.

A new conventional wisdom is arising that distribution reform is required much earlier in the reform process than has been practiced over the last decade. We subscribe to that view, but we caution that distribution reform – whether pushed early or late in a broader process of electric power reform – can unfold in a manner that violates textbook reformers' intentions. In most situations where political regulators are torn between conflicting policy goals and regulation is thus unstable, gaming must be expected. As regulators bounce back and forth between demands for universal service, affordable power for all, business competitiveness and economic efficiency, firms with particular abilities to play ahead of and around unstable rules will prosper. Those distribution districts that have relatively more paying customers and fewer traditionally subsidized consumers will be cherry picked for initial privatization by the better informed. National dual firms, like those in Delhi, which are better able to exercise political influence than their competitors will be more likely to risk investments that require continuing transfers from state treasuries. Private local distribution networks will emerge to flourish where they can aggregate high value users and also persuade regulators to allow them to wheel their excess power across external grids without burdensome system charges. In all these cases, where politics renders wholesale textbook distribution unrealistic, the least solvent elements in the system will remain in the hands of the state – ever less amenable to sustainable reform. While restructured distribution must undergird efficient electricity growth, new recipes for reform that do not anticipate the conflicts that power politics always generates will again disappoint expectations.

Creating and sustaining constituencies for reform

Incumbent utilities are usually powerfully connected to political elites and thus are a strong conservative element in the process of reform. Even when the incumbents stand to gain from reform – for example, in the case of China's Huaneng Power – they favor an insider style of reform that relies on opacity and propagates inefficiencies. In addition to these organizational barriers to reform, the state-dominated system has bequeathed expectations about favorable tariffs that can be difficult to unseat. With electric service intrinsic to modern economic growth, opponents of reform can easily point to the risks of change to magnify wariness about bold experiments with uncertain outcomes. (Indeed, worldwide no event caused a greater setback to the case for market reform than the power crisis in California. Prior to California's meltdown, reformers pointed to England and Wales as positive examples; after, opponents pointed to California while reformers were forced to engage in complicated explanations for why the lessons of California would not apply locally.) And unlike telecommunications, there are no technological wonders akin to Moore's Law, wireless or the Internet that allow new entrants to create new markets and gain share easily, drive down costs and tariffs, and disrupt the established institutional system while demonstrating the tangible benefits from change.

Faced with these difficulties, special attention is needed to building and sustaining political coalitions that favor reform. In part, the variation in outcomes from the many diverse attempts to reform the power sectors examined in this book reflects the range of efforts to create coalitions for reform. Brazil's first round of reforms in the early 1990s occurred not simply because reformers had a strong mandate for change. They softened the opposition to selling several distribution enterprises by offering special loans from the federal government to fund large projects that politicians could use as examples of the benefits of reform. In Mexico, the fullest efforts at restructuring – begun in the late 1990s and extending to today – have largely failed because the effort to bring change to the power sector arrived at the same time that the Mexican political system was fragmenting, which made it especially difficult for the federal government to create a winning coalition for reform. When the PRI had complete control over Mexican governance it could normally muster the votes needed for policy change of any magnitude. (Indeed, many PRI policies were codified in the constitution rather than simply adopted as legislation. In a truly contested democracy, it is much less likely that any single party would be able to marshal the votes needed to alter the constitution.) The only one of the four democracies that we have studied that has been able to sustain a consistent electoral majority is South Africa, and the lack of urgent need for new power in the 1990s meant that the ruling African National Congress did not need to use its majority for much in this area.

The various attempts at reform underscore three false notions that have diverted attention away from the need to build politically viable reform coalitions. One is the prominent role given to experts – especially outside consultants – in the reform process. In most of the histories of restructuring that we examine in this book there is a moment when the experts are "called in" to develop a plan. Almost always those experts create plans with a tin ear for politics; the plans are not viable because they espouse technically correct ideas for a landscape whose contours reflect political rather than technical forces. In recent years India's pro-reform officials have deployed experts in a different way that has been much more effective – having established performance criteria, the Indian government has hired outside expert accountants to measure and assess performance against the agreed criteria. In that setting, independence and expertise assure that the books are clean and that performance is measured objectively. Expertise was not used as a substitute for politically informed judgments.

The second false notion is that stakeholder consultation is an effective means of creating a coalition. Many of these reform efforts – notably in Brazil and in South Africa – have been marked by extensive and broad-based efforts at stakeholder consultation. New World Bank guidelines for power sector reform also underscore the need for repeated stakeholder consultation. To be sure, such consultations can be an essential part of educating and building a coalition, but such consultation is no substitute for an active strategy to nurture a supporting constituency. Restructuring creates losers as well as winners, and with the incumbents already deeply entrenched through subsidies and interlocking relationships in fuel markets and in labor, the constituency for reform can be extremely weak. Among the active efforts that are perhaps most interesting from this volume are the systems of payments used in Brazil and India. In India, the financing system known as APDRP rewards the states that have done the best with reforms – as measured by independent experts – and thus aligns immediate financial reward with success at implementing policy changes that are favored by the center.

Third, we expected that investors themselves (especially foreign investors) might become a politically powerful constituency for reform.

Certainly the investment community, broadly, creates a strong magnetic field that guides reform – the golden straightjacket that has kept developing countries focused on the need for market-friendly rules. But aside from those broad influences it is striking how weak individual foreign investors seem to be as forces for continued reform. Investors, once they have sunk their investment, appear to care less about reform in abstract and more about the decisions that affect their particular investment. They seek predictability more than the abstract efficiency of a future market reform. Moreover, visible activism by foreign investors can also become self-defeating as such investors often polarize the debate and are easy prey for nationalists.

Attaining leverage outside the electric sector

The complex and interlocking nature of reforms that affect the power sector explain why fundamental reform of the most entrenched aspects of the system is such a slow process and why even concerted efforts at reform inside the power sector can be undone by external policies such as lax budgetary control and indifferent (or hostile) courts. In China, for example, concerted efforts to attract private investment to the power sector were undermined when the central government pursued expansionary monetary policy that gave state enterprises preferential access to cheap capital, which meant that privately financed generators had a much higher cost basis than state-connected plants.

The corollary to our attention to complementary reforms is that the greatest leverage on the electric power sector probably lies outside the sector itself. Indeed, experts on the power sector need to become more savvy about finding leverage in this larger firmament of policy choices. The studies in this volume suggest that the single most important reforms lie in finance – notably, the application of hard budget constraints on state-owned enterprises. In some of the cases, labor reforms have also created an opportunity to boost economic efficiency by cutting costs. In others, improvement in corporate governance has been essential to creating a context for encouraging joint investment since outside firms usually want local partners to help manage risks but need protection to ensure that their partnership does not run amok. Stronger competition law can tame the dominance of small numbers of well-connected firms in emerging energy markets, which in turn can create opportunities to new entrants. These complementary reforms, in many cases, have required sailing directly into strong political headwinds, with success coming often only during brief punctuated periods of crisis – usually a severe financial crisis when reformers have a strong mandate for change.

Building appropriate regulatory institutions

The creation of independent power regulators is one of the striking institutional changes in developing countries in the last decade. Training programs that focus on building regulatory capacity in developing countries often use as their starting point the experience of regulators in the OECD nations, where there is a long tradition of regulation and large cadres of regulation experts.

In practice, however, the tasks of electricity regulators in the OECD and the developing countries differ sharply and may actually be diverging. In the OECD, notably the United States, the traditional practice of regulators has involved reviewing investment proposals from regulated utilities and deciding on fair rates of return. The targets of their review have had audited books, usually subjected to the accounting standards of publicly traded companies. Regulators have faced difficulties of asymmetrical information about the true costs of new capital projects and operations, but in large and diverse markets with competitive equipment suppliers and capital markets such problems have not been severe. Fuel costs are usually determined in competitive markets and easily passed to customers. Where power systems are in transition from fully regulated supply to roles for markets in forming prices, regulators are increasingly focusing on the new task of spotting and taming the abuse of market power.

Regulators in developing countries worry about quite different problems. Their jobs are viewed as highly political, and in most cases that we examined they must make decisions with an eye to what will survive political scrutiny. Indeed, the actual authority of regulators has varied substantially and in ways that reflect the contours of political and organizational power in the executive branch of government that delegates its authority to the regulator. In Brazil, the regulator's authority included the right to set tariffs under some circumstances. In Mexico, the authorities were much more limited to review of proposed projects but not control over tariffs. (The difference in these outcomes reflects, in large part, the political power of those who could lose authority from tariff-setting regulators. In Brazil, the regulated units were highly fragmented, with many controlled by individual states that the Federal government sought to bring into line. In Mexico, the incumbent was mainly a single all-powerful enterprise, CFE, that, if upset too severely, could retaliate by supporting political opponents using enormous funds that the enterprise and its labor union had stashed away for that purpose. Moreover, in Mexico the central government's finance ministry is powerful and demands continued control over the full portfolio of financial issues, including electricity tariffs.)

Even when these regulators perform tasks that are closest to those of their colleagues in advanced industrialized countries – such as reviewing the reasonableness of PPAs offered to IPPs – the challenges are daunting. In reviewing PPA proposals the regulator faces overwhelming problems of asymmetrical information because the IPPs they review are often first-of-a-kind and the applicant will claim (probably correctly) that experience elsewhere is not a proper guide. Our own survey of capital costs of IPPs, for example, found huge variation across the developing world (Woodhouse, 2005). The regulator will probably not know the true cost of the equipment installed, especially if contemporary changes in trade rules make it possible to import unfamiliar equipment from overseas. The regulator, aware of his own fragile authority, will be wary of allowing politically sensitive yet essential risk premia that private investors demand.

Thus it is not clear to us how much of the OECD regulatory experience actually applies in countries where dual markets prevail, the "rule of law" is weak, strong consumers have incentives to abandon the system, and regulatory independence rests on a shallow foundation. We suggest that efforts to build regulatory capacity in developing countries may be particularly relevant if they engage more fully regulators from other developing countries in an effort to compare experiences across similar settings, rather than attempting to glean useful lessons from the OECD settings. At present, however, many of the capacity-building programs are designed with the false notion that there is much useful knowledge to transfer from the OECD to the developing world.

Conclusion

The studies in this book reveal electric power systems in five countries that are all quite different from the old state-owned enterprises that dominated during an era of more complete state control over the economy. Even in South Africa, the country that has been required to do the least in reform because it has survived the longest on the legacy of over-building from the earlier era, the power system is in the midst of migration to a new industrial form.

The political factors that interfere with the ideal operations of economically sound models are the unavoidable legacy of the past institutional practices. They are not simply "barriers" that can be cleared with enough political will. Economists and investors must consider the likelihood that fragmented and transitory systems are reasonably stable political economic orders.

None of these five countries illustrates the idealized textbook form of market-based power systems that had been espoused as a final goal of reformers and is evident today in only a few (mainly industrialized country) jurisdictions. As piecemeal and contested reforms have proceeded across varied jurisdictions, the very concept of what now constitutes the reform template has become cloudy. Rather than a textbook reform, we have suggested that reforms have unintentionally created an alternative system – a "dual market" – with its own peculiar dynamics and industrial organization. We have suggested that this industrial form may prove to be quite stable politically, if not economically efficient. It has spawned a class of specialized firms that are talented at combining skills of efficient management with the political connections necessary to operate for profit ventures in a state-laden electricity system.

We also find that reformers have concentrated their efforts on the parts of the electric business that are least prone to natural monopoly – namely, generation of bulk electricity. But the largest inefficiencies and the greatest difficulties for reform lie elsewhere – in the distribution systems that, in most cases, have remained in the hands of the state and are politically prized (although often economically insolvent) assets because they are the point of connection between the power system and politically-influential retail customers. Reform of distribution systems remains the largest unmet task for reformers. Success on that front requires reforms in a host of other areas – capital markets, law, administration, labor, public finance, and industrial organization more generally. Those broader reforms have proved very difficult to adopt; yet they offer greater leverage over the power system than have most power-specific reform programs.

Bibliography

African National Congress, Reconstruction and development program. Johannesburg: Umanyano Publications. 1994.

Agrawala, P., Personal Discussions, R. Tongia, Editor. 2003.

Ahluwalia, M. S., Report Of The Expert Group (on) Settlement Of SEB Dues. Ministry of Power: New Delhi. 2001.

Ahluwalia, M. S., *State Level Performance Under Economic Reforms In India.* Center for Research on Economic Development and Policy Reform (CREDPR): Palo Alto. 2001.

Ahluwalia, S. S. and G. Bhatiani. Tariff Setting in the Electric Power Sector - Base paper on Indian Case Study in TERI Conference on Regulation in Infrastructure Services. New Delhi. 2000.

Aneel, Quality of the Electricity Supply, www.aneel.gov.br. 2003.

Apt, J. "Competition Has Not Lowered U.S. Electricity Prices." *The Electricity Journal* Volume 18, Issue 2, March 2005, Pages 52–61.

Asia Pacific Energy Research Centre, Electricity Sector Deregulation in the Asia Pacific Region. Tokyo: Asia Pacific Energy Research Centre. 2000.

Averch, H. and L. L. Johnson. "Behavior of the Firm Under Regulatory Constraint." *The American Economic Review* 52, 1052–1069. 1962.

Bacon, R. W. and J. Besant-Jones, "Global Electric Power Reform, Privatization and Liberalization of the Electric Power Industry in Developing Countries." Energy & Mining Sector Board Discussion Paper Series, No. 2. Washington, D.C.: The World Bank Group. 2002.

Bacon, R., "Global Energy Sector Reform in Developing Countries: A Scorecard." Report 219, ESMAP, 1999.

Baer, W., *A Economia Brasileira.* Nobel, São Paulo. 1995.

Bakovic, T., B. Tenenbaum, and F. Woolf, "Regulation by Contract: A New Way to Privatize Electricity Distribution?" World Bank Working Paper No. 14. 2003.

Bardhan, P., *The Politics of Economic Reform in India, in Poverty, Agrarian Structure, and Political Economy in India.* Oxford University Press: New Delhi. 2003.

Bastarrachea, S. and J. Aguilar, "Evolución de la Industria Eléctrica en México," in *El Sector Eléctrico de México.* CFE y Fondo de Cultura Económica. 1994.

Bayman, S., Return of the Big Bet: U.S. Business in India, in US-India Business Council - 27th Annual Meeting. Washington, DC. 2002.

Beck, U. I., *La Societé du Risque*, Aubier, Paris. 2001.

Berrah, N., Lamech, R., and Zhao, J., Fostering Competition in China's Power Markets. World Bank Discussion Paper No. 416. 2001.

Berrah, N., Jianping Zhao, Fostering Competition in China's Power Markets, World Bank Discussion Paper No. 416. 2001.

Bharadwaj, A. and R. Tongia, Distributed Power Generation: Rural India - A Case Study. Submitted for publication. 2003.

Bidwai, P., "The other Enrons," in *Frontline*. 2002.

Bradley, Jr., R. L. "The Origins of Political Electricity: Market Failure or Political Opportunism?" *Energy Law Journal* 17, 59–102. 1996.

Bratton, W. and J. A. McCahery, "Comparative Corporate Governance and the Theory of the Firm: The Case Against a Global Cross-Reference," 38 *Columbia Journal of Transnational Law*. 213, 219–220. 1999.

Breceda, M., "Debate on the Reform of the Electricity Sector in Mexico," North American Commission for Environmental Cooperation. 2000.

Brennan, T., K. Palmer and S. Martinez, *Alternating Currents: Electricity Markets and Public Policy*. Resources for the Future, Washington, D.C. 2002.

Brown, R. E. and M. W. Marshall, "The Cost of Reliability," *Transmission & Distribution World*. 2001.

Business Map: The electricity supply industry: economic and social effects of restructuring. Johannesburg. 2001.

Cambridge Energy Research Associates. "Mexico's Supreme Court Ruling: Opening Pandora's Box?" *CERA Insight*. 2002.

Camozatto, I., "A Trajetória do Setor de Energia Elétrica de 1980," *Memória de Eletricidade*, Rio de Janeiro. 1995.

Carbajo, J. and S. Fries, "Restructuring infrastructure in transition economies." Working Paper No. 24, European Bank for Reconstruction and Development. 1997.

Carneiro, D. D. and E. M. "Modiano, Ajuste Externo e Desequilíbrio Interno: 1980–1984," in Abreu, M. P. *A Ordem do Progresso: 100 anos de Política Econômica na República*, Campus, Rio de Janeiro. 1990.

Carreón Rodríguez, V. G. "Las Tarifas en el Sector Eléctrico Mexicano", *Boletín División de Economía*. CIDE. 2003.

Carreon Rodríguez, V. G. and J. Rosellón, "El sector eléctrico mexicano: La necesidad de una reforma structural," *Ejecutivos de Finanzas IMEF*, Año XXXI, No. 4. 2000.

Carreón Rodríguez, V. G. and J. Rosellón, "The Economic Rationale of the Structural and Regulatory Reform of the Mexican electricity Sector," Working Paper STDE-199. Centro de Investigación y Docencia Económicas, A.C. 2000.

Carreón Rodríguez, V. G. and J. Rosellón, "La Reforma del Sector Eléctrico Mexicano: Recomendaciones de Política Pública". *Gestión y Política Pública*, Volumen XI, Numero 2. 2002a.

Carreón Rodríguez, V. G. and J. Rosellón, "Incentives for Expansion of Electricity Supply and Capacity Reserves in the Mexican Electricty Sector". Working Paper STDE-219. Centro de Investigación y Docencia Económicas, A.C. 2002b.

CEA, All India Electricity Statistics: General Review 2005. Central Electricity Authority, New Delhi. 2005.

CEA, Fourth National Power Plan. Central Electricity Authority, New Delhi. 1997.

CESC Limited, *The Story of Electricity in the City of Calcutta.* 2001.

Chen, B., J. Kimball Dietrich and Yi Fang, eds., *Financial Market Reform in China: Progress, Problems and Prospects.* Westview Press, Boulder Colorado. P.5. 1999.

China Electric Power Yearbook, China Electric Power Publishing House, Beijing, China, various years.

China Statistical Yearbook, China Energy Yearbook. Beijing, China, various years. (Chinese)

Choukroun, S., *Enron in Maharashtra: Power Sector Development and National Identity in Modern India.* University of Pennsylvania, Philadelphia. 2001.

Christie, R., *Electricity, industry and class in South Africa.* London: Macmillan. 1984.

Dailiami, M. and R. Hauswald, "The Emerging Project Bond Market: Covenant Provisions and credit Spreads," World Bank Policy Research Working Paper 3095. July, 2003.

Davies, M and G. Steyn, Electricity in South Africa. *Financial Times Business Limited.* London. 1998.

de Castro, A.B and F.E.P. De Souza, "A Economia Brasileira em Marcha Forçada," *Paz e Terra*, Rio de Janeiro. 1985.

de Oliveira, A., Internacionalisation du capital et développement économique: L'industrie pétrolière au Brésil, D.Sc., Université de Grenoble, France. 1977.

de Oliveira, A., ed., *Power System Performance: Options and Opportunities for Developing Countries.* COPED, CEC, Luxembourg. 1992.

de Rosenzweig, F. and J.C. Femat, *Mexican Electricity Sector: Is it moving forward?.* Mimeo. 2003.

Deloitte Touche-Tohmatsu, "Sustainable Power Sector Reform in Emerging Markets: Financial Issues and Options," Joint World Bank/USAID Policy Paper. June, 2004.

Demsetz, H., "The Cost of Transacting," *The Quarterly Journal of Economics 82*, 33–53 1968.

Department of Minerals and Energy. White Paper of Energy Policy for the Republic of South Africa. Pretoria. 1998.

Department of Minerals and Energy. Electricity Distribution Industry Restructuring Blueprint Report. Pretoria. 2001.

Department of Minerals and Energy / Department of Public Enterprises, Options for reform of the electricity supply industry in South Africa. Internal Government Paper. Version 3.0, July, Pretoria. 2000.

Department of Minerals and Energy, Draft policy and strategy for electricity supply industry reform for the Republic of South Africa. Internal government paper. Version 5, April, Pretoria, 2000.

Devapriya, K.A.K. and H. Wilhelm Alfen, Role of Institutional Arrangements in Financing Project Companies in Asiab draft working paper, Oct. 2, 2003.

Development Research Center of State Council, Strategic Study of Chinese Electric Power Structure Reform and Sustainable Development. Report submitted to the Energy Foundation and W. Alton Jones Foundation. October, 2000. (Chinese)

Development Research Center, Strategies for China's Electricity Reform and Renewable Development (White Paper). Prepared for China Sustainable Energy Program, The Energy Foundation. 2002.

Dias Leite, A., A Energia do Brasil, Nova Fronteira, Rio de Janeiro. 1997.

Dingley, C., Electricity for All.: the Needs and the Means. Monograph. Department of Electrical Engineering, University of Cape Town. 1990.

Diniz, E., "Empresariado, Estado e Políticas Públicas no Brasil: Novas Tendências no Limiar do Novo Milênio," in Ferraz, Crocco e Elias, Liberalização Econômica e Desenvolvimento: modelos, políticas e restrições, Futura, São Paulo. 2003.

D'Sa, A., Power Sector Reform in India - an Overview. International Energy Initiative, Bangalore. 2002.

Dubash, N. ed., Power Politics: Equity and Environment in Electricity Reform; World Resources Institute (WRI), Washington D.C. 2002.

Dubash, N. K. and S. C. Rajan, "The Politics of Power Sector Reform in India," World Resources Institute, Washington, DC. 2001.

Dubash, N. K., "The public benefits agenda in power sector reform," Energy for Sustainable Development 2, 5–14. 2001.

Eberhard, A and van Horen, Poverty and Power: Energy and the South African State. Pluto Press, London. 1995.

Econ. Electricity Price Scenarios for South Africa. A report to the Department of Minerals and Energy, South Africa. Oslo. 2002.

Electricity Supply Commission Annual Reports 1923–1935, South Africa.

Eletrobrás, Plano Decenal de Expansão, Rio de Janeiro. 1999.

Eletrobrás, Relatório Sintético de Diagnóstico do Setor Elétrico, mimeo. 1998.

Emmons, W. M. "Franklin D. Roosevelt, Electric Utilities, and the Power of Competition." The Journal of Economic History, 53, 880–907. 1993.

Energy Information Administration, "World Electricity Installed Capacity by Type, January 1, 2003," International Energy Annual, Posted June 24, 2005.

Eskom. Proposals for the restructuring of the electricity supply industry in South Africa and implications for Eskom. Confidential internal document. 16/7/90. 1990.

Eskom. Annual Report. 1990, 2001, and 2003.

Eskom Act, 1987. Government Printer. Pretoria, 1987.

Estache, A. and M. Rodriguez-Pardina, "Light and Lightning at the End of the Public Tunnel: Reform of the Electricity Sector in the Southern Cone," Policy Research Working Paper No. 2074, Washington, D.C.: The World Bank, 1999.

Estache, A. and M. Rodriguez-Pardina, "Regulatory Lessons from Argentina's Power Concessions," Viewpoint Note No. 92, The World Bank Group, Sept. 1996.

Esty, B. and W. L. Megginson, "Creditor Rights, Enforcement, and Debt Ownership Structure: Evidence From the Global Syndicated Loan

Market," *Journal of Financial and Quantitative Analysis*, Vol. 38, No. 1, pp. 37–59. 2003.

Ferreira, P., On the Efficiency of the Argentinean Electricity Wholesale Market, Seminario No. 09/02. June 6, 2002.

Finon, D., T. Arnt Johnsen and A. Midttun. "After the grace period: Economic and political challenges when electricity markets fact the investment phase." Mimeo.

Fridley David ed. *LBNL: China Energy Databook v. 5.0*, LBNL-47832, May 2001.

Furtado, C, Formação Econômica do Brasil, Cia. Editora Nacional, São Paulo. 1972.

Goldemberg, J., E. Lebre la Rovere and S. Teixeira Coelho. "Expanding Access to Electricity in Brazil." *Energy for Sustainable Development.* 8(4): 86–94. 2004.

Gray, P., "Private Participation in Infrastructure: A Review of the Evidence." Washington, D.C.: The World Bank 2001.

Green, J., Managing Risks in International Power Projects, 672 PLI/Comm 669, Practising Law Institute. 1993.

GTRDC, "Guangdong Provincial Electric Power Market Reform and Future Development," Working Paper, PESD, Stanford University. 2003. (Chinese)

Guangdong Energy Techno-economic Research Center, 1999. Guangdong Electric Power Development and Future Trend. Paper presented at the Forth China Energy Project Workshop of CISAC, Stanford University, November 1999. (Chinese)

Guasch, J. L. *Granting and Renegotiating Infrastructure Concessions.* World Bank, 2004.

Guasch, J. L. and P. Spiller, Managing the Regulatory Process: Design, Concepts, Issues, and the Latin American and Caribbean Story. The World Bank, 1999.

Gupta, J., J. Vlasblom, and C. Kroeze, An Asian Dilemma: Modernizing the electricity sector in China and India in the context of rapid economic growth and the concern for climate change. Vrije Universiteit, Amsterdam, Report number E-01/04. 2001.

Hall, P. A. and D. Soskice eds., *Varieties of Capitalism: The Institutional Foundations of Comparative Advantage.* 2001.

Harris, C., "Private Participation in Infrastructure in Developing Countries: Trends, Impacts, and Policy Lessons," World Banks WP No. 5, 2003.

Harris, C., et al., Infrastructure Projects: A Review of Cancelled Private Projects, Public Policy for the Private Sector Note NO. 252, The World Bank, 2003.

Heller, T. C. and D. G. Victor, A Political Economy of Electric Power Market Restructuring: Introduction to Issues and Expectations, PESD Working Paper #1, 2003.

Heller, W. B. and M. D. McCubbins, "Politics Institutions, and Outcomes: Electricity Regulation in Argentina and Chile," *Policy Reform* 1, 357–387, 1996.

312   Bibliography

Hellman, J. S., "Winners Take All: The Politics of Partial Reform in Postcommunist Transistions," World Politics 50, no. 2, January 1998.

Henisz, Witold J. "The Institutional Environment for Infrastructure Investment," presented at The International Society for the New Institutional Economics Third Annual Meetings: Washington D.C. September 17, 1999.

Henisz, W. J., Zelner, B. A., and Guillen, M. "The Worldwide Diffusion of Market-Oriented Infrastructure Reform, 1977-1999," The Wharton School WP, October 24, 2005.

Henisz, W. J. and Zelner, B. A., "Interest Groups, Veto Points, and Electricity Infrastructure Deployment," International Organization 60, 263-286, Winder 2006.

Hofmaenner, A., A history of energy research in South Africa. PhD thesis. ETH, Zurich. 2002.

Hollingsworth, J. Rogers et al., Contemporary Capitalism: The Embeddedness of Institutions 1997.

Ibge, Estatísticas Históricas do Brasil, Rio de Janeiro. 1986.

IEA, World Energy Outlook. 2002.

IEA, México Energy Outlook Paris, 2002.

IEA, Electricity Market Reform: An IEA Handbook, OECD/IEA, 1999.

IEA, Electricity Reform: Power Generation Costs and Investment, OECD/IEA, 1999b.

IEA, World Energy Outlook 2002: Energy and Poverty, Paris, France, September 2002.

International Finance Corporation, Project Finance in Developing Countries, International Finance Corp., 1999.

Irwin, T., M. Klein, G. E. Perry, and M. Thobani, Dealing with Public Risk in Private Infrastructure, The World Bank, 1997.

Jadresic, A. and F. Fuentes "Government Strategies to Reduce Political and Regulatory Risks in the Intrastructure Sector," paper presented at Private Infrastructure for Development: Confronting Political and Regulatory Risks, Sept. 8–10, 1999, Rome, Italy.

Jamash, T., Mota, R., Newbery, D. and Pollitt, M. "Electrcity Sector Reform in Developing Countries: A Survery of Empirical Evidence on Determinants and Performance," World Bank Policy Research Working Paper 3549, March 2005.

Jiang, S., Ouyang, C., "Strategic Structural Adjustment of the Electric Power Industry during the 9th Five-year Plan Period," in SPC (Comp.), Summary of the Electricity Industry Performance during the 9th Five-year Plan. China Electric Power Press, Beijing, pp. 218 – 232, 2002 (Chinese)

Jiménez San Vicente, A., "The Social and Economic Cost of Structural Adjustments in Mexico". Masters Degree Thesis, Harvard University. 1999.

Jiménez San Vicente, A., "The Political Economy of Tax Collection in Mexico, 1970-2000," PhD Thesis, London School of Economics. 2002.

Joskow, P., "Deregulation and Regulatory Reform in The U.S. Electric Power Sector," mimeo, MIT, 2000.

Joskow, P. L. and R. Schmalensee, "Incentive Regulation for Electric Utilities," Yale Journal of Regulation 4, No. 1, 1986.

Joskow, P. L. and R. Schmalensee, *Markets for Power: An Analysis of Electrical Utility Deregulation.* The MIT Press, 1983.

Kanungo Committee, G.o.O., Report of the Committee on Power Sector Reform of Orissa, Ministry of Power of the Government of India. 2001.

Kessides, I. N. Reforming Infrastructure: Privatization, Regulation, and Competition, World Bank Policy Research Report, 2004.

Kornai, J., "Hardening of the Budget Constraint: The Experience of the Post-socialist Countries," *European Economic Review*, 45(9) :1573–1600 (2001). (chapter 1)

Kornai, J., "Understanding the Soft Budget Constraint," available at <http://post.economics.harvard.edu/faculty/kornai/papers/understanding.pdf> as accessed Nov. 19, 2005.

La Porta, R., F. Lopez-de-Silanes, A. Shleifer and R. Vishny, "Investor protection and corporate governance," *Journal of Financial Economics* 58, 3–27, 2000.

Lal, S., Political Factors Affecting Power Sector Reform in India - An Internal (World Bank) Discussion Note, The World Bank: New Delhi. 2003.

Lamech, R. and K. Saeed, "What International Investors Look For When Investing In Developing Countries: Results from a Survey of International Investors in the Power Sector," World Bank, Energy and Mining Sector Board Discussion Paper No. 6, 2003.

Levy, B. and P. T. Spiller, *Regulations, Institutions, and Commitment* New York., Cambridge University Press, 1996.

Levy, B. and P. T. Spiller, "Regulatory Commitment: A Comparative Analysis of Telecommunications Regulation," *Journal of Law, Economics & Organization*, vol. 10, 201–246, 1994.

Lieberthal, K. and Oksenberg, M., *Policy Making In China – Leaders, Structures, and Processes*, Princeton University Press, Princeton, New Jersey. 1988.

Lieberthal, K., "China's Governing System and Its Impact on Environmental Policy Implementation," *China Environment Series*, Issue 1. Woodrow Wilson Center, Washington, D.C. 1997.

Lima, M, "Petróleo, Energia Elétrica e Siderurgia: A luta pela Emancipação," *Paz e Terra*, Rio de Janeiro. 1975.

Lopez-Calva, L. F. and J. Rosellon, "The Benefits of Privatization: Evidence from México," Universidad de las Americas, Puebla, Mexico, 2002a.

López-Calva, L. F. and J. Rosellon, "On the Potential Distributive Impact of Electricity Reform in Mexico". Working Paper. CIDE. 2002.

Mahalingam, S., Power to the Regulator, in *Frontline*. 1998.

Manibog, F. Dominguez, R., and Wegner, S., "*Power for Development, a Review of the World Bank Group's Experience with Private Participation in the Electricity Sector*," The World Bank, Washington, D.C. 2003.

Marquard, A & A. Eberhard, Towards energy equity, efficiency and environmental sustainability in South Africa: policy challenges. *Energy for Sustainable Development*, Vol IV, No 4, pp 3–7. 2000.

May, M., T. C. Heller, and C. Zhang, Electricity Industry Development and Global Warming Impact: Case Studies of Three Chinese Provinces. Prepared for EPRI, Stanford University, November 2002.

Mc Kinsey, D. And D. Mookherjee 'The Distributive Impact of Privatization in Latin America: Evidence from Four Countries," *Economia*, vol. 3, no. 2, Spring. 2003.

McElroy, M., Industrial Growth, Air Pollution, and Environmental Damage. In *Energizing China: Reconciling Environmental Protection and Economic Growth.* Harvard University Press, Cambridge, MA. 1997.

Medeiros, R., O Capital Privado na Reestruturação do Setor Elétrico, M.Sc., COPPE. 1993.

Megginson, W. L., R. C. Nash and M. Van Randenborgh, "The Financial and Operating Performance of Newly Privatized Firms: An International Empirical Analysis," *The Journal of Finance*, 49:2, 403–452, 1994.

Memória da Eletricidade, A Eletrobrás e a Historia do Setor de Energia Elétrica no Brasil, Rio de Janeiro. 1995.

Merrill Lynch & Co. 2002. "Energy Reform Mexico". México, D. F.

Meyer, J. W. and B. Rowen, "Institutionalized Organizations: Formal Structure as Myth and Ceremony," *American Journal of Sociology* 83 (2):340–363, 1977.

Millan, J. "Power Sector Reform in Latin America: Accomplishments, Failures and Challenges," Economic and Political Weekey, December 10, 2005.

Ministério de Minas e Energia, Balanço Energético Nacional, Brasília. 2000.

Ministry of Coal, Annual Report 2004–05. 2005, Ministry of Coal, Govt. of India: New Delhi.

Ministry of Electric Power Industry, Electric Power Industry in China, China Electric Power Press, Beijing. 1996. (Chinese)

Ministry of Finance, Economic Survey 2001–02, Ministry of Finance (Economic Division), Govt. of India: New Delhi. 2002.

Ministry of Finance, Economic Survey 2003–04, Ministry of Finance (Economic Division), Govt. of India: New Delhi. 2002.

Ministry of Finance, Economic Survey 2004–05, Ministry of Finance (Economic Division), Govt. of India: New Delhi. 2005.

Ministry of Power, 2001–02 Annual Report, Ministry of Power, Govt. of India: New Delhi. 2002.

Ministry of Power, Blueprint for Power Sector Development. New Delhi, 2001.

Ministry of Power, Discussion Paper on Rural Electrification Policies. Ministry of Power: New Delhi, 2003.

Minor, M. S., The Demise of Expropriation as an Instrument of LDC policy 1980–1992, of *Journal of International Business Studies* 1:25, 1994.

Mlambo-Ncguka, P, Electricity supply industry (ESI) vision and objective. Electricity Supply Industry Reform Workshop, Midrand, 3–5 April, 2000.

Mlambo-Ngcuka, p., Minister of Minerals and Energy, press conference July 31, 2001, Pretoria.

Moran, T. H., Political and Regulatory Risk in Infrastructure Investment in Developing Countries: Introduction and Overview, preliminary draft presented at "Private Infrastructure for Development: Confronting Political and Regulatory Risks, Sept. 8–10, 1999, Rome, Italy.

Morgan, G. and S. Tierney, "Research Support for the Power Industry," *Issues in Science and Technology*, Fall 1998.

National Electricity Regulator, Lighting up South Africa: a century of electricity serving humankind. National Electricity Regulator and Open Hand Press, Pretoria. 2001.

National Electricity Regulator, Electricity Supply Handbook of South Africa. National Electricity Regulator, Pretoria. 2001a.

National Electrification Economic Study, Financing requirements of national electrification scenarios. Finance and Tariffs Working Group. National Electrification Forum. Johannesburg. 1993.

National Energy Regulator, National Integrated Resource Plan. Pretoria. 2002.

National Institute of Public Finance and Policy. Conference Summary, in *India: Fiscal Policies to Accelerate Economic Growth.* X New Delhi: National Institute of Public Finance and Policy. 2002.

Newbery, David M., "Regulatory Policies and Reform in the Electricity Supply Industry," Cambridge Working Papers in Economics 9421, Department of Applied Economics, University of Cambridge. 1995.

Newbery, D. M., *Privatization, Restructuring, and Regulation of Network Utilities.* The MIT Press, 1999.

Padmanaban, S. and J. Totino, *Energy Efficiency in Indian Agriculture,* USAID-India: New Delhi. 2001.

Paixão, L. E., Memórias do Projeto RE-SEB, Masao Ohno, São Paulo. 2000.

Parikh, K. S., *The Enron Story and Its Lessons,* Indira Gandhi Institute of Development Research. 1996.

Personal communication: Eberhard interview with Eskom Treasury Department, January 27, 2003.

Personal communication: Eberhard interview with Kevin Morgan, the then-secretary of the privatization study, 28 January 2003.

Pinheiro, AC, F. Giambiagi and J. Gostkorzeqicz, O desempenho Macroeconômico do Brasil nos anos 90, in AC Pinheiro, and M. Mesquita, A Economia Brasileira nos Anos 90, BNDES, Rio de Janeiro. 1999.

Planning Commission, Annual Report 2001–02 on the on the Working of State Electricity Boards & Electricity Departments. Planning Commission, Govt. of India: New Delhi. 2002.

Planning Division of the Ministry of Electric Power, 1996. Report on Electricity Supply and Demand in China, in Planning Division of the Ministry of Electric Power, ed., *Reform and Planning in the Power Industry,* Beijing: China Electric Power Press, 1996. (Chinese)

Powell and Starks, "Does Reform of Energy Sector Networks Improve Access for the Poor?" Washington, DC: The World Bank. 2000.

Powers, L. F., New Forms of Protection for International Infrastructure Investors, in Managing International Political Risk Theodore M. Moran ed., 1998.

Prayas, India Power Sector Reforms Update, Issue 1. 2001, Prayas: Pune.

Radebe, J., Press release by the Minister of Public Enterprises, dated August 10, 2000.

Rajan, A. T., Power sector reform in Orissa: an ex-post analysis of the causal factors. *Energy Policy,* 28(10). 2000.

Rao, M. G. and N. Singh, Intergovernmental Transfers: Rationale, Design and Indian Experience. Center for Research on Economic Development and Policy Reform (CREDPR): Palo Alto. 1998.

Rao, N. V., India's Labor Laws Remain Inflexible. 2000.

Reddy, M. T. Development in the Power Sector in Andhra Pradesh. in Prayas-Focus on Global South – Event on Power Sector Reforms. 2000. Mumbai.

Rodríguez y Rodríguez, G., "Evolución de la Industria Eléctrica en México" in El Sector Eléctrico de México, México, CFE y Fondo de Cultura Económica. 1994.

Rosellón, J., "Pricing Electricity Transmission in Mexico," in Repsol YPF-Harvard Kennedy School Fellows 2003–2004 Research Papers, William Hogan, editor, Cambridge, MA, Kennedy School of Government, Harvard University, April 2005.

Rosellón, J. and J. Halpern, "Regulatory Reform in Mexico' Natural Gas Industry. Liberalization in the Context of a Dominant Upstream Incumbent", Policy Research Working Paper, The World Bank, 2537. 2001.

Ruet, J., "The Limited Globalisation of the Electrical Sector: From The Pre-Eminence Of The States To The Relative Come back Of The Centre," in From globalization to local development in India: questions of scale, Landy, editor. Manohar Publishers: New Delhi. 2003.

Ruet, J., Winners and Losers of State Electricity Board Reforms: An Organizational Analysis. Center de Sciences Humaines: New Delhi. 2001.

Rufin, C., U. Srinivasa Rangan and R. Kumar, "The Changing Role of the State in the Electricity Industry in Brazil, China and India." American Journal of Economics and Sociology. 62(4), pp. 649–675. 2003.

Sankar, T. L. and U. Ramachandra, Regulation of the Indian power sector. ASCI Journal of Management, 29(2). 2000.

Sankar, T. L., Fiscal Impact of Electricity Board's Overdues on States' Finance, in India: Fiscal Policies to Accelerate Economic Growth. New Delhi: National Institute of Public Finance and Policy. 2001.

Sankar, T. L., Towards a People's Plan for Power Sector Reform. Economic and Political Weekly, October 5, 2002: p. 4143–4151.

Schiffer, M. and B. Weder, "Catastrophic Political Risk versus Creeping Expropriation: What determines private infrastructure investment in less developed countries?" University of Basel, July, 2000.

Secretaría de Energía, "Proposal for the electricity sector modernization". México, D.F. 2002a.

Secretaría de Energía, "Prospectiva del Mercado de Gas Natural 2002–2011". DGFPE. México. 2002b.

Secretaría de Energía, "Prospectiva del Sector Eléctrico 2002–2011". DGFPE. México. 2002c.

Secretaría de Hacienda y Crédito Público, "Programa Nacional de Financiamiento al Desarrollo, 2002–2006". Mexico. 2002.

Shah, T. and Tewari, D. D. "An assessment of South African prepaid electricity experiment, lessons learned, and their policy implications for developing countries," Energy Policy 31, 911–927. 2003.

Shao, H., A Critique of Electricity Grid Price Reform. *China Energy* No. 1, 33–39. 1998. (Chinese)

Shao, S., Z. Lu, N. Berrah, B. Tenenbaum, and J. Zhao, *China: Power Sector Regulation in a Socialist Market Economy.* World Bank, Washington, D.C. 1997.

Shirley, M. M. and P. Walsh, "Public versus Private Ownership: The Current State of the Debate," Mimeo.

Shleifer, A. and R. W. Vishny, "A Survey of Corporate Governance," *The Journal of Finance* 52:2, 737–783, 1997.

Shy, O. *The Economics of Network Industries,* Cambridge University Press. 2001.

Singh, N. and T. N. Srinivasan, *Indian Federalism, Economic Reform and Globalization.* 2002, Center for Research on Economic Development and Policy Reform (CREDPR): Palo Alto.

Sinton, J. E. and D, Fridley, Growth in China's Energy Consumption. *Energy Policy,* 28, 671–687, 2000.

Skidmore, T. E., Brasil: de Getúlio a Castelo, *Paz e Terra,* Rio de Janeiro. 1969.

Smil, V., *Energy in China's Modernization: Advances and Limitations.* M. E. Sharpe, New York, New York. 1988.

SPC, Main Report in SPC (Comp.), *Summary of the Electricity Industry Performance during the 9th Five-year Plan.* China Electric Power Press, Beijing, 29 – 174. 2001. (Chinese)

Srinivasan, T. N., India's Fiscal Situation: Is a Crisis Ahead? 2001, Center for Research on Economic Development and Policy Reform (CREDPR): Palo Alto.

State Power Corporation, Report on Electric Power Industry during the Ninth Five-year Plan. China Electric Power Press, Beijing, China. 2002.

State Statistical Bureau of China. China Statistical Yearbook, various years. China Statistical Publishing House, Beijing, China.

Steyn, G., A competitive electricity market for South Africa: the need for change and a strategy for restructuring South Africa's electricity supply industry. Paper prepared for the Department of Minerals and Energy. Pretoria. February, 2000.

Steyn, G., Governance, Finance and Investment: Decision making and risk in the electric power sector. DPhil, University of Sussex. 2001.

Stigler, G. and Friedland, C., "What Can Regulators Regulate? The Case of Electricity," Journal of Law and Economics, Vol.5, 1-16, October 1962.

Stiglitz, J., "The Private Uses of Public Interests: Incentives and Institutions," *Journal of Economic Perspectives* 12, 3–22, 1998.

Streek, W. and K. Yamamura eds., *The Origins of Nonliberal Capitalism,* 2001.

Surrey, J., *The British Power Experiment,* Earthscan, London. 1996.

Sweeney, J. L. "The Response of Energy Demand to Higher Prices: What have we Learned?" *The America Economic Review* 74, 2 pages 31–37. May 1984.

Sweeney, J. L. *The California Electricity Crisis,* Hoover Institution Press. 2005.

The Economist, Happy Anniversary? Special on India's 50, in *The Economist.* 1997.

Theron, P (ed). Proceedings of the ANC National Conference on Electrification. Elan Press, Cape Town. 1992.

Theron, P, A. Eberhard, and C. Dingley, Electricity provision in the urban areas of South Africa: towards a new framework. *Urban Forum* Vol 2, No 2, 1992.

Tinto, E, Restructuring South Africa's Electricity Supply Industry. MPhil. University of Cape Town. 2002.

Tjiong, H. I., T. Heller and D. G. Victor, "Electricity Restructuring and the Social Contract." PESD Working Paper #15, 2003.

Tongia, R. and R. Banerjee, Price of Power in India. *Energy Policy*, 26(7): p. 557–575. 1998.

U.S. Agency for International Development (USAID) Innovative Approaches to Slum Electrification. Washington, DC: USAID. 2004.

Velasco, M. *Surviving a Power Crisis*, Polistrat International, 2006.

Velloso, J. Paulo dos Reis, Estratégia Industrial e Retomada do Desenvolvimento, José Olympio, Rio de Janeiro. 1992.

Vernon, R., *Sovereignty at Bay: The Multinational Spread of US Enterprises*, 1971.

Victor, D. G. "Power Sector Reform in Developing Countries: Crafting Markets and Providing Access for the Poor." UNDESA 2005, 2006.

Vogel, D. *National Styles of Business Regulation: A Case Study of Environmental Policy*. Beard Books. 2003.

Wamukonya, N., 'Power Sector Reform in Developing Countries: Mismatched Agendas'. In: Wamukonya, N. (ed): *Electricity Reform: Social and Environmental Challenges*. United Nations Environmental Programme, Roskilde. 2003.

Wamukonya, N., "Power sector reform in developing countries: mismatched agendas." *Energy Policy* 31, 1273–1289. 2003.

Wang, T., Y. Zuo, D. Zeng, L. Tang and J. Zhang, Liaoning Electric Power Industry Development and Greenhouse Gas Emissions Abatement Policy, Report submitted to China Energy Project, Institute for International Studies, Stanford University, Stanford, CA. 2001. (Chinese)

Wang, X., G. Chai, Review of Economic Policy in the Electricity Industry During the 9th Five-year Plan and Future Prospect. In SPC (Comp.), Summary of the Electricity Industry Performance during the 9th Five-year Plan. China Electric Power Press, Beijing, pp. 266–277, 2001. (Chinese)

Wang, W. *Research Report on China's Photo Voltaic Industry Development*, The Chinese Renewable Energy Development Program Office, Beijing, October 2004.

Wang, X., X. Ni and A. Feng, Evolution of the Chinese Investment Financing System: Problems and Reform Directions, in Guo Shuqing eds. *Investment Financing System Moving toward Market Economy*. Reform Press, Beijing. P. 53. 1998. (Chinese)

Wells, L. T., "Private Foreign Investment in Infrastructure: Managing Non-Commercial Risk," paper presented at Private Infrastructure for Development: Confronting Political and Regulatory Risks, Sept. 8–10, 1999.

Wells, L. T. Jr., The New International Property Rights: Can the Foreign Investor Rely on Them?, in *International Political Risk Management: Looking to the Future* (Theodore H. Moran and Gerald T. West, eds., 2005

Williamson, J. and R. Zagha, From the Hindu Rate of Growth to the Hindu Rate of Reform, Center for Research on Economic Development and Policy Reform (CREDPR): Palo Alto. 2002.

Williamson, J., ed. *The Political Economy of Policy Reform*. Washington, D.C.: Institute for International Economics, 1994.

Wilson, R., "Market Architecture", Stanford University, mimeo. 1999.

World Bank, *The Private Sector in Infrastructure: Strategy, Regulation, and Risk*. 1997.

World Bank (2002b), *Private Participation in Infrastructure: Trends in Developing Countries in 1990–2001, Energy, Telecommunications, Transport, Water*, World Bank , 2002.

World Bank, *Why Liberalization May Stall in a Mature Power Market: A Review of the Technical and Political Economy Factors that Constrained the Electricity Sector Reform in Thailand 1998–2002*, Energy Sector Management Assistance Program 2003.

World Bank, *China Power Sector Reform: Toward Competition and Improved Performance*. World Bank, Washington, D.C. 1994.

World Bank, *Clear Water, Blue Skies: China's Environment in the New Century*. Washington, D.C. 1997.

World Bank, Reforming Infrastructure. Washington, D.C. 2004.

World Bank, *2005 World Development Indicators*, the International Bank for Reconstruction and Development. 2005.

World Bank, Bureaucrats *in Business: The Economics and Politics of Government Ownership*, pp. 81–92. Oxford University Press, 1995.

World Bank, *India - Power Supply to Agriculture*. Energy Sector Unit, South Asia Regional Office, Washington, DC. 2001.

World Bank, *World Development Report 2002: Building Institutions for Markets*. Oxford University Press, 2002.

Wu, G., 2003. Retrospect and Perspective of Rural Electrification in China. http://www.drcnet.com.cn/html_document/guoyan/inoth/2003-01-24. (Chinese)

Wu, J., 1999. *Contemporary Chinese Economic Reforms*. Far East Press, Shanghai. (Chinese)

Xinhua News Agency, http://www.sp.com.cn/html/gndt/c2.htm, http://www.sp.com.cn/html/yaowen/y0429.htm (Chinese)

Xu, Y., *Powering China: Reforming the Electric Power Industry in China*. Ashgate Publishing Company, Burlington, VT. 2002.

Yang, M., China's rural electrification and poverty reduction. *Energy Policy* 31, 283–295. 2003.

Yarrow, G., "A Theory of Privatization, or Why Bureaucrats are Still in Business," *World Development*, 27, 157–168, 1999.

Zelner, B.A. and W.J. Henisz "Politics and Infrastructure Investment," McDonough School of Business, Georgetown University; and The Wharton School, University of Pennsylvania, September 2000.

Zeng, L, L. Chen, B. Su, Guangdong Electric Power Development and Future Trend. Paper presented at the Forth China Energy and Global Environment Workshop of CISAC, Stanford University, November 1999. (Chinese)

Zhang, C., T. Heller, and M. May, "Carbon intensity of power generation and CDM baseline: case studies of three Chinese Provinces." *Energy Policy* 33:4, 451–465, March 2005.

Zhang, C., M. May and T. Heller, "Impact on global warming of development and structural changes in the electricity sector of Guangdong Province, China." *Energy Policy* 29, 179–203. 2001.

Zhou, D., Y. Guo, Y. Shi, and J. Logan, "Electric Power Options in China." Prepared for the Pew Center on Global Climate Change, May 2000.

Zhu, C., W. Li, F. Yang, and D. Ogden, Overview of Institutional and Market Reforms and Future Prospective in China's Utility Sector. Report of Lawrence Berkeley National Laboratory submitted to China Sustainable Energy Program, The Energy Foundation. 1999.

Zhu, C., Fifty years of structural reform in the Chinese electric power industry. National Electric Power Information Net. 2003. (Chinese)

Index

ABT *see* Availability Based Tariffs
Accelerated Power Development and
  Reform Program (APDRP) (India)
  154, 302
accounting 270, 276–7
  India 133
AES 51, 145, 146, 158
African National Congress (ANC) 223,
  302
  aggressive electrification program 279
  criticism of fiscal conservatism 228
  economic philosophy 227
  formation of government 227
  split on the matter of power distribution
    reforms 244
Agência Nacional de Energia Elétrica (Brazil)
  see Aneel
agricultural power consumption
  China 89
  India 124, 126–7, 130
    accounting 130 agricultural power
      tariffs
    India 126, 130
    Mexico 188
Ahluwalia, Montek Singh 137, 150, 157
Alliant 287
Alstom 281
Álvarez, Luis Echeverría 183
AMEU (South Africa) *see* Association of
  Municipal Electrical Undertakings
  (South Africa)
AMFORP 34, 40
ANC *see* African National Congress
Andhra Pradesh (India) power sector
  reforms
  see also Delhi power sector reforms;
    Orissa . . . IPPs 148
  restructuring without privatization 147–8
  subsidies 293
Aneel (*Agência Nacional de Energia Elétrica*)
  (Brazil) 51, 55, 57, 59, 72
  suspension of regulatory authority 67

Antitrust Federal Commission (Mexico) *see*
  Comisión Federal de Competencia
  (Mexico)
APDRP *see* Accelerated Power
  Development and Reform Program
  (India)
Argentinean power sector reforms 18
asset shifting 287
Association of Municipal Electrical
  Undertakings (AMEU) (South Africa)
  242
assured energy 55
Availability Based Tariffs (ABT) 164

Basu, A. K. 153
Bechtel 287
Bharat Heavy Electricals Limited (BHEL)
  281
BHEL *see* Bharat Heavy Electricals Limited
BNDES *see* National Bank for
  Development (Brazil)
Brazil
  constitutional reforms 49
  Ministry of Mines Energy (MME)
    58
  role in privatization 52–3
  political economy 46
Brazilian power sector
  1970s 43–4
  historical development 34–5
  privatization 58
  treaty with Paraguay 42
Brazilian power sector reforms 31–3, 72–5
  see also São Paulo power sector
    reforms2001 drought 66–72
  effects 33
  dual market system 33, 54–7
  marginal reforms 46–9
  problems 59
British power sector reforms 5–6
BSES 145, 146, 150, 159